D1243285

Wildlife
of AUSTRALIA

Wildlife
of AUSTRALIA

Louise Egerton and Jiri Lochman

JACANA BOOKS

ALLEN&UNWIN

Jacana Books, an imprint of
Allen & Unwin
83 Alexander Street
Crows Nest NSW 2065
Australia
Phone: (61 2) 8425 0100
Fax: (61 2) 9906 2218
Email: info@allenandunwin.com
Web: www.allenandunwin.com

National Library of Australia
Cataloguing-in-Publication entry:

Wildlife of Australia / Louise Egerton, Jiri Lochman.

   978 1 74114 997 5 (hbk.)

   Includes index.

   Zoology – Australia – Pictorial works.

   Other Authors/Contributors: Lochman, Jiri.

591.994

Designed and typeset in Australia by saso content & design Pty Ltd
Printed in China at Everbest Printing Co
Maps created by Ian Faulkner

This book is intended as a source of information. While every
care has been taken in compiling the information contained herein
neither the authors nor the publishers can be held responsible for
any adverse reactions contrary to the information offered. The
reader is advised to consult with a medical health professional
should you be injured by any animal encounter.

Photographs on
page 1: Western Pygmy Possum
page 2/3: Motorbike Frog
this page: New Holland Honeyeater

CONTENTS

ACKNOWLEDGEMENTS

We would like to thank the following experts for generously giving up their time to read sections of this book.

Dr Gerald R. Allen, Western Australia Museum; Marion Anstis, herpetologist and author; Professor Andrew J. Beattie, Dept. of Biological Sciences, Macquarie University; Dr Walter Boles, Curator, Ornithological Dept., Australian Museum; Dave Britton, BSc. (Hons), Collection Manager, Entomology, Australian Museum; Paul D. Brock, Natural History Museum, London; Professor Gerry Cassis, School of Biological, Earth and Environmental Sciences, University of New South Wales; Dr Sue Churchill, field biologist; Dr Andrew Claridge, Mammologist, New South Wales National Parks and Wildlife Services; Dr Hal Cogger, John Evans Memorial Fellow, Australian Museum; Ricki Coughlan, Grad. Cert. App. Ornithology, avian consultant, guide and presenter, Redtail, Sydney; Dr Chris Dickman, Director, Institute of Wildlife Research, Sydney University; Dr Eric Dorfman, Director, Eklektus Inc., Wellington, New Zealand; Dr Mark Eldridge, Dept. of Biological Sciences, Macquarie University; Michael Elliott, BSc. (Hons), Centre for Biodiversity and Conservation Research, Australian Museum; Dr Karen Firestone, School of Biological, Earth and Environmental Studies, University of New South Wales; Dr Fred Ford, New South Wales National Parks and Wildlife Services; Dr Tony Friend, Principal Research Scientist, Fauna Conservation Program, Dept. of Environment and Conservation, Western Australia; Dr Clifford B. Frith, author and ornithologist, north Queensland; Dr Peter Fullagar, CSIRO Research Scientist, retired; David Geering, Regent Honeyeater Recovery Coordinator, Dept. of Environment and Conservation, Dubbo; Denise Lawungurr Goodfellow, biological/indigenous tourism consultant, bird-watching/natural history guide, Northern Territory; Dr Mark Greco, Centre for Plant and Food Sciences, College of Health and Science, University of Western Sydney; Dr Brian Green, Adjunct Research Fellow, Applied Ecology Research Group, University of Canberra; Phillip Hadlington, New South Wales Forestry Commission, retired; Dr R.B. Halliday, Research Fellow (Acarology), CSIRO Entomology; Dr Kath Handasyde, Dept. of Zoology University of Melbourne; Dr George Hangay, author and entomologist; Associate Professor Rob Harcourt, Macquarie University; Dr David Hollands, rural doctor, wildlife photographer and author; Dr Greg Holwell, Research Fellow, Department of Biological Sciences, Macquarie University; Dr Paul Horner, Curator of Terrestrial Vertebrates, Museum and Art Gallery of the Northern Territory; Ian Hutton, author and Curator of Lord Howe Island Museum, Lord Howe Island; Tessa J. Ivison, B.Appl.Sc., natural history consultant; Dr Stephen Jackson, Project Officer—Animal Welfare, New South Wales Dept of Primary Industries; David James, BSc. (Hons), Acting Senior Project Manager/Ecologist, Australian Museum; Associate Professor Darryl Jones, Griffith School of Environment, Griffith University; Diana Jones, BSc. (Hons), Executive Director, Western Australia Museum; Dr Leo Joseph, Director of the Australian National Wildlife Collection, CSIRO; Professor Richard Kingsford, School of Biological Earth and Environmental Sciences, University of New South Wales; Dr Gerald Kuchling, School of Animal Biology, University of Western Australia; Dr Naomi Langmore, Senior Research Fellow, School of Botany and Zoology, Australian National University; Dr Ivan Lawler, School of Tropical Environment Studies and Geography, James Cook University of North Queensland; N.W. Longmore, Collections Manager: Birds and Mammals, Museum Victoria; Professor Michael Mahony, School of Environmental and Life Sciences, University of Newcastle; Dr Richard Major, Senior Research Scientist, Australian Museum; Darryl McKay, Southern Ocean Seabird Study Association; Dr Robert Mesibov, Honorary Research Associate, Queen Victoria Museum and Art Gallery and School of Zoology, University of Tasmania; Graham Milledge, Arachnology Collection Manager, Australian Museum; Dr Max Moulds, Senior Research Fellow, Australian Museum; Dr Timothy

Moulds, Senior Environmental Consultant, Subterranean Ecology (Scientific Environmental Services); John Nielsen, BSc. (Hons.), entomologist; Dr Richard Noske, Senior Lecturer in Biology, School of Science and Primary Industry, Charles Darwin University; Dr Penny Olsen, Australia National University; Anthony Overs, ornithologist; Bruce Pascoe, Curator of Zoology, Alice Springs Desert Park; Dean Portelli, BSc. (Hons), School of Biological, Earth and Environmental Science, University of New South Wales; Dr Mark Read, Manager, Species Conservation Unit, Great Barrier Reef Marine Park Authority; Dr David Rentz, Honorary Research Fellow, CSIRO Entomology; Dr Jacqui Richards, Australian Wildlife Conservancy; Peter Roberts, birdwatcher and author; Peter Rowland, author and ornithologist; Dr Bronwen Scott, Victoria University; Dr Jim Shields, Wildlife Manager, State Forests of New South Wales; Professor Rick Shine, School of Biological Sciences, University of Sydney; Graeme Smith, entomologist; Dr Courtenay Smithers, Senior Fellow, Australian Museum; Dr Helen Stevens, Charles Sturt University; Dejan Stojanovic, ecologist, Birds Australia; Phil Straw, B.Appl.Sc., consultant avian and wetlands ecologist, Avifauna Research and Services; Gerry Swan, herpetologist and author; Dr Noel Tait, Honorary Research Fellow, Biological Sciences, Macquarie University; Dr Anthea Taylor, School of Biological Sciences, Monash University; Dr Aleks Terauds, Wildlife and Marine Conservation Section, Biodiversity and Conservation Branch, Dept. of Primary Industries and Water, Hobart; Julianne M. Waldock, BSc., Technical Officer, Dept. of Terrestrial Zoology, Western Australian Museum; James Walker, entomologist, Australian Quarantine and Inspection Service; Dr Scott Whiting, Biomarine International, Charles Darwin University; Dr Mary White, palaeobotanist and author; Steve Wilson, wildlife photographer, author and herpetologist; Dr David Yeates, Australian National Insect Collection, CSIRO Entomology; Paul Zborowski, photographer, author and entomologist; Mark Ziembicki, BSc. (Hons), School of Earth and Environmental Sciences, University of Adelaide and Biodiversity Conservation Unit, Dept. of Nature Resources, Environment and the Arts, Northern Territory.

We are also grateful to the following people for their assistance: Dr Matthew Colloff, Research Scientist, CSIRO Entomology; Judith Gillespie, Curator, Western Plains Zoo; Professor Barrie Jamieson, University of Queensland; Martyn Robinson, naturalist, Australian Museum; Dr David Root, Senior Lecturer, Macquarie University, retired; Ted Taylor, Treasurer, Entomological Society; Nigel Weston, Ecological Services Unit, Australia Zoo Wildlife Warriors Worldwide; Dr Leigh Winsor, Facilities Management Office, James Cook University.

The authors and publisher would also like to thank to the photographers who contributed their work to this book, without which a project of this magnitude would not be possible.
Note: t (top), b (bottom), c (centre)

Hans and Judy Beste (30 images): 22/23, 40t, 40b, 41, 55, 58, 63, 82, 83, 84t, 111, 114, 158, 170, 183, 186, 188, 189, 206, 211b, 214, 218, 219, 233b, 235b, 239b, 243, 281, 308b, 347b; Rob Drummond (14): 121, 168, 187, 204t, 204b, 207, 208, 210t, 224, 226, 230, 234, 235t, 241; Marie Lochman (13): 18, 20, 69b, 250, 259, 263, 266, 268, 270, 273, 289b, 336, 368; Gunther Schmida (13): 314, 315t, 315b, 316, 317c, 317b, 318, 319t, 319b, 320t, 321, 322, 391; Stan Breeden (9): 38, 81, 203, 205, 228, 229, 283t, 301; Dave Watts (9): 26, 27, 51, 62, 97, 118, 123, 182, 220; Geoff Taylor (5): 96, 98, 99, 100, 103; Wade Hughes (3): 292t, 329t, 356; Peter Marsack (2): 191, 341t; Simon Nevill (2): 169, 190b; Alex Steffe (1): 122; Clay Bryce (1): 80; Eva Boogaard (1): 95; John Kleczkowski (1): 248; Bill Belson (1): 217t; Raoul Slater (1): 232; Peter Roberts* (1): 209.

* All the above listed photographers, except for Peter Roberts, are represented by Lochman Transparencies.
All images not credited above were taken by Jiri Lochman.

We would also like to thank Marie Lochman and Fred Magro for all their help and support.

NOTES ON CAPITAL LETTERS

In this book the common names of some animals are spelt with capital letters, while others are not. Those with capitals refer to species; those in lower case refer to *groups* of animals. For example, 'kangaroos' but 'Eastern Grey Kangaroos'.

BY MIKE ARCHER

What a wonderful book! It directly tackles the most awesome threat to the future survival of Australia's animals—ignorance about what is out there: the extraordinary mansion of biodiversity that is Australia's natural inheritance. Because of its ancient Gondwanan origins and 35 million years of evolution in isolation, ours is the only biota in the world profoundly unlike those of any of the other continents. Apart from the equally isolated but frozen Antarctica, Australia is the only continent that hasn't been linked by land or ice bridges to other continents over that period of time. Hence, while North America, Europe, Asia, Africa and even South America have shared lions, camels and elephants, none of those lands have ever had kangaroos, wombats or koalas—they are part of the vast legacy that is unique to Australia.

Unfortunately, as we spend more and more time living in cities and less time in the bush where Australia's animals live, our awareness of just how magnificent this legacy is steadily dwindles. Each generation is aware that a bit more land is destroyed and a few more species have been nudged into oblivion during its watch. They know this because the media notes threats to conservation that are happening now, but not what was happening 100, 50 or even 25 years ago. Because our personal timeframes are much too short, we fail to see that these contemporary, relatively minor generational losses, when added up since the arrival of Europeans, have become monstrous. Louise Egerton's and Jiri Lochman's book, sparkling with hundreds of beautiful visual moments and descriptive text, reminds us all that our globally unique animals are things we should and must not forget. If we do, we'll stop caring; if we stop caring, much that defines Australia's national identity and international appeal will be lost.

Unlike many other books about Australia's animals, this one is novel for another reason—it gives space to all the different kinds of animals that make up our complex ecosystems such as the lizards, frogs, fish, insects, spiders and snails rather than just the cute, furry or feathered ones. As a child growing up in the boreal forests of Appalachia in North America, I certainly noticed the conspicuous birds and mammals, including the American Opossums, although it was many years later before I realised this curious mammal was North America's only representative of the great group of mammals known as marsupials that became so fantastically diverse in Australia. But I don't recall a thing about the much smaller creatures such as the insects and molluscs that must have been struggling to survive, unnoticed, beneath my feet. When I returned to Australia in 1967 as a doctoral student in the Western Australian Museum, the whole biological spectrum of Australian creatures suddenly popped up in front of me, often on expeditions to remote places—and I was blown away; I'd never seen things like this before. I worked every day with Australian experts on every conceivable group of creatures, some of them microscopic—and we were all in love with the animals we studied. *Wildlife of Australia* does this for others who may not have noticed the little but no less fascinating creatures in our ponds, streams and underfoot. Without these treasures of biodiversity, there would be none of the cute and furry critters who in one way or another all depend on them.

But this is not just a beautiful compendium of Australian animals—it's much more than that. It also introduces the reader to aspects of the lives of these animals, their relationships to other creatures (including alien species that make their lives doubly hard) and to their whole environment. No creature exists in nature without vital ties to and interactions with other things. This is why conservation of these animals will not work unless the webs of beneficial inter-dependencies are secured.

And now there is the challenge of climate change—a familiar process over the last 35 million years but now uniquely challenging not only because of the extraordinary speed of change, but because of the way we have altered the bush, reducing its resilience by cutting it up into fenced blocks surrounded by agricultural land that in the most part is hostile to native animals. Best estimates are that for every degree change in average annual temperature, every animal will need to shift its range by on average 100 kilometres (62 miles). If temperatures eventually rise 5°C (41°F) as predicted, conservationists anticipate that our animals will need to shift their ranges by on average 500 kilometres (300 miles) from where we find them now. Given the way we have carved up much of Australia into a tapestry of tiny little fenced-in boxes, enabling most of these species to shift their ranges will be a major challenge. But no effort will be made if we cease to care, and we won't care if we aren't aware. That is why this book will be a valued addition to every household where tomorrow's Australians are growing up today. They need to know and care about what is in this book or that is the only place where it is going to survive.

Mike Archer
8 February 2009

Professor Michael Archer is Dean of Science
at the University of New South Wales.

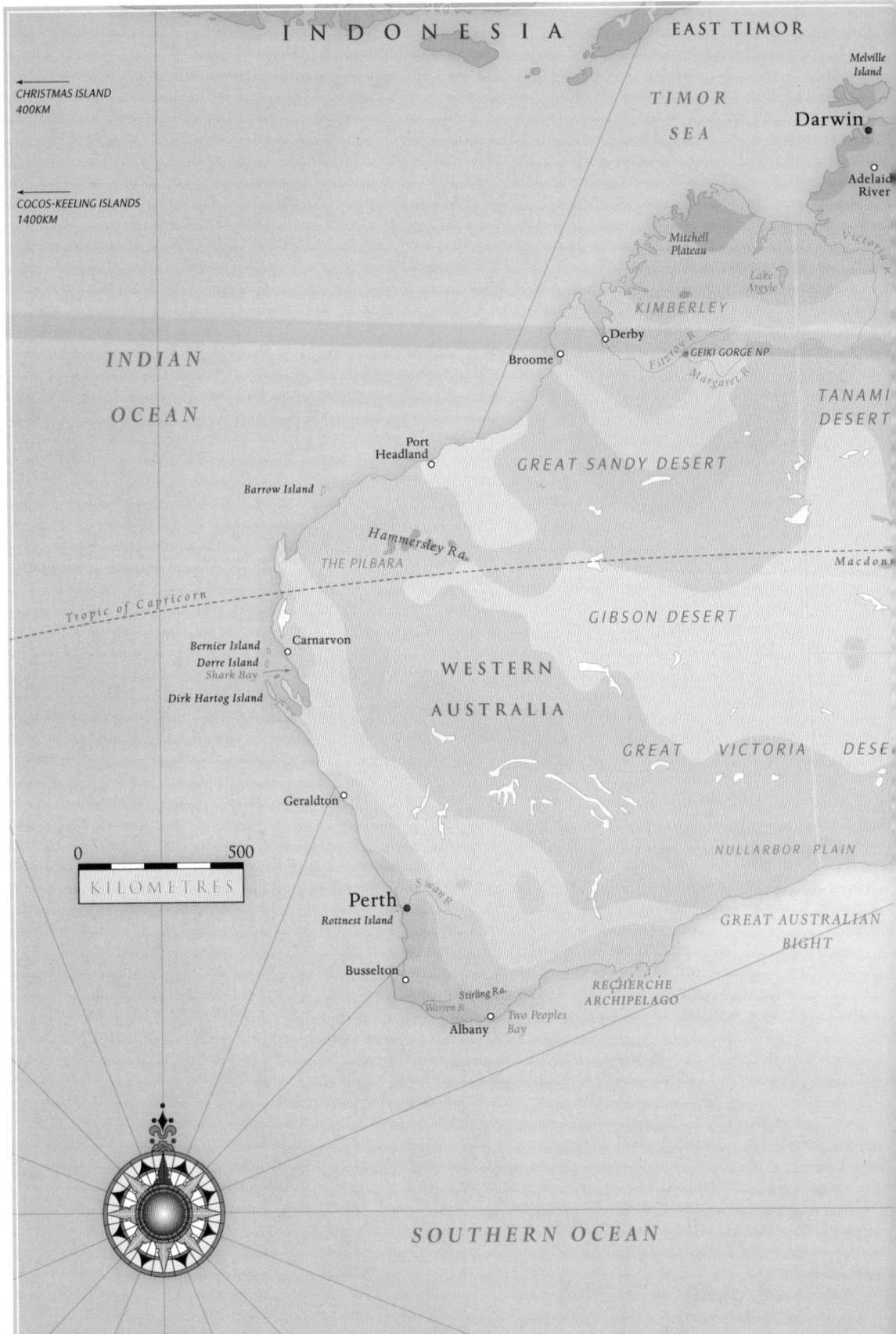

INDONESIA

EAST TIMOR

CHRISTMAS ISLAND
400KM

COCOS-KEELING ISLANDS
1400KM

*Melville
Island*

TIMOR

SEA

Darwin

*Adelaid
River*

INDIAN

OCEAN

*Mitchell
Plateau*

Victoria R.

*Lake
Argyle*

KIMBERLEY

Derby

TANAMI
DESERT

Fitzroy R.

GEIKI GORGE NP

Broome

Margaret R.

*Port
Headland*

GREAT SANDY DESERT

Barrow Island

Hammersley Ra.

THE PILBARA

Macdon

Tropic of Capricorn

GIBSON DESERT

Bernier Island
Dorre Island
Shark Bay

Carnarvon

WESTERN

Dirk Hartog Island

AUSTRALIA

GREAT   VICTORIA   DESE

Geraldton

NULLARBOR PLAIN

0   500

KILOMETRES

Perth

S Wan R

GREAT AUSTRALIAN
BIGHT

Rottnest Island

Busselton

Stirling Ra.

RECHERCHE
ARCHIPELAGO

Warren R.

*Two Peoples
Bay*

Albany

SOUTHERN OCEAN

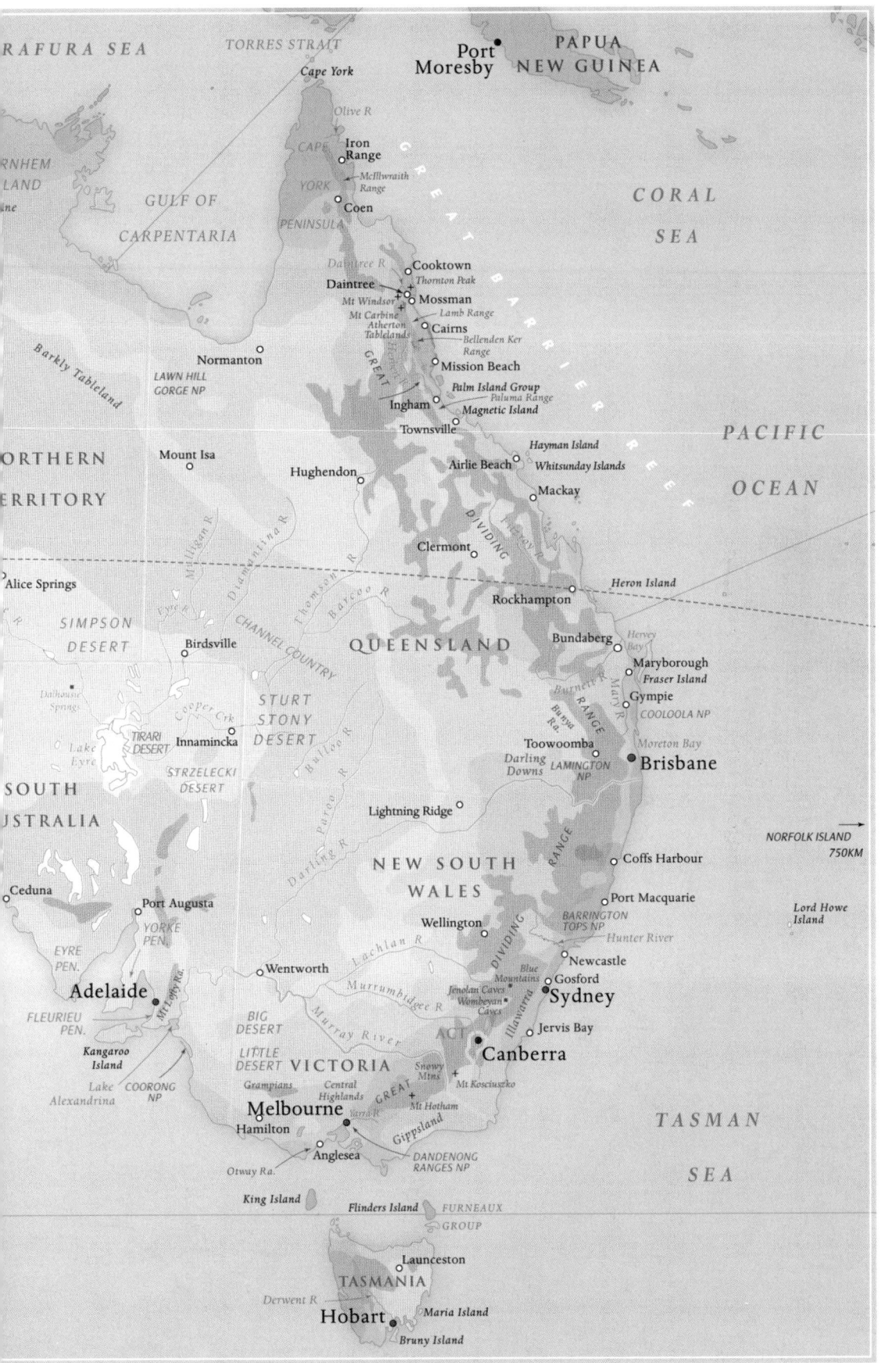

By world standards, many Australian animals look, well, a bit strange. Take kangaroos, Koalas, the Platypus, the Southern Cassowary or the Gippsland Giant Worm. Extraordinary as they are, these animals are well adapted to their habitat but through what evolutionary hoops have these creatures jumped? It is almost as though the wildlife of Australia has experienced a separate evolution from the rest of the world, and so, indeed, to a large extent it has.

The continent of Australia today carries a precious and irreplaceable cargo: a cornucopia of life forms. There are so many different species of animals living in Australia; many are not even named or described and every year scientists discover more.

Not only is there enormous diversity among Australian animals; many, too, are endemic to the continent. Animals are said to be 'endemic' to a place when they are restricted to that location. This usually happens as a result of ancestors having evolved in isolation over a vast span of time. The majority of animals living on the Australian continent today exist naturally nowhere else on Earth.

At first glance this land, with its vast expanses of dry scrubby vegetation, might seem an unlikely setting for an explosion of biodiversity but something very special happened here way back in prehistory: a series of events that resulted in a remarkable fauna.

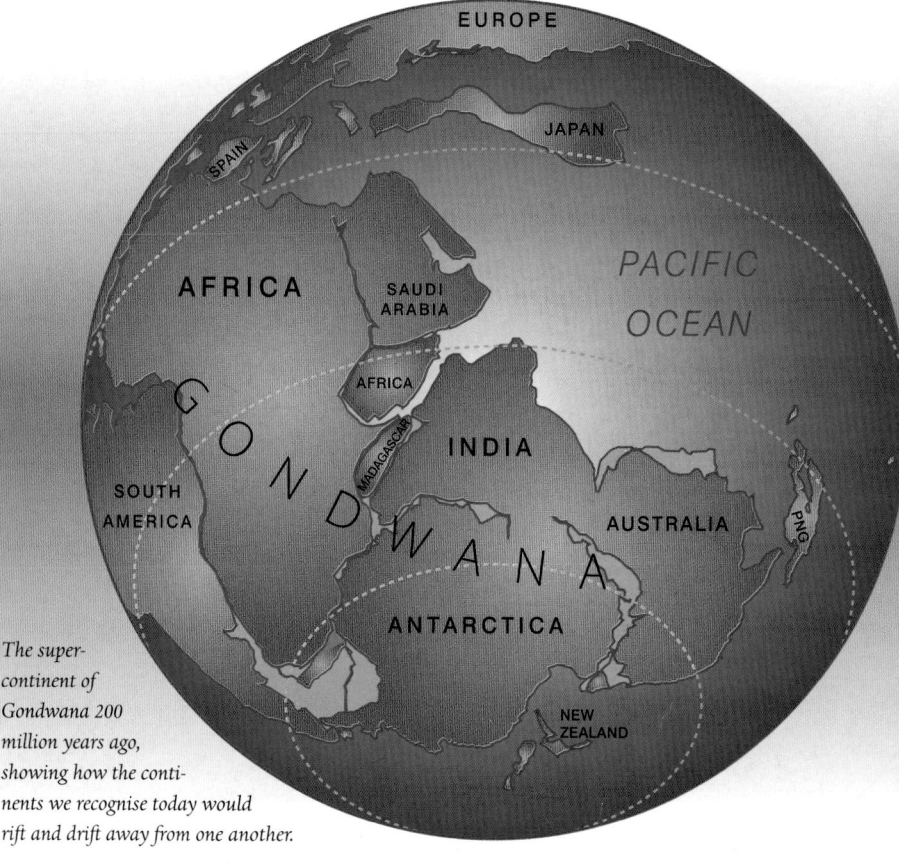

The super-continent of Gondwana 200 million years ago, showing how the continents we recognise today would rift and drift away from one another.

A Continental Ride

Two hundred and fifty million years ago Australia was part of a super-continent called Gondwana. It was one of only two supercontinents in the whole world; there were no small ones then and only one ocean, the Pacific. At this time Gondwana extended from the South Pole to equatorial regions. Australia lay near the Pole but the climate there was very different from today. It fluctuated between cool and warm temperate conditions and, despite months of winter darkness, vast swampy areas of the supercontinent were blanketed in lush vegetation and teemed with wildlife.

About 130 million years ago Gondwana began to break up into some of the continents we recognise today: South America, Africa, Antarctica, India and Australia. Continents sit upon monumental 'plates' of crust that drift across the world's surface. They are powered by convection currents in the mantle of the Earth, where partially melted rocks display a degree of plasticity. This amazing phenomenon is known as 'plate tectonics'.

The Australian continent shared a 'plate' with New Guinea and India. When the supercontinent of Gondwana began to break up, a rift formed between the Indian/Australian Plate and Antarctica. The Indian end of the plate moved north, eventually crumpling up against the Asian Plate to form the Himalayas. The Australian end of the plate was slowly ripped away from Antarctica but did not break completely free until about 38 million years ago.

Because the Australian end of the plate remained attached to the Antarctic Plate, as did the South American Plate, there are some striking connections between the fauna of South America and Australia. Animals were able to migrate between the two land-masses, via Antarctica. One of the most obvious conse-quences of this is the presence of marsupials in both South America and Australia today.

The Green Ringtail Possum, a resident of Australia's northern rainforests. The presence of possums in both South America and Australia hints at a shared evolutionary history. Many millions of years ago the two continents were geographically linked to one another via a third: Antarctica.

Despite fluctuations, the climate on Gondwana remained relatively stable and benign over tens of millions of years. The early plants of swampy habitats gave way to predominantly coniferous rainforest. Huon Pines, Bunya Pines, Hoop Pines and the recently discovered Wollemi Pines, as well as Antarctic Beeches, are all ancestors of Gondwanan forest species, as are tree ferns and cycads.

Mass Extinctions Open the Way for New Developments

Up until around 65 million years ago, the coniferous forests were inhabited by dinosaurs but around this time the diversity of dinosaurs declined significantly, and they were not alone. Many marine groups, such as ammonites—a diverse group of molluscs that dominated the world's oceans during this time—underwent mass extinctions.

Many scientists believe that these mass extinctions were due to a single cataclysmic event: a meteor of enormous proportions. The impact catapulted solid and vaporised rocks up into the atmosphere. The energy released by the initial crash and those that followed as debris returned to Earth raised the temperature of the atmosphere, igniting wildfires across the globe. Evidence of tsunamis, earthquakes and intense volcanic activity at the edges of the world's tectonic plates around this time suggest that plumes of particles and dust darkened the sky and blotted out the sun, resulting in plummeting temperatures on Earth.

Whatever the cause, whole suites of animals vanished from land and sea. There were, however, survivors. Among them were birds which had previously evolved from small carnivorous dinosaurs, their feathers arising from modified scales. Turtles, crocodiles and lungfish also made it through the crisis in their watery domains and so did a number of small spineless creatures, such as insects. Also scurrying about, very likely at night, were some inconspicuous, small, furry animals: the mammals.

Mammals Burst from Cover

A multitude of niches previously occupied by extinct species now lay vacant for survivors to adapt to and fill. With the demise of the dinosaurs, the three major groups of mammals—the egg-laying monotremes, the marsupials, and the placentals—were free to exploit these ecological niches. With an evolutionary burst, they diversified and spread out.

The Australian fossil record for Gondwanan mammals is sketchy. Only a few are known from Australia before it split completely away from Antarctica 38 million years ago. One was found at Lightning Ridge in New South Wales. It is the opalised jaw of a platypus-like creature dated at 110 million years old. Today the egg-laying monotremes are only known from five species. Two, the Platypus and the Short-beaked Echidna, live only in Australia. The other three species are rare and endangered echidnas from New Guinea.

Ancient marsupial fossils have been discovered from China and North America but there is no certain record of marsupials from South America before 70 million years ago. The first marsupials to be found in Australia date from 55 million years ago. While the marsupials died out in the northern continents and Africa about 15 million years ago, they flourished in Australia and South America. The American Opposum re-invaded North America approximately three million years ago. In Australia the marsupials diversified into a menagerie of forms and came to dominate the continent's mammal fauna.

Despite evidence of non-flying placentals (those other than bats) in Australia 55 million years ago, this group of mammals did not survive on the continent until it was invaded much later by rodents and later still by groups brought in by humans. Placentals are the dominant group of mammals in the rest of the world but in Australia, it would seem, they were out-competed by the marsupials.

The Short-beaked Echidna is a survivor of a line of mammals known as monotremes. Monotremes are curious mammals because they lay eggs. Only five species exist today, all of which live in either Australia or New Guinea, but they were once much more widespread.

The Gondwanan Ark Drifts North

After Australia and New Guinea cut loose from the Antarctic Plate about 38 million years ago, it drifted north, leaving in its wake the newly formed transatlantic cold oceanic current. On board the Australian continent were the ancestors of many of today's inhabitants. These included frogs, fishes, turtles, crocodiles, birds, bats, snakes, lizards and marsupials. Free of contamination from invasive species, Australia's living cargo evolved in splendid isolation as the continent drifted into warmer latitudes.

It is hard to believe now but 55 million years ago much of Australia was covered in rainforest. The flowering plants that form the majority the world's vegetation today were well established. Having first appeared in the fossil record 125 million years ago, they had evolved in the rift valleys and gradually diversified and spread out into forests formerly dominated by conifers.

Enticed by the nectar and pollen from the flowers of these rainforest plants, herbivores developed new adaptations to reach them and predators followed. New forms of flying insects filled the skies. To catch these, the ground-based spiders extended their web-making skills to large aerial silk constructions slung between branches. The birds evolved spectacular flying skills to feast on darting insects. A number of the mammals, too, took to the trees; in Australia many of these were possums and gliders.

Frustratingly, there is a yawning gap in the fossil record of Australian

The semi-arid landscape of north-western Queensland looked very different 15 million years ago. Its rich rainforest supported a great diversity of possums as well as ancestral thylacines (centre), some strange kangaroos, including a flesh-eating species (bottom left-hand corner), and large, quadrupedal marsupials (bottom left).

REPRODUCED WITH KIND PERMISSION FROM THE ARTIST, DOROTHY DUNPHY

mammals between 55 and 26 million years but we do know that this island continent underwent a series of climatic fluctuations and that, as a consequence, there were successions of extinctions and evolutionary bursts.

Fossils from central Australia and north-western Queensland dating from 25 to 15 million years ago reveal a rich assemblage of wildlife. These animals were living in a landscape of rainforests, lakes and streams. There were prototype wombats and possums living alongside giant pythons, marsupial lions and four-footed, sheep-sized marsupial browsers known as diprotodontids. In the waterways swam catfish, lungfish, crocodiles and turtles.

Evidence of tree-dwelling, leaf-munching koalas at this time suggests the existence of eucalypts living in the rainforests. Very gradually Australia was beginning to dry out. From about 15 million years ago, its rainforests were giving way to more open, drier forests that came to dominate the continent.

The Drying Continent

Although the world as a whole proceeded to undergo a series of warm, wet greenhouse-like conditions interspersed with dry, cold periods, the overall climatic trend for Australia was towards a cooler, drier continent. This was driven by several global and some local events. The break-up of Gondwana impacted profoundly upon the world climate but the cold circumpolar current that resulted and whips around Antarctica to this day particularly affected Australia. Eventually the extensive formation of ice caps in Antarctica would compound the cooling and drying effects upon its continental neighbour. Australia continued to drift northwards towards tropical latitudes but the influence of the rain-bearing westerlies diminished. Eventually the northern edge of the Australian plate buckled up against the southern edge of South-east Asia, pushing a line of mountains up along New Guinea's longitudinal axis. These mountains received monsoonal rains that might otherwise have fallen in Australia.

Around 10 million years ago, the dense, broad-leafed forests of central Australia were being replaced by forests with she-oaks and eucalypts: plants better adapted to dry conditions. Five million years ago the continent's rainforest had retreated to refuges where wet conditions still prevailed. The wet tropical rainforests of north-eastern Queensland today are just such a refuge. Here ancient flowering plants still support a dwindling group of animals from a time when much of the continent was clad in rainforest.

Rodents were notably absent from the fauna of Gondwana. The first rats and mice only made it into Australia about 5 million years ago.

A eucalypt woodland. It seems likely that the eucalypts evolved from rainforest cousins in response to the drying of the Australian continent. Today there are about 800 species and they dominate the Australian landscape. Found in habitats as diverse as sub-alpine regions, forests, woodlands and the arid inland, they are absent from rainforests, yet they belong to the Myrtaceae, a family of plants that are commonly found in rainforests.

They came in several waves from the north. By this time Australia and New Guinea were closing in on the Indonesian archipelago and migration of species became possible.

It was around 5 million years ago, too, that the drought-tolerant wattles and saltbushes appear in the pollen record. While some rainforest animals were able to adapt to the new conditions, others died out, including many of the possums. About 2.5 million years ago grasses became commonplace and with them came a burst in diversity of grazing animals, among them many different kinds of kangaroos.

In fact kangaroos of a sort had lived in the rainforests. One of the earliest known species ate flesh. Others, known as rat-kangaroos, were omnivores and had bounded across the rainforest floors in profusion. The sole survivor from this group, the Musky-rat Kangaroo, still forages for

food on tropical rainforest floors in north-east Queensland. When grasslands became extensive, most Australian rainforest kangaroos became extinct. Those that survived underwent changes to their teeth, digestive systems and skulls, in response to new sources of food.

Around 1.5 million years ago some of the grazing kangaroos became enormous; so, too, did the wombats and many birds, including one called a Mihirung which was three times bigger than today's Emu. The largest marsupial ever to have lived, a species of *Diprotodon*, was from this time: it was a thick-set, four-legged, rhinoceros-sized plant eater. The predators of these large animals took the form of marsupial lions and thylacines. Scavengers were also large. Among them was a more robust and bigger form of today's Tasmanian Devil and a 5m (16ft)-long goanna. The reign of the megafauna, however, was short lived. It is possible that climate change drove them to extinction but it is also possible that humans contributed to their demise.

The large number of grazing kangaroos that we associate with Australia's wide open spaces have been part of the landscape for less than five million years. They evolved from rainforest cousins in response to the proliferation of grasslands as the continent began to dry out.

The Arrival of Humans

Over the last two million years Australia has experienced a series of glacial–interglacial periods. Glacial phases imposed cool, dry conditions on Australia. With sea levels low at such times, land bridges existed between Tasmania in the north and New Guinea in the south. It was from the north that the first Aborigines migrated into Australia some time prior to 60,000 years ago.

Animals from many ancient Gondwanan lineages are still to be found in Australia. Despite the fluctuating climatic conditions, this continent's geological stability and its isolation for 40 million years following the break-up from Gondwana provided a unique opportunity for evolution to take place without external influences.

One of the last arrivals in Australia to be deemed a native of the country was the Dingo. It was probably brought to Australia by seafarers from the north about 4000 years ago. Being a hunter of large prey, it is possible, although by no means certain, that it out-competed the Thylacine on the Australian mainland.

Since European settlement, just over two hundred years ago, the rate of extinction of native species has been exceedingly high. Among the mammals alone, we have lost 18 species, more than any other nation on Earth in the same amount of time. Another nine formerly mainland mammal species survive now only on islands.

Many species of possums disappeared with the shrinking of rainforests in Australia but this tiny Honey Possum survives in south-western Australia to this day. It relies on the pollen, nectar and sap of a suite of native heathland plants that have adapted to drying conditions on the continent.

The Story So Far

So, in a nutshell, that's the story so far . . . but it isn't over yet. The world is in perpetual motion. Tectonic plates grind against one another, crash into one another and move apart as seafloors spread. Extinctions and speciations roll on through the millennia. Mountain ranges go up and down, so do oceans. Climates lurch from greenhouse to ice-age conditions.

We have some idea of what lies ahead. The dire warnings of climate change are consistent with the Earth's history but this time our own activities are instrumental in its occurrence. The speed and ferocity with which this change has come upon us will

undoubtedly take a toll on our natural world. It could even overwhelm the human race. But we may be able to do something to stem the worst effects.

Let's stop cutting down our carbon sinks—the forests. Let's curb our desire for manufactured goods. Let's look to a future of renewable energy sources. And let's try and keep ourselves, our beautiful world and the magnificent array of creatures, the like of which we shall never see again, alive and safe. There's a lot at stake for both ourselves and our fellow species.

Several species of Australian frogs have disappeared in recent years. Scientific researchers are trying to find out more about where and how frogs such as this Roth's Tree Frog from northern Australia live. Furthering understanding about how animals survive in the wild can provide valuable clues that will help us to help them to survive the future.

Mammals

Most of the world's mammal fauna belong to a group known as placentals but more than 50 per cent of Australia's land mammals are represented by an extraordinary group known as marsupials. Still more curious, and even rarer, are the monotremes: a tiny group of five species found only in Australia and New Guinea.

All mammals are warm-blooded animals that produce milk to feed their young but not all bear offspring in the same way. Placental mammals, such as ourselves, give birth to very well-developed young, having carried them internally for a long time, oxygenating and feeding them by diffusion across the placenta.

Marsupials are found only in Central and South America, New Guinea and Australia; all landmasses that were once part of the supercontinent of Gondwana. The animals in this group of mammals bear live offspring at a very early stage of development. There is rarely a placenta. Although the young are fully formed when they are born, they are minute, hairless and blind. They develop slowly, suckling within the protection of their mother's pouch over a long period before acquiring independence.

Australia has the greatest diversity of marsupials in the world and 99 per cent of them are nocturnal. Koalas, wombats, kangaroos, bandicoots, possums, gliders and the carnivorous dasyurids are all marsupials.

Monotremes are very unusual mammals. They lay eggs; a characteristic associated more with birds, reptiles and frogs than mammals. The name 'monotreme' means 'one opening' and these animals have just a single body cavity through which faeces, urine and eggs must pass. Females incubate their eggs for 10 days before they hatch. Although monotremes do wean their young, they have no nipples; the mother's milk simply oozes from her mammary glands through her skin.

Of the five known species of monotreme existing in the world today, four are echidnas; the fifth is the Platypus. Echidnas are known in New Guinea and one species is commonly found in Australia. The Platypus is wholly Australian and occurs nowhere else in the world.

In total, there are about 320 species of mammals currently living in Australia or Australian waters. The majority of these animals are descendants of those that were present on the continent when it broke away from Gondwana 40 million years ago. However, about 80 species are bats and many of their descendants would have arrived in Australia on the wing. Others, such as the rodents, reached the continent from Asia, and over the last 200 years or so just under 20 species have been introduced into the country.

PREVIOUS PAGE *The pouch of this Squirrel Glider is clearly visible as it volplanes through the canopy.*
RIGHT *Riding piggyback on its mother, this young Koala is still feeding on her milk. Gradually it will gain confidence and develop a taste for gum leaves.*

Platypus

In 1798, when a dead animal with a torpedo-shaped, thickly-furred body, four webbed feet, a large duck-like 'bill' and a broad, flattish tail arrived in England from Australia, zoologist were perplexed. Nearly everyone thought it was a fake, produced by the deft hand of a taxonomist who must have sewn a duck's bill onto a mammal's body. This delightful little creature is in fact very real and it can still be seen in some of eastern Australia's rivers today.

A Platypus dives for food, propelled by its webbed front feet and steered by its partially webbed rear feet and its tail. The soft fur is waterproof. Underwater it keeps its eyes, ears and nostrils closed, and feels its way about with its sensitive bill. As it runs out of air, it surfaces, its cheek pouches hopefully full of food. Prey is ground up on plates within the Platypus's mouth before swallowing.

Mostly nocturnal, the Platypus probes for food underwater, foraging for up to 12 hours through the silt and gravel with its bill. This remarkable organ is not horny, as it is in ducks. It is covered in soft, highly sensitive skin that picks up the minute electrical pulses generated by the muscles of larvae, worms and yabbies.

Platypuses excavate sleeping burrows in the banks of rivers and live solitary lives except during the breeding season (July to September). Females initiate courtships, chasing and playing with males in the water. Smaller than the males, females are only about 43cm (17in) long and normally weigh 1–1.5kg (2–3lb). Couples nuzzle and stroke one another with their bills, with females cautiously avoiding the hollow horny spurs on the ankles of males' hindlegs. These spurs, which are supplied with venom from glands in the male's thighs, are probably weapons for fending off other males during the breeding season.

After mating, the female constructs a complex nesting burrow, 8–30m (26–98ft) long, at the end of which is a chamber lined with wet vegetation. Here she lays one to three leathery little eggs. She curls her body around them to keep them warm and after 10 days the tiny, fully-formed young hatch. The young stimulate the mammary glands on mother's belly and milk oozes from their skin. For up to four months they will suckle before leaving the burrow in late summer.

A Platypus emerging from its burrow before sliding quietly into the water. This is a rare sight as the Platypus has a shy and wary nature. It excavates its burrow with the strong claws of its front feet, while the back ones provide stability. If a Platypus can withstand massive floods and avoid the attention of goannas, pythons, Foxes, birds of prey and even crocodiles in the north of its range, it may live for 16 years.

Short-beaked Echidna

There's no mistaking this spiny land dweller as it ambles along on its four splayed feet. In a country teeming with ants and termites, specialising in a diet of these creatures has proved extremely successful for the Short-beaked Echidna. Although elusive, it lives in every habitat in Australia, from the parched deserts through woodlands and forests to the snow country and, unusually for an Australian marsupial, it is active during the day rather than at night.

> **MAMMAL EGGS**
> The Short-beaked Echidna and the Platypus belong to the smallest and rarest group of mammals: the curious, egg-laying monotremes.

The Short-beaked Echidna is about the size of a rugby ball. When under threat, it rolls itself into a prickly ball or digs directly down into the ground with the rotational force of its front claws. This vanishing act, together with its beautifully camouflaged form and colouring, gives an echidna the freedom to forage in daylight and saves it from the need to make a burrow, except during cold winter months and when housing its young.

Echidnas have robust digging claws for ripping open termite mounds and ant nests in both hard ground and rotten wood. Their cylindrical, long tongue, housed in a Pinocchio-like snout, is highly flexible and is used to investigate the narrow channels of ant and termite habitats. Hapless prey become stuck to the saliva and are lapped up fast.

In winter the usually solitary echidnas may join 'trains' of other echidnas, all following a female in season. A line of up to 10 male suitors of diminishing size may follow a single female as she wafts her scent behind her. Over several weeks males jostle one another. The dominant male eventually digs himself into position next to his prickly sweetheart to mate, carefully avoiding her spines.

Three to four weeks later the female lays a single egg directly into her pouch, where she incubates it for 10 days. Then a naked, translucent but well-formed 'puggle', smaller than a fingernail, pierces its shell with its miniscule egg tooth. Once hatched it clings to its mother's hairs as it feeds from her milk patches. After 45 days its growing spines are so uncomfortable the mother leaves her puggle in a burrow but she will continue to suckle it for another five months.

Koala

Koalas look like small round cuddly bears with fluffy ears, but there is more to this iconic Australian animal than meets the eye. Firstly they are no more bears than kangaroos are. They are nocturnal, tree-dwelling marsupials whose closest living relatives are the wombats.

Koalas normally spend up to 19 hours a day asleep, their bottoms wedged firmly in the fork of a tree, their heads slumped forward on their chests. As dusk approaches they rouse themselves to feed almost exclusively on the leaves of gum trees (eucalypts). They show distinct preferences for certain species and even for individual trees, and they often sniff leaves before eating them, presumably testing for palatability.

The lethargic nature of Koalas is a direct result of their diet: gum leaves have very little nutritional value and contain toxins. Tender young leaves may be better for them to eat but they often grow at the tips of small branches that cannot sustain a Koala's weight. They must chew the leaves to a pulp with their molars before despatching them into a specialised gut that separates the useful from the useless components and

Despite their dumpy shape, Koalas are surprisingly agile, even with a baby on their back. They climb trees by maintaining a vice-like grip with the tips of their stout claws. Males are larger than females but size, colour and coat thickness vary with location. A mature southern male is usually 11–12kg (24–26lb); its northern-most counterpart may weigh only half that. Southern Koalas have thick, dark grey coats, often with rust-coloured bellies, while those of northerners are short, woolly and silver grey.

NIGHTMARE LOVE

'Docile' is not a word that springs to the mind of anyone who has heard Koalas mating. The male's deep, low growls and heaving bellows, accompanied by the electrifying screams of the female, put one more in mind of an axe-murderers' convention.

Koalas are too large to move through the canopies of open woodlands so they must come to ground each night to find new feeding trees. Males also move around on the ground quite a bit during the breeding season in search of females. The bare patch in the middle of this male Koala's chest is a gland that exudes a smelly scent. He rubs his chest on trunks and branches to signal his presence to other Koalas. The range over which these mostly solitary animals forage often overlaps with that of others, so scent marking is a good way of communicating who is where.

is full of microbes to help break down the tough foliage. Digestion is slow, with some food particles spending up to eight days in the gut.

Koalas are restricted to eucalypt woodlands across a broad swathe of eastern and south-eastern Australia. Although widespread, populations are fragmented, variable in size and may change with time. At their western extremity they border semi-arid land, where they are susceptible to drought. Others are affected by bushfires. Before European settlement, Aboriginal hunting and predation by dingoes kept populations in check but today land clearance is a greater threat—it has wiped out much of the Koala's habitat, especially in New South Wales and Queensland. However, some populations in the south-east have been so successful that they would have eaten themselves out of existence had they not been carefully managed by wildlife experts.

Females breed once a year, commencing at two years of age. After a 35-day pregnancy they give birth to one (very rarely, two) blind, naked, barely-formed miniature Koala, less than half a gram (⅟₆₀oz) in weight. Remarkably, the baby crawls, using its front claws, up its mother's fur into her pouch and latches on to the smaller of two teats. Within three months, it weighs 50g (1¾oz). At about six months it has fur and pokes its head out of the pouch. At this stage the young Koala acquires the microbes it will need to digest gum leaves later by eating some of its mother's poo.

Many Koalas are infected with a bacterium called *Chlamydia,* which can cause diseases. Sometimes these affect the eyes, resulting in a form of conjunctivitis called pink-eye, or the bladder may be affected, giving rise to incontinence, but *Chlamydia* is best known for causing infertility in females.

Although this can reduce fecundity in populations, there are many long-term wild populations where infection persists but only at low levels, probably because Koalas have developed a degree of immunity or the strain of *Chlamydia* in the population is only mild. While infection is mainly sexually transmitted, mothers may pass *Chlamydia* on to their young; equally they may also pass on their immunity.

TIME TO MOVE OUT

Koalas breed in late spring or summer. Once a baby is born, any sneaky attempt by its sibling of the previous year to suckle from its mother will be met by a cuff around the head, signalling it is time to move on and move out. Female young usually remain around their mother's home range but males disperse and at such times may fall prey to eagles, owls, dogs and cars.

Wombats

Australia's bear-like wombats are solid and muscular, and seem unlikely marsupials. All three species are native to the country and are nocturnal. None stand higher than a human's knee but the Northern Hairy-nosed Wombat weighs up to 38kg (84lb) and is the largest burrowing herbivore in the world. Its cousins, the Southern Hairy-nosed Wombat and the Common Wombat, are a little smaller.

A Common Wombat on the move. Despite its bumbling appearance, wombats are flexible and, if needs be, fast. They can swim well, scratch behind their ears with their back foot and run at 40kph (25mph) for over 150m (165yd). In the safety of captivity they have lived for 26 years but in the wild 15 years is a more realistic lifespan.

The body of a wombat is supported squarely by four short sturdy legs at the end of which are slightly cupped feet with long powerful claws designed for digging. Wombats are inveterate burrowers. They excavate elaborate tunnels up to 60m (200ft) long with twists and turns and descents to 10m (33ft). Some tunnels end in blind alleys that widen out into sleeping chambers. Outside the entrance, a wombat usually scoops out a sitting spot where it may sunbathe or rest in the early morning before retiring for the day.

Wombats are solitary animals and, although the two hairy-nosed species are said to be more docile, Common Wombats may be quite

A wombat's pouch opens from the back to prevent soil excavated by the front paws being flicked into it. Here a mother exercises a variation on pelvic floor exercises as she relaxes her pouch muscles, lowering the undercarriage to allow a wide-eyed inquisitive young wombat a peek at the world beyond. It is from the safety of the pouch that the young wombat starts to graze. As mother moves forward, it crops where she has been.

aggressive with one another. The Common Wombat is widespread in the forests of south-eastern Australia, including Tasmania. It is rarely seen but its presence is made evident by its cube-shaped calling cards prominently displayed on raised features such as rocks, branches and even toadstools. It also deposits scats outside the entrances to its burrows to signal its residence.

The hairy-nosed species can be distinguished from the Common Wombat by their distinctly square snouts, larger ears and soft fur. Both live in dry country. While populations of Southerns are scattered throughout the semi-arid grasslands and woodlands of South Australia and just into Western Australia (plus a recently discovered population in the south-western corner of New South Wales), the Northerns have become the focus of considerable recovery efforts as they teeter on the brink of extinction with only about 115 animals known from a single 300ha (740ac) of semi-arid woodland near Clermont in Queensland. These animals usually stay close to their

SARCOPTIC MANGE

Wombats are often infected by sarcoptic mites, which dig in beneath the skin and cause intense irritation. To alleviate the itch, the wombat rubs itself raw. As successive generations of mites continue to feed on the blood serum (the clear fluid in blood), the wombat weakens and may succumb to secondary infections and even liver or kidney failure. Sick wombats may be encountered during the day, as their senses, including their eyesight, can be affected.

burrows when feeding and use prescribed runways and tunnels.

All wombats are vegetarians. Their teeth have no roots and continue to grow throughout the animal's lifetime and, like our fingernails, can become very long. These teeth are tailor-made for snipping off plant roots and blades of grass. Wombats also have a split lip that allows them to reach the choicest young picks of a plant close to the ground.

Common Wombats mate at any time of year. Females usually bear only one young, which suckles in the pouch for six or seven months. A young wombat hones its excavation skills inside its mother's burrow. When it first ventures outside, the foray is tentative and brief but soon the young wombat accompanies its mother into the open to graze close to the home.

Young wombats are extremely playful. They rush about and roll around, occasionally jumping on their mother, but at this time they are vulnerable to attacks from dogs and Dingoes, so at the slightest hint of danger they bolt for the burrow. After 15 months they are weaned and ready to establish their own home. They may renovate a vacant burrow, dig their own or share one with other juveniles.

COMFORT ZONE

Tunnel-life temperatures differ from those of outside. For the Hairy-nosed species the burrow provides welcome respite from the heat; for the Common Wombat, which often inhabits snow country, it is a relatively cosy shelter when temperatures plummet in winter.

BUM CRUSHER

As wombats tunnel, their stout rump fills the burrow's circumference. Intruders have been known to be crushed to death by the wombat's behind, squeezing them up against the roof of their burrow.

A Common Wombat's burrow is large enough for a child to crawl through. On emerging at night, a wombat often takes time out to get its bearings, sniffing the air for scents, scratching and rubbing itself against branches before setting out on the night's foraging.

Brushtail Possums

Possums are nocturnal tree-dwelling marsupials that feed mostly on leaves, blossoms and fruits. The toes of these expert climbers are arranged to give them a firm grasp and their claws generally grip like ice-picks. In most cases, their long tails are prehensile and act as a fifth limb, providing balance and support during tricky manoeuvres between branches. Of the 24 species of Australian possums, six belong to the brushtail family.

Brushtails feed one or two young in a forward-opening pouch that contains two or four teats. After four or five months young brushtails exchange the warmth, safety and on-tap meals in the pouch for a more awkward existence, clinging onto their mother's back. After several months of being poked in the eye and jabbed by twigs, they settle for complete independence.

Common Brushtails and their Relatives

Most Australians are familiar with the ubiquitous Common Brushtail Possum. It has availed itself of the larders of roses, fresh young leaves and vegetables we call parks and gardens, and adopted our lofts for daytime dens. Highly communicative, they partake in wild pursuits and raucous exchanges of blood-curdling gutteral gasps, rasps and purrs. On a tin roof their nocturnal maraudings evoke a herd of elephants and frequently awaken slumbering humans below.

This adaptable possum has managed to exploit all but the most tree-less and arid regions of the continent. About the size of a cat, its dark

The Mountain Brushtail Possum is an inhabitant of the wet forests of the Great Dividing Range. Recent morphological work has divided this species into two separate ones: the northern species in this photo is now known as the Short-eared Brushtail Possum.

A head-first descent presents no problem for this Common Brushtail Possum. With the sturdy grip of its claws and the flexibility of its muscular tail, it moves amongst trees with confidence and agility.

fluffy tail is only weakly prehensile. Although most individuals are grey to brown, there are regional variations. The undersides are pale and in males, chest glands ooze a scent that stains the fur yellow to brown. Rubbing this scent onto branches is how they mark their territories.

Despite its similarity, the Mountain Brushtail Possum is a different species from the Common Brushtail. It has a less pointy nose, smaller ears, thicker fur and some adults weigh in at a hefty 4.5kg (10lb). It prefers the thickly forested coastal ranges of eastern Australia, while the Common Brushtail lives in drier forests and woodlands.

Cuscuses

Cuscuses look a little like small arboreal bears but they are nothing of the sort. They are possums with round faces, small ears and partially naked prehensile tails that curl up like springs when the animal is still or travelling, but extend to wrap around branches when a firm grip is required.

Cuscuses are mainly New Guinean possums. A few species extend as far north as the Indonesian island of Sulawesi but to the south Australia hosts two species on Queensland's northern-most tip of Cape York Peninsula.

The Common Spotted Cuscus is relatively widespread within the rainforests, mangroves and strips of gallery forest on the Cape. It sleeps in the canopy of a tree, shrouded in leaves and twigs. At night, and sometimes during the day, it searches for fruits and blossoms.

With the exception of a pale chest, this Common Spotted Cuscus has a uniformly grey coat, which identifies it as a female. Only males display the piebald colouring.

About the size of a Common Ringtail, Scaly-tailed Possums are thicker set and heavier. Their furless, highly prehensile tails provide sufficient grip to take their own body weight of up to 2kg (4lb).

Occasionally it descends to the ground to reach new habitat.

The smaller, lighter-weight Southern Common Cuscus lives only in the tropical rainforests of the McIlwraith and Iron ranges north of Coen on the Peninsula's eastern seaboard. It is hard to spot, partly because it lives almost exclusively in the canopy and is active only at night, and partly because, unlike the Spotted Cuscus, it sleeps in a tree hollow. Also, its grey-brown body with a dark dorsal stripe provides excellent camouflage.

Scaly-tailed Possum

The Scaly-tailed Possum lives in the remote northerly and eastern parts of the Kimberley in Western Australia, where temperatures soar and rain falls heavily during the Wet. Its home is a landscape of deeply fissured sandstone ridges and gorges, open woodlands and vine thickets. It snoozes away the day in cool rock crevices but clambers into trees and up vines after sundown to nibble leaves, blossoms and fruits, and to snatch the odd protein-rich creepy crawly that crosses its path.

Young Scaly-tails are usually born during the Dry season (March to August) and spend the first five months in their mother's pouch. In three months they are fully weaned and able to look after themselves. Owls, pythons, Dingoes and quolls all dine on Scaly-tailed Possums, given the chance.

Ringtail, Striped and Leadbeater's Possums

All these possums have tapering, lightly furred tails, two digits opposing three on their forelegs for a strong grasp and teeth that are well adapted for grinding up the cellulose in leaves.

Common Ringtail Possum

It may take a while for you to find a Common Ringtail Possum but they are there on the outskirts of our towns and cities. They are much shyer than Common Brushtails but they do live in our parks and reserves, or even gardens adjoining bushland. Throughout eastern Australia, including Tasmania, they are common in eucalypt forests, coastal and riverine vegetation, and rainforests.

Keep a look out for their nests (dreys). Common Ringtails build these dreys in trees, usually only 4–5m (13–16ft) above the ground. They consist of a big ball of twigs lined with bark and grasses. They are easily mistaken for large birds' nests but there is only a small opening. Ringtails have several dreys and alternate between them, sometimes sharing their quarters with another Ringtail.

The Western Ringtail Possum, confined to the south-western corner of Western Australia, is considered a different species. It has disappeared from much of its original habitat, hunted down by Foxes and Cats and rendered homeless by land clearing. It is now considered rare and endangered.

The Common Ringtail Possum weighs no more than a kilo (2½lb). It is grey to ginger above and pale beneath, with a distinctive white-tipped tail. Along the underside of the tail is a strip of bare, ribbed skin that provides traction when the possum is hanging on, or in need of support while stretching across a span.

TWO-POO POSSUM

The Common Ringtail Possum is vegetarian. Its diet of buds, blossoms and tender new leaves is not particularly nutritious. To eke out every bit of goodness, it eats it twice. A soft pellet, called a caecotroph, is voided from the night's feeding inside the drey and then eaten, creating the hard fibrous pellets disposed of the next night on the ground.

Rock Ringtail Possum

This possum dwells within the remote escarpment country of the Top End, from the Kimberley in Western Australia to western Queensland. It is a sociable possum that lives in family groups and shelters by day in rock crevices where it is safe and cool. At night it scales trees and forages on leaves, flowers and fruits. Researchers have been surprised to find that the males of this species appear to be monogamous and partake in their share of parental care.

Striped Possum

Despite its striking fur coat of black and white stripes, this agile possum is rarely seen. It travels at speed through the branches in the woodlands and rainforests of northern Queensland, searching for insects, its major source of food. It is especially fond of grubs, which it scrapes out of rotting wood with a pair of stout incisors on its bottom jaw and a long, bony fourth finger and claw before slurping them into its mouth with its flexible long tongue.

At night it is highly active and noisy as it crashes through the leaves of the canopy and leaps between branches, but it spends the day asleep, curled up in a leaf-lined hollow or even in the centre of an epiphytic fern.

A Striped Possum arches its tail to give it balance while making a steep descent. Its enormous fourth fingers and claws are indispensable tools for extracting grubs from rotten timber.

AMERICAN RELATIVES
The possums that live throughout New Guinea and Australia are distant relatives of the opossums of the Americas.

Leadbeater's Possum

The stronghold of this small endangered possum is the tall, wet forest of Victoria's Central Highlands but it has also been recorded in Snow Gum woodlands and swamplands. It feeds primarily on plant and animal secretions but also takes creepy crawlies that lurk on and under leaves, branches and the bark of trees and bushes. It requires a thick understorey of wattles from which it takes sap and is dependent on nesting hollows high up in trees.

Extended family members live together in colonies. There is usually only one breeding pair in the colony; others are there to assist in protecting the territory and the group. The forest tree hollows essential to the well-being of Leadbeater's Possum take at least 120 years to form. Habitat containing such trees is susceptible to logging and fires. Currently being monitored by ecologists, there are fears for this little possum's survival.

The lively little Leadbeater's Possum resembles a Sugar or Squirrel Glider but this species has no gliding membrane. It weighs less than 200g (7oz) and measures little more than 30cm (12in) from nose to tail tip. A distinctive black stripe runs down its grey back and its tail darkens towards its tip and fluffs out into a club-like shape.

The Rainforest Possums

Five possums are confined to the rainforests of north-eastern Queensland. They are restricted to the uplands, where they occur as a number of isolated populations. Such a diversity of medium-sized mammals in so small a space is remarkable. Known as the Wet Tropics, Australia's northern rainforests are recognised as a world hot-spot for biodiversity of plants and animals, and the possums' habitat is accordingly protected by World Heritage listing.

All five possums are about the size of a Common Ringtail. Four are Ringtail Possums. The fifth is a coppery form of the Common Brushtail Possum.

Daintree Ringtail

The Daintree Ringtail Possum lives on just three rainforest-clad uplands within the greater Daintree region: Mt Carbine Tableland, Mt Windsor Tableland and Thornton Peak. In these highly restricted regions, it appears to be quite common.

These possums are solitary, pairs coming together only to breed. They travel slowly and jump small, safe distances. They usually feed high in the canopy on leaves and fruits, occasionally coming to ground to access suitable trees. During the day they curl up in a nest constructed in a hollow or in a large epiphytic fern if hollows are unavailable.

Herbert River Ringtail

The brown and white patterning of this possum is distinctive. Its long tapering tail, sometimes with a white tip, is naked along much of the underside. A solitary possum, it moves slowly through the treetops, feeding mostly on young leaves and resting in a built nest or curling up in a large epiphytic fern or orchid clump. It lives in the dense rainforest canopy in the gorge country of the Herbert River's headwaters. A separate population

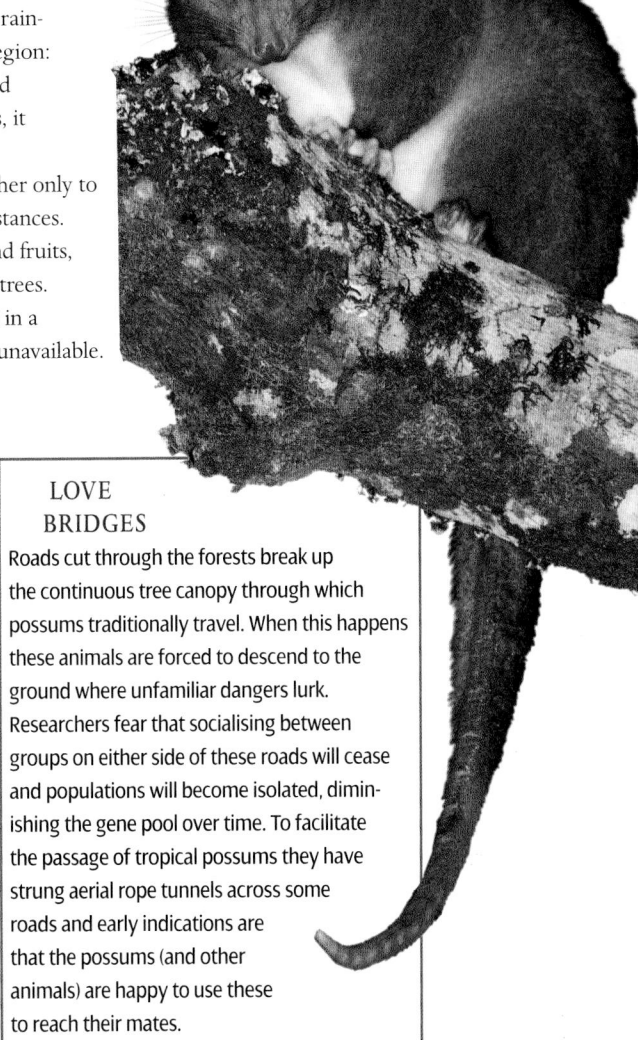

In 1945 the Daintree Ringtail Possum (right) was recognised as a subspecies of the Herbert River Ringtail and then in 1989, on the basis of differences in chromosomes, it was pronounced a distinct species. Its caramel colouring is reminiscent of a young Herbert River Ringtail Possum but there is a dark stripe running down its back and the prehensile tail is darker.

LOVE BRIDGES

Roads cut through the forests break up the continuous tree canopy through which possums traditionally travel. When this happens these animals are forced to descend to the ground where unfamiliar dangers lurk. Researchers fear that socialising between groups on either side of these roads will cease and populations will become isolated, diminishing the gene pool over time. To facilitate the passage of tropical possums they have strung aerial rope tunnels across some roads and early indications are that the possums (and other animals) are happy to use these to reach their mates.

has been found in the rainforest of the Lamb Range behind Cairns and another on Mount Lee west of Ingham.

Green Ringtail Possum

Green Ringtails live as far south as the Paluma Range, south of Ingham, and in rainforest at elevations as low as 300m (1000ft) above sea level. These possums eat leaves almost exclusively, especially those of figs, but they take ripe fruit from these trees as well. They move quickly, making use of vines rather than risk jumping. These ringtails will come to ground to find new habitat, some of which is being fragmented, especially on the Atherton Tableland, by development.

Lemuroid Ringtail Possum

Lemuroids are most abundant at high altitudes and never occur below about 450m (1500ft). They need a lot of rainforest because they are canopy dwellers that rely upon mature trees with a continuous network of branches through which to travel and hollows where they can shelter by day. Where fragmentation of habitat has occurred, populations have disappeared.

A passing resemblance to the Madagascan lemurs is responsible for the name of these possums. While they have similar round heads, short snouts, small ears and forward-facing eyes, lemurs are primates and therefore unrelated. The possums have bushy, prehensile tails and most are a charcoal grey to brown colour with a yellowish tinge underneath. However, in a population isolated on the Carbine Tableland west of Mossman there are some rare beauties with white coats.

Lemuroids rarely come to ground. Vestigial flaps along their flanks that suggest a close affiliation with Greater Gliders enable them to leap small distances between dense leaf clusters. Sometimes they can be heard crashing overhead at night. They feed almost entirely on rainforest leaves, preferably on the young shoots of trees growing on the basalt-rich soils that commonly cap rainforest-clad peaks. Lemuroids are quite social animals, sharing sleeping quarters, gathering at feeding trees and resting in small family groups. Their strong musky scent, no doubt used in communication, can sometimes be detected from ground level.

Having spent up to four months in the pouch, this young Herbert River Possum will ride piggyback on its mother for a couple of weeks before being left at the nest from which it will gradually venture out alone.

The Green Ringtail Possum has no need of a hiding place when sleeping since the greenish tinge of its fur, with the dark zigzag marking down its back, provides effective camouflage. It simply tucks itself up into a ball, and drops off to sleep.

Gliders

Gliders are possums that have evolved loose flaps of skin or membranes (known as a patagium) between their legs. As they leap from branch to branch they stretch out their limbs and the membrane unfolds like a handkerchief, enabling them to parachute onto trees or bushes. With subtle adjustments of this membrane they can change direction and speed.

A Yellow-bellied Glider looks out from a feed of eucalypt blossoms. This large glider requires extensive dense forests of mature trees to support it throughout its life.

All six Australian species are nocturnal, sleeping by day in tree hollows. Naturally enough, they are inhabitants of woodlands and forests. Only the Sugar Glider is found in Tasmania where it may have been introduced in the mid 1800s.

Greater and Yellow-bellied Gliders

With their long, pendulous, fluffy tails, the two largest gliders, the Greater and Yellow-bellied, look superficially similar when perched high in the treetops, but Greater Gliders are more solitary and quieter. They are also larger, being up to 1.3k (3lb)—compared with about 700g (1½lb) in the Yellow-bellied Glider—and 1m (39in) from

A Greater Glider with a dark chocolate coat and contrasting white
chest. This species can be all dark or
all pale or a combination of any
colour in between. The Greater
Glider eats only eucalypt leaves and
has a special stomach to contend
with the high levels of toxins and
cellulose. Its larger, furry ears set it
apart from the Yellow-bellied Glider.

RARE AS MAHOGANY

Rediscovered in 1989, having not been seen since 1886, the
Mahogany Glider was only confirmed as a distinct species
from the Squirrel Glider in 1993. Rare and highly endangered,
this species lives in northern Queensland in a discontinuous
ribbon of lowland rainforest, no wider than 15km (9mile) at
any point.

nose to tail tip. The coat colours of Greater Gliders
vary from creamy white to the darkest brown, or a mix
of any shade in between. Their ears are well furred
and, unlike other gliders, their membrane extends only
to the elbow (rather than to the wrist); nevertheless,
they can cover 100m (330ft) in a single glide.

The Greater Glider inhabits woodlands and forests on
both sides of the Great Dividing Range. Like the Koala,
it eats only eucalypt leaves. It has evolved a special colon
to break down the heavy load of cellulose. This relatively poor diet may account for its placidity.

Yellow-bellied Gliders measure about 70cm (28in)
from nose to tail tip. They live in small family groups
and are loud, active and acrobatic. They may hang
upside down or even run along branches upside down.
Their distinctive creamy yellow fronts contrast
markedly with their overall darker colouration, and their
ears are furless.

Most Yellow-bellieds live in the dense wet forests of
the eastern seaboard but several populations are
isolated in the higher-altitude rainforests of northern Queensland
where temperatures remain relatively cool.

For food they rely heavily on the sugary fluids that ooze from
plants and insects known as manna, honeydew and lerps. To access
eucalypt sap they gnaw the bark with their incisors to 'bleed' the tree
and they return regularly to tap these sites, leaving heavily scarred
trees. Protein from pollen and invertebrates supplements this high-
carbohydrate diet.

Dependence on hollows in mature trees and
a diversity of plants means that Yellow-bellied
Gliders need home ranges of 30–70ha
(75–175ac), and so protection of extensive
forest habitat is essential to their survival. By
contrast the home range of Greater Gliders
may be only 1 or 2ha (2½ or 5ac) but they
remain faithful to their patch, building dozens
of dens within this limited area. Being sedentary, they are prone to the impacts of logging.

HAVING A LIE-IN

During inclement weather smaller gliders sometimes curl up
in a nest for a few days together. As their metabolism slows
and their body temperature drops they become torpid. This
is an energy-saving survival strategy. The social Feathertail
Gliders are particularly susceptible to cold and frequently
bed down with companions in a feather and fur-lined nest.

Sugar and Squirrel Gliders

Sizes and tails distinguish Sugar Gliders from Squirrel Gliders. Sugar Gliders are about 38cm (15in) long, half of which is tail; Squirrel Gliders are nearly twice as big. Both are grey with a dark stripe on the forehead that runs down the back. Both, too, have long, thick bushy tails but the Sugar Glider has a white tip and the tail of the Squirrel Glider is decidedly thicker at its base.

Sugar Gliders occur in a broad coastal band from the Kimberley region of north-western Western Australia across to the eastern seaboard and down into and throughout all but innermost Victoria, just reaching into south-eastern South Australia. They also inhabit Tasmania. Still quite common in wooded areas of south-eastern Australia, they reside in a range of tree terrains, including remnant trees alongside roads and rivers. They chew into the bark of wattles and gums to release the sap and take nectar pollen, manna and invertebrates. Squirrel Gliders share a similar diet and habitat, although they avoid the wetter forests and so are absent from northern Australia and Tasmania but reach into some of the dry woodlands west of the Great Dividing Range.

Both gliders live in family groups and are highly territorial. They leave messages with scent markings and vocally, uttering

A Sugar Glider feeding on the sap oozing from the bark of a eucalypt tree. It cuts the bark with its teeth and maintains the flow of sap by keeping the wound open. Sugar Gliders are social creatures and up to 12 individuals have been found nesting together. They usually choose small, slit-shaped hollows into which they can squeeze but larger predators cannot.

A Squirrel Glider caught in the spotlight. Note the thick base of its tail, a feature that distinguishes it from the smaller Sugar Glider. The rippling folds of its membrane, edged with white, are just visible. When taking to the air its legs stretch out and the membrane unfolds, allowing it to glide up to 60m (226ft). As it splats onto a vertical trunk unharmed, the elongated claws of its fourth and fifth 'fingers' gain an instant purchase. Powerful Owls love gliders for dinner and so these possums must remain alert at all times.

The prehensile tail of the Feathertail Glider wraps strongly around twigs and branches as this tiny marsupial, no bigger than a House Mouse, manoeuvres through bushes and trees. This glider is an amazing acrobat. It catapults itself fearlessly off branches and spirals down like a fluttering leaf with its membrane taut and limbs out-stretched. Its thin, flexible tail bears stiff bristles that stick out in a single plane like a quill. On landing, sharp claws provide a good grip but Feathertails can also land on smooth vertical surfaces as they have minute suction pads on the soles of their feet.

Three little Honey Possums (right) get stuck into a bottlebrush blossom. Banksias are another favourite. These miniature marsupials weigh only 9g (⅓oz) and would fit into the palm of a child's hand. In relation to other possums, they are a bit of an anomaly and in fact may be the sole survivors from an otherwise defunct line of marsupial evolution.

whirrings, gurgles and high-pitched barks; when alarmed Sugar Gliders hiss or yap. Both gliders gather leaves to make nests in tree cavities and have several dens; some may be conveniently located for seasonal food, others are favoured for their thermal qualities. Multiple use of hollows may be a means of parasite control. It also serves to confuse predators: ever-vigilant forest owls must decide which hollows to stake out.

Sugar and Squirrel Gliders produce one or two young each year. After a couple of months in the pouch they are left in the nest and at four months they are weaned. Sugar Gliders live for up to 12 years, while six years is average for Squirrel Gliders, which may explain why there is a greater abundance of Sugar Gliders.

Feathertail Glider

These tiny delightful gliders occupy forests and woodlands south and east from the top of Queensland to wooded areas around Adelaide in South Australia. They favour tall wet eucalypt forests with a well-developed understorey in which to build their nests from bark and leaves. They visit flowers nightly, using their brush-tipped tongue to soak up nectar and sweep up pollen. They also lick up honeydew, manna and lerps and snatch invertebrates.

Honey Possum

This unique little marsupial lives in the sandy heathlands of south-western Western Australia, where a profusion of native shrubs provide a year-round supply of its only food: nectar and pollen. No other mammal takes nectar feeding to this extreme. The only equivalent among vertebrates is the hummingbirds of the Americas, which of course have the advantage of flight. The Honey Possum has no need of claws but has very flexible feet and a prehensile tail for clambering about. To penetrate flowers it has a pointy nose and a sheathed 18mm (¾in)-long flexible tongue, brush-tipped and shaped for nectar extraction. Its few teeth act as a scraper for pollen picked up on the tongue.

Honey Possums sleep in disused birds' nests or tiny hollows and can live on 100m² (1075sq ft) their whole life provided there is sufficient food. They appear to breed in response to mass flowerings, weaning two or three young over a 10-week period, first in mother's four-teat pouch and then at the nest, after which they learn the ropes from mum. In common with most species of kangaroos, Honey Possums can put a pregnancy on pause in the event of poor conditions or unavailable space in the pouch.

Pygmy-possums

These are the smallest of all the possums. They have long slender prehensile tails and all but the Mountain Pygmy-possum live in trees or shrubs. They are quick, agile and have an acute sense of smell, perfect attributes for catching insects, an important source of food for most species. All the pygmy-possums build nests.

The tiniest of all pygmy-possums is the Little Pygmy-possum, which weighs a mere 10g (⅓oz)—less than half a teaspoon of sugar. It is usually found by accident, while splitting wood or dismantling old buildings. More common in Tasmania, it also occupies pockets of mallee and eucalypt forests in the southern part of the mainland. Inside its pouch there are four teats but the suckling young soon outgrow their miniscule haven and must stay in the nest or ride piggyback on mother.

Another rarely seen species is the Long-tailed Pygmy-possum, which inhabits the rainforests and trees at the edge of the coastal plains of north-eastern Queensland. There is still much to discover about this species, which is also known from the rainforests of New Guinea.

A reddish tinge to the upper body and a pure white chest and belly distinguish the Western Pygmy-possum from its eastern counterpart. While both average a nose to tail tip length of 16–18cm (6–7in), the Western species weighs a mere 13g (½oz) as against 24g (¾oz). It feeds among the dense flowering shrubs that grow in open woodlands, mallee heath and dry forest in the south-west, southern South Australia and western Victoria. Recently a population has also been discovered in south-western New South Wales.

Eastern Pygmy-possum

The Eastern Pygmy-possum is a solitary animal that is rarely seen but it is quite common in bushland where year-round native flowers proliferate. About the size of a House Mouse, it has dark bulging eyes and big ears. Its brush-tipped tongue is an evolutionary adaptation to obtain nectar from blossoms.

This little possum lives in the heaths, swamps, forests and subalpine

The Eastern Pygmy-possum has a long brush-tipped tongue, ideally suited to lapping up nectar and gathering pollen from native flowers. Among its favourites are the flowers of banksias, bottlebrushes and eucalypts.

woodlands of south-eastern Australia, including Tasmania. Its has a prehensile tail that is fattened at its base to act as a food storage deposit for when flowers are unavailable or during cold weather when it may go into torpor for up to six weeks.

It rests by day in a globular nest of woven shredded bark and grass, tucked into a crevice or tree hollow. Between spring and autumn it may produce two litters of four young. These offspring spend six weeks in the pouch. They develop quickly and may be ready to breed the following season.

Mountain Pygmy-possum

The first living Mountain Pygmy-possum was discovered only in 1966—in a ski hut at Mount Hotham in the Victorian Alps. Another came to light three years later in the Snowy Mountains. Previous to these discoveries, this little marsupial had been known only as a fossil from the Wombeyan Caves in New South Wales.

Slightly bigger than the Eastern Pygmy-Possum, it is recognised by its long tail, which is almost 1½ times its body length and scaly, with only its fat base covered in hair. Sometimes it carries its tail curled up like a watch spring. The Mountain Pygmy-possum is confined to the high mountains of south-eastern Australia and occurs only at altitudes of over 1400m (4500ft), which is often above the snowline. The only other mammals able to live at the summit of Mt Kosciuszko is the Dusky Antechinus. Unlike its tree-dwelling cousins, this mountain species scurries about on boulder fields and throughout high-altitude shrubby heath. It is usually found around tors and boulders that provide shelter and are used by Bogong Moths, an important source of food.

It is one of the only Australian species that truly hibernates. Its nest, built deep beneath rocks, becomes blanketed with snow in winter. Hibernation has been recorded for as long as seven months. In spring it mates and in November four young are born. They are carried in the pouch for four to six weeks and weaned at eight to nine weeks. These little marsupials can live up to 11 years in the wild.

> ### SKIING DOWN AND SCRAMBLING UP
> Male and female Mountain Pygmy-possums usually live apart. Only in the breeding season do males scramble up the mountain to court females. Every year hibernating possums must share their tiny patches of snow country with skiers. Since the construction of man-made tunnels beneath roads has prevented squashing of their 'highways', the survival rates of these endangered animals have improved. However, global warming may pose new threats.

Throughout most of the year Mountain Pygmy-possums pick berries and seeds with their nimble forepaws but when the Bogong Moths arrive at their summer-time caves and crevices the possums feast on these, building up fat reserves.

Bettongs, Potoroos and the Musky Rat-kangaroo

None of these small hopping marsupials stand much higher than 40cm (16in), although they vary in weight from 600g (21oz) or so in Musky Rat-kangaroos to a few kilos (5lb) in the Rufous Bettongs and Long-footed Potoroos. They all have slightly prehensile tails and some of them use these to carry nesting material.

ROUND AND ROUND WE GO
Small hopping marsupials of the undergrowth feed on truffle-like fungi and disperse the spores in faecal pellets, which helps spread them around. These fungi aid trees to absorb nutrients and water, and the trees in turn provide fungi with sugars for growth, so there's at least a three-way association happening in this natural system.

Members of this group have a broad diet, many relying quite heavily on underground fruiting, truffle-like fungi. All of them have a highly developed sense of smell and are able to detect food beneath the surface. They excavate the fungi by rapidly scrabbling with their large, powerful foreclaws, sometimes ploughing through the leaf litter nose-first like little bulldozers.

Potoroos

The potoroos are solid little hoppers with slightly stooped backs and pointy Roman-like noses. Their fur is thick, soft and grizzled, varying from dark grey to rufous brown, and their tails, which are shorter than their bodies, are tapered and only lightly furred. These animals are cautious and remain under cover until dusk, when they usually venture out to feed. They like soft friable soil that is easy to dig and from which they recover fungi, grubs, roots and tubers.

The Long-nosed Potoroo lives in the dense undergrowth of coastal heathlands and dry and wet eucalypt forests in Tasmania, and in pockets along the east coast of the mainland. The elusive Long-footed Potoroo was first described by biologists only in 1980, although specimens had been inadvertently collected and mislabelled a decade or so before. First discovered in the forests of far East Gippsland in eastern Victoria, two other small populations have since been found in the Berry Mountains in north-eastern Victoria and the far south-eastern corner of New South Wales.

This photograph of a female Gilbert's Potoroo showing her joey where to find food is very rare because this species is one of the most endangered mammals in the world. Believed to be extinct for 115 years, it was rediscovered in 1994. The only known wild population lives on the slopes of Mount Gardner in Two People's Bay Nature Reserve outside Albany in Western Australia and is estimated at between 25 and 50 individuals.

Bettongs

Bettongs require large home ranges of 45–100ha (110–250ac) within woodland communities. Many of these areas have been cleared for farming or grazing, so perhaps it is little wonder that all five species of bettong have been in decline ever since European settlement.

The small Northern Bettong, perhaps the most fungus-dependent of all the bettongs, is known from only four isolated localities along the western edge of the Wet Tropics in north-eastern Queensland, within a narrow band of tall open woodland between rainforest to the east and savanna woodland to the west.

The Burrowing Bettong once inhabited the drier parts of Australia, west of the Great Dividing Range, and was probably the most widespread mammal in Australia prior to European settlement. Now it lives only on some offshore islands of Western Australia. Known by early settlers as the Boodie Rat, it was considered a pest. Boodies eat fallen fruits and seeds, termites, underground tubers and probably fungi. Despite being able to breed three times a year, Foxes and Cats have destroyed mainland populations, except within enclosures where these feral predators have been eradicated.

Historically widespread throughout arid and semi-arid regions of south-eastern Australia, the Brush-tailed Bettong is now thought to be extinct but some tiny populations of a subspecies, the Woylie, in south-western Australia have become the target of conservation efforts. Fox baiting and translocation of animals is helping re-establishment and recovery in a few reserves and forests.

Nevertheless, this species occupies only a small percentage of its historic range.

In Queensland and north-east New South Wales the Rufous Bettong hangs on in grassy understoreys beneath dry and wet eucalypt forests and woodlands, while a population on the

A Burrowing Bettong emerges from its tunnel and checks its surroundings before venturing out into the open to feed. This bettong is an inveterate burrower. Preferring firm moist soils (but never in rainforest) to collapsible sand, it excavates elaborate tunnels, some quite deep and with many entrances. It is highly social and shares its subterranean maze with many (some say up to 60) companions. Western Quolls, Brush-tailed Possums and even Rabbits have also been known to curl up and 'sleep over' in these handy burrows.

Victoria–New South Wales border has become extinct. Until recently, the Tasmanian Bettong has had to face fewer adversities. Although extinct on the mainland, the lack of Foxes (until 2000/01) and limited Rabbit populations may account for this bettong's continuing presence in nutrient-poor dry eucalypt woodlands across the eastern half of the island state.

Musky Rat-kangaroo

The Musky Rat-kangaroo of tropical rainforests may look similar to the bettongs and potoroos but it is in fact the sole survivor of an ancient and otherwise extinct line of evolution that thrived in Australia's rainforests 20 million years ago, when the forests were far more widespread than they are today. The telltale signs of a different lineage lie in its possession of a big fifth toe on its hind foot (all other hoppers have four) and its quadrupedal galloping, rather than hopping, gait. The opposable toe provides a grasp and this animal does sometimes climb. Also unusual is its ability to bear twins, even triplets, instead of a single offspring.

Apart from the Numbat, the Musky Rat-kangaroo is the only small- to medium-sized marsupial that is normally active during the daytime, which means you have a chance of seeing one if you visit its habitat. About the size of a Rabbit, it has a beautiful dark rich-coloured coat and a naked, scaly tail. It forages through the leaf litter for rainforest fruits, fungi and invertebrates. If you're very lucky you might see it perform a class act as it collects nesting material in its mouth and forepaws, deposits it on the ground, then kicks it up with its back legs into its coiled tail.

> ### SOUTH-WEST IMMUNITIES
> Many native mammals in south-western Australia have developed an immunity to a poison found in a group of native pea plants belonging to the genus *Gastrolobium*. Monofluoroacetic acid, more commonly known as 1080, is highly toxic to exotic mammals, both vegetarians like Rabbits and Goats, and carnivores, such as Cats and Foxes. Several native mammals that elsewhere have become extinct or are highly endangered, continue to survive in the south-west and their immunity is, at least in part, attributed to the occurrence of these plants in some areas.

Kangaroos and Wallabies

No animal is more symbolic of Australia than the kangaroo; it even features on the nation's coat of arms—well, at least one species does, the Red Kangaroo. There are, however, another 27 species of kangaroo and wallaby, and not all of them live on the wide open plains of the inland like the big Red.

A female Eastern Grey Kangaroo with her joey. At this stage joeys are highly active, tumbling out of mum's pouch to hop around and graze but darting back to safety at the slightest hint of danger. Like most young mammals, they are extremely flexible, as the hindlegs poking out of the pouch illustrate.

Perhaps the most curious and impressive aspect of kangaroos and wallabies is how they move. Frogs and a few small desert mammals hop but the kangaroos have evolved a physique that makes hopping an exceedingly fast and highly efficient means of getting around. It is said that a Red Kangaroo can outpace a race horse.

In 'big roos' most of the weight is concentrated in their hindquarters, where the tendons of their massive hindlegs, large muscular tail and the lower back are able to store elastic energy. Once in its stride a hopping kangaroo expends virtually no energy. As it lands on the ground the impact is stored in its body and powers its next hop off the ground.

Mature male kangaroos spend can smell when a female is ready to mate. Three to five weeks after a coupling, females give birth to a fully formed but tiny kangaroo the size of your smallest fingernail. Naked and pink it tenaciously pulls itself up its mother's fur with the sharp little claws of its front paws to reach the safety of her pouch. Once inside, it locates one of her teats and attaches itself. Here it stays, putting on weight for six to 11 months (depending on species). In the last few months before it is fully weaned the flexible gangly joey somersaults and catapults itself in and out of the pouch with little thought for mum.

Red Kangaroos

This is the biggest marsupial in the world. A mature male may stand 2m (7ft) tall and his muscular form is an impressive sight. Males are red or, more precisely, a rufous brown. Females are sometimes reddish, too, but more often they are a bluish grey. Dark points on the end of their limbs, a pale tail, a bare nose and white cheek patches help to distinguish the Reds.

These kangaroos feed on grass in the open woodlands and on the vast flat inland plains of mallee, saltbush and mulga. Unable to survive without fresh water, they must travel long distances in times of drought in order to drink. When food and water are in short supply or when predation is high you may see only one or two animals, but when conditions are good large groups (mobs) graze together by night and laze about in the shade through hot days.

Mobs consist of family members of various ages and sex. Dominant males are recognised by their large size. Mature females with their joeys may stay slightly aloof from the mob. Only after a tiny embryonic youngster is born and has safely ensconced itself in mum's pouch, will a female accept the advances of a male. Joeys remain in the pouch suckling for eight months and are fully weaned at 12 months.

> ### SMALL DISASTERS
> While the larger kangaroos and wallabies have mostly benefited from farmers sowing crops, digging dams and sinking bores, much of Australia's inheritance of small hopping marsupials has disappeared without anyone much noticing . . . until very recently. Many of these extinctions have been from the arid and semi-arid inland.

A female Red Kangaroo with her joey in the dim light of dusk. The bluish grey fur of the female is only slightly tinged with red but in the much larger male this red- or rufous-coloured fur predominates.

> ### A PREGNANT PAUSE
> In poor conditions, or if a joey has yet to leave the pouch, many female kangaroos can put their pregnancy on hold. Technically known as embryonic diapause, this remarkable survival mechanism is a way of saving lives (the embryo's) and saving energy (mum's).

Imagine this . . . seeing a mob of kangaroos streaking across a paddock from your window. This photograph of Western Grey Kangaroos in motion illustrates beautifully the way these animals move; their muscular thighs power their long legs and feet as they jump, while their tails provide balance.

This aerial shot captures the powerful muscular body of a Euro in motion. Like all of the wallaroos its limbs are shorter and broader than the other large kangaroos and to suit their rocky habitat the soles of their hind feet are granulated to give them a firm grip on boulders and rock piles.

Wallaroos

Wallaroos are quite large kangaroos: males stand over 1m (39in) high and may weigh more than 40kg (88lb); females are almost half this size. Most are stocky and broad chested with shaggy-looking fur. They live in rocky country, on escarpments and stony hills. Although they inhabit all mainland states, their habitat is fragmented.

Most widespread are two subspecies of the Common Wallaroo. The so-called Eastern Wallaroo lives among the outcrops on the slopes of the Great Dividing Range, while the Euro inhabits patches of suitable habitat across a vast stretch of the continent that reaches all the way to the west coast and up into the tropical north. While Eastern Wallaroos are generally grey, Euros are more reddish.

A smaller, northern species, known as the Black Wallaroo, is a shy, dark-coloured animal, confined to a small area of the steep Arnhem Land escarpment and its sharply dissected plateau.

All these wallaroos are solitary animals that shelter by day in the deep shade of rocky outcrops, coming down the slopes to feed on grasses at night. Only when food is especially abundant do several animals graze together.

Most kangaroos must find fresh water every day to stay healthy. Although they may benefit at times from the dams and bores installed by farmers in semi-arid regions, drought often takes a heavy toll on the large kangaroos. This powerful male Euro has had to dig a deep hole to access water from the surrounding parched land.

There is also a so-called Antilopine Wallaroo that lives in tropical woodlands but, apart from its shaggy-looking fur, this animal looks and behaves more like an Eastern or Western Grey Kangaroo. Slender and long limbed, the tan-coloured males and smaller, greyer females laze about by day under shade trees and graze on open grasslands at night. During the Wet mobs may even feed during the day to take advantage of so much green pick.

Western and Eastern Grey Kangaroos

Unless you are in the Top End, these are the roos you are most likely to see. The two distinct species look alike, although Western Greys have woollier fur and are darker, especially on their faces and forepaws. Males of both species weigh about 65kg (143lb) and females about 30kg (66lb).

An important distinction between the species is the length of their reproductive cycles. Pregnancies in Western Greys are shorter and so is the time joey spend in the pouch.

Greys are mostly nocturnal but they sometimes feed at either end of the day, especially when it is overcast. They emerge from woodlands and forest shelters to graze in adjacent open grasslands.

Agile Wallaby

Found across Western Australia, the Northern Territory and Queensland, Agile Wallabies are the most common tropical kangaroos. Often occurring around river systems, they shelter in the understorey of open forests and woodlands throughout the heat of day. They are social

> WHEN WALLABIES
> ARE ROOS
> 'Wallaby' is just the name used to describe a small kangaroo.

A pair of young male Agile Wallabies practising their boxing and sparring. When they grow up they may come to real blows while vying for females. Body blows are inflicted mostly to the belly by powerful hindlegs as the muscular tail briefly takes the entire weight of the animal.

animals and at dawn and dusk small groups of up to 10 animals can often be seen feeding out in open country. When there is an abundance of food, groups may come together to graze in large mobs.

Agile Wallabies graze on grasses, browse on leaves and sometimes take fruit from trees. They have strong claws for digging out juicy roots and 'agile' forepaws to manipulate food. Medium-sized and sandy-coloured, they can be distinguished by a white thigh stripe and a dark face stripe that runs through the eye to the muzzle, underscored by a white chin strap.

The grey fur of the Red-necked Wallaby is tinged with red on its neck, shoulders and forelegs and often on its tail and lower hind-quarters. It has a white cheek strap and often a dark stripe down the centre of its face.

Red-necked Wallaby

Red-necked Wallabies are common inhabitants of south-eastern eucalypt forests from southern Queensland to eastern South Australia. In Tasmania and on the islands of Bass Strait they are known as Bennett's Wallabies. Males stand about 80cm (31in) high and weigh about 20kg (44lb). They are more heavily built and slightly larger than females.

These robust wallabies usually rest alone in the shrubby under-storey of the forest by day, venturing out into grassy areas to graze in the evening. Here, where grass is plentiful, groups of up to 30 animals may gather. Farmers often consider this wallaby a pest as it fails to discriminate between native grasslands and improved pastures.

Swamp Wallaby

The Swamp Wallaby is classified separately from other large kangaroos and wallabies on account of its chromosomes; curiously it has only 10 while all the others have 16. It is quite big, averaging about 15kg (33lb) and standing 70cm (28in) high and, unusually, males vary little in size from females. Their dense fur may be dark grey to orange-brown depending on region. The front of the face is dark, as is the tail and the ends of all four limbs.

Parma Wallaby

You will be extremely fortunate to see the pretty little Parma Wallaby in the wild as it has not fared well in its native habitat. It lives in limited numbers in the eucalypt forests of New South Wales where it hides by day in the understorey and hops through worn-down runways out to open areas at night to feed. Parma Wallabies stand about 50cm (20in) high and weigh 3.5–5kg (8–11lb); males are larger than females. As they hop, they keep their body relatively horizontal and their tail, which is sometimes tipped with white, curled upwards in a shallow U-shape.

Tammar Wallaby

Your best chance of seeing this little wallaby is on Kangaroo Island in South Australia. Once common across much of the southern mainland, populations have succumbed to predators and the destruction of their dense scrubland habitat. Little more than 50cm (20in) high and with thick grey-brown fur, the Tammar hides under a blanket of low bushes by day, venturing out to feed on grasses only at night.

The Nailtails

There were once three species of nailtails but the Crescent Nailtail, a one-time woodland inhabitant of the outback, has been driven to extinction by land clearance, introduced competitors (Rabbits) and predators (Foxes, Cats and humans). The Bridled Nailtail teeters on the brink of extinction but captive breeding programs are underway and may save the day. Only

The Swamp Wallaby has forsaken the open grasslands for a life in the woodlands and forests of the eastern and south-eastern mainland. It is a hardy and relatively common solitary animal that feeds on whatever the forest has to offer: fungi, bracken, leaves and sedges.

Nailtails derive their name from a horny projection at the end of their tails. Less than 1cm (⅓in) long, the purpose of this curious fingernail-like feature remains a mystery.

A Bridled Nailtail dashing away. These wallabies stand about 50–80cm (20–32in) high and weigh 4.5–9kg (10–20lb), with females being considerably smaller than males. Sandy brown to grey, this wallaby is easily distinguished by the white line or 'bridle' that runs around its shoulders, from the back of its neck and under its forearms.

the Northern Nailtail on the floodplains of northern Australia is holding its own. Although mostly solitary, it sometimes feeds with Agile Wallabies. By day it rests hidden in a hollowed-out scrape beside tufts of tussock grasses.

Western Brush Wallaby

Standing 1.2m (47in) high and weighing 5–7kg (11–15lb), this pale grey kangaroo has a long tail with a crest of black hairs towards its end. Dark fore and hind feet explain its other name: Black-gloved Wallaby. A native kangaroo of the south-west, the Western Brush Wallaby grazes on flat, fairly open land in jarrah forests, woodlands, mallee and heathlands. When alarmed, it moves with agility and speed, keeping its body close to the ground. Until the advent of Fox baiting, this wallaby was disappearing at an alarming rate.

Black-striped Wallaby

The Black-striped Wallaby is another medium-sized wallaby with a white thigh stripe, but this shy animal lives in forests with dense under-storey (either vine thickets or wattles) in Queensland and northern New South Wales. In groups of up to 20 animals it hides out by day in the gloom and shadows, moving out to graze at night. The black stripe that runs from between its eyes, over its head and half way down its back is distinctive.

Whiptail Wallaby

This elegant pale grey wallaby has fine features and a slender, tapering and very long tail, tipped with black. Delineating a dark face is a broad white cheek stripe that runs from below the eye to the nose. Whiptails feed on understorey grasses, ferns and herbs in dry woodlands among the undulating hills on both sides of the Great Dividing Range, from Cooktown in Queensland to northern New South Wales. Often active by day, you may see mobs of up to 50 individuals. Males take two or three years to become sexually mature. Access to females is competitive and usually must be fought for.

Quokkas

Quokkas stand about 50cm (20in) high and weigh only about 3kg (7lb). They have small rounded ears, coarse hair and a much shorter tail than most wallabies. Like many of the small marsupials, they were once widespread on the mainland in the south-west and, until 1960, Quokkas still inhabited swamps around Perth. The scrub thickets they need for cover, however, have been stripped away and introduced predators have found them easy prey. The best place to see them today is on Rottnest Island, off the coast from Perth, Western Australia.

This female Quokka and her joey are among the few resident Quokkas left on the mainland. Stripped of the thick cover that these animals need for protection, most have disappeared or live only on islands off the west coast.

The attractive Spectacled Hare-wallaby is named for the circles of red fur around its eyes. It weighs around 4.5kg (10lb) and stands less than 50cm (20in) tall. It has thick salt-and-pepper fur tinged with red, which provides superb camouflage as it hops through the hummock grasslands and the understorey of open woodlands and tall shrublands.

Hare-wallabies

There used to be five species of these little round wallabies but two (Central and Eastern) have completely disappeared since European settlement. For the three remaining species, help is on the way but their survival continues to be threatened by Foxes and Cats. In the Northern Territory and Western Australia the Spectacled Hare-wallaby's habitats are fragmented but Queensland still retains some suitable land.

The Rufous Hare-wallaby or Mala, standing only 30–36cm (12–14in) high and weighing less than 2kg (4lb), once hopped about the spinifex deserts of the Northern Territory, the Great Sandy and Gibson deserts of Western Australia, and the north-western parts of South Australia, but Foxes and fire wreaked havoc on their populations. Today they survive only on a few islands in the north-west of Western Australia or in captive colonies on the mainland.

Despite its similar appearance, the Banded Hare-wallaby comes from a completely different evolutionary line. Once an inhabitant of the mainland, it was unable to survive the encroachment of introduced predators and is now found on only two islands—Bernier and Dorre in Shark Bay, Western Australia.

The Banded Hare-wallaby, so named for its darkly banded rump, shelters, sometimes in the company of others, beneath the dense cover of low shrubs. To reach open feeding grounds of grasses and shrubs, it moves along worn-down runways.

Pademelons

These charming hunched little kangaroos with their dark eyes and shiny black noses live in dense understorey at the edges of rainforests. They are always a delight to encounter. Wary and shy, they may stand their ground if you stay still long enough.

To insulate itself from the cold winter weather the Tasmanian Pademelon has a much thicker coat than mainland pademelons. It is also darker, which affords it the best camouflage in its cool-temperate rainforest habitat.

Pademelons divide their attention between feeding upon fallen leaves and fruit on all fours and popping upright constantly to look and listen for danger. In all three species their brown fur is tinged a rusty red in certain places. As the names suggest, the red fur of Red-necked Pademelon is on its upper neck, shoulders and upper forelimbs while that of the Red-legged Pademelon is on its hindlegs, specifically the thighs, but also on the forearms, at the base of the ears and on the cheeks. A helpful distinguishing mark is the pale stripe on its upper lip.

The Tasmanian Pademelon is confined to that state but once inhabited the southern mainland. Sometimes known to as the Red-bellied Pademelon, its rufous tones are to be found, not surprisingly, on its belly, with hints around the eyes and at the base of the tail.

All the pademelons have long muscular tails that provide support when moving slowly. Against an adult human's leg they stand somewhere between knee to mid-thigh height. Females are generally smaller, with Red-necked females weighing as little as 2kg (4lb) while Tasmanian males may attain up to 9kg (20lb).

Tree-kangaroos

A kangaroo up a tree may seem like a fanciful notion but these animals really do exist. In fact there are 10 tree-kangaroo species in the world but only two live in Australia; the others inhabit New Guinea.

Both Bennett's Tree-kangaroo and Lumholtz's Tree-kangaroo live only in Australia's north-eastern Queensland tropical forests but fossils of extinct tree-kangaroo species have been found from Wellington and the Hunter Valley in New South Wales to as far south as Hamilton in Victoria, and these date back to around 2 to 5 million years ago. Such findings suggest these areas were once covered in rainforest.

Lumholtz's Tree-kangaroo lives in the high-altitude rainforests of the Atherton Tableland and the Bellenden Ker Range, while Bennett's Tree-kangaroo lives further north in the Daintree River area in lowland vine forests, gallery forests and up into highland rainforests. Bennett's is the largest tree dweller in Australia: 75cm (30in) tall when upright, with an 85cm (33in)-long tail.

Although arboreal, tree-kangaroos do not have prehensile tails or the opposable thumbs of possums, attributes advantageous to a tree-dwelling lifestyle. An ancient branch of the possums descended from the trees a long time ago and became ground-dwelling kangaroos but the tree-kangaroos, it would seem, moved back up into the trees. Since there is no going back once an evolutionary adaptation has been lost, they have had to do without both prehensile tails and opposable thumbs. Nevertheless, they are capable climbers and can jump from tree to tree. Compared with the ground roos, they have long, muscular forearms and short hindlegs. They have developed granulated soles on their feet and powerful claws to help them grip branches.

A young Lumholtz's in a Bird's Nest Fern. We know very little about reproduction and growth rates in the wild but we do know that a mature female tree-kangaroo can produce a single young each year and youngsters probably stay close to their mothers for up to two years. While arboreal pythons are traditional predators of young tree-kangaroos, these days they are more likely to be lost to cars and dogs when they come to ground.

A Lumholtz's Tree-kangaroo, with its seemingly impossibly long and cylindrical tail. Each night tree-kangaroos raise themselves from their daytime 'roosts' high up in a branch to feed on the leaves, and sometimes fruits, of rainforest trees. They clamber along branches on all fours, with alternating steps (ground kangaroos can only move their hindlegs together . . . except when swimming).

Rock-wallabies

Throughout mainland Australia rock-wallabies live on rocky escarpments and outcrops but many of the 16 species have extremely limited ranges. Several are confined to just a few isolated outcrops. By day they shelter in caves and crevices. At dusk they move down towards the lowlands in search of food.

Given the beautiful markings of Yellow-footed Rock-wallabies it is hardly surprising that this species was once the target of the fur trade. Their thickly furred tails are distinctively marked with black and grey rings and tinged with rich sandy tones. Thanks to Fox controls, these rock-wallabies still exist in large colonies. They live in the Flinders Ranges of South Australia and on a few rocky outcrops in semi-arid New South Wales and Queensland.

Rock-wallabies vary considerably in size from 1–12kg (2–26lb). They are remarkably agile and negotiate the uneven surfaces of their terrain with ease. Their short toenails and the granulated pads of their hind feet grip smooth or slippery surfaces and their long cylindrical tails give them balance.

As with other kangaroos and wallabies, pregnant females can put embryo development on pause until the previous offspring ceases to suckle. Most young stay in the pouch for about six months, after which mum leaves joey in a rocky den while she forages. Bored and curious about the world beyond, a joey may wander from its den

only to find itself the unwelcome attention of an eagle. A traditional predator of rock-wallabies (as are pythons), eagles now compete with Dingoes, Cats and Foxes. Foxes especially are a danger when rock-wallabies attempt to cross open pasture or crop fields in the lowlands where once there was the cover of native plants. If they are unable to reach populations on neighbouring outcrops, inter-breeding may cease and gene pools will dwindle over time. However, where Foxes are controlled, populations often recover and recolonisation may occur.

An elusive Short-eared Rock Wallaby, standing a mere 40cm (16in) tall, soaks up the last of the sun's rays. While the deep shade of dens can be pleasantly cool on hot days, rock-wallabies often sunbathe outside their entrances when temperatures drop.

The Queensland Rock-wallabies

Many rock-wallaby species are endemic to Queensland. While their occurrences are patchy because of their need for rocky places, their distributions dot the state's eastern edge from north to south.

The northernmost species, the Cape York Rock-wallaby, lives in a tiny region of tropical woodlands and vine thickets on Cape York Peninsula. Godman's Rock-wallaby inhabits the Cooktown area and, at its southernmost limit, hybridises with the Mareeba Rock-wallaby on the Atherton Tableland. Sharman's Rock-wallabies occupy a small area behind Ingham and the Allied Rock-wallabies, to their south, live on rocky outcrops among open woodland and are widespread in suitable habitat west of Townsville and on Palm and Magnetic islands. Their range abuts that of the

Western Australia's little Monjon is almost entirely nocturnal. It stands a mere 30cm (12in) tall and weighs just over 1kg (2lb). Only discovered in 1978, it was first photographed in 1985 by Jiri Lochman.

The colouring and markings of this Black-footed Rock-wallaby, photographed on the islands of the Recherche Archipelago in Western Australia, are typical of the species. The Black-footed Rock-wallabies are the most widespread of all the rock-wallabies, being present in various forms in three different states. Some live in the Kimberley, some on southern islands and some in the Macdonnell Ranges of Central Australia. Another race, now considered a separate species, is the Purple-necked Rock-wallaby that has a discontinuous distribution across the dry grasslands and open woodlands of western Queensland.

Unadorned Rock-wallabies. Further south and inland, near Clermont, are Herbert's Rock-wallabies and there are tiny scattered colonies of Proserpine Rock-wallabies feeding on the leaves and fruits from vine thickets in dry rainforest areas around Airlie Beach. Some Proserpines have been translocated to Hayman Island in the wake of development on the mainland.

The Brush-tailed Rock-wallaby of south-eastern Queensland, New South Wales and Victoria was once hunted by fur traders and farmers. Its recent alarming disappearance from many localities has prompted considerable conservation efforts. It stands over 50cm (20in) tall and its thick dark coat graduates to a rufous brown towards the hindquarters and tail. Weighing 5–11kg (11–24lb), it is an agile rock hopper and lives in small groups, grazing on grasses and browsing on low shrubs, usually at night.

Remote Locations

In the wild, remote country of the north-west and the Top End a few rock-wallabies have escaped many of the dangers of human settlement, although large-scale grass fires remain a threat. At dusk small groups of Short-eared Rock-wallabies make their way down from the rocky hills and ledges of the Kimberley and Arnhem Land escarpment into the savanna country to feed. The cat-sized Nabarlek or Little Rock-wallaby emerges from the sandstone and granite hills and deeply fissured gorges to nibble on ferns, sedges and grasses.

The tiny Monjon that lives only in the sandstone gorges and rock piles of the Mitchell Plateau in the Kimberley and a few islands off the coast, feeds mainly on the fresh and dry leaves of various rainforest trees. Another western inhabitant is the relatively large Rothschild's Rock-wallaby from the Hamersley Ranges and some offshore islands.

Small Marsupial Predators

Australia has a large family of predatory marsupials known as dasyurids. Many of them are small and resemble the shrews of the northern hemisphere. Despite their size they have formidably sharp teeth, voracious appetites and will tackle prey larger than themselves.

Young Brush-tailed Phascogales curl up together in the nest while mother goes foraging. If they get too cold in her absence they may go into torpor until her return. By mid-summer they will be weaned. Males will disperse away from home; females usually remain closer.

Small dasyurids have bright beady eyes, long, curved front claws for digging, pointy noses for reaching into crevices and holes and dexterous forepaws for handling prey. They are generally nocturnal, or at least crepuscular.

Males are larger than females. While some females have shallow pouches, others have none and still others develop mere abdominal folds to protect their young. Teats number four to 12 and litters are generally large.

These little marsupials shelter and raise their young in nests hidden in hollows, holes and tufts of vegetation. To make them snug they line them with grass, leaves and/or shredded bark. Owls are their traditional predator but Cats are as great a threat these days.

THUMPER STUMPER
When alarmed, phasogales thump a branch or the ground to alert others to possible dangers.

In many species the mating season is a two- or three-week annual synchronised event. Males of many species live only through one breeding season. With their energy spent in marathon sexual activity, their immune system weakens and they succumb to disease. This phenomenon is common among phascogales, antechinuses, Kalutas and some populations of dibblers.

The Agile Antechinus is well named. While insects, spiders, small lizards and berries are its usual fare, it is not averse to a sip of banksia nectar. This common, but rarely seen, inhabitant of south-eastern Australia's heathlands and forests is the smallest of all the antechinuses, rarely weighing more than 30g (1oz).

Phascogales

Phascogales are lively marsupials that look a bit like small squirrels. They have a lightweight, long, grey body, short legs and a tail that, while initially furred like the body, sprouts out into a black fluffy brush. They live mostly in trees and can leap a couple of metres (6ft) between tree branches. Speedy and agile hunters, they snatch spiders, centipedes, insects, small mammals and birds.

The Brush-tailed Phascogale, known as the Tuan in Victoria and as the Common Wambenger in Western Australia, is about 20cm (8in) long, with a tail nearly as long; males weigh about 2kg (4lb). The Northern Brush-tailed Phascogale is about the same size. Between them they are scattered in low densities throughout all but the arid interior of Australia, commonly inhabiting dry sclerophyll forest in the south and monsoonal woodlands and forests in the tropics. Scurrying along branches, as fast on the underside as on top, they sometimes eat upside down, hanging from a branch by their hindlegs.

The much smaller Red-tailed Phascogale is confined to remnants of wandoo–casuarina woodland in Western Australia's wheatbelt. Although the brush remains black, the short fur on its tail is red. Less arboreal, it frequently hunts on the ground and is partial to House Mouse.

Antechinuses

Antechinuses are common but rarely seen. The 10 or so species vary in size from that of a mouse to a rat and, having brown-grey fur, they are often mistaken for these rodents. Most are adept climbers that move in a speedy, erratic fashion.

Antechinuses require good cover but they have adapted to many kinds of well-vegetated habitats: the Atherton Antechinus to tropical rainforests, Dusky Antechinuses to heaths, woodlands and forests and even snow country, the pale Fawn Antechinus to monsoonal woodlands and the Swamp Antechinus to the buttongrass sedgelands of Tasmania.

False antechinuses often inhabit more arid sandy habitats than antechinuses. This Fat-tailed Pseudantechinus lives along rocky ridges in Central Australia, predominantly in and around termite mounds. Its tail acts as a storage facility for food on which it can draw in times of drought. After cold nights it may sunbathe in the early morning sun to raise its body temperature, a behaviour commonly associated with reptiles.

A female Dusky Antechinus staggers awkwardly along, her litter of up to eight young hanging onto her teats in an open pouch. After a couple of months she will leave them in the nest and a month later they will be weaned and able to fend for themselves.

At an average of 16g (½oz) the Little Long-tailed Dunnart may indeed be small but it is no wuss. Here it displays determination and courage as it drags an equally ferocious predator, a centipede, from its lair.

SKIN-BREATHING MAMMAL

The rare Julia Creek Dunnart of Queensland gives birth to young that are no bigger than a grain of rice. Newborns are the focus of much scientific excitement as they can breathe through their skin. While this is not unusual in frogs, mammals have never before been known to do this.

Dunnarts

Dunnarts are not unlike antechinuses but they have bigger ears, large dark eyes and their hind feet are distinctly narrower. Most, too, are smaller, with many adults growing to no more than 10–25g (⅓–¾oz). Also, unlike antechinuses, quite a number of the 19 or so species inhabit arid and semi-arid regions. While some build their own nests, others shelter in other animals' burrows. Some dunnarts are common, such as the Fat-tailed Dunnart, but most are patchily distributed over limited areas.

Planigales

Planigales are tiny. The largest, the Common Planigale, usually weighs no more than 12g (⅖oz) while the Long-tailed Planigale, at no more than 6g (⅕oz), is the world's smallest marsupial. The distinctly flattened skull of all four species is an adaptation to a very specific but bountiful micro-habitat available only to the very small and intrepid: cracked earth.

Through the dry season, cracks appear on the parched claypans and saltpans of arid and semi-arid regions and on the baked floodplains and ephemeral lakes of the tropical north. In these cracks the miniature planigales take shelter from the blistering hot days and freezing night-time temperatures. With their wedge-shaped heads they are able to plough through leaf litter, part grass stalks and investigate narrow cracks in their search for prey.

The Kowari and Mulgaras

Three little plucky desert dwellers live exclusively in harsh arid country. They are the pale grey Kowari and two browner species of Mulgara.

The Kaluta has reddish brown shaggy fur and a relatively stumpy tail, fat at its base. This dasyurid lives among thick tussocks of spinifex in Western Australia's Pilbara region. Inquisitive, active and agile, it exploits every niche in its pursuit of invertebrates and small vertebrates.

Kowaris are scattered about the channel country of south-western Queensland and the scorching gibber plains of Central Australia. Mulgaras are from sandy spinifex country and live among sand dunes. All three species are distinguished by having black ends to their tails. In the Kowari, a full brush of black hairs encircles the end of its tail. In the Crest-tailed Mulgara, the black hairs form a crest along the top end of its tail. The longer, thinner tail of the Brush-tailed Mulgara ends simply in a tapering black tip.

Strong, agile and able to climb and jump, these animals emerge from their daytime burrows to hunt down large invertebrates, lizards, rodents and birds. They are also known to eat carrion. They communicate with odours produced by scent glands and mark territories and burrows with urine. These hardy little animals live for up to five years and carry their young attached to teats in rudimentary abdominal folds.

These little Kultarrs (or Wuhl-Wuhls) are engaged in a territorial dispute. Adapted for life in Australia's sandy arid centre, their long hind limbs might suggest these marsupials are hoppers but they actually bound very nimbly from front legs to hindlegs across the open spaces separating sparse vegetation. The long cylindrical tail, terminating in long dark bristles, provides balance and facilitates sudden changes of direction.

Dibbler

The Dibbler is a rare little dasyurid that lives only in one tiny spot of south-western Western Australia and on a couple of islands off the coast there. It needs thick unburnt ground litter in which to hunt and hide. While perhaps never common, it is hoped that changes to fire regimes may save dibblers from disappearing altogether.

A Wongai Ningaui, another small marsupial predator, despatches a weevil with its needle-like teeth. At barely 10g (⅓oz) and 14cm (5in) long, half of which is tail, this is the largest of the three ningauis. These desert-dwelling insectivorous marsupials shelter among clumps of spinifex, in hollow logs and under dense shrubs. Ningauis are lucky if they survive their first breeding season, when females raise five or six young. The Wongai is common throughout Australia's arid centre. The Pilbara Ningaui lives among the semi-arid grasslands of the Hamersley Plateau in Western Australia's Pilbara region and the Southern Ningaui inhabits semi-arid regions of southern Australia.

Quolls

The carnivorous quolls are native, Rabbit- to Cat-sized marsupials with beautiful white-spotted coats and naked pink noses that quiver as they sniff the air. Mostly solitary predators of forests and woodlands, they look for food at night, prowling along the ground and clambering into trees.

At 2–5kg (4–11lb), the Spotted-tailed Quoll is the largest native carnivore left on mainland Australia. It uses fallen trees as runways and often forages on rock faces and in trees where its long tail provides balance and ridges on its hind feet give grip. Bold white spots on its tail distinguish it from other quolls.

There are four species in Australia: the Eastern, Western and Northern Quolls, and the Spotted-tailed or Tiger Quoll. At 2–5kg (4–11lb), the largest of these is the Spotted-tailed Quoll; now the largest native carnivore left on mainland Australia. The Eastern and Western Quolls weigh 1–2kg (2–4lb) and the diminutive Northern Quoll, a mere 250g–1.2kg (½–2½lb). Adult males are usually larger than females.

Most quolls are partly terrestrial and partly arboreal. The Spotted-tailed Quoll uses fallen trees as runways and often forages in trees and on rock faces, where its long tail provides balance, while ridges on its hind feet give grip. Bold white spots on its tail distinguish this quoll from others. Most quolls scavenge. The smaller ones eat invertebrates, eggs and carrion but the Spotted-tailed Quoll will attack small wallabies, pademelons, possums, gliders and birds. Eastern Quolls eat grass, take blackberries and have adapted to pasture pests in Tasmania, while the Northern Quoll is not averse to fruit and nectar.

Male quolls maintain large territories. They breed annually from May to June or July. Pregnancies last three weeks. A quoll's pouch is rudimentary and cannot accommodate youngsters beyond a certain size. Mothers may drag youngsters along for a while, as they cling to her teats or belly fur, but when they grow too big she leaves them in a nursery den while she hunts. Here siblings may venture out briefly for a game of tag. At about five months they are weaned and on their own. In general, quolls live fast and die young. Some Spotted-tailed Quolls may make it to five years and smaller quolls to two or even three but some male Northern Quolls live only one year.

Since European settlement the range of all four quolls has shrunk due to degraded habitats, introduced species and altered grazing and fire regimes. The Eastern Quoll now lives only in Tasmania, mainland populations having crashed during the first decades of the twentieth century. The Spotted-tailed Quoll, once widespread across eastern Australia, is now restricted to patchy areas from eastern Victoria to southern Queensland. In Tasmania it remains widespread but not common and a separate smaller subspecies inhabits northern Queensland. The Western Quoll or Chuditch, once an inhabitant of the semi-arid regions of every mainland state, now hangs on in the jarrah forests, drier woodlands and shrublands of the south-west.

> ### SUNBATHING QUOLLS
> During the day quolls usually curl up inside hollow logs or trees, under rock overhangs or in caves. The Northern Quoll avails itself of damaged termite mounds. Sometimes, however, Spotted-tailed Quolls forage by day and even sunbathe, as does the Northern Quoll on occasions.

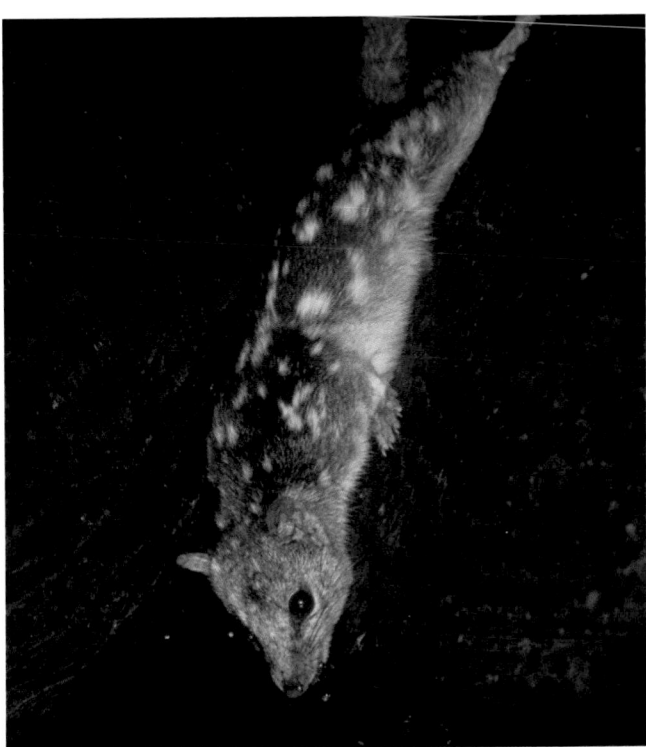

A little Northern Quoll reaches down into a pool of water to drink. Rarely is such a moment captured on camera. Northern Quolls (up to 1.2kg/2½lb) live in northern Australia, among rocky outcrops and open forests. Under threat from the Cane Toad invasion, populations have declined rapidly, although recent survey work suggests some populations are making a tentative comeback. So great has been the threat that in 2003 wildlife managers translocated some individuals to islands off Arnhem Land as a precaution against mainland extinction.

Tasmanian Devil

Only 450 years ago the Tasmanian Devil lived on the mainland but it was hunted out, probably by Dingoes, and now lives only in Tasmania. A forest dweller, it sleeps in dens, such as tree hollows, caves and wombat holes by day and feeds by night.

There's no mistaking a Tasmanian Devil. This thick-set marsupial, standing squarely on its four legs, weighs up to 12kg (26lb). Its overall black fur is marked with flashes of white, usually across its chest and front legs and on the rump. It has pink ears, a short thick tail and a wet, whiskered snout. Following the extinction of the Thylacine, the Devil has become the world's largest carnivorous marsupial.

Although Devils can run short distances surprisingly fast, they are built more for endurance, covering up to 16km (10mile) a night at a slow lope in search of food. Devils are kings of the carcass but they do not always wait for their prey to die. They have been persecuted by sheep farmers but, since they are reluctant to chase down their prey, they probably only take the weak and sick.

At 'Devil's restaurants' manners are dispensed with and a rowdy pecking order prevails, where Devils take precedents over quolls that must wait to take their turn. There is much snarling and teeth bearing. with blood-curdling growls and the whiff of meat drawing other Devils to the feast. Devils have powerful teeth and jaws and can dismember a carcass, consuming much of the bones and skin.

Domestic life is comparatively harmonious. Although solitary, their ranges overlap but fights are few. Despite much posturing and ritualised aggression, Devils rarely seriously harm one another.

Autumn is the breeding season and mothers will carry up to four young in their backward-opening pouch through the winter. After four months the young play around the den, tugging at each other's ears, growling, clambering over one another and developing their ambushing skills. By late December they are weaned and ready to hunt alone. Devils can live for up to eight years.

A DEVILISH CANCER

Populations of Tasmanian Devils are being decimated by a horrible disease, characterised by facial tumours, which threatens the future of the species. In 1996, a Dutch wildlife photographer came across some appallingly disfigured Devils near Mount William. In 2003, the issue spilled out into the public arena and a large team of scientists have been assembled to research the cause of what appears to be a highly contagious cancer. Since the discovery of the disease, Devil populations have declined by 50 per cent. Researchers are considering translocating healthy Devils onto an island to prevent the disease spreading. Having lost the Thylacine, the island state may be facing the extinction of the world's top marsupial predator once more.

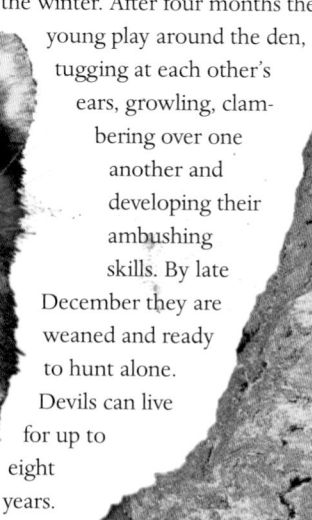

Bandicoots

Of the 11 species of bandicoots that were bounding around Australia when European settlers arrived, three are now extinct, five have severely diminished, and three are still sometimes found in the reserves and backyards of our city's outer suburbs.

Most bandicoots are about the size and shape of a rabbit but they have smaller ears, a medium-length tail and, most distinctive of all, a pointy nose that they poke into the ground to detect subterranean prey. Although they have long hindlegs they bound along on four legs rather than hopping on two.

Bandicoots are nocturnal marsupials that dig conical holes in the ground in a quest for spiders, insects and bulbs. Gardeners are often exasperated by the deep holes created in their lawns but these creatures actually provide a service since they rout out such grass pests as army worms and the larvae of cockshafer beetles.

The Northern Brown Bandicoot is a common occupant of bushy gardens around Brisbane. Strong and muscular, with males weighing up to 3kg (7lb), it is the largest of the bandicoots. Bandicoots live only a couple of years but reproduction is rapid. Females of this species can have several litters of six young in a year.

Many bandicoots broaden their diet to include roots of plants, berries and fungi. This opportunistic Golden Bandicoot is waiting to be served eggs . . . eggs being laid by a Green Turtle that has come ashore specifically to deposit them safely in the sand. Golden Bandicoots were once widespread across arid Australia but their home has shrunk dramatically to a couple of Western Australian islands and to a small part of the remote north-western Kimberley region.

To prevent soil and leaf litter being accidentally flicked into the pouch by their long front claws when digging, bandicoots have backward-opening pouches. They are famous for their short pregnancies: 12.5 days in the case of the Long-nosed and Northern Brown Bandicoots, the shortest of any mammal.

Bandicoots live where soils are easily dug. They sleep in depressions or grassy nests hidden in leaf litter and beneath clumps of tangled vegetation. Some prefer dry country but the Long-nosed and Northern Brown Bandicoots are found in rainforest. If alarmed they take off at speed zigzagging through the undergrowth, often uttering high-pitched squeaks.

Of all the bandicoots, the Western Barred Bandicoot is the smallest, with adults weighing no more than 300g (11oz). The dark stripes on its rump give it its common name. Now living only in the wild on two Fox- and Cat-free islands off Western Australia's coast, this species was once widespread throughout southern Australia.

Bilby

The Bilby has won a place in the hearts of many Australians, so much so that, come Easter, people often buy chocolate Bilbies in preference to chocolate Rabbits or eggs. The Bilby is actually a bandicoot. It has the same long pointed nose (but naked and pink) and the same strong digging forepaws for unearthing creepy crawlies but its ears are decidedly long and rabbit-like, indicating excellent hearing. It has a relatively long and slightly crested tail, black at first but white towards the tip and its body is covered in pale grey silky fur. Males are quite large, up to 50cm (20in) long, but all bilbies are delicately built.

The Bilby is rare. It lives in the arid and semi-arid woodlands and hummock grasslands of Western Australia, the Northern Territory and Queensland. It is a highly efficient burrower, excavating tunnels up to 3m (10ft) long and spiralling down 1.8m (6ft) deep. Here it rests through the scorching days. Being solitary, it shares its burrows only with its offspring or a mating partner.

Before the turn of the twentieth century Bilbies lived across 70 per cent of the Australian mainland, avoiding only the Top End and areas east of the Great Dividing Range. Despite being hunted by Aborigines, they began to disappear from parts of their former range only after settlers arrived. The trampling of soil by cattle, the competition from Rabbits for burrows and food, and the predation of Cats and Foxes was too much for the Bilbies. Despite a few failed attempts at releasing captive-bred animals, there have been some successes with releases into predator-proof fenced areas.

At nightfall Bilbies emerge from their burrows to feed on invertebrates, seeds and tubers. Fresh water may be hard to find but they obtain sufficient moisture from their diet. The availability of food dictates where they live and when they breed. Although they have eight teats in a backward-opening pouch, they usually raise only two or three young at a time.

Numbat

The Numbat is a boldly banded, bushy-tailed marsupial. Unlike most Australian marsupials, it is active during the day. It once lived throughout much of semi-arid southern and arid Central Australia but today it occurs only in a few woodlands and forests in the south-west, the wettest part of its previous range.

These siblings are about eight months old and have only just begun to venture out of their burrow. They are still suckling from their mother. Each day they will investigate their surroundings further and learn how to harvest termites. By summer they will have left their burrow to establish their own home range.

Numbats are small: adults of both sexes usually weigh around 500g (1lb) and grow 25cm (10in) long with a 20cm (8in)-long tail. They feed exclusively on termites, which they find mostly by smell. Termites move regularly to the outer limits of their nests for temperature control and it is at this time they are most accessible to Numbats, which synchronise their foraging activity to correspond with those of the termites'. In winter, they feed during the middle of the day; in summer, they feed in the early morning and late afternoon. The Numbats tear open the termite galleries and extract the insects with their extraordinary long, flexible and sticky tongue, to which the termites adhere. They then scrape these off on their palate.

Female Numbats establish quite large ranges, up to 50ha (125ac) each, while males roam through the ranges of several females during the mating season. Numbats need habitat with plenty of hollows in living trees or fallen logs in which to sleep and as boltholes for avoiding predators. Females excavate a nursery burrow 1 or 2m (40 or 80in) long and sloping down to a cosy, well-insulated nest. The tiny young are born two weeks after mating and attach themselves to mum's teats, which are initially couched in a circle of abdominal swelling, forming a depression into which the litter huddles. After a couple of weeks the swelling subsides and the young hang on tightly to the hair around the teats. Here they stay for the next six months. In late winter the mother leaves the litter in the nest, suckling them at night.

Soon after European settlement the distribution of Numbats shrank drastically, undoubtedly as a result of Fox predation. These delightful marsupials are now carefully monitored and protected in several Fox-free bushland reserves.

STICKY TONGUES

The Numbat is one of five unrelated groups of animals that have developed a very long tongue to help them reach social insects hidden in underground galleries. The other groups are the anteaters of South America, the Aardvark of Africa, the echidnas of Australia and New Guinea, and the pangolins of Africa and Asia. In all these groups of animals this adaptation has evolved independently.

The remarkably long tongue of a Numbat is covered with sticky fluid to which hapless termites adhere when the tongue is thrust into their narrow galleries.

Thylacine

The Thylacine was Australia's largest and most spectacular carnivorous marsupial. When Europeans arrived it had long disappeared from the mainland but it remained abundant in Tasmania.

The Thylacine weighed 25–30kg (55–66lb) and was about the size of a wolf. Its short, sandy fur was strikingly marked with dark tiger-like stripes across its back from its shoulders to its stiffly held tail. Females usually raised two or three pups each year in a backward-opening pouch that contained four teats.

MINIATURE THYLACINES

The Thylacine is often known as the Tasmanian Tiger. It was the last surviving species of a string of thylacine species that thrived in the rainforests of north-western Queensland 15 to 24 million years ago. From the famous fossil site of Riversleigh, remains of many different types of thylacines have been recovered, including miniature ones, no bigger than a man's hand.

Although the Dingo is often cited as the culprit of the Thylacine's demise on the mainland, over-hunting was the critical factor in Tasmania. When Europeans arrived in Tasmania (from which Dingoes were absent) the Thylacine was thriving there but, with the advent of sheep farming in the state, it became public enemy number one. In 1888, a government bounty was paid to shooters and by 1936 the last lone Thylacine died in Hobart Zoo.

Thylacines hunted at night, mainly wallabies and kangaroos in woodlands and forests. Whether they ambushed them or ran them down is unknown. In fact much about this animal remains shrouded in mystery. It was officially declared extinct in 1986. Occasionally a sighting is reported but none have been substantiated. The tragic tale of how humans drove this creature to extinction troubles the national conscience to this day.

Marsupial Moles

Perhaps the most curious of all Australia's marsupials are the marsupial moles. Approximately 12cm (5in) long with silky golden fur, these blind little burrowers pursue insects and their larvae through the loose sand of deserts.

The colour and texture of a marsupial mole's fur did not escape the attention of fur traders in the early part of the twentieth century.

There are two species of marsupial mole: one from northern Western Australia; the other from Central Australia. Almost indistinguishable, both have a snout protected by a horny shield, claws modified to miniature spades and a backward-opening pouch: all adaptations for a life spent tunnelling through sand.

Marsupial moles burrow about 10-20cm (4–8in) below ground level, occasionally coming to the surface, especially after rain, but they are notoriously difficult to find and, as a consequence, little is known about their life history.

Just how these elusive creatures are faring we really do not know but Foxes have an acute sense of smell and seem to be very successful at digging them out of sand dunes. To discover more, researchers are pooling their knowledge with that of Aboriginal people.

The Megabats

You will probably never forget the first time you see a colony of flying-foxes crossing the evening sky. Their large, dark, flapping silhouettes are suspiciously reminiscent of those vampire bats we have all seen at the movies but they are nothing of the sort. The flying-foxes are one of three kinds of megabats, all of which are vegetarians.

This Spectacled Flying-fox is an inhabitant of north-eastern Queensland's rainforests. It feeds on tropical fruits and is important to the health of these forests as it disperses the seeds of fruit-bearing trees. It has found itself at the very sharp end of fiendish and large-scale methods of eradication among some orchardists. These bats usually hang upside down by their toes but sometimes one leg is tucked under a folded wing for warmth or dryness or swung away from the body (as here) to reduce body temperature. Flying-foxes move along branches and climb vertical trunks using their toes and thumbs with four legs and their head uppermost. To avoid dirtying themselves they change position and hang right-side up to pee and poo.

Bats are nocturnal and they are the only mammals that actively fly. There are megabats, which are also known as fruit bats, and microbats. As the name suggests, megabats are mostly large. Flying-foxes are the best known but also in this group are the blossom bats and tube-nosed bats. Unlike microbats, megabats are born with their eyes open and with fur. Bats originated from a common ancestor but the megabats became differentiated from the microbats over 55 million years ago. It is thought that they originated from an early branch of primitive mammals that eventually became carnivores, whales, horses and rhinoceros.

All bats hang upside down because their pelvis and legs cannot support them. As their whole structure evolved for flight, their pelvis and back legs became too small for their muscular torso and their hip bones rotated so their 'knees' bend backwards. Their arms and fingers became thin and elongated to provide ribbing for the wings. The wings consist of a three-layered membrane stretched across the fingers of the hands leaving large, versatile thumbs free as stout claws. Another membrane usually stretches between the legs to the tail. The hairless wings are flexible, strong, waterproof and can self-repair if torn. They are used as fans for cooling, shawls

An Eastern Blossom Bat reaching in between the stamens of a bottlebrush with its pointy snout. Its tongue is covered in tiny protrusions that soak up fluids and, as it grooms, it eats any pollen that brushes onto its fur. Pollen is a valuable source of protein. Blossom bats roost quietly, hidden among foliage. They go into torpor for short periods each day to save energy.

for heating, raincoats for wet weather, cradles for youngsters, weapons for defending territories and deterring predators, but their essential role is to fly.

Weighing up to 1kg (35oz) and with a wingspan of up to 1.5m (59in), flying-foxes are impressive and highly visible. They live in large colonies called camps by day and stream across our skies in huge numbers at dusk. The much smaller, and solitary, tube-nosed bats weigh only about 50g (2oz). They are recognised easily by their tube-like nostrils, bulging eyes and the yellow spots on their wings, ears and nose. The blossom bats are tiny, only about 20g (¾ oz). They, too, are solitary.

Megabats can see and smell well and they use these senses to detect food but cannot hunt in total darkness like micro-

NOSY NEIGHBOURS

Flying-foxes are very social and hundreds may roost together in a daytime camp on a dozen or so large trees, often rainforest species but sometimes tall eucalypts, paperbarks or mangroves. Here they jostle for position, squabble, flap and groom. Visiting a camp is quite an experience. Usually located close to fresh water, the fetid, noisy community is continuously active and it's hard to believe that any member ever gets any sleep, especially during the breeding season when competition is at its height.

An Eastern Tube-nosed Bat roosts discreetly among the foliage and close to its next meal. Tube-nosed bats are so well camouflaged they look like dead leaves and sometimes they sway back and forth as if caught in a breeze to add a touch of authenticity. Tube-noseds are solitary animals and often settle close to fruiting trees. Where there's an abundance of fruit they may find themselves in the company of several others.

Little Red Flying-foxes roosting at their daytime camp. Flying-foxes are very social and hundreds may roost together on a dozen or so large trees, often rainforest species but sometimes tall eucalypts, paperbarks or mangroves. Here they jostle for position, flap and groom. Visiting a camp is quite an experience. Usually located close to fresh water, the fetid, noisy community is continuously active and it's hard to believe that any member ever gets any sleep, especially during the breeding season when squabbling is at its height.

bats. Flying-foxes and tube-nosed bats are fruit specialists that supplement their diet with blossoms. Flying-foxes squeeze the fruit against the roof of their mouth, swallow the nutrient-rich fluid and discard the skin and pulp. Tube-nosed bats have strong teeth for picking at fruit and tongues designed to penetrate tough skins. Blossom bats are nectar-feeders. All these bats help regenerate forests because they are important pollinators and agents of seed dispersal.

At the onset of the breeding season male megabats move to the edges of the colony where they mark out their territories by rubbing scent onto branches from their shoulders and muzzles. The colony becomes noisy as males squabble and courtships get underway. Megabats usually produce one youngster a year. Born in daylight, it quickly latches onto mum's teat where it remains for several weeks, even on nocturnal forages. When it is old enough to be left at the roost it joins a creche of other youngsters. Slowly the young experiment with their wings, clumsily at first, but under the guidance of adult males they acquire navigational and feeding skills.

Microbats

Meet the microbats . . . those tiny dark flitting creatures that catch the periphery of our vision as we stand in the dark. Slicing through the air at startling speed and on an apparently erratic course, they are no sooner seen than gone. Their mission is to catch night-time insects.

All of Australia's 70-odd microbat species, save one, are insectivorous, but catching flying insects in the dark is no easy task.

To locate their moving target with pinpoint accuracy micro-bats have evolved a special ability, known as echolocation; this also prevents them from bumping into things. They possess vocal chords that vibrate thousands of times a second, allowing them to emit through their mouth or nostrils high-frequency sound pulses. Many microbats have elaborate folds, lobes and wattles around their muzzles that control the output and direction of the sounds they emit. These pulses hit objects close to their flight path and bounce back to their sensitive ears. To receive the nuances of returning echoes the ears are big and finely

This Gould's Wattled Bat weighs no more than 15g (½oz) and is small enough to roost beneath peeling bark. It is an adaptable species that occurs throughout all habitats within its distribution range. Moths are its staple food, especially Bogong Moths for those that live in the high country of the mainland. It flies around the lower canopy level at high speed, zigzagging on a horizontal plane to catch prey.

sculpted, sometimes with corrugations and different shaped lobes. We do not hear the sound of the smaller bat species because the frequency of the pulses is usually too high in pitch for our ears to register them, but for the precision required to catch a tiny insect—for example, mosquitos—a bat's echolocation abilities are custom-made. When they catch prey they net it up in their wings before biting or swallowing it.

All bats have difficulty conserving energy. They must eat a lot because flying is energetically expensive and they cannot store much food in their little bodies as the extra weight uses up more energy. To maintain water and body heat they tend to hang out in warm, humid places. In fact, bats almost undoubtedly evolved in tropical climates. In colder regions where there is periodically little food to sustain them, microbats—which tend to go into daily torpor anyway—often extend this period of minimal breathing and heart rate into full-scale, long-

This delicate little Dusky Leaf-nosed Bat, weighing only 4g (⅛oz), displays a relatively modest nose leaf. Small enough to flutter between the leaves of tropical trees without damage, it flushes out moths and mosquitoes which it consumes in vast quantities.

A young Ghost Bat suckling from its mother. Ghost Bats weigh over 100g (3½oz) and are the biggest microbats in Australia. While they eat insects, they also hunt geckoes, frogs and small mammals, including other bats. As well as finding food by echolocation, they hang from branches and swoop upon unsuspecting earth-bound creatures, using sight and their enormous ears to locate prey. Once found throughout Central Australia they now occur only in the tropical north where there is access to warm, moist caves with roomy ceilings.

term hibernation during winter.

Traditionally most bats roost in caves, tree hollows and rock crevices. One or two are known to use birds' nests. Some bats take up residence in human constructions, such as mine shafts, overpasses, culverts, eaves and even drains. They might not seem very appealing domiciles to us but what matters to a bat is that the temperature and humidity are just right.

The reproductive strategies of bats are amazing. Sperm in humans cannot live longer than a few days but bats can keep their sperm alive and healthy throughout winter, stored in either the male's or the female's body. Females can also delay ovulation and embryo development. Bats give birth once a year, and within a species this is synchronised to occur when food supplies are most plentiful. In temperate areas this is usually spring; in winter there is rarely sufficient food to form effective sperm or feed a growing foetus and bat pregnancies are often long.

Mothers-to-be roost in microbat maternity camps. When the young are born they are naked, blind and up to 30 per cent the weigh of their mother. They attach to one of her two teats (occasionally twins are born) and cling onto her fur for the first few days as she flies and forages, after which they are left in nurseries, sometimes guarded by a few adults.

LYSSAVIRUS

In the past 10 years there have been a couple of human mortalities arising from a virus carried by sick bats, called Australian Bat Lyssavirus. This virus is a relative of rabies and people who handle sick bats, if scratched or bitten, could get infected. It is therefore important not to handle bats. It is also inadvisable to venture into bat caves as fungal spores and yeasts in their droppings can make humans ill and any disturbance to roosting bats can be fatal for the bats.

Like all insectivorous bats, this Western False Pipistrelle has very sharp teeth. Newborn bats have special recurved milk teeth that latch firmly onto their mother as she flies. It is possible to estimate a bat's age by its teeth as these wear down over a lifetime, which in some individuals has been known to be as long as 18 years.

BLIND AS A BAT

Contrary to popular belief, all bats can see quite well but in comparison with the megabats the eyes of the echolocating microbats are tiny.

Rats and Mice

Rats and mice are rodents renowned for their ability to gnaw through wood and insulation cable. They can also tackle food that other animals literally cannot crack, like nuts and hard-coated seeds. Squirrels, beavers, hamsters, gerbils and guinea pigs are all rodents but none of these are native to Australia. Australia does have, however, plenty of native mice and rats.

The Delicate Mouse weighs just 6g (⅕oz). It lives mostly on grass seeds but nectar from this flowering grevillea provides valuable carbohydrates. These tropical ground dwellers live among sand dunes and in open, often disturbed, land. Their populations fluctuate wildly. Litters of three or four babies are born, each one just a tiny 1g (½₅oz). They grow and are weaned quickly. Breeding can be continuous but sometimes it stops altogether. While food availability may explain this erratic behaviour to a point, other factors may also play a role.

Five million years ago a wave of rodents entered Australia from New Guinea. These animals diversified and spread across the continent to occupy every Australian habitat. Some took to the trees, some to the water, many live in the arid inland and some are rainforest specialists. Females of these so-called 'old endemics' have four teats. A much later wave of rats, the 'new endemics', have eight to 12 teats. When Europeans came to Australia they brought a third wave: the House Mouse, the Black Rat and the Brown Rat. In all, Australia has at least 60 species of rodents, although quite a few are within a whisker of disappearing forever.

Rodents are distinguished, above all, by a pair of large incisors at the front of the upper and lower jaw, which do all the gnawing.

The Common Rock-rat weighs an average of 36g (1oz) and is about 24cm (9in) long. It is the smallest of five species, all of which rely upon rock crevices for cover. Widespread across northern Australia in suitable habitat, it may suffer hardship during the wet season if nests are inundated and seeds, upon which it depends, become scarce.

Two or three pairs of molars at the back of the jaw do the humdrum business of grinding. The front of the strong incisors is coated with hard enamel, while the back is made of relatively soft dentine. The teeth are constantly worn to a chisel-like edge and, as they grow continuously, the edge remains razor-sharp throughout an animal's lifetime.

Mice and rats often live only one or two years and must therefore have a rapid life cycle. When there's plenty of food, some species breed continuously and some reach sexual maturity exceedingly fast. In times of

WHAT WE DON'T KNOW

We don't know nearly enough about our local rodents. In order to look after wild animals, we must first discover how they live. Since European settlement, we have lost 12 per cent of all Australian rodents and a further 20 per cent are endangered. Many of the extinctions and declines are among ground dwellers in arid and semi-arid areas. The introduction of predators, most especially the Cat, is undoubtedly responsible for much of this destruction. Another factor that affects small animals unable to move long distances is the large-scale fires that have replaced the Aboriginal practice of burning small patches.

Hopping mice have long, well-developed hindlegs on which they bounce with great agility and speed. Nocturnal, with big eyes, big ears and extremely long tails finishing in a brush of long hairs, these busy mice live in small social groups and share complex burrows up to 1m (39in) deep. There were at least nine species of hopping-mice 150 years ago. Today there are only five, of which Mitchell's Hopping-mouse, shown here, is one. Each species has made itself at home in a different habitat, mostly in arid and semi-arid Australia. Mitchell's lives in the mallee country of the south, the Dusky in inland dunes, the Fawn on the gibber plains and the Spinifex in the spinifex-clad sands of Central and Western Australia. Only the Northern Hopping-mouse inhabits tropical Australia.

The enormous stack of dead twigs that towers above this Greater Stick-nest Rat has probably been in the family for generations. Relatives live together and renovate and extend when necessary. At the time of European settlement there were two species of stick-nest rats. Both were vegetarians and fed upon the succulent chenopod shrubs that cover much of arid and semi-arid southern Australia but they could not compete with the large populations of grazing Rabbits and Sheep or the hunting pressures of feral Cats and Foxes. The Lesser Stick-nest Rat is now believed to be extinct, while the Greater Stick-nest Rat was lucky enough to inhabit the tiny Franklin Islands off the coast of Ceduna in South Australia. Introductions to several predator-free islands and one mainland reserve are showing signs that recovery of this species may be possible.

scarcity, however, populations crash. This boom and bust pattern is never more starkly illustrated than in Australia's drought-prone inland where seed production, upon which most rodents depend, is governed by unpredictable rainfall.

Keeping a Low Profile

Small mammals are on just about every bigger animal's menu so keeping a low profile is a life-or-death business. To this end most Australian rodents are nocturnal and many hide and nest in tussocks, under bark or tree hollows. For rock-rats the cracks between rocks provide the perfect boltholes but most ground dwellers dig burrows. These can be extensive, complex and linked to above-ground runways between patches of vegetation. Tunnel systems are usually communal and comprise nesting chambers and vertical pop-up holes. In arid regions some are up to 1.5m (59in) deep to escape both predators and above-ground temperatures.

Pebble Mounds and Stick Nests

The industrious pebble-mound mice are master builders. They carry thousands of small stones in their mouths and stack them with their agile front paws into mounds. Their miniature stony landscapes are dimpled with craters beneath which lie excavated communal burrows.

Best known is the Western Pebble-mound Mouse of the Pilbara region of Western Australia. Weighing a mere 15g (½oz) it carries stones half its weight to form mounds up to 9m² (97ft²).

The Greater Stick-nest Rat also builds communal nests, usually around bushes and under rock overhangs, but this time the construction is of interwoven dead branches lined with soft vegetation. Stick piles measure 2m (79in) in diameter and up to 1m (39in) high and may house up to 20 family members.

Tropical Rodents

In the tropical open forests and woodlands of northern Australia some rodents are more at home in trees. Tree-rats find daytime shelter in the hollows of standing and fallen trees and sometimes curl up in the leaf bunches of pandanus trees or palms. Long-tailed and frequently coming down to ground, the tree-rats feed mostly on the fruits and seeds of trees as they become seasonally available.

A well-known heavyweight of the Queensland rainforests is the Giant White-tailed Rat (.6–1kg/21–35oz). This frenetic nocturnal rodent rampages through every strata of the forest, from the canopy to the ground, sniffing out birds' eggs, cracking open the cases of rainforest seeds and killing insects. Tenacious and ever-resourceful, it has a reputation for being able to open tins of food.

With its luxuriant long tail and honey-coloured back, the Golden-backed Tree-rat is one of Australia's most beautiful native rodents. It weighs around 250g (9oz) and bears a passing resemblance to a squirrel but it is nothing of the sort. Rather more adventurous than other tree-rats, it will forage in grasslands, mangroves, around rocks, the edges of rainforests and even on beaches and it has a broad diet that extends from insects to leaves, flowers, fruits, seeds and grasses.

Taking to the Water

In the sweltering mangroves lives a small nocturnal rat whose life is ruled by the tides. The False Water-rat or Water Mouse nests at the edge of the high-tide mark among sedges and here it builds an enormous mud nest like a termite mound 60cm (24in) high and riddled with tunnels. At low tide it skedaddles between the mangrove roots sticking out of the mud, snapping up small crabs, mussels, molluscs and flatworms.

The slower, larger Broad-toothed Rat likes wet areas too, but its thick fluffy coat is designed for life in the high country in Tasmania and the

Perhaps Australia's most impressive rodent is the carnivorous Water Rat. About the size of a small Cat, it has thick, soft fur that is dark brown above and golden below, and its thick dark tail is distinctively tipped with white. Water Rats are quite common in creeks and rivers but quiet and mostly nocturnal. They look a little like a small otter, especially when swimming. With their partially webbed hind feet, a thick water-repellent coat and a tail that functions as a rudder they are superbly adapted for an aquatic lifestyle. They live in complex burrows in the banks of watercourses. Piles of unpalatable bits of discarded fish, insects and crustaceans at feeding areas are the work of Water Rats.

BAD PRESS

Australian native rats and mice are often ignored or, worse, maligned—perhaps because we associate them with the plagues and diseases of non-native species. They are, in fact, beautiful and interesting animals.

---

mainland. These gentle creatures creep through covered runways alongside gullies in alpine woodlands and wet heaths, feeding mostly on succulent grasses and occasionally picking up fungi, seeds and leaves.

The New Endemics

The so-called 'new endemics' came into Australia only one to two million years ago. They have scaly tails and all belong to the genus *Rattus*. Their future looks much more secure than that of many old endemic's.

One of the most widespread of the new endemics on the mainland is the solitary Bush Rat, a nocturnal inhabitant of forests, woodlands, rainforest, heaths, coastal scrub and even snow country. Its 16cm (6in)-long body is covered with soft, dense fur, that is grey to brown and paler below. Its tail is slightly shorter and its feet pink. Bush Rats feed on insects, fungi, leaves, fruit and seeds. They often live for only one year, especially males, and their dependence on thick leaf litter renders them vulnerable to fires, but they can produce three or four litters of usually five young each year and they are sexually mature within four months, so populations tend to recover quickly.

The range of Swamp Rats often overlaps that of Bush Rats, although they are absent from Western Australia and common in Tasmania where Bush Rats are absent. They prefer swamps, heaths, buttongrass moorlands and sedgelands. Not unlike the Bush Rats but darker, stockier and with dark feet, their staple diet consists of grasses and sedges supplemented with insects, fruits and seeds.

Other new endemics include the Dusky Rat, which feeds on the corms of sedges and seeds in the wetlands of the Top End, the paler shiny-coated Pale Field-rat that feeds along the watercourses of grasslands, and the Cape York Rat, a rainforest specialist that forages in leaf litter. The Canefield Rat, which occurs naturally within grasslands of open forest and rainforest, has become a scourge to cane farmers and outbreaks of Long-haired Rat populations on the Barkly Tableland and Channel Country of western Queensland occasionally cause alarm.

Sea Lions and Fur Seals

Sea lions are amphibious mammals that feed in the sea but breed on land. Their body plan is derived from land-based animals but modified for life in the sea. The southern coasts and islands off Australia are home to three species: the Australian Sea Lion, New Zealand Fur Seal and Australian Fur Seal. The rarest of these, the Australian Sea Lion, is endemic to Australia.

Only about 8500 Australian Sea Lions haul out (come to land) in South Australia and 3500 in Western Australia. One of the best places to see them is at Seal Bay on Kangaroo Island in South Australia. Here you will find them snoozing and basking on a sandy beach as if they hadn't a care in the world. The truth is, they are often exhausted after several days of constant diving for food at sea.

In another part of this large island, at Cape de Couedic, colonies of New Zealand Fur Seals lie just beyond the splash zone on rocky shelves. The slightly upturned, pointy nose of fur seals distinguishes them from the blunter-nosed sea lions. New Zealand Fur Seals are widespread. They live around Western and South Australian coastlines, in New Zealand and on subantarctic islands.

An Australian Sea Lion pup seeks out its mother's nipple. After three to four months its black coat will moult to the colour of its mother's. At about 18 months it will cease to suckle and moult again, thereafter moulting every 18 months. Adult males (bulls) become chocolate brown. Many pups die in their first two years. Some are crushed by bulls; others fall victim to sharks, disease or rough weather.

The name, 'fur seal', is derived from the two layers of fur which give them additional insulation. The inner layer traps air so their skin remains dry, even during diving.

Australian Fur Seals breed on a handful of islands in the Bass Strait. Biggest of the three Australian residents, males weigh up to 360kg (57st) and females 110kg (17st). On land they lumber forward, swaying their head from side to side as they shift their weight from side to side and move one front flipper at a time. Male New Zealand Fur Seals weigh up to 180kg (28st) and females only about 50kg (8st); being relatively light, they can canter on their four flippers.

All three resident seals propel themselves through water with their front flippers. Their back flippers, which stretch behind them when swimming like rudders, rotate forward on land to provide balance. This is a characteristic of the family otariids. A second family, the phocids or so-called 'true seals', swim by undulating their hind flippers; these are unable to rotate forward, so phocids can only wriggle when on shore, their hind flippers stretching out behind them like fish tails. Another feature of otariids is their external, protruding ears, which are not apparent in phocids.

Sometimes the Subantarctic Fur Seal, which breeds on Macquarie Island in the Bass Strait and on subantarctic islands, visits Tasmania and mainland Australia. Its dark back with contrasting yellow chest, particularly obvious in the males, distinguishes it from other fur seals. Occasionally, too, members of the true seals visit Australia's southern seas, and even haul out. Among them are the enormous Southern Elephant Seal, which breeds on Macquarie and Heard islands as well as on some subantarctic islands. At 3500kg (630st)

Seals have thick blubber layers around their bodies that keep them warm in cold water but on land they easily overheat. Sitting upright, like this New Zealand Fur Seal, is one way to catch the breeze; raising a lazy flipper from the prone position is another less strenuous strategy. If all else fails, taking a dip in the ocean is a sure way of cooling down. The prominent ears on this fur seal identify it as a member of the otariid family.

and with their bulbous proboscis, males are unmistakable. Another visitor, especially to Tasmania, is the fierce reptilian-looking Leopard Seal, renowned for its consumption of penguins and other seals. This large dappled grey seal breeds on pack ice. It is so adapted to an oceanic existence that its front flippers have become useless for moving on hard surfaces.

Seals hunt for days at sea, spending 90 per cent of their time diving. These Australian Fur Seals can dive to depths of 200m (650ft) propelled by their fore flippers. To reduce the pressure on their bodies and to reduce buoyancy, they empty, rather than fill, their lungs before diving. With their torpedo-shaped body and considerable flipper power they are agile, graceful and fast, which is just as well since an important part of their winter diet consists of the exceptionally fast-swimming squid. They also eat fish, octopuses, crustaceans and other marine invertebrates.

Baleen Whales

Although whales live their entire life in water and look like enormous fish, they are mammals. Were they fish, we might never see them as they would not need to surface for air. In recent years, Australians have been excited and delighted to witness the return of Humpback and Southern Right Whales to their coastal waters in the wake of banned commercial whaling.

A breaching Humpback Whale. Humpbacks often propel themselves out of the sea, twisting and flopping back with a mighty splash. Why they do this, we have yet to understand: perhaps they are communicating, dislodging parasites or just having fun. They also pop their head above the surface ('spy hopping'), maybe looking for predators, and slap their tail flukes or pectoral fins hard on the water surface, producing a loud crack and a plume of spray, perhaps as a deterrent. Rolling belly-up may be a stretching exercise or a means of avoiding the attentions of an over-attentive male or an insistent hungry calf.

Humpbacks and Southern Rights are baleen whales. Instead of teeth they have a row of long, horn-like plates called baleen, or whalebone, suspended from the top jaw. These act as sieves for catching copepods and shrimp-like crustaceans called krill. These tiny creatures swarm in their billions in the Southern Ocean. Baleen whales round up these swarms and gulp them into their cavernous mouths. As their mouths close, their tongues push upwards squeezing out the water through the baleen sieves but retaining the nutritious krill. The long pleats beneath

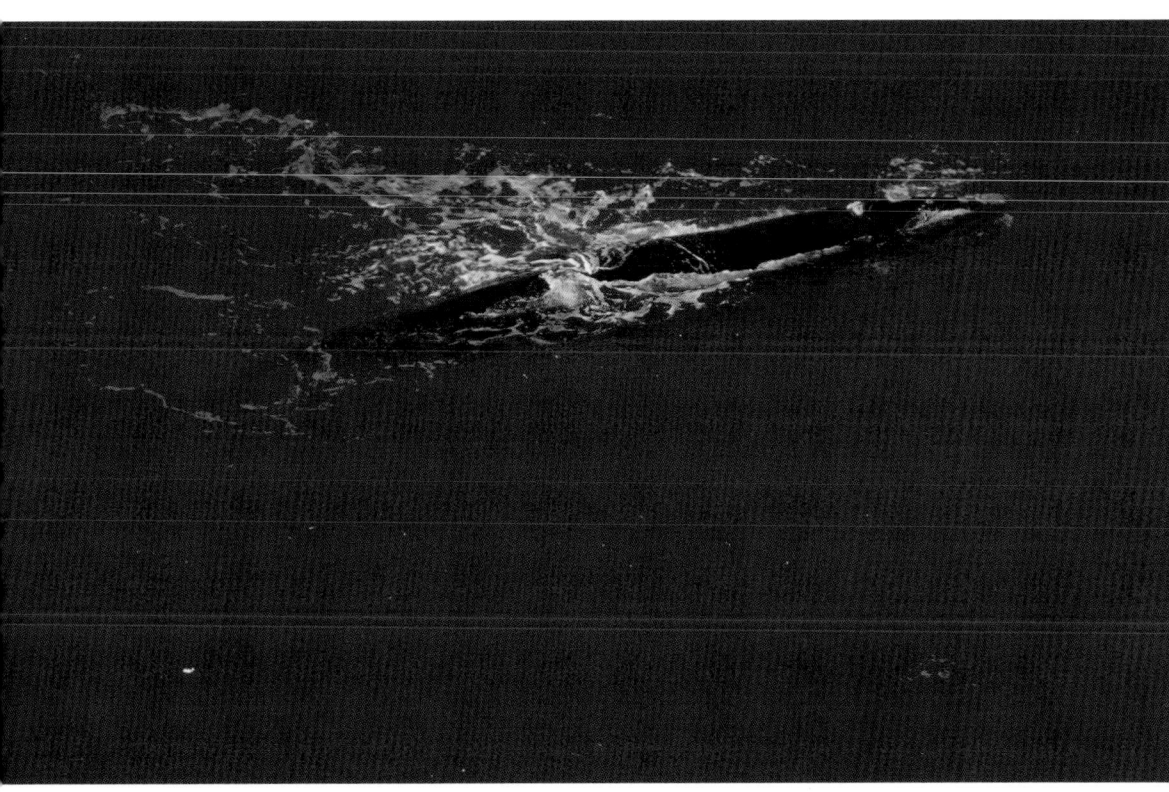

the lower jaw of Humpbacks bulge as the mouth takes in extra volume.

In the southern hemisphere Humpbacks migrate from the cold-water feeding grounds of the Southern Ocean in late April and move up the west and east coasts of Australia through shallow coastal waters to mate and calf. They travel close to the shore and it is possible to see them from any number of headlands. Hervey Bay in Queensland and Rottnest Island near Perth are two favourite whale-watching spots. Around August, they begin the return journey south, usually spearheaded by the newly pregnant females, with mothers and newborn calves bringing up the rear.

In recent years Southern Rights have been appearing regularly in southern Australian waters. They arrive around late May and stay until early October. Here they mate and breed. It is possible to see them from cliffs around Tasmania, in South Australia and along the Great Australian Bight. Victor Harbor near Adelaide is another popular destination for watching these whales.

Although these huge whales can live 60 or 70 years, they grow and reproduce slowly. At about 10 years they begin breeding; pregnancies last about a year and

Although not much longer than a Humpback Whale (about 18m/59ft), a Southern Right Whale weighs twice as much as 80t due to a broader, bulkier body. The V-shaped plume of water that it blows out when surfacing (the 'blow') distinguishes this species and the arrangement of raised white patches of rough-ened skin on its head, called callosities, help researchers identify individuals.

SINGING WHALES

When the eerie calls of Humpback Whales were first recorded in 1971, the world sat up and listened. Never before had such melodious and complex songs been heard from a mammal. The tuneful clicks, squeals, hoots, moans or groans in a rising or falling cadence are performed in 'phrases' strung together to form recurring themes. Singers are usually males. They sing during the breeding season, whether to sere-nade females or warn off other males, or both, we still do not know. Sometimes several males sing in unison, and continue to do so even when songs change, as they sometimes do.

weaning a further year. Southern Rights produce one calf every three years. The bond between mother and calf is constantly reinforced by touching and making sounds. Calves are unable to suckle underwater, so they nuzzle one of two of their mother's mammary slits to stimulate her to spurt rich, thick milk into their mouths. A calf receives at least 100L (22gal)

of milk a day and puts on weight very rapidly to acquire a thick layer of blubber before reaching Antarctic waters. The mother, however, fasts in the absence of food.

Between 1900 and 1965, around 200,000 Humpbacks were slaughtered and by the mid-1960s, with only hundreds left, whaling was no longer viable. Since then, Humpbacks in the Southern Ocean have made a comeback and populations are now nearly half those of pre-whaling times.

Southern Right Whales acquired their name from nineteenth-century whalers who considered them the 'right' whales to catch as they were slow and buoyant and provided valuable oil and baleen. Between 1820 and 1850, about 26,000 animals were slaughtered. In 1978, Australia banned whaling and today all whales are protected in Australian waters.

Other baleen whales that live around the Australian continent include Fin, Antarctic, Minke, Dwarf Minke and Blue Whales. The Blue Whale is frequently seen off southern Victoria and South Australia, as well as off Perth. At 30m (98ft) long, it is the largest animal ever to have lived.

The Humpback Whale's upright tail fluke indicates a deep dive. It is the fluked tail that propels whales and dolphins through water. Unlike fish, tails are horizontal to the body and move up and down rather than vertical and swept from side to side. The flippers or pectoral fins of whales and dolphins provide balance and direction.

Toothed Whales and Dolphins

Apart from baleen whales, all other whales have teeth. Although numerous, they are undifferentiated, peg-like teeth, good for grasping only. Toothed whales can also be distinguished from baleen whales by their single, rather than double, blowhole.

Most toothed whales are highly social and live in groups called pods. In shallow coastal waters, six to 20 animals often form a pod but more pelagic (ocean-going) species often gather in their thousands.

Sperm, Pilot and Killer Whales

At 11–18m (36–59ft) long, the Sperm Whale is the largest of the toothed whales. Its enormous oblong head, often scarred by the flailing tentacles of giant squids, contains a huge brain: six times that of a human's. It lives in deep waters at the edge of Australia's continental shelf, where it dives for hours on end in pursuit of octopus, fish and squid.

Sperm Whales often travel in large pods. The males migrate to Antarctica in the summer months to feed, leaving 'nurseries' of females and calves in the warmer waters. Once a major target of whalers, today

A Gray's Beaked Whale, photographed near Busselton, Western Australia. Beaked whales are rarely seen and, as a consequence, poorly understood. It is estimated that there are 12 species inhabiting deep Australian waters. Usually no more than 5 or 6m (16 or 20ft) long, they do indeed have a distinctive beak. In most species, only the males have teeth and then only on the lower jaw, suggesting they are used for fighting or sexual display rather than feeding. Gray's dive deeply for squid, seafloor crustaceans and starfish, which they suck into their mouth.

The bold black and white patterns of Killer Whales are instantly recognisable and males are easily distinguished from females by their tall triangular dorsal fin, which grows to 1.8m (6ft) high. Female Killers cannot become pregnant until they are 15 years old and each pregnancy takes about 16 months. On average they give birth every five years and at 60 years of age they cease breeding but they remain with their pod. They can live for 90 years. Males only live about 60 years.

FINDING THE ENEMY AND FINDING LUNCH

Toothed whales sense their world through sound. They hear exceptionally well and emit sonar clicks that echo back from surrounding objects to their two separate ear bones. Echoes from 100m (320ft) can be detected with accuracy and the range and configuration of objects is assessed precisely because the ears hear individually. This sophisticated mechanism, known as echolocation, is similar to that used by microbats but we have yet to learn exactly how it works. There is a hypothesis that these animals may be able to stun their prey by echolocation.

they are protected and believed to be in good numbers.

Pilot whales are also toothed whales. Pods are often lead by a so-called 'pilot'. Males are about 6.5m (21ft) and females notably smaller. Pods of 50 or so family members sometimes swim close to shore and occasionally they become stranded along Australia's beaches. In deep offshore waters they gather in hundreds. Short-finned Pilot Whales prefer Australia's warmer northern waters, while Long-finned Pilot Whales live in the cooler southern waters. The female Short-finned Pilot Whale is one of the few mammals, other than humans, known to undergo menopause. Although she can live for 60 years, she ceases to bear young at 30 to 40 years of age but acts as a wet nurse to younger whales thereafter.

Killer Whales are formidable predators of seals, penguins and other whales. Their jaws can crush large bones and their teeth can tear flesh. Living in small pods led by a dominant female, they often work together to herd prey. They also patrol shores where there are penguin and seal colonies.

Dolphins

Dolphins are small toothed whales. With beak-like mouths and sharp cone-shaped teeth they pluck fish and squid from the water, tossing them down their throat whole, tail-first and very likely alive.

Many dolphin species ply the deep offshore waters of Australia but they are rarely seen, except by sailors and fishermen. Pods of bottlenose dolphins, however, inhabit many of Australia's sheltered bays, harbours and estuaries. These animals can live for 45 years. When a female gives birth to her 1m (39in)-long single calf tail-first, attendant dolphins nudge the newborn up to the surface for its first breathe. It suckles from its mother for at least a year and, stays close to her for several more years. Before it can hunt for itself, it is babysat by other dolphins while mother goes fishing. Why some whales and dolphins help one another is not fully understood. A quite plausible explanation is that altruistic behaviour towards individuals benefits the whole pod and thereby increases the survival of all its members.

Common Dolphins are found around Australian coasts and often swim in the Bass Strait, sometimes in large numbers. They occasionally enter Port Phillip Bay in Victoria. Smaller than Bottlenoses, these fast-swimmers have elegant yellow and pale grey hourglass markings on their flanks, which contrast with dark grey above and white below. They

A pair of Indo-Pacific Bottlenosed Dolphins. Grey above, paler below, with a bottle-shaped snout, a rounded forehead and a characteristic 'smile', Bottlenoses grow to about 3m (10ft) long. In places like Jervis Bay in New South Wales resident pods of 50 or so animals are star attractions, regularly delighting tourists with their playful antics and animated whistles and squeals.

Mass strandings of live whales and dolphins are a common phenomenon worldwide. Theories abound as to why they occur. Scientific work suggests the whales have made a navigational error. If you come across stranded live whales or dolphins contact your state's wildlife authority immediately. Do not go near them unless you have been properly trained as even an accidental knock by a whale's tail can be dangerous.

pursue fish, squid and octopus, and work in pods, often at night, to round up large schools of sardines, pilchards and anchovies.

Dolphins have been hunted for food and for bait and killed because they compete for fish or simply for 'sport'. Thousands of Common Dolphins are caught each year in nets and countless deaths occur from eating plastic. There is mounting evidence, too, that industrial waste in the form of heavy metals and polychlorinated biphenyls (PCBs), as well as bacterial and viral pollution from sewage outfalls, are killing dolphins. While Australian law protects dolphins, we could all do more to help.

In Monkey Mia in Western Australia it is possible to come face to face with a friendly pod of Indo-Pacific Bottlenose Dolphins, a species of warm shallow waters. Dolphins are playful and communicative, with a seemingly extensive vocabulary. Their curiosity often brings them close to human beings and we respond with equal inquisitiveness. Although most dolphins have binocular vision, they can use just one eye to examine objects. The dolphin on the left in this picture is clearly trying to assess what is on offer.

Dugong

A less likely candidate for mermaid-hood than the 350kg (55st) torpedo-shaped dark brown body and head of a Dugong would be hard to find. Yet this is the animal that appears to have inspired the over-active imagination of so many poor, deluded, homesick sailors.

True, females have a visible nipple beside each short paddle-shaped flipper, and certainly they have a gentle disposition, but a broad, flat, bristly muzzle, tiny eyes and elephant hide seems a far cry from the half woman–half fish mythological mermaid.

Dugongs are marine mammals that inhabit the world's shallow tropical waters. They are found throughout the northerly waters of Australia, from Shark Bay in the west to Moreton Bay in the east, and beyond. They are slow-moving vegetarians that graze on seagrasses, tearing them out by the roots and creating clouds of silt as they plough through beds of vegetation. About 2.5–3.3m (8–11ft) long, they have a whale-like tail, square head, with nostrils to the fore and a mouth on the underside. They are sirenians, a group to which the mantees of the northern hemisphere belong.

Throughout their range Dugongs are under threat. Where herds of a hundred or more once grazed, you are lucky to spot a pair or a sole animal. Traditional predators include sharks, crocodiles, Killer Whales and people. Once hunted for their oil and flesh, today they are protected in Australian waters except where traditional hunting rights prevail.

The shallow bays of northern Australia remain a last stronghold for dugong populations. Despite conservation efforts, entanglement in fishing nets cause many deaths and sediments from rapid coastal development on Queensland's east coast sometimes smother their food.

A young Dugong stays close to its mother for up to two years. It will be up to eight more years before it is able to mate. Pregnancy lasts a year and suckling a further year. Although Dugongs can live up to 70 years, they only breed every three to seven years. Their slow rate of reproduction is problematic as it hampers recovery of locally declining populations. The species is listed by the International Union for Conservation of Nature (IUCN) as vulnerable to extinction.

DRIVE CAREFULLY

In some places, such as Moreton Bay, Dugongs are often killed by boats hitting them. Wildlife agencies have instituted measures to make boats go slow in recognised Dugong areas.

Introduced Herbivores

When animals come into a new environment, they may die out, unable to survive the new conditions, or thrive on opportunities presented by their new home. Many of the mammals introduced to Australia have flourished at the expense of native wildlife and the country's agriculture.

DESPERATE MEASURES

There are constant efforts to keep populations of introduced species in check. Biological weapons prepared in the laboratory for use against Rabbits have received the greatest publicity and probably had the greatest effects. In 1950, the *myxoma* virus that causes myxomatosis, a disease of American Rabbits, was released as a biological control on Australian rabbits. Initially it was very effective but about 2 per cent of the Rabbits developed resistance. By 1996, when the Rabbit *calici* virus was released, populations had climbed again to 300 million. In dry areas the new virus has been very effective but work now underway to biologically sterilise Rabbits may hold the key to a more effective and humane solution.

With no traditional predators to control their population growth, the newcomers upset the delicate natural balance of whole ecosystems and native plants and animals decline. This scenario plays out all over the globe. Australia, sadly, is one of the worst cases.

Rabbits and Goats

One of the earliest introductions has transpired to be one of the most devastating, both for the farmers who were driven off their land and for the environment. Rabbits, brought to Australia as food on the First Fleet, did not establish themselves at first but with later releases for sport they proliferated and spread across the continent to all corners but the tropical north.

Rabbits are a Mediterranean species accustomed to a hot dry climate and poor soils and it is in the marginal semi-arid and arid regions of Australia where the greatest damage has been done. Rabbits cannot handle long grass so when sheep became the mainstay of the Australian economy, the massive expansion of sheep farming greatly assisted the spread of Rabbits. As the sheep grazed down the vegetation, the rabbits fed and bred at a rate of knots. At their peak, in the 1880s and '90s, an estimated 800 million Rabbits were eating Australia out of house and home . . . literally.

Rabbits don't just eat plants; they kill them. They nibble out seedlings, pare down saplings, ringbark shrubs and trees, dig up roots

Who could believe that such a cute furry animal could wreak such havoc? Given some fresh young shoots and another bunny to play happy families with, Rabbits intended for the pot ironically starved out humans and wildlife alike. Their master stroke: a rapid reproductive cycle. They can breed at four months and produce four or five litters of five or so bunnies each year. In times of plenty, populations boom. In times of drought, populations crash, but never entirely.

and prevent plants from seeding and regenerating. Hordes of ravenous Rabbits under the pressures of high population and drought can render a landscape plant-less: no crops, no pasture, no food or cover for native wildlife.

Overgrazing leads to dust storms, erosion and invasion of weeds. Rabbits compound the land-altering effects of over-stocking by Sheep, as do feral Goats. Farmed for their milk, hair and meat, domestic Goats have escaped or been set free over time to roam the country. They, too, reproduce rapidly. By 1996 there were 2.6 million feral Goats stripping out whatever vegetation they could find, mostly in semi-arid land but also on hills and rocky outcrops, where they out-competed species such as rock-wallabies.

Herds and Hooves

With the advent of the car, animals brought to Australia for transportation, such as Horses, Donkeys and Camels, were cut loose. Herds of all these animals now compete with native wildlife for food across the land. The Camel has relatively soft feet but the hard hoofs of Horses and Donkeys on a continent of ancient fragile soils and precious little fresh water have eroded and denuded landscapes beyond our imagination.

In the monsoonal north herds of imported Swamp Buffalo charge through the floodplains, churning up the pristine waters of places like Kakadu National Park, polluting it with their dung and spreading weeds.

There are now six species of introduced deer browsing through Australia's woodlands, heaths, shrublands and forests, ringbarking trees with their antlers and eroding the soil. Innocent as these animals are, they have become a hazard to the well-being of native plants and animals in a country that still has a lot of endemic life to lose. Australians are now facing the monumental conundrum of how to save native species without cruelty to the animals they introduced and without massive costs to taxpayers.

Goats are herd animals and their hard hooves trample vegetation and erode soils. They can eat tough plants that other animals literally cannot stomach and they can browse on two legs to maximise their reach. Like Rabbits, they inhibit the growth and regeneration of plants. They can also invade places that other herbivores cannot reach. Sure-footed and nimble climbers, they are most at home in rocky terrain and so they compete directly with rock-wallabies for both food and shelter.

Feral Pigs are black, hairy and relatively long-legged omnivores. Males have enlarged canine teeth that form robust tusks capable of harming even humans They wallow in squelchy places, like waterholes, swamps, floodplains and watercourses, and, with their cartilage-toughened snouts and fine sense of smell, they root out small animals, underground tubers and bulbs, eggs and carrion. In doing so they muddy fresh waters, trample nests and shelters, erode banks and kill plants. Feral Pigs are now widespread wherever there is suitable habitat, except in Tasmania.

Introduced Carnivores

It has been believed for a long time that the extinction of species is the result of a combination of forces. While this may be so in some instances, Australian experience shows that it is not always the case. There have been 18 native mammal extinctions since the arrival of the First Fleet. Of these, 16 are the direct result of predation by introduced feral Cats and/or Foxes.

Dingoes are wild dogs, descendants of the Indian Wolf. They consume anything from large invertebrates to animals as large as feral Pigs and Swamp Buffaloes. Males often travel long distances and hunt alone but sometimes they join packs to bring down large prey, such as Sheep, feral Goats and kangaroos. Dingoes have learnt to scavenge around campsites. If taunted or teased with food, they may attack.

THE DINGO FENCE

The dependence of early settlers on Sheep for their livelihood soon brought them into conflict with Dingoes and a government bounty encouraged their perse-cution by trapping, shooting and poison-ing. During the 1880s, in an effort to exclude Dingoes from the fertile plains of the south-east, a 8500km (5200 mile)-long fence was constructed. Parts of the great Dingo Fence can still be seen today. It stretches from near Toowoomba in Queensland through desolate arid country to the Great Australian Bight. Despite this bold plan, Dingoes still live on both sides of the fence.

Dingoes

One of earliest introduced species to these soils was the Dingo, often thought of as native. Dingoes came to Australia about 4000 years ago with Asian seafarers. Whether they came as companions, food or as guard dogs is uncertain. Aboriginal people adopted Dingoes to help them hunt and to keep them warm on cold nights.

The descendants of runaway Dingoes populated every environment on the Australian mainland, although they never reached Tasmania. Being a descendant of the Wolf, they became the top predators and Dingoes prey mostly on large animals, such as kangaroos and wallabies. Over tens of thousands of years some form of equilibrium was achieved between Dingoes and other native animals but with the arrival of two more exotic predators—the Cat and the Fox, this equilibrium has been upset.

Cats

No amount of protestation by Cat lovers can alter the predatory nature of Cats. Whether feral, stray or domestic, Cats hunt wildlife by day and night. They stalk birds, skinks, geckoes, small and baby mammals, frogs, snakes and virtually anything that moves. It is estimated that domestic Cats alone kill about 100 million native Australian animals every year.

Many feral Cats are the progeny of farm Cats that were deliberately bred to suppress mice, rats and Rabbit plagues. Others were dumped as kittens. Feral Cats now roam the deserts, forests, mountains, beaches and urban bushlands of every state and territory.

We now know that the Cat's impact on native wildlife is truly enormous. Feral Cats have driven several species of native rodents and small marsupials and many ground-dwelling birds to extinction and they have been attributed with destroying some populations of threatened native animals, such as bilbies, Rufous Hare-wallabies and Numbats. The ground-dwelling Painted Button Quail is also a sitting 'duck' for a Cat.

Foxes

The Fox turned the tables on colonial Australians when it ceased to oblige them as a quarry to hunt and focused its attention on their tender young lambs and poultry instead. When Rabbits overran the country, Foxes were hot on their trail and populations of the two species remain inextricably entwined. For Australia's native wildlife, especially its medium-sized mammals and ground-dwelling birds, the Fox—now widespread throughout the mainland except for the tropical north—is the biggest threat. Six small macropods are now extinct and an additional five survive only on islands that remain Fox-free; the distribution and abundance of many others have drastically declined.

THE DYNAMICS OF WILDLIFE MANAGEMENT

If you drastically reduce Rabbit populations, will Foxes, Dingoes and Cats turn their attention to hunting native wildlife? If you control Foxes, Dingoes and Cats, will you be promoting the proliferation of Rabbits? These and many more dilemmas face wildlife managers and illustrate just how much we still have to learn about how the natural world interacts.

A lone hunter of stealth and intelligence, the Fox takes medium-sized ground-dwelling mammals, reptiles and birds. In times of scarcity it switches to berries, frogs, mice and carrion. It has been implicated in the extinction of many native species and the decline of the Greater Bilby, Eastern Barred Bandicoot, Bridled Nailtail Wallaby and Green Turtle. Any recovery program of a native animal without eradication of Foxes within its release area is nowadays considered doomed.

BIRDS

Of the 800 bird species that live or regularly visit Australia, 600 or so breed here. Many live nowhere else in the world and are, therefore, said to be endemic to Australia. This high level of endemicism suggests that there have been massive independent evolutionary developments on this continent.

There is much lively debate about the origin of Australia's birds. The world's birds are divided into two groups: the passerines and non-passerines. Until the advent of molecular biology in the 1970s it was assumed that Australia's passerines had originated elsewhere and reached the continent on the wing. DNA analysis now reveals that almost all Australian passerines are more closely related to one another than they are to species elsewhere in the world, suggesting the existence of early native ancestors that are believed to have been living on Gondwana around the time when Australia broke away from the supercontinent.

Passerines are sometimes referred to as perching birds or songbirds. They are accomplished weavers, able to construct elaborate nests, and their voice-box has a unique musculature that allows them to sing complex songs. They perch with three toes facing forward and one backwards, and the ligaments in their toes are designed to 'lock' when the birds are at rest or asleep on a branch.

Over half of Australia's birds are passerines and it is entirely possible that today's lyrebirds, treecreepers, fairy-wrens, grasswrens, honeyeaters, monarchs, pardalotes, thornbills, shrike-tits, fantails, woodswallows, birds of paradise and bowerbirds evolved either on Gondwana or on the landmass of Australia and New Guinea after it split from Gondwana about 45 million years ago. So while Australia's robins, wrens, warblers and flycatchers may strongly resemble northern hemisphere species of the same name, they are not related. They have simply developed similar characteristics to deal with similar environmental conditions. Their common names are misleading. They were bestowed upon them by early settlers, who recognised their similarity to birds of their homeland but did not to know about this separate evolution.

Of course some songbirds have colonised Australia from elsewhere. For example, starlings, mistletoebirds, pittas, sunbirds, swallows, larks, reed-warblers, cisticolas, white-eyes and thrushes. These birds all arrived from Eurasia in comparatively recent times.

Non-passerines are unable to sing sweet complex songs or to weave elaborate nests. Among them are the flightless birds, penguins, waders, waterbirds, waterfowl, seabirds, owls and birds of prey, moundbirds, quails, pigeons, parrots and cuckoos. Many of Australia's non-passerines, too, are believed to have derived from Gondwanan descendants, including the emu, cassowary, parrots and cockatoos, moundbirds, frogmouths and some raptors.

PREVIOUS PAGE *Australian Pelicans.*
RIGHT *A male Victoria Riflebird displays his yellow gape to attract female attention.*

Emu

These extraordinary looking creatures are Australian born and bred. They evolved from a group of flightless birds that ran around Gondwana 50 million years ago. Today emus roam across savanna woodlands, open inland plains, deserts, forests, coastal regions and even the snow country of mainland Australia.

Emus are nomadic, forever on the search for food and water. They usually travel in small groups but in times of drought they congregate at waterholes, sometimes in their hundreds, where there is good feed.

Emus have long filamentous grey-brown feathers that fall around their back and shoulders like giant shaggy shawls, and tufts and wisps of shorter feathers sprout untidily from the top of their head and along their bluish-black neck. They stand up to 2m (79in) tall, with females being larger than males. The wings of Emus are greatly reduced and incapable of flight, but they have long, powerful legs and can run exceedingly fast in open country: up to 65kph (40mph) in short bursts.

With the strong claws on their forward-facing toes an adult Emu can defend itself or its offspring from a Dingo attack. Emus are constantly alert and can hear and see well. A special membrane pulls across the eye to protect its surface from dust. In the breeding season their windpipe develops into a thin-walled, 30cm-long throat pouch that can deliver a deep guttural boom for a kilometre (3300ft) across the plains.

Anyone who has picnicked at Healesville Sanctuary on the outskirts of Melbourne in Victoria will tell you that Emus are incurably inquisitive, especially about food. In an environment where pickings can be slim, it's smart to be omnivorous. In the wild they eat fruit, grass shoots, flowers, leaves, seeds and insects but they won't say no to a sandwich or to a field of wheat. This latter propensity infuriates farmers.

FENCING THE FLIGHTLESS

Emu populations have increased since European settlement. In 1932 the Western Australian government resorted to shooting Emus with machine guns and erected thousands of kilometres of vermin-proofed fencing to protect wheat fields. Despite this, their numbers continue to rise, mainly because of the considerable reduction in populations of animals that prey on Emus.

It is the male Emu that raises the chicks. Here an attentive father eyes off an intruder. He has been left with up to 13 eggs each measuring about 13x9cm (6x4in) to incubate. For 55 days he will hardly eat, drink or defecate. Within hours of hatching, the well-formed chicks in their downy cream and brown stripes will be moving around but they won't be able to shake off dad until they are fully grown and ready to breed at about 18 months of age.

Southern Cassowary

In a very restricted area of north-eastern Queensland lives one of the world's three cassowary species. Cassowaries are primarily New Guinean tropical rainforest birds but they share many characteristics with the Emu, including their Gondwanan heritage.

OSTRICH ON THE RUN

Australia's third flightless bird is the African Ostrich, which was introduced into South Australia as a farm animal in 1869 to supply the fashionable hat trade. After the First World War the birds were released and became feral. Today a few individuals still eke out a living in the Flinders Ranges, South Australia.

They are flightless but have long legs and feet that are extremely powerful. The dagger-shaped claw on one toe is a mighty weapon; it is also indispensable for sifting through leaf litter. Females are larger than males—weighing up to 60kg (132lb) to his 35kg (77lb), and, like the Emu, it is the male that undertakes incubation and parental duties.

The long glossy black quills that drape most of a cassowary's body are offset by blue and red skin on the head, neck and pendulous throat wattles from which a resonant boom is emitted, especially during courtship. The horny helmet on the top of an adult's head, known as a casque, is distinctive. Certainly used for penetrating vine thicket, it perhaps serves other functions yet to be discovered.

Naturally shy birds, Cassowaries live solitary lives browsing through the rainforest, plucking small animals, carrion and fallen fruits from the forest floor. They need extensive areas of undisturbed rainforest to survive because they depend on a year-round fruit supply. By consuming the fruits of many different trees, they disperse the seeds in their droppings and effectively re-forest their habitat.

Pressures from agriculture, shifting human populations and tourism have fragmented their habitat, especially in places like Mission Beach, once a lowland cassowary stronghold and now a burgeoning tourist destination. The contact with humans is also leading to cassowary road casualties and dog attacks. Fewer than a thousand survive in north Queensland's rainforest and these magnificent birds are now on the national endangered species list.

An ever-wary male Southern Cassowary looks out for its charges as they investigate the understorey for food. These chicks started life in brown and buff stripy down and will not be sexually mature for two or three years. Provided they stay healthy and do not meet with misadventure, they may live for 40 years.

WARNING!

Never feed cassowaries as some individual birds have come to expect food handouts and a few people have consequently been attacked.

Penguins

Most penguins live in Antarctica or on sub-Antarctic islands so Australia is fortunate to have, in the Little Penguin, a resident species. It nests in colonies around Tasmania, on islands of the Bass Strait and all along the mainland's southern coast from Western Australia up to New South Wales. Weighing a mere 1kg (2lb) and standing only 40cm (16in) high, it is the world's smallest penguin.

A Little Penguin on its way from the sea to its burrow. Its spindle-shaped body and webbed feet are adaptations to a life spent swimming in water. A layer of down locked beneath a similar blanket of outer feathers traps air to give the penguin insulation in freezing water temperatures.

Like all penguins the Little Penguin is flightless and amphibious, feeding in the sea but resting and nesting on land. Using its powerful short flippers as propellers it dives in pursuit of fish, often sardines or anchovies, sometimes squid and crustaceans.

Unlike the subantarctic penguins that nest in the open, the Little Penguin lives in a sandy burrow, which it excavates under vegetation or rocks. Here the female usually lays two eggs in late winter, and she and her partner take turns to sit on them while the other goes fishing. After a month's incubation the young penguins hatch and the chicks grow rapidly. Within six weeks they are fledged and the parents are free to moult.

Outside of the breeding season birds may stay at sea for several days but they do eventually return to their burrows. They come to land only after dusk, waddling up the shore, fat with fish, to find their burrow. At Philip Island, 60km (37mile) south-east of Melbourne, it is possible to witness the delightful sight of rafts of penguins gathering in the surf before coming up onto the shore each night.

Grebes

Like penguins, grebes are diving waterbirds but they live in freshwater lagoons, dams and swamps and occasionally in estuaries or salt lakes. As they fly at night they are rarely seen out of water.

A Great Crested Grebe sitting on eggs. Grebes nest discreetly among reeds at the water's edges. Both sexes gather soggy weeds into large mounds that sometimes float but remain tethered to standing vegetation. The downy chicks have stripy markings on their heads and bodies. They enjoy riding on their parents' backs but can swim almost immediately and will even go diving, launching themselves from under their parents' wings.

Of the three species found in Australia, the cosmopolitan Great Crested Grebe is the largest at about 40cm (16in) long, while the Australasian Grebe and Hoary-headed Grebe are only about 26cm (10in) long.

Sometimes grebes pluck midges from the water's surface but these birds are accomplished swimmers and divers. Their toes are lobed and underwater they provide excellent propulsion as they snap up small fish, insect larvae, molluscs, yabbies and prawns. The smaller species may prospect from the surface before diving upon their target, while the Great Crested Grebe, with its dagger-like bill, often undertakes high-speed chases after fish of up to 20cm (8in) long. Plants, too, form a portion of a grebe's diet.

> **DABCHICKS**
> Many of the world's grebes are commonly referred to as dabchicks.

The Great Crested Grebe is found throughout the world. It favours large bodies of deep, clear water, edged with dense aquatic vegetation. The Australasian Grebe from the Pacific area and recently self-introduced into New Zealand is widespread throughout Australia, including Tasmania, but it rarely visits inland lakes, whereas the native Hoary-headed Grebe is more nomadic and may breed in colonies on ephemeral inland lakes but is scarce in the tropical north outside of Kakadu National Park.

The elegant Great Crested Grebes are famous for their courtship rituals, which start with a long distant two-note call to attract attention and evolve into an elaborate water 'dance'. The pair mirror each other's movements, fanning out their head ruffs, proffering weed to one another and paddling across the water's surface at high speed and in unison, their bodies stretched out almost vertically.

SIEVING YOUR FISH BONES

Young grebes are fed their own feathers by their parents and, once adult, they continue to swallow them. This curious habit may be a preventative measure to avoid choking. Inevitably grebes swallow a lot of fish bones. These could easily puncture their intestine. If feathers accumulating at the beginning of the intestine were to form a sort of open-weave basket, food could pass through but indigestible large fish bones might be caught and periodically regurgitated.

BOB OR FLY

At the slightest hint of disturbance, the Great Crested and Australasian Grebes bob underwater but Hoary-headed Grebes are more likely to fly off.

From a distance and in their plain, non-breeding plumage, the Australasian and Hoary-headed Grebes are hard to tell apart. Like all grebes, they appear to have no tail and tend to sit low in the water. In breeding plumage, however, the Australasian Grebe (top) colours up with a chestnut nape and a striking yellow spot between the eye and bill, while the head and upper neck of the Hoary-headed Grebe (bottom) turns black and is streaked with white plumes.

Petrels, Albatrosses and Shearwaters

These birds spend their entire lives at sea except when nesting on offshore islands. Magnificent flyers, many of them ply the wild Southern Ocean that encircles Antarctica, coming north to feed at nutrient-rich upwellings along the edge of southern Australia's continental shelf, especially during winter.

The Shy Albatross breeds only on three small islands off Tasmania. With a wingspan of 2.5m (8ft) it has little need to flap its wings, preferring to conserve energy by sailing on wind currents. It may stay at sea without touching land for several years after fledging. Among nesting Shy Albatrosses there is a high rate of egg loss and chick mortality, with some pairs successfully raising just one fledgling every three years. Populations are therefore sensitive to the loss of even a single adult.

Essentially southern hemisphere birds, many breed on islands in the Bass Strait and especially on Australia's subantarctic Macquarie Island, where four of the world's 21 albatross species nest.

Although rarely encountered, except at sea, these seabirds are a large group collectively known as tube-noses because of the tube-like nostrils on their upper bill. Tube-noses possess many adaptations for life at sea. Equipped with long, narrow and pointy wings they can ride the updraughts from the heaving waves of the ocean and travel huge distances. The wingspan of the Wandering Albatross that breeds on Macquarie Island can reach a staggering 3.5m (11½ft). It has been recorded travelling at speeds of up to 80kph (50mph) and for a distance of 15,000km (9300mile) in a single foraging trip.

Tube-nosed seabirds feed on fish, squid, crustaceans and plankton and to this end the large hook on their bill is invaluable. To rid themselves of the excessive salt that comes from their food, they have salt glands behind the eyes that excrete a saline solution that is twice the concentration of seawater. All the fish oil they eat is stored in their stomach and serves to energise them on their long fishing trips. It is also regurgitated as a high-calorie diet for their chicks, which often have to wait days or even weeks for a feed.

These seabirds nest colonially, either on the ground or in burrows. Monogamy is the general rule and pairs work together to build the

The Southern Giant-Petrel breeds on Macquarie Island, south of Tasmania, and during winter and spring it can be seen soaring over Australia's southern seas. It is a large aggressive seabird 90cm (35in) long with an enormous bill on which the tube-nose is quite prominent. A predator of seal and penguin colonies, it also scavenges behind boats and at sewage outfalls and is strong enough to tear open the beached carcass of a whale.

nest, incubate the chicks and time-share feeding and chick-sitting duties. They are long-lived and, not withstanding misadventure, large albatrosses may live for up to 50 years. This longevity is just as well since most tube-nosed seabirds reproduce very slowly. They lay only a single egg and most of the larger seabirds take a long time to attain sexual maturity—up to seven years in albatrosses.

Australian shearwaters are commonly referred to as muttonbirds because they were once eaten by early settlers, and even today young Short-tailed Shearwaters are hunted on the windswept Furneaux Islands in the Bass Strait. Millions of this species breed in Tasmania and the Bass Strait each spring before undertaking their annual epic trans-equatorial migration to summer feeding grounds in the Gulf of Alaska and the Bering Sea.

With up to 55 species of petrels, nine albatrosses and nine shearwaters flying around Australia's temperate coasts, it is notoriously difficult to tell species apart, especially as they are nearly always on the wing. If you are a good sailor, why not take a pelagic boat trip out to see these birds in their natural habitat?

SEABIRD RESCUE

Long-line fishing is killing seabirds at an unsustainable rate. The lines, up to 130km (19mile) long and strung with thousands of baited hooks, are run out of the back of fishing boats and remain on the surface for 20 or 30 seconds before sinking. Petrels and albatrosses attempt to take the bait. In doing so, they often become hooked and are dragged under the water and drowned. Seabird ecologists from the Australian Antarctic Division in Hobart have developed a new long-line that is embedded with minute lead particles. The increased weight sinks the line as it hits the water, making the bait unobtainable to all but the smallest diving-petrels, thereby drastically reducing seabird mortality.

During summer Wedge-tailed Shearwaters are commonly seen from the cliff tops of Australia's eastern and western coasts foraging for their young, which they raise in 2m (78in) long, sandy burrows beneath vegetation or rocks. Most shearwater species nest on Australia's offshore islands but the Wedge-tailed, Fleshy-footed and Short-tailed Shearwaters sometimes nest on the mainland, albeit in low numbers.

Australian Pelican

The Australian Pelican is the continent's largest waterbird. Standing a metre (39in) high and with a wingspan of 2.7m (9ft), it is an impressive but docile bird. Pelicans are fishers commonly seen on sheltered bodies of shallow fresh and salt water throughout Australia. As well as fish they eat crustaceans, carrion and even small birds; they are also not above taking handouts from fishermen.

Despite their bulk these birds are remarkable fliers. They may have to take off from water by running across the surface but once airborne a few flaps usually lift them on to a current of warm, rising air. In this way they attain great heights and travel long distances.

Pelicans nest in colonies on coastal and inland islands. Males and females gather together a scrappy nest of sticks and weeds on the ground. Good rains inland often trigger breeding. As the dry depressions of clay-pans and salt lakes fill with water, the eggs of crustaceans and fish burst into life. One of Australia's great natural history mysteries is how pelicans and other waterbirds know when it has rained in the interior. These rare events draw birds from all over the country and the massive shallow and normally dry Lake Eyre in South Australia suddenly comes alive with up to 15,000 pairs of pelicans busily nesting within days of arrival.

Breeding pairs share food gathering and the incubation of their one or two eggs. Their hatchlings are born naked, pink and gangly but, once feathered, they waddle about and greet their instantly recognisable parents on their return from fishing expeditions by thrusting their bills deep into their parent's gullet to feed. Within 60 to 70 days they are flying and must learn to fish for themselves.

An Australian Pelican paddles along on huge webbed feet. It fishes in shallow water, using its cavernous bill-pouch as a scoop. Lifting its head from the surface, water drains out of the bill while the luckless fish are thrown directly down its throat. Pelicans often feed in small groups, herding fish together into tight shoals before sweeping the water in unison to net the confused victims.

Gannets and Boobies

Gannets and boobies are a family of seabirds, 70–86cm (27–34in) long, with webbed feet, pointed wings, dagger-sharp bills, keen eyesight and a remarkable habit of plunge diving for their prey. They spend their lives at sea feeding on fish and squid and nesting on islands, reefs, atolls or cays.

Gannets and boobies are a family of seabirds, 70–86cm (27–34in) long, with webbed feet, pointed wings, dagger-sharp bills, keen eyesight and a remarkable habit of plunge diving for their prey. They spend their lives at sea feeding on fish and squid and nesting on islands, reefs, atolls or cays.

The Australasian Gannet is a familiar sight off the southern coasts of the mainland and around Tasmania, whereas boobies are tropical birds. The Brown, Masked and Red-footed Boobies are widespread throughout the world's warmer oceans, and all of them nest on islands off northern Australia. The most common is the Brown Booby. The rare and endangered Abbott's Booby is struggling to survive on the Australian territory of Christmas Island—a dot in the Indian Ocean closer to Java.

The massive bill and body shape of gannets and boobies is easily recognised. Boobies have facial skin and throat patches and some have

This adult Australasian Gannet is focusing on life beneath the waves. Once prey is located its body will fold into a living dart, with the wings against its body and the bill pointing seaward. It then drops from the sky, dives, pursues its quarry underwater propelled by its webbed feet and wings, and snags it from behind on the backward-raked serrations of its bill. Within seconds the fish is devoured and the gannet is flapping out of the water, heading skyward once again.

brightly coloured feet. Watching these birds dive is an absorbing sight. They may fish singly or, when targeting shoals, in groups. To withstand the impact of plummeting into water at speeds of up to 60kph (35mph), they have a network of internal air sacs that act as shock absorbers. Once underwater, flaps block their nostrils to stop water getting in. It takes a long time to hone the consummate skills of these aerial bombers and young birds grow up slowly. Many do not acquire the sleek plumage of adults for several years and young gannets do not attain sexual maturity for four to seven years.

Gannets and boobies are colonial nesters. Some nest on the ground but Abbott's Boobies nest in the canopy of large rainforest trees and Red-footed Boobies nest as high as possible, although only shrubs are sometimes available on Coral Sea islands. Breeding pairs share duties, including the incubating of eggs. They cement their bond with greeting rituals and some partners stay together for more than one season.

A female Brown Booby with her chick. Brown Boobies lay two eggs several days apart but only one hatchling, usually the older, survives. The younger sibling misses out on most of the food and is gradually edged out of the nest, where it is likely to be gobbled up by predators.

Tropicbirds and Frigatebirds

These tropical seabirds nest on islands and cays off northern Australia. Both are spectacular birds, especially in flight.

Tropicbirds look rather like terns but mature birds have two long, thin central tail feathers that trail behind them; these are called streamers. Both Australian species are white with black markings around the eye and on the wings. The 46cm (18in)-long Red-tailed Tropicbird has a red bill and 40cm (16in)-long red streamers, while the 40cm (16in)-long White-tailed Tropicbird has a yellow bill and 45cm (18in)-long streamers that are usually white but occasionally yellow.

Tropicbirds are ocean fliers that travel at great heights. When feeding they hover over prey before plunging into water with wings half closed and they take flying fish on the wing. They are often attracted to ships in the hope of a quick and easy meal.

Frigatebirds spend much of their life in the air. They have long, narrow, angular wings and deeply forked tails and are brilliant fliers, soaring, twisting and turning through the sky. The Greater Frigatebird is up to 1m (3ft) long with a wingspan of 2.3m (7ft); the Lesser Frigatebird is about 80cm (31in) long with a 1.8m (6ft) wingspan. At breeding time male frigatebirds are particularly impressive as their red throat patches blow up like huge balloons, a captivating sight to female frigatebirds no doubt.

Frigatebirds have a ferocious hook at the end of their bills. They snatch baby turtles, carrion and flying fish from the water's surface on the wing, never landing on water. They also spend much of their time robbing boobies and terns of their catch by outmanoeuvring and harassing them in mid-air until they disgorge their food.

A Red-tailed Tropicbird sits on a solitary egg. Tropicbirds return to the same island breeding area each year. The nest is usually nothing more than a scrape on the ground in the shadow of a cliff or the shade of a bush. Tropicbirds often fall victim to cyclones and storms.

Cormorants and Australasian Darter

Australia is home to five species of these fishers of seas, estuaries and rivers. The Black-faced Cormorant rarely visits the mainland, nesting on southern offshore islands, while the Pied and Little Pied Cormorants, as well as the Little Black and Great Cormorants, are widespread and common. Only the Pied Cormorant is absent from Tasmania, making it no further than the Bass Strait.

These angular, skinny-looking birds with hooked bills sit low in the water and dive for fish. Underwater their long necks and sleek bodies stretch out as their webbed feet, set well back on the body, provide propulsion from behind. To reduce drag, they usually hold their wings close by their sides.

Cormorant feathers are not waterproof so it is common to see these birds holding their wings out to dry after fishing excursions. Becoming wet to the skin reduces buoyancy and therefore energy expenditure underwater, allowing them to stay down for longer.

Were Australia's cormorants to stand obligingly side by side (which they usually do not) it would be easy to tell them apart. The largest of the five is the Great Cormorant at 90cm (35in) tall, followed by the Pied, the Black-faced, the Little Black and, lastly, the 60cm (24in)-high Little Pied Cormorant. Greats and Little Blacks are black all over; the Little Pied and Pied are black and white, as is the pelagic and range-restricted Black-faced Cormorant. Only the Black-faced and Little Black Cormorants lack yellow bills when mature.

The Australasian Darter is another diving bird that shares many characteristics with cormorants. Although it

These Pied Cormorants are distinguished from Little Pieds by their yellow or orange facial skin which colours up in the breeding season. Like all cormorants, they are colonial nesters. They may nest inland, in mangroves or islands, either on the ground or in trees.

looks superficially similar, it is distinctly thinner and it has a long, S-shaped neck, a narrow head and a dagger-straight bill. Its dark plumage is streaked with white and there is a distinct yellow throat pouch. Darters fish in sheltered coastal and inland waters. They use their bill to skewer fish, which they then throw up off their beak to catch and swallow.

An adult male Darter with its characteristic bright yellow throat pouch holds out its wings to dry. Darters are sometimes known as Snake-birds because, when swimming, their sinuous head and neck poke up above the water's surface while their body remains submerged.

Herons, Egrets and Bitterns

Australia is home to 14 of these graceful long-necked, long-legged waders. They quietly stalk the shallows of swamps, estuaries and mangroves for worms, crabs, frogs, aquatic larvae and fish. Their keen sight and fine-pointed bill, edged with serrations for holding slippery customers, twinned with patience, concentration, stealth and lightning reactions, conspire to make them masterful spear-fishers.

The White-faced Heron is one of the boldest herons. It is often seen in paddocks or on playing fields and golf courses after rain; it may even prospect in garden ponds. It feeds on fishes, tadpoles and crustaceans, as well as grasshoppers, small rodents and birds. Like other herons and egrets, it sometimes stirs the water to lift fine silt and reveal disturbed prey or chases it with uncharacteristic haste.

Probably the most common and widespread heron or egret in Australia is the slate grey White-faced Heron, which stands 65cm (26in) tall on yellow legs and has a white face and dark bill. It is sometimes confused with the taller, darker grey White-necked or Pacific Heron (80cm/31in) that is commonly seen on floodplains, but it lacks its snowy white head and neck and its grey legs. In northern Australia the less aquatic Pied Heron (45cm/18in) is smaller than both. It has a white head and neck and dark back and wings but its bill and legs are yellow. The Pied heron is a particularly opportunistic species that has recognised the bounties of sewage ponds, stockyards and recently burnt areas. Along northern Australia's rivers and coasts lives the impressive Great-billed Heron.

The egrets are quite simply all-white herons. The regal Great Egret stands 1m (3ft) high and, being the largest, forages in relatively deep water. Next in size is the Intermediate Egret (67cm/26in), followed by the Little Egret (62cm/24in). The two former remain mostly still while foraging, poised to strike unsuspecting prey. The Little Egret is more active in shallower water.

Eastern Reef Egrets (65cm/26in) investigate rocky coasts, exposed reefs, estuaries and islands of all but parts of the southern coast and Tasmania. Although the plumage of one form is characteristically white, there is, confusingly, a dark grey form but its habitat helps identify it.

Bitterns are shy, and mostly nocturnal, inhabitants of dense reeds and grasses around water. Despite their relatively short legs and streaky brown plumage, they are also herons. Camouflaged by their plumage and their habit of freezing with their long bill pointing skywards at the slight whiff of danger, all of Australia's three bittern species are notoriously hard to spot.

Breeding and Nesting

During the breeding season herons and egrets acquire long plumes. These are especially impressive among the egrets. Lacy shawls of modified feathers hang from the back, wings and breast of Great, Intermediate and Little Egrets. Most striking are the soft orange breast and back feathers, with matching head crest, of the Cattle Egret, a cosmopolitan species that has made itself at home in Australia's paddocks, where it snatches insects from grass disturbed by grazing cows.

Herons and egrets nest in trees overhanging water. Breeding colonies are usually small, although heronries can be lively noisy places numbering thousands of birds at times. Nests comprise platforms of twigs in treetops and frequently become the unwelcomed attention of birds of prey. When breeding pairs are not attending to domestic matters, they preen, waterproofing their feathers with powder down (see page 217) like cuckoo-shrikes, and removing grease and other gunk. Their sleek, immaculate appearance bears witness to its effect.

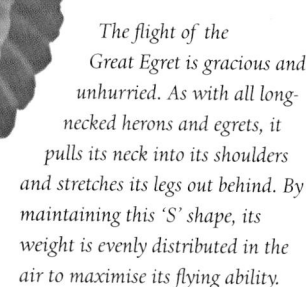

The flight of the Great Egret is gracious and unhurried. As with all long-necked herons and egrets, it pulls its neck into its shoulders and stretches its legs out behind. By maintaining this 'S' shape, its weight is evenly distributed in the air to maximise its flying ability.

THE BUNYIP'S BOOM

Australia's early white settlers, unnerved by the spooky sounds around lagoons and creeks at night, adopted the Bunyip creature of Aboriginal folklore as their own. More often heard than seen, the deep gurgling boom of the strange bittern birds may well account for all the stories and legends.

During the breeding season Cattle Egrets transform from entirely white birds into a finery of orange plumes. Their bills, and even their eyes, turn from yellow to red and their legs from grey to red.

Ibises and Spoonbills

Perhaps surprisingly, ibises and spoonbills belong to the same family but their long legs, body shape and preference for wetlands are common to both. In fact these birds often nest together in large numbers across the river systems of south-western and south-eastern Australia.

A Straw-necked Ibis in typical swamp habitat. Ibises and spoonbills often nest together and breeding colonies can be packed. Low trees, shrubs and reed beds surrounded by water are favourite sites for building twig nests, lined with bark or vegetation. Straw-necked Ibises mostly breed along the river systems of south-eastern Australia, although colonies also form around ephemeral lakes when they fill with water.

It is the bills that set ibises and spoonbills apart. While that of ibises is a long, robust, downward-curved bill, a spoonbill's bill is . . . well, spoon-shaped (although flat). The different shapes require different foraging techniques. An ibis probes deep down into the substrate whereas a spoonbill swishes its bill through water and the top layer of soft sediment. Both bills are sensitised to detect the small movements of aquatic prey.

Ibises

Ibises are generally more commonly seen, especially the Australian White or Sacred Ibis. All three Australian species have traditionally fed in grasslands, ideally when the ground is soft after rain. Flocks of ibis will rid a crop of its pestilential grasshoppers and caterpillars in no time at all. While draining of wetlands has probably reduced the occurrence

Compared with the Royal Spoonbill, this Yellow-billed Spoonbill has a slightly longer bill with a narrower 'spoon' that sweeps smoothly through the shallows for water bugs and yabbies. The less widespread Royal Spoonbill has a shorter, wider-tipped bill, whose sweeps are punctuated by erratic interludes, which may account for its greater fish-catching ability; it also eats more aquatic plants.

of the two rarer species, the irrigation of fields, golf courses and football ovals has expanded the feeding range of the Sacred Ibis. In fact it has adapted so well to human modifications of the landscape, it is not unusual to see it in cities foraging in the garbage bins of parks and snatching leftovers from garden restaurants.

At about 75cm (30in) long, the Sacred's mostly white body contrasts with a naked black head and neck, black wing tips and rather alarming unfeathered scarlet 'armpits'. The Straw-necked Ibis, the most widespread species, especially on floodplains, is a little smaller. Its upper-parts are mostly dark but with a green and purple iridescent sheen that glints in sunlight. Only its neck and underparts are white. Its name comes from the straw-colour plumes that hang from its lower fore-neck. Smallest and rarest is the Glossy Ibis (53cm/21in), a mostly inland inhabitant, whose entirely dark body shimmers with bronze, purple and green iridescence.

Spoonbills

Australia's two spoonbill species are quite common in northern and eastern Australia and they often occur, and even nest, together. While both are white and have remarkably long spatulated bills, the Yellow-billed Spoonbill has a yellow bill and matching yellow legs, while the Royal Spoonbill has a black tail with matching black legs. Spoonbills sweep their bill from side

---

SKY FLIGHT

It is not uncommon to see flocks of ibis and spoonbills flying in 'V' formation as they travel to and from breeding grounds or migrate in response to rainfall and flooding. Unlike herons and egrets, they extend their neck while flying.

to side through the water in search of frogs, yabbies, molluscs, aquatic insects and fish. It is unusual for two such similar birds to forage so close to one another but subtle differences in the selection of their food and method of collection obviate competitive squabbling.

Standing out from the crowd is the enormous Black-necked Stork or Jabiru, Australia's one and only stork. Graceful and elusive it stands 1.2m (4ft) high on long spindly legs and has a wingspan of 2.2m (7ft). Moderately common in wetlands of northern Australia, it becomes increasingly rare in New South Wales. Adults have bright red legs and females can be recognised by their yellow iris. Its 30cm (12in) dagger-straight bill is used to spear frogs, eels, snakes, rodents, birds, fish and crabs in wet meadows, mangroves and estuaries.

Swans, Geese and Ducks

In a dry land of unpredictable rain Australia's waterfowl have evolved to take advantage of the good times to breed. They do not follow the patterns of annual migration to and from breeding and feeding grounds so characteristic of the swans, geese and ducks of the northern hemisphere; rather they have developed a nomadic lifestyle based on regional droughts and floods.

There are 19 native species of waterfowl in Australia. Some may have evolved from ancestors living millions of years ago when wetlands in Central Australia were plentiful but the continent has been drying out gradually ever since. Diminishing habitat further for these birds over the last 200 years has been the drastic alteration of precious natural water flows to meet the needs of farmers, pastoralists and those in cities and towns.

For visitors from the northern hemisphere, accustomed to white swans, the funereal plumage of Australia's Black Swan is a bit of a shock. The Swan River, upon which Perth was built, was so named for its high density of Black Swans and this species remains the bird emblem of Western Australia.

Swans and Geese

Among Australia's native assemblage are two geese and a swan. Black Swans are common throughout Australia on large bodies of permanent fresh or brackish water with plenty of emergent and submerged vegetation. Like most of the country's waterfowl, they travel long distances, usually at night. Male and female swans bond for life. Each year the pairs gather reeds and sedges into raised sodden mounds; these nests are usually well hidden in dense vegetation. They may raise up to ten fluffy grey cygnets, protecting them fiercely through their first few months.

Magpie Geese cluster at a billabong fringed with spike-rushes, a Dry-season refuge. Here they feed on aquatic plants, the hook on their bill ripping the bulbs out of the mud. Come the Wet, the spike-rushes will flourish and be harvested by the geese for nesting mounds.

FLY BYS GET THE GUN

While New South Wales, Queensland and Western Australia have banned duck shooting altogether, other states lag behind. Despite heavy fines for shooting protected species, poor and inexperienced shooters make mistakes. Most at risk is Australia's rare Freckled Duck, a nondescript bird (at a distance) that is easily confused with the common Pacific Black Duck, with which it often circles over wetlands.

The Pacific Black Duck is one of Australia's most common and widespread ducks in natural and man-made waterways. Introduced Mallard Ducks often interbreed with this native species. Hybrids, not surprisingly, display features of both species.

For many Australians the Magpie Goose is synonymous with Kakadu National Park, the wetland jewel in the nation's crown. In the Wet season of the north these birds disperse in vast numbers across the floodplains. On close inspection this gawky goose looks faintly odd. The large knob on the top of its head and the partially webbed feet indicate a separate and, possibly extremely ancient, lineage from that of other geese.

Magpie Geese are depicted on Aboriginal rock paintings and were obviously an important source of food. They remained widespread and plentiful until

settlers along the lower reaches of the rivers of New South Wales and Victoria began draining their wetlands for pasture and agriculture, and shooting and poisoning the geese as crop pests. Now eradicated from most of the south, they continue to breed in large numbers in the wetlands of the north.

Among the rarest geese in the world is the Cape Barren Goose that lives on Australia's southern windswept offshore islands from Western Australia to Victoria. It is a pale grey goose with red legs, black feet and a distinctive yellow flap of skin on its upper bill. Originally a grazer of native tussock grasses and speargrasses, it took to the clovers and sweet new pastures of settlers and paid the price. By the 1950s, their numbers had plummeted but a degree of protection in recent years has increased populations to an estimated 20,000 birds.

Duck Habitats

Land cleared for crops, pastures, dams, golf courses and football fields has expanded the feeding grounds of many of Australia's grazing waterfowl; among them, the Australian Wood Duck, the Magpie Goose, Black Swan, Plumed Whistling-Duck and the Australian Shelduck. Other waterfowl have different needs. For Australia's dabblers—Grey and Chestnut Teal, Freckled Ducks, Pacific Black Ducks and Hardheads—shallow fresh water holds the greatest culinary promise since they must reach the bottom when they up-turn to find weeds and invertebrates. Diving ducks, like the Musk and Blue-billed Ducks, prefer deep, permanent water in which to 'fish'. Pink-eared Ducks and Australasian Shovelers rely on surface-dwelling inverte-

A male Musk Duck is recognised by its leathery chin pouch, an indispensable accessory to his elaborate courtship performance. Musk Ducks usually swim out in deep water, their body sitting low on the surface. They are accomplished divers, remaining submerged for 20 to 30 seconds per foraging trip.

brates, such as midges, which they strain out of the water through the fine plates along the edge of their long spatula-shaped bill. Specialised flaps on the bill of the Pink-eared Duck refine the water flow.

Top Duck Locations

For many Australian ducks, flooding triggers breeding. Floodwaters fan out over huge distances on this relatively flat continent. Coongie Lakes in South Australia is an extensive mosaic of lakes, billabongs and swamps, and the terminus for floodwaters of the north-west tributary of Cooper Creek in Queensland's Channel Country. Although parts are dry for most of the year, there are persistent waterholes and billabongs fringed by red gums and coolabah trees. When episodic inland downpours or monsoonal waters from the north burst their banks, the plains of lignum and cane grass beyond begin to flood. As the water spills into the shallow depressions of claypans and saltpans, thousands of Grey Teal are among the first to respond.

Flooded swamps with dense stands of lignum are highly prized, providing good cover for breeding. The temporarily wet claypans and saltpans, while lacking substantial cover, provide a nutritious soup of freshly hatched, wriggling invertebrates, irresistible to ducks. Pink-eared and Australian Wood Ducks, and even the elusive and rare Freckled Ducks, soon arrive. A surprising number of Australian ducks nest in tree hollows and pretty soon the river red gums become hot property.

Another major waterfowl habitat is the Barmah–Millewa forest. This is a 60,000ha (150,000ac) floodplain dominated by river red gums in the Murray–Darling Basin. When the floodwaters arrive here so, too, do the Pink-eared Ducks, Australian Shelducks, Grey and Chestnut Teal, Pacific Black Ducks and Wood Ducks, all looking for suitable nesting hollows and a good feed. Other wonderful places to see large numbers of wildfowl in southern Australia are Moulting Lagoon in Tasmania, the Coorong in South Australia and the Swan River Plain lakes in Western Australia.

A male Australian Shelduck. This handsome, solidly built duck is the largest of all the native ducks (73cm/29in). Females are distinguished by white eye-rings and white at the base of their bills. Shelducks reside on coastal saline lakes and estuaries in the southern part of the continent but often move inland to breed.

Tropical Ducks

Large expanses of northern Australia are annually inundated by monsoonal rain and there is a small suite of tropical native waterfowl that do not venture far south. Among them are the delightful Plumed and Wandering Whistling-Ducks, so-named for their whistling calls. They are pretty, long-necked upright ducks with upswept flank plumes, most distinct in the Plumed Whistling-Duck. Equally charming are the tiny Green and Cotton Pygmy-geese that swim among the waterlilies of rivers, deep lagoons and dams. No more than 38cm (15in) long, they have a delicate appearance with only their small bill bearing even the slight resemblance to a goose which, indeed, they are not.

A pair of Australian Wood Ducks accompany their chicks to the water's edge. The male is bringing up the rear. Unlike most ducks, this species nests in tree hollows, which can be many metres up. For duck-lings leaving the nest for the first time, there's only one way to go . . . down. Having fluttered and flapped their way to the ground, the brood follow their parents on what may be a lengthy walk to the nearest water, where they will swim right away.

In the Top End, Radjah Shelducks are often seen in pairs sifting through the mud of mangroves or even puddles for invertebrates.

Eagles, Hawks and Falcons

These raptors or birds of prey are predators at the top of the food chain. Their sharp, curved talons, powerful feet, stout hooked bills and keen eyesight are perfect attributes for catching prey as it runs, swims and flies. Their hunting style is well suited to Australia's wide open spaces. Little wonder then that there are 24 species of native raptors. While some, like the Osprey and the Peregrine Falcon, range across the world, others are endemic.

A juvenile Wedge-tailed Eagle stands poised to take the plunge. At 1–1.2m (3–4ft) long and with a wingspan of up to 2.5m (8ft), this is Australia's largest raptor and the fourth largest in the world. It is quite commonly seen soaring high in the sky above remote country. The much smaller, but also common, Little Eagle (45–55cm/18–22in) is easily confused with other brown hawks. Its 'trousered' legs, however—the hallmark of true eagles—distinguishes it when at rest.

Identification of Australian raptors is often vexing, especially since juveniles are slow to acquire their adult plumage and birds of the same species are often paler in drier habitats. As a rule, females are larger than males but this, too, can be tricky to distinguish from a distance.

Raptors usually breed in spring, courting one another in the sky with spectacular acrobatic feats such as cart-wheeling together through the air with talons locked. While most hawks and eagles build huge nests of twigs, the falcons pinch those of other birds, often members of the crow family. For such substantial birds, egg sizes are surprisingly small: that of the White-bellied Sea-Eagle is largest at 80mm (3in), while Collared Sparrowhawk eggs are a mere 38mm (1½in).

Eagles and hawks soar and glide for long periods and sometimes at great heights. Their broad, rounded wings are often splayed at the tip. Falcons are given to bursts of breathtaking speed. Their relatively narrow wings have a pronounced bend at the wrist joint and their feathers rarely splay out at the pointed tips.

Kites

The big Black and Whistling Kites (55cm/22in) are opportunistic hawks that prey upon weak and injured animals. Scavengers and carrion feeders, they are often first on the scene of bushfires. The forked-tailed Black Kites have a more tropical distribution and flock together. The rather solitary dishevelled Whistling Kite is often heard screaming across water where it commonly hunts. The endemic Square-tailed Kite (50cm/20in) prospects around the canopies of lightly timbered country. It snatches mostly small birds, such as honeyeaters and nestlings, from foliage.

Australia has two small kites (35cm/14in), both of which are predominantly white with pointed wings like falcons. They hunt rodents, small reptiles and grasshoppers in open country. The Black-shouldered Kite is fairly commonly seen perched on roadside wires, while the mostly nocturnal Letter-winged Kite—named for the 'M' or 'W' black markings on its underwing—is rarely seen.

Goshawks

The goshawks are a little smaller than the big kites and their wings are more rounded with feathers at the tips less splayed. Their tails are long and rounded. They have long yellow legs, powerful talons and red or yellow eyes. The barred undercarriage of adults camouflages them well among the foliage of mangroves, forests and woodlands from which they ambush prey. Although the Grey Goshawk is indeed grey, there is also a snowy white form. Australia's rarest and most threatened bird of prey is the endemic Red Goshawk of coastal and riverine forests in northern and north-eastern Australia.

Fish-eating Ospreys (50–66cm/20–26in) live around estuaries, coastal inlets and freshwater rivers and lakes. The distinctive dark stripe through the eye identifies the species from the juvenile White-bellied Sea-Eagle, another fishing raptor commonly seen soaring along the coasts of southern Australia. Adult Sea-Eagles (75–85cm/30–33in) are unmistakeable in their black and white livery. A more commonly seen raptor in the tropical north is the Brahminy Kite, with its gorgeous russet-coloured body and white head and neck. While Ospreys plunge into water, Sea-Eagles and Brahminy Kites snatch their catch from the surface with their feet.

A Brown Goshawk with a freshly killed Nankeen Heron. This fairly common raptor sometimes ventures into towns and cities to take domestic fowl. Males (40cm/16in) are considerably smaller than females (55cm/22in). It is easily confused with the smaller Collared Sparrowhawk (30cm/12in) but has more robust legs and a fiercer stare bestowed by a heavy brow ridge. It also lacks the long toes that are indispensable to the Sparrowhawk's capture of birds on the wing.

Harriers and the Pacific Baza

Two harriers occur in Australia. Characterised by long legs, tails and wings, and an owl-like facial disk, both the Swamp and the Spotted Harriers fly close to the ground scouring the surface for small birds and mammals. The Swamp Harrier nests on the ground or in marshes, while the Spotted— unlike all other harriers—nests in trees. For a bird of prey, the docile Pacific Baza or Crested Hawk (38–43cm/15–17in) is unusual since native figs supplement its diet of tree frogs and stick insects. A tree dweller in the dense forests of northern and eastern coastal areas, its striking head crest, large yellow eyes and stripy abdomen are unmistakable.

A pair of Brown Falcons at the entrance to their nest. The Brown Falcon (40–50mm/16–20in, with tail almost half) has a broad diet that includes insects, snakes, lizards, small birds, mammals and carrion. Soaring from a height, it looks down to locate its prey before swooping at speed to snatch it from the ground. A noisy hunter, it screams harshly and may agressively harass other raptors to give up their prey. It also hunts on foot, running after its quarry.

Falcons

Of the world's 37 species, six are found in Australia and four have evolved here. Black head markings in the form of 'side-burns', 'moustaches' or 'helmets' are a feature of these, the fastest and most dare-devil fliers in the world.

Although falcons are renowned for their ability to capture birds in mid-air, the Nankeen Kestrel (30–35cm/12–14in) and Brown Falcon (40–50cm/16–20in) rarely perform this feat. The Australian Hobby or Little Falcon (30–35cm/12–14in), however, does snatch swallows, insects and microbats on the wing, and will even eat its prey in mid-air. It also

The Nankeen Kestrel is a small, beautifully marked falcon that is commonly seen hovering, sometimes descending in 'steps', before dropping quickly on its prey.

often flies low at speed and at dusk picking off small ground-dwelling birds from grazing flocks. More robust than the Nankeen but similar in size and with a black head and back, it hunts in open woodlands, along watercourses and on farms.

The Black Falcon (45–55cm / 18–22in, with its tail almost half its length) is the largest of the Australian falcons but it is not common. Typically it soars over open and sparsely vege-tated dry plains, feeding on flying insects and pouncing on ground-dwelling mammals and birds. It is more of a carrion-eater than any of the other falcons.

The handsome Peregrine Falcon (36–50cm / 14–20in, with a tail less than half its size) is the world's fastest bird. Although similar in size to the Brown and Black Falcons, it is stockier with a black hood, broad rump and tail. A ferocious hunter, especially of flocking birds such as pigeons, seabirds and parrots, it is famous for its stomach-lurching dives. With wings half closed, it hurtles down on its prey at speeds of up to 180kph (110mph), knocking it out instantly with its feet or snapping its spinal chord at the neck with a single bite.

The elusive and rare Grey Falcon is found only in Australia's arid inland. Soft grey above and still paler below, with dark wing tips, it is a true desert dweller. Travelling nomadically, it feeds almost exclusively on birds and breeds in trees near water.

Traditionally Peregrine Falcons nest on the ledges of escarpments and cliffs, close to water, but some pairs adopt the ledges of tall buildings in cities while others, where stony forma-tions are lacking, choose hollows or abandoned stick nests in trees.

Moundbirds

These large hen-like birds belong to the megapode family. They are remarkable for the way in which they incubate their eggs. Instead of nests, they build enormous mounds. Two of the 22 species—the Australian Brush-turkey and the Malleefowl—are endemic to mainland Australia; a third, the Orange-footed Scrubfowl, is found in northern Australia and throughout the South-east Asian and south Pacific regions. All other family members live on islands to the north of Australia. Such distribution suggests that these birds evolved in that part of the world.

Australian Brush-turkeys are widespread across eastern Australia from the tip of Cape York Peninsula to Sydney. Males and females (70cm/28in) have the same bright bare skin on their head and neck but the yellow base of the male's neck billows out into a bulbous wattle during the breeding season. Notice the robust feet and legs, a feature of the megapode family; mega meaning 'big' and pod meaning 'foot'.

The Orange-footed Scrubfowl (40cm / 16in) is fairly common in the rainforests of Australia's tropical north. Here it picks through the leaf litter for tasty morsels. Its mound is huge—about 10m (11yd) in diameter—but it is usually used by several pairs. Scrubfowls form lifelong partnerships. They sometimes cause quite a commotion as they flap up noisily into trees and squawk loudly.

Indispensable to the construction of megapodes' incubation mounds are their strong, stout feet and legs, which they also use to scratch through leaf litter and soil to recover invertebrates and vegetable matter for food. Their heavy bodies make them ill-suited to flying, yet they will fly up if disturbed and to roost in trees.

Megapodes often add new layers of vegetation to an existing mound. As the freshly heaped vegetation begins to rot down and ferment, the temperature in the mound rises, as in a well-built compost heap. Females visit the mound and lay eggs one at a time into it. The eggs are big: 90x60mm (4x2in) in Malleefowl. The male monitors the heat in the mound and rakes vegetation off or on to maintain optimum incubation temperature.

Females lay a lot of eggs; up to 20 or more. In the case of the Brush-turkey, this amounts to twice the female's own weight. Once egg-laying is complete the female departs the mound. She may return many times to lay more eggs. The male is left to continue monitoring and controlling the temperature of the mound by adding or removing material each day. However, when the eggs are ready to hatch, the male plays no further part. The young break out of their eggs fully

BIRD ARCHITECTS

Early colonists, seeing the huge mounds of the megapodes for the first time, believed they were looking at Aboriginal burial mounds.

HARNESSING NATURE'S HEAT

Some megapodes that live outside of Australia do not build mounds. They simply lay their eggs in burrows on beaches or in the soil of geothermal areas. Sand-laid eggs are incubated by the heat of the sun, while eggs laid in geothermal areas are warmed from beneath by volcanic heat.

A pair of Malleefowl (60cm/24in) hard at work. These large gentle birds pay continual attention to their finely sifted mounds. Despite their beautiful plumage being well camouflaged against the dry red-brown ground of their mallee habitat, Foxes—with their excellent sense of smell—are a constant threat, especially to the chicks and eggs.

fledged and, without parental assistance, they work their way out of the mound. They immediately take off into the bush and are able to fly within 24 hours.

Although megapodes are mostly forest birds, the Malleefowl has adapted to the dry sandy inland of southern Australia. Mallee is a type of semi-arid woodland consisting of low-growing eucalypts. While both the Brush-turkey and the Orange-footed Scrubfowl have learned to exploit the detritus left by humans and are moving closer into our suburbs, the Malleefowl in its remote habitat is under siege from shrinking habitat, the incursion of introduced herbivores and predators.

COOL GUYS AND HOT CHICKS

Recent research has confirmed what some Australian Aborigines already knew: the temperatures at which Brush-turkeys' eggs are incubated determines their sex. At 34°C (93°F) an equal number of male and female chicks hatch but at 31°C (88°F) more males hatch and at 36°C (97°F) more females hatch. While this phenomena is well known in reptiles, from which birds have evolved, the sex of birds was, until recently, believed to be determined at the time of fertilisation.

Quails and Button-quails

The cryptic plumage of these dumpy, short-tailed ground birds makes them hard to spot in their natural habitat. If alarmed, they crouch down and explode from cover only as a last resort, flying low and rarely far. They are well represented in Australia, especially the button-quails, with seven of the world's 14 species living here. There are three native quail species and one introduced.

Despite similar appearances and habits, 'true' quails and button-quails are not closely related and do not share a common ancestry. The only visual anatomical difference is a hind toe in true quails that is absent in button-quails. True quails belong to a worldwide family of patridges, grouse and pheasants that are active by day; the origin of the predominantly nocturnal button-quails remains a mystery. Often, however, in nature, unrelated groups develop similar adaptations in response to similar ways of life.

True quails and button-quails scratch a living—literally—from the ground, feeding on seeds and insects. They nest in a depression or 'cup' on the ground, lined with grass, tucked in beside or beneath

The reddish and heavily spotted Painted Button-quail (16–20cm/ 6–8in) likes a dry habitat with a dense leaf litter in which to search for insects and seeds. It is an inhabitant of heaths, dry eucalypt forests and sandstone ridges. It was once, but is no longer, common around Sydney.

The endemic Stubble Quail is traditionally an inhabitant of open grassy areas, floodplains and saltbush but it has availed itself of the food and cover provided by cereal crops. It can be recognised, close-up, by the long white 'eyebrows' and streaked flanks. The orange throat of this individual signifies it is a male.

PITY THE PLAINS-WANDERER

The shy, quail-like Plains Wanderer (16–18cm/6–7in) is in a group all of its own. It is extremely rare and there are fears for its survival. Like true quails, it has a fourth hind toe, and it shares the role reversal behaviour of the button-quails, but its posture is more upright, its neck more distinct and narrower and its yellowish legs are longer. It prefers to run rather than fly and lives on the open semi-arid plains of inland New South Wales, Victoria and Queensland, where clearing of its native grasslands has reduced its range to critical levels.

clumps of vegetation. They may be flushed from their habitat singly, in pairs or small groups.

Quails

The common Stubble Quail (18cm/7in) is the only species in either group that can be legally hunted. It can be distinguished by its loud whirring wingbeat and the longer distance it flies (up to 500m/550yd) compared with other quails before dropping back down into cover. It is found in Queensland, much of the south-east and south-west of the country, in Tasmania and on King Island in the Bass Strait.

The slightly larger Brown Quail (18–20cm/7–8in) skulks around the rank grasslands of swamps and moist coastal heaths, venturing into stubble fields and pasture grasses. If disturbed it runs quickly with its neck outstretched. It occurs in northern, eastern and south-western Australia, and in Tasmania, where it is known as the Swamp Quail.

THE FLOPPY-PLUMED QUAIL

Introduced into Tasmania in the 1880s, the Californian Quail (23–24cm/9in) now lives only on King Island, among the low coastal scrub. The male bears a dark tufted head-plume that flops forward over its chestnut crown and contrasts with its striking black and white head markings, the grey breast and the buff, white and chocolate lattice patterning of its abdomen.

The small, dark King Quail (13–15cm/5–6in) also lives in rank grass-lands near swamps. Found throughout southern Asia and in New Guinea, it is quite common in northern Australia but rarer along the eastern seaboard and south to the Mount Lofty Ranges near Adelaide.

Button-quails

Despite their name, button-quails are not necessarily smaller than the true quails. Five of Australia's seven button-quails are endemic. The Red-backed Button-quail (11–15cm/4–6in) that inhabits swampy areas of north and north-eastern Australia also occurs in New Guinea and the Solomon Islands while the widespread Painted Button-quail occurs in New Caledonia.

An unusual feature of button-quails is the role reversal of the male and female. The female is bigger and brighter and it is she who initiates courtships and fights for territory. After she has laid her four or so eggs in a cup-shaped nest on the ground, she wanders off to court another mate, leaving the male to incubate the eggs and care for the young.

> ### CLUTCH COUNTS
> While button-quails usually lay up to four eggs, the true quails often lay a far larger number; up to 14 eggs in Stubble Quail.

The larger and more colourful of this pair of Black-breasted Button-quails is the female on the left. These birds scratch through the dense leaf litter looking for invertebrates and maybe seeds. The leaf litter is essential to their livelihood and may be derived from vine thicket rainforest, brigalow scrub or hoop pine plantations. Living only in a restricted area of south-eastern Queensland and north-eastern New South Wales, a loss of 90 per cent of their habitat in Queensland has left Fraser Island as an important stronghold.

> ### QUAIL QUEST
> To find button-quails, look for circular scrapes on the ground where they have been foraging or listen for a low, resonating booming call—especially at night. If disturbed, they zigzag rather than attempt a weak, short-distance flight.

Rails and Crakes

The rails and crakes are a worldwide family of small- to medium-sized hen-like swamp dwellers. They are generally secretive birds that lurk in dense vegetation near water. Some are nocturnal; others come out to feed only at dawn and dusk. A few have become semi-tame and will feed in the open, sometimes in public gardens. Of Australia's 20 species, five are endemic, one of which is extremely rare.

The Buff-banded Rail (28–30cm/ 11–12in) is quite common but, being shy, it is rarely seen. The pale stripe above the eye and the buff band across its breast are distinctive. Similar, but smaller and with relatively long, purple to pink bill, is the much rarer Lewin's Rail (20–23cm/8–9in), an inhabitant of reeds in the woodland swamps, tidal creeks and saltmarshes of eastern and south-eastern coastal areas.

Most rails and crakes have colouring that blends in with their background, although small patches of bright plumage are common. Some have a shield of skin where the forehead meets the base of the stout bill. They have powerful, quite long legs with unwebbed but strong and long toes, perfect for skulking around in squishy weeds and mud. Their tails are short and often flick up jerkily, revealing a white patch beneath. The wings are short and rounded. Reluctant fliers, their flight is laboured and clumsy looking with legs dangling awkwardly from their body. Two Australian species are entirely flightless.

Rails and crakes are more often heard than seen. Each species has its distinctive raucous cry. Most eat plant shoots and roots as well as fish, frogs, snails, worms and insects. Nests are bowls of vegetation around the margins of water. Some birds fashion a canopy of bent stems to camouflage and shelter the nest; others build launch pads to the water. Some members have lobed toes and swim well, and a few, such as the almost sparrow-sized Baillon's Crake, dive for food.

Where They Live

Largest of these birds is the common Purple Swamphen (45cm/18in), a familiar bird to most Australians. The flightless Tasmanian Native-hen is as big and robust but has more restrained colouring, a yellow bill and a white patch on its flank. Once a resident of the mainland—before Dingoes were introduced, it is now endemic to to Tasmania. It grazes in pastures close to water and, although mostly active at night, semi-tame birds will venture into the open during the day if there is dense cover nearby. It runs fast and swims well, even underwater. Equally large is the Chestnut Rail that lives in the dense mangroves of the Top End and Kimberley coasts. This species builds its nest of sticks in the hollows or prop roots of mangroves above the high tide level.

Despite being poor fliers, a number of rails are nomadic. The Black-tailed Native-hen (32–38cm/13–15in), for example, may fly inland to nest after good rain and it has a reputation for popping up in numbers in places not previously frequented. Several species have a tropical distribution; for instance, the little White-browed Crake (18–20cm/7–8in) that inhabits the coastal lagoons, swamps and mangroves of the Top End and Cape York, and the very timid Red-necked Crake (24–29cm/9–11in), which is confined to the watercourses of rainforests in north-eastern Cape York.

Purple Swamphens are widespread throughout Australia. They often boldly gather around lakes in town and city parks. They have huge, strong toes with which they dig plant roots out of the mud and construct substantial nest mounds. With their bill they stab at frogs, worms and snails and sometimes they take the eggs of other birds.

BACK FROM THE BRINK

Almost as rare as hen's teeth is the Wood Hen confined to the world heritage-listed Lord Howe Island, located 700km (435mile) east of Port Macquarie in New South Wales. The ancestors of this now flightless bird flew to the island and thrived in the lush subtropical rainforests until 1788 when the crew of the HMS *Supply* discovered the culinary delights of woodhen. The island was settled in 1834 and the shy brown woodhen became hunted by humans, introduced owls, Cats and Pigs alike, until it teetered on the brink of extinction. When a captive breeding program got underway in 1978 there were less than 30 birds left. Today, there are over 100.

The cosmopolitan Coots are among the most sociable members of the rail family. They are enthusiastic swimmers and happily up-end or dive for food. Outside the breeding season rafts of birds gather on open water, even on artificial dams and lakes. Nests are floating mounds of vegetation, tethered to standing rushes. The white facial shield and white bill distinguishes the adult Coot from the shyer but common Dusky Moorhen, whose facial shield and bill is red, tipped with yellow.

Brolga, Jacana and Bustard

These three native Australian birds display curious modes of behaviour. The elegant Brolga is Australia's only endemic crane. The Australian Bustard is a wanderer of the country's wide open spaces, and the Comb-crested Jacana is a bird of the lily-strewn wetlands with a reputation for walking on water.

One Brolga gets all of a-flutter and before you know it the whole group is shimmying around the swamp. Brolgas form life-long partnerships and a little exuberance keeps the bond strong.

Brolga

Since cranes are wetland birds, it is a credit to Australia's only true crane, the Brolga, that it survives in this dry continent. Its stronghold is the monsoonal north, but Brolgas also live in desert regions thanks to the bores sunk by station owners for their stock.

Brolgas use their bills to unearth the rhizomes of bulkuru sedges. They supplement this staple diet with small fishes, frogs, snakes and aquatic invertebrates. In the Wet, they disperse across the floodplains but, come the Dry, these shrink so they congregate at permanent waterholes and swamps.

In flight, Brolgas stretch their necks and legs fore and aft. Their broad wings beat deeply and they trumpet as they go. Like all the world's cranes, Brolgas dance, and it's catching. As one bird flaps and lifts off the ground, another gets the bug. The courtship dance is elaborate, a rare and magnificent sight; pairs bounce towards and away from each other, tossing about sticks and grass and flinging their necks back to point their bills skyward.

The Comb-crested Jacana (right) is also known as the Lotus Bird or Lily Trotter, and its reputation for walking on water has also earned it a fourth name, the Jesus Bird. In fact it treads carefully on floating vegetation, most particularly waterlily pads. Its remarkably long toes distribute its weight evenly over the floating leaves, preventing it from sinking.

Comb-crested Jacana

The dainty Comb-crested Jacana (23cm/9in) lives in the clear, still waters of well-vegetated billabongs and lagoons in northern and

The remarkable contortions of a male Bustard performing his nuptial dance is captured in the last rays of the setting sun. Having chosen a highly visible open space, the bustard inflates his breast sac with air until it almost reaches the ground, then fans out and raises his tail over his back, fluffing out his throat and breast feathers. While swinging his breast sac from side to side, he struts in front of the female, releasing a low pumping sound through his closed bill.

subtropical eastern Australia. It is a familiar sight in the floodwaters of the Top End, including Kakadu National Park. Jacanas glean insects and seeds from the underside of lilies and other vegetation. Weak fliers, they are more likely to dive in the face of danger.

Roles are reversed among male and female Jacanas, with the larger, more colourful females defending territories, initiating displays and taking several mates, while males build the flimsy floating nests of vegetation, incubate the eggs and care for the young alone. The eggs of the Comb-crested Jacana are quite beautiful: caramel-coloured and decorated with dark treacle squiggles. These eggs can float, which is just as well since nests are often almost submerged. If danger threatens, the male gathers up the entire brood under his wings; the chicks' skinny long feet dangle from his feathers as he carries them to safety.

Australian Bustard

This iconic bird of the outback stands up to 1m (39in) high—the female a little smaller—and weighs over 3kg (7lb). It roams the open grasslands of Australia's interior and coastal plains. Elusive and well hidden by its cryptic plumage, in many parts of its range it is nomadic and appears to follow the bounty of seeds, fruit, grasshoppers, molluscs, frogs, rodents and small birds that result from good rains.

Bustards may suddenly appear in large numbers, either to feed or breed. They have been reported to gather in flocks at the margins of fires to snap up fleeing or dead creatures.

For breeding purposes bustards adopt what is called an 'exploded lek'. A lek is a gathering of male birds that meet to perform courtship displays designed to win over females. They are 'exploded' in the sense that the performers are spaced out, sometimes up to 1km (⅗mile) apart. Females then choose the biggest and most impressive performers.

After the frenzied excitement of lekking, females select a sheltered nest site on the ground in which to lay one, occasionally two, large eggs. They incubate the eggs alone and care for the fluffy striped young that become mobile almost immediately.

Early settlers recorded flocks of thousands of bustards but these birds have now disappeared from large parts of southeastern Australia. They remain common only in parts of the arid interior and savanna grasslands of the north.

Waders

Each year up to two million wading birds, sometimes known as shorebirds, migrate to Australia from their Alaskan and eastern Siberian summer breeding grounds in the northern hemisphere.

The first migrants reach northern Australia in late August. Some stay there; others move further south. By Christmas, numbers are at their peak in south-eastern Australia. When March arrives they are on their journey home again, joined on their excursion in April by those that stayed in the north of the country. Some long-distance migrants over-winter in Australia for their first year and a few, like the small Red Knots (25cm / 10in), over-winter in New Zealand.

These long-distant travellers come to our shores to avoid the rigours of the northern winter. Having survived their extraordinary long and strenuous flight, those still in their breeding plumage moult. Gradually they put on weight as they feed in the estuaries and permanent swamps

No birds fill the sky with such profusion as migrating waders do. Each species has a breeding and a non-breeding plumage. When they arrive in Australia birds may be in one or the other, or in an intermediary stage. For amateur birdwatchers, the speckles, streaks, scallops and bars of these birds' muted browns, greys, blacks and whites makes identification notoriously difficult.

The strange-looking Beach Stone-curlew (55cm/22in) patrols the tideline of beaches and mudflats, looking for crabs and other marine invertebrates. Its cousin, the Bush Stone-curlew (55cm/22in), skulks around Australia's sparse open woodlands. Stone-curlews, sometimes also known as 'thick knees', reside permanently in the Top End of Australia. They are nocturnal birds that rely on their cryptic plumage to keep them safe but, with the advent of Foxes, feral Cats and four-wheel drives, the range of both species has contracted north.

around Australia's coasts. A number will even travel to inland saltpans and floodplains in times of heavy rain. There are curlews, Whimbrels, godwits, greenshanks, knots, tattlers and sandpipers. Some waders also migrate to Australia from less remote locations. For example, Latham's Snipe (24–26cm/9–10in) comes from Japan and the Double-banded Plover (18–19cm/7in) arrives from New Zealand.

Species identification among these peppery plumages of browns and greys can be bewildering but the bill of each has a slightly different size and shape, reflecting the different ways in which they feed. Short-billed waders often feed on the surface, pecking from the mud, like the small Red-necked Stint (15cm/6in). The orange-legged Ruddy Turnstone (21–25cm/8–10in) flips over small stones, shells and seaweed with its very slightly upturned, wedge-shaped bill to recover hidden marine invertebrates on rocky shores. Long-billed waders, like Bar-tailed Godwits (38–45cm/15–18in), make full use of their bill to probe deep into the mud. The large, downward-curving bill of the Eastern Curlew (55–61cm/22–24in) is sensitive to the slightest movement of mud dwellers. This variety of feeding techniques to access different prey minimises competition within mixed flocks of waders.

MARATHON FLIGHT

Until recently it was thought that Bar-tailed Godwits leaving Victoria for their northern-hemisphere summer breeding grounds in Alaska stopped off in northern Australia. However, in 2007, some godwits were fitted with the latest satellite tracking technology, which revealed a very different story. It seems that these quiet birds travel from Victoria directly to the northern end of the Yellow Sea in China, a journey of 10,000km (6000mile), in a miraculous nine-day non-stop flight.

Resident Waders

Australia has a number of resident waders of its own. They, too, move around but, with Australia's less marked seasonal differences, their migrations tend to be less extensive and less predictable. Many of these waders are plovers, plump medium-sized birds with longish legs and relatively short bills.

The solid blocks of white, black and rusty red plumage common to many native plovers make them easy to identify, especially as their plumage stays the same all year round. Their gait, too, is distinctive. Most plovers catch their food by sight, pursuing prey with rapid little steps before stopping and plucking it from the surface. Many bob their heads when doing so.

Plovers frequently nest in exposed places. To divert a predator's attention from a nest, a plover often runs away from it while dragging a seemingly broken wing along the ground. The predator, thinking the bird is an easy target, gives chase rather than plundering the nest.

Some of the small plovers are known as dotterels in Australia. Among them are the widespread Black-fronted Dotterel (16cm/6in) and the Red-capped Dotterel (15cm/6in) that commonly inhabits the margins of inland salt lakes. The pretty Red-kneed Dotterel (18cm/7in) scours the vegetated margins of fresh or mildly saline waterways. Still rarer is the endemic and sedentary Hooded Plover (19–21cm/7–8in) that lays its eggs in the dunes of southern Australia's sandy beaches, leaving them vulnerable to four-wheel drives, humans, dogs and horses.

Not all waders are associated with aquatic habitats. Australia's Inland Dotterel (20cm/8in), for example, lives in stony arid country, where it covers its eggs with sand before it leaves to

THE FLAMINGO CONNECTION

Twenty million years ago Central Australia was green and lush with extensive wetlands being grazed by flamingos. While Australian flamingos are now extinct, the related Banded Stilt has adapted to the prevailing drier conditions and migrates inland only after flooding.

The Black-fronted Dotterel (top) and the Red-kneed Dotterel (bottom) are both endemic waders. The Black-fronted Dotterel is commonly seen around fresh and brackish waters throughout Australia. The black 'V' on its breast, the red eye-ring and bill and the black broad strip through the eyes are distinguishing features. The Red-kneed Dotterel has a dark eye-ring and a black breast that graduates to a rusty orange colour on the flank.

forage. The larger endemic Banded Lapwing (25cm/10in) lives on the rough ground of dry plains. It is a common inhabitant of ploughed fields and grazing pastures, especially in Western Australia. The Masked Lapwing or Spur-winged Plover (35cm/14in) is a more familiar equivalent in eastern Australia.

The Banded Lapwing (right) is a fairly common resident, especially in poorly grassed areas where it feeds on caterpillars, grasshoppers and other insects. The Masked Lapwing, or Spur-winged Plover (bottom) with its distinctive bright yellow facial wattles, is traditionally a bird of open grasslands. It has, however, adapted well to improved grasses and is now frequently seen on suburban golf courses and playing fields. Its harsh, clattering cry is often heard during the nesting season, especially at night. Both of these birds defend their nests fiercely; the Spur-winged Plover uses a horny spur on its wing joint to see off intruders.

Nesting Waders

The nests of breeding waders are often mere scrapes in the ground but these are defended vigorously, often by diversion tactics, such as the broken wing strategy (see page 153), but sometimes with direct attacks. Many of the eggs are beautifully marked and blend in perfectly with their background.

While waders are sociable feeders, they usually nest in solitary pairs. Australia's endemic Banded Stilt (36–45cm/14–18in), however, is an exception. This elegant wader mysteriously appears on rare occasions when heavy rains fill the saltpans of inland Australia. Within days tens of thousands of Banded Stilts are nesting on shallow spits and islands, fattening up on a nutritious broth of brine shrimp. These minute crustaceans burst from eggs that have lain dormant for years, spirited into life by the floodwaters. While the waters remain, the brine shrimps clone themselves (reproduce asexually) and the stilts continue to breed. With up to 50,000 birds producing clutches of three to five eggs, the fluffy white chicks are gathered into crèches and overseen by male adults as the females continue to lay. This massive collective reproduction event is rare; the next opportunity may not arise for another decade. The end can be grizzly: as the waters recede predatory Silver Gulls invade the colonies and pick off the eggs and chicks.

COUNTING WADERS

At Australia's three major wader feeding grounds, the bird counts are impressive: up to 337,500 at Eighty Mile Beach on the north-west coast between Port Hedland and Broome; 250,000 in the Coorong, South Australia; and 236,000 in the Gulf of Carpentaria in northern Australia. On one remarkable and rare occasion recently, 2.8 million Oriental Pratincoles (23cm/9in) were recorded on Eighty Mile Beach. These birds flock into north-western Australia at the beginning of summer and move inland in pursuit of insect swarms. Built more like swallows than their wading relatives, and with forked tails, pointy wings and wide mouths, they can snatch flying insects with acrobatic agility.

RAMSAR SITES

In 1971 a convention was held in a small Iranian town called Ramsar to discuss the increasing loss of ecologically important wetlands across the globe. Eighteen nations, including Australia, signed a commitment to list their sensitive wetlands and to co-operate in an effort to conserve them. The Ramsar Convention was the first wildlife conservation international treaty ever to be signed. Today there are 152 participating signatories representing over 1600 wetlands, of which about 60 are in Australia.

While cosmopolitan Pied Oystercatchers are a fairly common sight around Australia's sandy beaches, this Sooty Oystercatcher is an endemic species that confines itself to rocky shores. The jet-black plumage, red legs and eye-ring are unmistakable. Its bill is designed for opening mussels and prising limpets off rocks. Usually seen in pairs, the parents tutor their offspring in shellfish manipulation.

Gulls, Skuas and Terns

If you are picnicking at the beach, expect to be joined by a mob of Silver Gulls, Australia's most widespread and common gull. Cast your eyes seaward and you may see terns plunge-diving into the waves. The skuas are mostly ocean-fliers, robbers of other seabirds, but some venture into Australia's bays and estuaries. The gulls, skuas and terns are web-footed social birds given to feeding in flocks and resting and nesting in colonies.

There's no mistaking Australia's Silver Gull (41cm/16in), at least not the adults, with their bright red bills, legs and eye-rings. Motley brown and grey juveniles, with their dark bills and legs, are usually easy to pick among the flock. The slightly hooked, multi-purpose bill of all gulls is well suited to their opportunistic habits of taking other species' eggs, small birds and invertebrates. They scavenge along beaches, at sewage outflows and garbage tips, as well as fishing in flocks upon shoals out at sea.

In addition to the ubiquitous Silver Gulls, two other larger gulls are often seen in Australia. Most familiar is the endemic Pacific Gull (63cm/25in) that nests in loose colonies on offshore islands and headlands along southern coastlines, from west to east. The black and white adults have yellow legs and chunky bill tipped with red on both mandibles. Juveniles are often mistaken for another species as their fawn plumage—which persists for four years—is so different from that of the adults.

The cosmopolitan Kelp Gull (57cm/22in) arrived in Tasmanian waters in the 1940s. It is expanding its range and population northwards. Its lighter bill with just one red spot on the lower mandible distinguishes it from the Pacific.

Skuas and Jaegers

Skuas and jaegers are solid gull-like birds of cold-water seas. The Brown Skua (61–66cm/24–26in) even nests on the Antarctic continent. Several skuas and jaegers visit Australia's southern oceans. Their pointy wings and two projecting tail feathers (not always obvious) give them great acrobatic skill, which they exploit as sky pirates, chasing and harassing other seabirds to regurgitate their catch, ready for the steal. At seabird colonies they take eggs and young birds. Sometimes they rest on water near beaches but they rarely come to shore.

Terns

Terns are more slender-built birds than gulls. Mostly white, with legs set further back on their compact cigar-shaped bodies, long narrow wings and sharply pointed bills, they are expert plunge divers, best suited to feeding on fish and squid at sea. Most widespread is the Crested Tern (45cm / 18in), often seen resting on sandy spits or rocky reefs around all coastlines. A striking and not uncommon sight is the large black-capped Caspian Tern (53cm / 21in), with its impressive 7.5cm (3in)-long scarlet bill, diving with marked concentration in estuaries. The tiny Fairy and Little Terns (22–26cm / 9–10in) nest on sandy beaches, their shallow scrapes strung out in loose colonies that are easily disrupted by high tides and people. The Whiskered Tern (26cm / 10in) is extremely unusual as it prefers inland wetlands and nests on floodplains where it builds a floating nest.

Terns become darker in colour in tropical Australia. Both the Sooty and Bridled Terns are dark on top and white below. Notoriously difficult to tell apart, the Bridled Tern (36–42cm / 14–17in) flies into coastal areas, whereas the Sooty (40–46cm / 16–18in) spends all but its breeding time on the tropical seas. Three entirely dark, smooth feathered terns, known as 'noddies', nest mostly on tropical islands. Unlike other terns, noddies nest in trees and, rather than dive, they skim the water's surface catching flying and jumping fish.

The Arctic Jaeger (40–45cm / 16–18in) arrives at the beginning of summer from its breeding grounds in the tundra and moors of Russia, Canada, Alaska and northern Europe. Only on the wing is this magnificent flyer easy to distinguish from other skuas and jaegers, but it also ventures into coastal wetlands further than any other members of this group.

A pair of Crested Terns with their chick. These medium-sized birds with their distinctive scruffy tuft of short black head feathers nest in huge colonies in the dunes and shingle behind the beaches of small islands.

A NOD'S AS GOOD AS A WINK

The vigorous head-nodding of excited males executing their courtship performance has given the noddies their name.

Pigeons and Doves

Of the 22 species of pigeons and doves that live in Australia, 15 are found nowhere else in the world and another five are found only in New Guinea and adjacent islands. New Guinea is part of the same landmass as Australia. During ice ages, when seas were low, a land bridge existed between the two countries. With no barrier to migration or genetic mixing at such times, it is possible that pigeons, or at least some species of pigeons, evolved in this part of the world.

The Rose-crowned Fruit-Dove is one of several colourful fruit-doves that feed on the fruits of the rainforest. The deep green on the backs and wings of fruit-doves blends in with the lush, shiny leaves, while patches of bright yellow, purple, red and orange on breasts, crowns, shoulders, bellies and the undersides of tails and wings mimic the fruits of rainforest trees.

> **WHAT'S IN A NAME?**
> A dove is really just a small pigeon.

Australia's pigeons may be divided broadly into those that rely on fruit and forage mostly among vines and trees in the rainforest, and the ground-dwelling seed eaters of dry, open country. They range in size from the 50cm (20in)-long Topknot Pigeons and Wompoo Fruit-Doves to the dainty 20cm (8in) ground-living Diamond Dove.

Rainforest Pigeons

Only in extensive stretches of undisturbed rainforest can fruit-doves find year-round fruit. The magnificent Wompoo feeds in the canopy of trees, as do the diminutive Superb and Rose-crowned Fruit-Doves (22–24cm/9–10in). All are highly coloured birds, especially the males.

The Brown Cuckoo-Dove is a common but discreetly plumaged pigeon of the east-coast rainforests. Its soft reddish-brown plumage and

One of several black and white rainforest fruit-doves, the White-headed Pigeon is a common inhabitant of eastern Australia's rainforests. Confined to monsoonal forests growing at the foot of escarpments in the Top End is the half-black, half-white Banded Fruit-Dove. The Torresian Imperial-Pigeon is a white bird except for the black in its wings and tail. Once a winter migrant from New Guinea, it has taken a fancy to the fruits of Australia's cultivated Carpentarian Palms and is now a permanent resident in Australia's monsoonal forests and the gardens of Darwin.

unusually long tail provide excellent camouflage when it sits quietly on branches at the forest's edge. Although large, it is easily overlooked, but its pretty, soft three-note call is pure pigeon.

From south of Sydney to Cape York small flocks of Topknot Pigeons travel across paddocks and lightly wooded country to reach the fruits of figs and Bangalow Palms in gullies of remnant

The rotund 40cm (16in)-long Wonga Pigeon waddles along at the edges of rainforest gullies foraging for fallen fruits and seeds on the ground. Endemic to Australia, it ranges from Cape York to Victoria. Emerald Doves have a similar lifestyle at the edge of more tropical forests.

LOVEY DOVEY

Pigeons bob their heads as they walk and, when courting, males put on quite a performance. Puffed up, they persistently stalk their paramours, flashing their iridescent wing patches as they glint in the sunlight. Tree-dwelling pigeons also woo with impressive aerial displays that involve whirring their wings.

A Common Bronzewing, one of several dry-country birds with iridescent wing patches.

The beautiful colouring of the small Spinifex Pigeon (20cm/8in) blends in with its iron-rich sandstone habitat. It is found in rocky, spinifex country in central and northwestern Australia, and suitable parts of the Top End. Only the more adaptable and commonly seen Crested Pigeon (31–35cm/12–14in) lays claim to such an impressive head crest.

rainforest. Their large grey bodies are offset by rusty red and grey head plumes that flop about like miniature cavalier hats, and, at close quarters, their scarlet eye-rings and bills are distinct. They are excitable birds that pivot, swing and flap their broad wings as they reach to pick off berries at the end of branches. Their mating performances entail much bowing, entwining of necks and displaying of crests.

Seed-eating Pigeons

One of the most soothing sounds of the bush is the gentle cooing of the Peaceful Dove. It epitomises the nature of this quiet, innocuous, ground-dwelling seed-eater. Many of these seed-eating pigeons are native to Australia and survive in dry country. They cannot afford exuberant colours but must blend with their surroundings.

Dry-land pigeons must drink regularly; at dusk and sunrise large numbers gather at waterholes or bores that have been sunk for stock. Some, especially ground-nesters, are becoming rare as they lose cover and contend with new predators. Some tree nesters, however, such as the Crested Pigeon—possibly Australia's most common pigeon after the worldwide city-dwelling feral Rock Pigeon, have expanded their range into wheat country and from small towns into our cities.

FRESH FROM THE FIRE

Bush fires in Australia are common, natural occurrences. For seed-eating pigeons the new grasses that spring up after a fire are a bountiful source of food.

Cockatoos

Cockatoos are large, noisy parrots with heavy-duty bills and head crests. Their bills are capable of cracking open the hardest of seed coats. As with most parrots, they nest in tree hollows and form life-long partnerships with their mate. Australia has 13 species of cockatoos, most of which are black, white or grey.

Black-Cockatoos

Not surprisingly, the six species of black-cockatoos are primarily black, with all but the Palm Cockatoo having bright-coloured tail panels and, usually, ear-coverts (small feathers behind the cheeks). These large funereal birds are a spellbinding sight as they fly with slow, deep wingbeats in small flocks, crying loudly. At 65cm (26in) in length, the Yellow-tailed Black-Cockatoo of south-eastern Australia and the more northerly and inland Red-tailed Black-Cockatoo are the largest, while the Glossy Black-Cockatoo is nearly half a metre (20in) long.

The black Palm Cockatoo (54–64cm / 21–25in), with its spiky head crest and red cheek patches, is a spectacular bird that is found only at the tip of Cape York. Its pickaxe-like top mandible is designed to crack open the massive tough fruits of the pandanus palms, a widespread plant of the region.

Pink and / or Grey Cockatoos

Galahs (34–38cm / 13–15in) are abundant and widespread pink and grey cockatoos that usually feed in flocks on the ground. During rain they swing precariously from telegraph wires, washing away dirt and uncomfortable parasites from between their feathers. Traditionally inland birds,

Each black-cockatoo specialises on different foods according to the size and shape of its bill. This Yellow-tailed Black-cockatoo (above) has the hardware to tackle banksia cones. In south-western Western Australia the Long-billed or Boudin's Black-Cockatoo extracts seeds from the large urn-shaped fruits of marri gums (both endemic to the area), while in the same region the Short-billed or Carnaby's Black-Cockatoo specialises in the hard fruits of local hakeas and dryandras. The rare Glossy Black-Cockatoo of eastern and South Australia prises tiny seeds from she-oaks. New on the menu for some black-cockatoos are the seeds of radiata pine, plantations of which are proliferating.

HANDY CLAWS

All parrots have two claws that point forwards and two that point backwards, giving them good grasp and dexterity; they are able to cling onto a branch with opne foot and hold fruit in the other.

There are few Australians who wouldn't recognise a Galah. This inquisitive one is inspecting a potential nesting hollow. Tree hollows are in great demand among almost all parrots and many other native animals, too.

they have ventured into towns and cities and are now a familiar sight on lawns and grassy verges, where they dig up roots, nibble seeds and pluck out shoots.

The Gang Gang (33–36cm / 13–14in) is a grey-coloured cockatoo of the cool eucalypt forests of south-eastern Australia. Creaking like old doors, these gorgeous birds sit in trees, splitting open the cones of pines or feeding on berries. Look for the male's bright red head with his wispy quiff.

The Pink or Major Mitchell Cockatoo (35–40cm / 14–16in) is a rare bird of the outback. Its delicate shades of pink and salmon plumage are exquisite. It feeds on the seeds of wattles and native pines in dry country but never strays far from water.

Another slender member of this group is the mostly grey Cockatiel (32–33cm / 13in). Well known as a caged bird, in its natural habitat of inland Australia it forages on native grasses. It is highly nomadic, travelling in large flocks across open country following the rains and ensuing plant growth.

CREST FALLEN

Cockatoos are highly sociable birds and their crests are expressive means of communication.

Sulphur-crested Cockatoos are quite common, even in bushy suburbs. Flocks commute daily from arboreal roosts to feed on berries, seeds, flowers and nuts on the ground. They rest in the heat of the day in trees before a late-afternoon 'tea' and the flight back to their roosts.

White Cockatoos

The magnificent Sulphur-crested Cockatoo (45–50cm / 18–20in) is flourishing in wooded parts of northern and eastern Australia, including Tasmania, and a small population also exists in Perth. Easily mistaken for Sulphurs and only slightly smaller are the Long-billed, Little and Western Corellas. The white crests of corellas are almost indiscernible at times but a flush of red between the eyes and bill and on the throat, as well as blue skin around the eyes, is apparent on close inspection. These inland birds move towards the coast during drought and some have established in several major cities.

Lorikeets and Rosellas

Australia's lorikeets and rosellas are among the most colourful parrots in the world. Many, too, are common and easily found throughout the continent. There are six lorikeet and six rosella species. In the outer suburbs of most cities you are likely to find at least one of each.

Lorikeets (22–28cm / 9–11in long) and rosellas 25–38cm / 10–15in) are similar in size and both are colourful but several telltale characteristics set them apart.

Lorikeets

Lorikeets are social birds that dart across the sky in flocks at speed. Their swift direct flight is courtesy of pointed wings and a tapered tail, both features absent in rosellas. Lorikeets feed on nectar and pollen, which they collect with a thick brush-tipped tongue. Dependence on flowering trees can lead to a nomadic lifestyle but many lorikeets commute daily to and from communal roosting sites. Their presence is often revealed by their excitable screeches.

The familiar Rainbow Lorikeet is a brilliant bird of the wet timbered areas of eastern and south-eastern Australia, including the lower reaches of the Murray River. A subspecies, the Red-collared Lorikeet, lives across the Top End through to the west coast; it has a red collar across the back of its neck and a dark green lower belly. Often feeding with the Rainbows are the smaller Scaly-breasted Lorikeets (23cm / 9in), distinguished by their scaly yellow and green breast plumage and green heads.

The three smallest and primarily green lorikeets are hard to spot among the foliage of flowering trees. The Purple-crowned Lorikeet lives in the woodlands, dry forests and mallee of southern Australia, from west to east. The red-capped, red-billed Varied Lorikeet, which is

This pair of Rainbow Lorikeets are inspecting a hollow as a possible nesting site. The demand among wildlife for good nest hollows is exceedingly high and lorikeets must compete with Sugar Gliders, phascogales, other parrots and introduced Common Mynas, Starlings and Honey Bees. Once ensconced and breeding, invading Honey Bees may still force birds off their nests, young may be lost to goannas and kookaburras, and nestlings to tree snakes.

The little Musk Lorikeet (23cm/9in) has distinctive splashes of scarlet on its cheeks, forehead and at the tip of its black bill. It occurs in pairs and small flocks in the south-eastern corner of Australia, including southern and eastern Tasmania.

streaked with yellow and has a white eye-ring, is found in northern Australia, sometimes occurring in large numbers in response to an abundance of food. The red-faced, dark-billed Little Lorikeets inhabit the woodlands of eastern and south-eastern Australia.

Rosellas

Rosellas are more reserved than lorikeets and they forage for seeds, fruits and flowers on the ground, flying up to shrubs and trees for safety. They have distinct cheek patches in blue, yellow or white and the feathers along their back are edged with a contrasting colour to give a scalloping effect that provides useful camouflage when viewed from above. Their tails are long, broad and rounded at the end. They fly shorter distances than lorikeets and with a rising and falling rhythm.

In the forests and woodlands of south-eastern Australia three blue-cheeked rosellas, the Crimson, Yellow and Adelaide Rosellas, hybridise where their distributions overlap. In densely populated areas the Crimson Rosella, with its startling cerulean blue, black and crimson plumage, is familiar but in the woodlands of the Murray River Basin it is replaced by the Yellow Rosella, while in the parks and gardens of Adelaide and the hills and ranges beyond lives the intermediate coloured Adelaide Rosella.

Isolated in south-western forests and woodlands is the multi-coloured Western Rosella, with yellow cheek patches. The Eastern Rosella of the south-east looks very similar but has white cheek patches. White cheeks and a black head distinguish the Northern Rosella, and the Pale-headed Rosella is a north-eastern species.

EGGS WITH NO FRILLS

Parrots' eggs are almost round and plain white. No camouflage is needed for eggs laid in a tree hollow and the traditional oval shape of an egg can be dispensed with when there is no chance of it rolling away.

The Green Rosella is endemic to Tasmania and a few islands in the Bass Strait. While dark above, the yellow head, blue cheeks and greenish yellow underparts are very noticeable. Note the parrot's ability to hold food, a handy adaptation afforded by the arrangement of its toes.

Other Parrots

In addition to the cockatoos, lorikeets and rosella, many other parrots live in Australia. In fact, evidence suggests that the southern supercontinent of Gondwana, of which Australia was a part, was the epicentre of parrot evolution. Today the country has 50 or so species and you will find several in practically every terrestrial habitat on the continent.

If parrots can find year-round food and suitable nesting sites they are likely to be sedentary but many parrots have to travel far and wide to find these resources. Tasmania's Blue-winged, Swift and rare Orange-bellied Parrots migrate annually across the Bass Strait to over-winter on the mainland.

A male Australian King-Parrot. Although absent from Tasmania, these sleek tall-forest birds love the wet timbered ranges of the east coast and their pipping calls are often heard celebrating rain after a dry period.

Rainforest Parrots

Several gorgeous Australian species feed on a smorgasbord of rain-forest fruits, seeds and nectar. The spectacular, deep-bodied Eclectus Parrots (40–43cm / 16–17in) live isolated on a couple of rainforest-clad ranges in north-eastern Cape York Peninsula. Feeding in the canopy of

This magnificent parrot is a male Eclectus Parrot; the female is equally stunning but is primarily scarlet with a bright blue belly. For a long time, these differences in colour led people to believe they were entirely different species. Eclectus Parrots nest deep in the hollows of rainforest trees. As they gather at dusk to roost, their harsh screeches carry across their remote rainforest country. This species also lives in New Guinea and on islands to the north.

the same area are flocks of smaller Red-cheeked Parrots. The diminutive but stocky Double-eyed Fig-parrot (15cm/6in) —our smallest parrot—occurs in three disjunct patches of rainforest along the east coast; its southernmost subspecies is Australia's most endangered parrot. Widespread and common throughout eastern Australia is the regal Australian King-Parrot, whose range extends into heavily timbered high country, wet eucalypt forests and even the suburban bushland of Sydney.

Dry-country Parrots

Throughout the inland, plant seeds are a widely available source of food so it is not surprising that many Australian parrots have adapted to the native grasses and other dry-country vegetation. They still depend, however, on a regular supply of water for drinking and today the dams and bores of farms and cattle stations in previously dry areas supplement natural waterholes. These have favoured many dry-land birds like Galahs and Australian Ringnecks, who drink often from cattle troughs.

Despite this boon, Australia's inland mallee and woodlands have been extensively cleared, heavily grazed, frequently burnt and inundated by feral animals and plants. Sensitive species with specialist lifestyles, such as the Hooded, Golden-shouldered and now extinct Paradise Parrots, have not coped well. Those with a more generalised lifestyle have survived better. For example, the four distinct forms of the opportunistic Australian Ringnecks, with their broad diet and fast flight, can find widely dispersed food and will breed whenever conditions are good. One of

NOVEL NESTING SPOTS

In tree-less landscapes small parrots often adopt hollowed fence posts for nesting. In the tropical savannas, where large termite mounds abound, the specialised Hooded Parrot of the Top End and the Golden-shouldered Parrot on Cape York Peninsula tunnel into these structures to nest. The Rock Parrots of southern and south-western coasts nest along shores in the crevices of rocky offshore islands. The Night Parrot and the Ground Parrot, both nocturnal birds, live and nest under thick vegetation but, as many ground dwellers have discovered, this lifestyle, with the arrival of feral Foxes, Pigs and Cats, puts them at serious risk.

the most successful parrots of the outback is the highly nomadic Budgerigar.

Parrots rarely stray far from water, and riverine habitats provide essential shelter in the form of eucalypts and other trees growing along the banks, providing shade, roosts and nesting sites. Ringnecks, Blue Bonnets, Regent and Mulga Parrots follow these gums through arid lands. The Superb Parrot that feeds in the mallee country skirting Australia's only extensive river system, the Murray–Darling region, forages wherever it can find food, often in close proximity to permanent water and nests in old craggy river red gums.

NEW HOPE

With no confirmed sightings of the nomadic, ground-dwelling Night Parrot since 1990, the find of a dead bird in Queensland's Channel Country in November 2006 has revived hopes that there are still some individuals left of this elusive and unusual bird of the arid regions.

The delicate pastel shades of the slender, long-tail Princess or Alexander's Parrot are unusual among Australia's dazzlers. Rare and endemic, this is an elusive nomad of the central and western deserts.

The world's most famous cage bird, the Budgerigar is endemic to the country's semi-arid centre. Highly nomadic and gregarious, these little parrots form immense flocks, converging on waterholes to drink at dawn and dusk and on seeding grasses to feed. In times of plenty they breed up fast and furiously, raising several broods in succession and becoming sexually active at only three months.

Cuckoos

Contrary to popular belief, not all cuckoos lay their eggs in other birds' nests but 11 of Australia's 12 species do. Only the large Pheasant Coucal raises its own young. At 70cm (28in) long, much of which is tail, it is Australia's largest cuckoo while the Little Bronze-Cuckoo, on the other hand, is barely bigger than a sparrow.

The distinct horizontal bars on the breast and belly of this Shining Bronze-Cuckoo (16–18cm/6–7in) are typical of many cuckoos. The name 'bronze' comes from the bird's greenish bronze iridescent plumage that 'shines' or glints in the light. The bird shown here breeds in Australia but there is a green-headed subspecies that is occasionally seen passing through mainland Australia as it migrates via Norfolk and Lord Howe islands between New Zealand, where it breeds, and New Britain and Solomon Islands, where it over-winters.

Parasitic cuckoos stake out nests under construction by their hosts from a safe distance. In some species, such as the Eastern Koel, the male waylays the busy parent some time during its egg-laying period, while the female nips into the nest, evicts one egg and pops out one of her own. Most Australian cuckoos supplant a host's egg with their own, but some, like the Channel-billed Cuckoo, just deposit an egg in the nest, leaving the young to be reared alongside its foster siblings.

Often, the size, colour and pattern of a cuckoo's egg match those of its host and, while open-nest builders may detect the difference and toss it out, those in dimly lit domed nests often do not. Once the cuckoo hatches, it heaves its host's eggs or nestlings up to the edge of nest on its broad back and tips them overboard. It then becomes the sole recipient of all food brought to the nest by its foster parents. After leaving the nest, it is still fed by its foster parents and may even be fed by birds of other species.

Cuckoos have an undulating flight: several wingbeats followed by a shallow swoop with closed wings. They mostly eat insects, especially hairy caterpillars. Australian cuckoos are mostly migratory, moving southwards in spring to breed. Some, like the Oriental Cuckoo, reach northern Australia from as far afield as Eurasia. Others migrate from New Guinea or from within the continent.

In the south, the call of cuckoos is a sound of summer. Each species' call is distinctive and, while they are keen to be heard

The central shaft of a Pheasant Coucal's feathers has overlapping scales that help it slip through the tangled sharp grasses of swampy areas. A large tropical and sub-tropical cuckoo of north-western, northern and eastern coastal regions, it is a reluctant flier that is, unfortunately, often found as road-kill. Unlike other Australian cuckoos, it raises its own young. Its well-hidden nest is close to the ground, protected by a thatch of overhead grasses and open at two ends to leave room for its long tail and head to poke out during incubation.

Despite the intimidating appearance of the hawk-sized Channel-billed Cuckoo with its massive bill, it is a fig specialist. Its arrival in northern and eastern Australia each summer causes an almighty hullabaloo among the local bird population. It lays its eggs in the nests of Australian Magpies, Pied Currawongs and crows and it is, not surprisingly, frequently mobbed.

to attract mates, they are less keen to be seen. A parasitic lifestyle requires subterfuge. Cuckoos are solitary. Most sit still hidden on branches. To break up their outline, heavy barring on their breast, belly and beneath their long tails is a common feature.

Two Noisy Cuckoos

The widespread Pallid Cuckoo is usually heard before it is seen. A repetitive volley of loud insistent rising notes presents an opportunity for an observer to track the sound to the bird. Often it is perched quite prominently but its plumage serves as a disguise.

Two large noisy migrants from South-east Asia and New Guinea to northern and eastern Australia are the Eastern Koel and the Channel-billed Cuckoo. While the Channel-billed Cuckoo has a harsh grating call, the male Koel drives people mad as it whoops up the scale with loud insistent notes, even in the dead of night. Entirely black with a red eye, it sits hidden in the canopy of tall trees, sometimes in parks and gardens, courting heavily streaked females that look completely different.

Common Cuckoos

Most cuckoos prefer well-forested areas but the widespread pale grey-brown Pallid Cuckoo (30cm/12in) that lays its eggs in the nests of honeyeaters, robins, whistlers and woodswallows, remains elusive even in the open country it favours. Another common species, sometimes seen in the forests and woodlands of eastern and south-western Australia and Tasmania, is the Fan-tailed Cuckoo (25–27cm/10–11in). Adults are slate grey above, fawn below with an orange-flushed breast and a yellow eye-ring. Juveniles are heavily barred, as is often the case with juvenile cuckoos.

Kingfishers and Kookaburras

There are ten species of kingfishers in Australia. Although we associate king-fishers with rivers, several species live in dry country, including the Laughing Kookaburra, a bird synonymous with the bush and, once heard, never forgotten.

Nothing personifies the sound of the Australian bush more than the cackling dawn and dusk chorus of kookaburra families declaring their territorial rights throughout timbered eastern and western Australia—and even the outer suburbs of our cities. Despite its large size and land-based lifestyle, the Laughing Kookaburra is a king-fisher. Mostly cream and brown to blend in with its woodland habitat, its shape and the hint of kingfisher blue in its wings belie this affinity.

Kingfishers have round dumpy bodies, short tails and long dagger-like bills. Most fly low and fast, darting across our vision as a streak of magnificent iridescent blue. Australia's tiniest kingfisher, the 12cm (5in)-long Little Kingfisher of the Top End and northern Queensland, is the world's second smallest, while the Laughing Kookaburra, at 45cm (18in) long and half a kilo (18oz), competes with the African Giant Kingfisher for the title of the world's largest.

Breeding pairs of kingfishers share the daunting task of excavating nest holes with their powerful and seemingly shockproof bills. The river-dwelling, cobalt blue and orange Azure Kingfisher (17–19cm / 7–8in) scoops out its nesting chamber at the end of a tunnel dug into the side of a river bank. Little Kingfishers (11–12cm / 4½in) excavate holes in rotten branches or the bases of epiphytic ferns. Kookaburras, which live in woodlands and forests, nest in tree hollows or termite mounds. Termite mounds are also favoured by Australia's Forest, Yellow-billed, Collared and Sacred Kingfishers, especially in the north where they are plentiful. Perhaps the mounds act as incubators, saving the parents the work.

Many Sacred Kingfishers (19–23cm/7–9in) migrate from northern Australia in summer to breed in the south. A few cross the Bass Strait to Tasmania. They feed mostly on insects and reptiles and occasionally fish. Breeding pairs excavate nests in trees and arboreal termite mounds in paperbark swamps, mangroves, woodlands, forests and even on golf courses and in parks.

Kingfishers have excellent eyesight. They perch over water or solid ground and pounce or dive onto their targets. Diving kingfishers catch fish with a tweezer-like grip. To avoid spines in the fins, they swallow fish head-first and feed their young similarly. To subdue troublesome prey, all kingfishers whack their prey senseless against a branch or rock.

Northern and Inland Kingfishers

Many of Australia's kingfishers live in the north. The gorgeous Yellow-billed Kingfisher (18–21cm/7–8in) forages for insects, worms and small reptiles at the edges of rainforests and swamps on Cape York Peninsula. The Little Kingfisher dives into water or snatches prey from the forest canopy of the north's mangroves and rainforests. The Collared Kingfisher lives only in mangroves. Common in the north, too, are the Azure and Sacred Kingfishers. Azure Kingfishers also inhabit the rivers and creeks of eastern Australia, including Tasmania, all year round, while Sacred Kingfishers are a relatively common sight along the waterways of southern Australia during the summer breeding season.

Not surprisingly, the Red-backed Kingfisher (20–24cm/8–9in) that patrols the dry watercourses of the semi-arid inland is found only in Australia. It feeds on skinks, spiders, grasshoppers and snakes and sometimes nests in the hard vertical banks created by earth movers.

Many people are unaware that Australia has two kookaburras. In northern Australia the Blue-winged Kookaburra occupies a similar habitat to that of the Laughing Kookaburra. Only very slightly smaller, the Blue-winged is paler with a blue rump and blue in its wings, pale eyes and a much chunkier bill giving it a top-heavy appearance. Its family chorus, which is more grating and hoarse, almost shakes the leaves off the trees.

In most kingfishers both sexes incubate and feed the young. Kookaburras, however, live in families of five to seven birds. Residing in the same extensive territory all year round, all members partake in its defence. Come spring a single pair will nest while the others—mostly siblings from the previous year—help to incubate the eggs, discourage visitors and feed the young. This so-called 'co-operative breeding' is quite a common phenomenon among Australian birds.

Each year the Buff-breasted Paradise-Kingfisher crosses 800km (500mile) of sea from New Guinea to breed in the rainforests of north-eastern Queensland through the Wet season. Bird enthusiasts from all over the world travel to Australia to see this brilliant blue and orange bird with its large red bill and long white streamer tail feathers.

Owls

Australia is inhabited by nine species of owls. These nocturnal predators fit into two groups: the masked owls, with their heart-shaped facial disks, dark eyes and relative long legs; and the hawk owls, with a more hawk-like appearance, shorter legs and yellow eyes.

These hunting birds are highly attentive. Their hearing is acute so they are able to detect the slightest rustle. Their sight is excellent and their pupils can dilate or contract independently. Exceeding the normal scope of an animal's vision, a flexible neck can rotate their head almost 180 degrees. Owl plumage is soft, permitting them a silent approach on prey, which is despatched with the clenching of sharp, powerful talons as they puncture vital organs.

Masked Owls

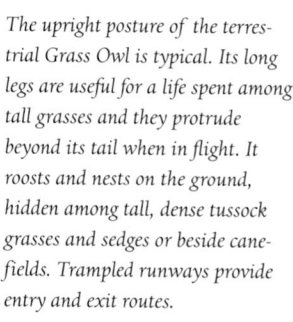

The upright posture of the terrestrial Grass Owl is typical. Its long legs are useful for a life spent among tall grasses and they protrude beyond its tail when in flight. It roosts and nests on the ground, hidden among tall, dense tussock grasses and sedges or beside canefields. Trampled runways provide entry and exit routes.

Even on the darkest nights masked owls can locate their prey accurately due to the dish shape of their facial disc, and the sweep of feathers that encircle it, funneling even the faintest sounds to their ears, which are set asymmetrically in order to pinpoint the direction of sound. In Europe the cosmopolitan Barn Owl (33–35cm/12–14in) has adapted especially well to farm life where there are plenty of rodents, to which it is partial, open paddocks with trees for hunting and, traditionally, barns for roosting and nesting. Barn Owls proliferate throughout Australia's woodlands during rodent plagues but populations fall during prolonged droughts.

> ### OWL WATCH
>
> Owls may be hard to see at night but white splashes of poo below overhanging branches are often clues to an owl's favourite perch. Compressed pellets of bones, feathers and fur, too, are a giveaway as owls regurgitate the indigestible bits of their prey.

There is a larger, more heavily built species of masked owl called, confusingly, a Masked Owl (37–47cm/15–19in). The paler form is distinguished from the Barn Owl only by a more obvious ruff around the facial disk and denser feathering on the legs. The darker form, however, is visibly distinct. Mainland Masked Owls are widespread but uncommon. In Tasmania the dark form is moderately common and robust enough to take Rabbits. Masked Owls often use caves, especially on the Nullarbor Plain and in Tasmania.

The terrestrial Grass Owls (32–38cm/13–15in) live in the swamps, floodplains, saltmarshes and canefields of northern and eastern Australia, and sometimes the north-eastern inland. Although considered rare, loose colonies may form. The majority of their prey consists of rodents, which they snatch from the ground like hawks. Only rarely do they take birds or insects.

Two dark masked owls that live in the tall dense forests of the east coast depend upon large home ranges and deep roosting hollows or caves. From southern Queensland to the Dandenongs in Victoria the Sooty Owl (40–48cm/16–19in) snatches gliders and ringtails from the canopy, while the Lesser Sooty Owl (33–37cm/13–15in) of north-eastern Queensland's mountainous rainforests pounces mainly on smaller creatures. Both have very large dark eyes and an eerie whistle that sounds like a bomb dropping. The Lesser, sometimes called the Silver Owl, is more heavily speckled.

> **TELLING THE SEXES**
> While female hawk owls are usually smaller than males, those of the masked owl group are generally larger.

The Barking Owl (40cm/16in) is a hawk owl, so-named for its 'woof, woof' call. It lives on the edges of forest patches with nesting hollows and adjacent open ground for good hunting, often in wetter areas. A broad diet of rosellas, Rabbits, starlings, Sugar Gliders and large insects are on its menu.

Hawk Owls

From its perch midway on a euca-
lypt this little Southern Boobook
(23–36cm / 9–14in) watches and
listens for the slightest sign of an
insect, small bird or small mammal.
It may pounce to the ground, hawk
from the air or snatch its prey from
surrounding vegetation. This is
Australia's most common owl.
Its soft but distinct 'boo-book' call
echoes through the country's dry
eucalypt forests and woodlands.

Australia's largest and most impressive owl is the Powerful Owl (60–66cm / 22–23in). Recent radio-tracking of this forest giant of south-eastern Australia has shown that it has a vast home range, up to 6000ha (15000ac). Within this area it hunts quite large prey, especially Ring-tailed Possums and gliders.

The large Rufous Owl (45–55cm / 18–22in) roosts in the dense vegetation of Australia's tropical rainforests, paperbark forests and mangroves in the Kimberley, Top End and north-eastern Queensland. Finely barred and reddish brown, this owl is a versatile hunter with a broad diet that includes flying foxes, large birds and flying insects.

Frogmouths and Nightjars

Despite their appearance and nocturnal habits, frogmouths and nightjars are not owls. They have weak feet incapable of grasping large muscular prey and no long sharp talons with which to puncture it. Instead they trap prey in their wide, open mouths.

The cryptic plumage of the Tawny Frogmouth (32–46cm/13–18in) is a great disguise for avoiding predators. Even the stick nests of these birds can afford to be exposed on the fork of a horizontal branch. Frogmouths probably bond for life and both partners participate in nest building and incubation of the eggs.

Frogmouths

The frogmouths are a curious-looking mob with spiky tufts of long straight bristles sticking out around their enormously wide mouths. They hunt from low branches or fence posts, pouncing on ground-dwelling spiders, snails, frogs, insects, worms, small birds and rodents. Their soft plumage allows for a silent assault, the prey netted in their broad flat bills, which snap shut like steel traps.

Two Australian species have limited northern distributions and are better known in New Guinea but a third, the Tawny Frogmouth, is endemic to Australia and common throughout the forests and woodlands of all states.

> **DOMESTIC ARRANGEMENTS**
>
> Tawny Frogmouths breed in spring. They make a stick nest on horizontal branches and the male incubates the eggs by day while the female takes on night duty.

Tawny Frogmouths are usually a motley grey, although northern Australian birds tend towards rufous brown. Their greatest claim to fame is the remarkable camouflage its plumage affords. In times of danger, the Tawny Frogmouth sticks its bill in the air, flattens its plumage, closes its eyes and remains stock still. In this way it looks just like part of the tree on which it is perched.

It is possible to see frogmouths in the outer suburbs of any city as they hunt moths that gather around street lights. If you hear a low monotonous hooting resonating through the still night air, chances are you are listening to a Tawny Frogmouth.

Similar in size is the Marbled Frogmouth that lives only in the rainforests of far north Queensland and on the Queensland–New South Wales border. The larger Papuan Frogmouth is confined to Cape York Peninsula. Both species have bright orange eyes.

Nightjars

The Spotted Nightjar (29–32cm/11–13in) lives in dry, open country, including mallee, heath, mulga woodlands and gibber plains. Its rufous markings blend in with the iron-rich soils on which it roosts and nests. Its moth-like flutterings are sometimes caught in the beam of headlights or the glow of campfires or street lights.

Nightjars nest and rest in scrapes on the ground and hunt on the wing. The subtle variations in the mottled plumages of each of Australia's three species provide masterful disguises among the ground colours of their different habitats. They are skilful night-time fliers, able to dive steeply, twist and roll on long wings, deftly trapping mosquitoes, flying termites, beetles, crickets and fireflies in their enormously wide gapes.

The Large-tailed Nightjar (25–28cm/10–11in) is a northern tropical species that rests in the gloom of rainforests, monsoonal vine thickets

and dense mangroves by day, venturing out into open habitat at night to hawk for insects. It sits tucked into a bed of fallen leaves, safely camouflaged, calling 'chop, chop' during the breeding season or when demarcating territory.

Although nightjars are rarely seen, the White-throated Nightjar (32–37cm / 13–15in) of eastern Australia's coastal ranges is in fact quite common from Cape York to Melbourne. Large, long-winged and dusky grey, it roosts in among twigs and leaves of woodlands, forests and heaths and on the ridges of open ground. Sometimes seen feeding on roads or in campsites, its call is a clear 'puk, puk, puk, puk, puk', starting slow and rising as it accelerates.

> ### BRISTLY MOUTHS
> Why frogmouths, some night-jars and the Owlet-Nightjar have long, straight bristles around their mouth remains a matter of conjecture. It is generally thought that these have a sensory function that helps in the capture of prey.

Australia's smallest nocturnal bird is the 20–25cm (8–10in)-long Australian Owlet-nightjar. It has huge dark eyes, facial whiskers, long legs and tail and well-developed feet with claws. It roosts and nests in tree hollows and stumps and feeds on flying and ground-dwelling insects. Widespread across all states, it is especially common in the arid centre provided there are timbered waterways close by.

Bee-eaters, Dollarbirds and Pittas

The colourful plumage of all these birds hints at their tropical origins.
The Rainbow Bee-eater and the Dollarbird are aerial acrobats and summer
visitors to southern Australia, while the unrelated pittas are ground dwellers
of dense rainforests.

If you catch a glint of iridescent green, blue and purple flashing through the sky you may be looking at a Dollarbird. On close inspection this 30cm (12in)-long rather dumpy looking bird has a dark brown head, an olive back and soft brown and turquoise underparts. This photo shows a young bird, yet to acquire its bright red bill and feet.

Dollarbirds

Dollarbirds (30cm / 12in) fly from Indonesia and New Guinea into northern and eastern Australia for the summer breeding season. They nest in the hollows of tall trees, usually stationing themselves on the borderline between a wet forest and open space. Here they sit on high branches with good aerial views to prospect for prey, which mostly consists of flying insects but occasionally they take small birds and ground-dwelling invertebrates.

At dawn and dusk, even in the leafy suburbs of some cities, the gutteral grumblings and cackles of Dollarbirds can be heard as they execute aerial courtship flights from prominent perches. They are members of the roller family, so named for their mid-air barrel rolls and looping flight, performed to impress prospective partners and indispensable in the pursuit of nimble prey.

Bee-eaters

The slender Rainbow Bee-eaters are most commonly found in northern Australia, New Guinea and on the islands of eastern Indonesia. While some remain in northern Australia to breed, others migrate south for the breeding season, travelling in flocks by night. Their arrival in southern Australia signals the start of summer.

Perched on fence posts, fallen trees and telegraph wires in open country, their beautiful plumage is hard to miss. From these lookouts they hawk insects, a skill for which bee-eaters have inestimable talent.

Bee-eaters nest in colonies in the sides of banks, several birds co-operating together to raise a single brood. They chose banks with sandy or friable soil that is easy to excavate. The female props herself on her wings as her feet cycle away, pushing the earth from under her. The hole extends into a 1m (39in)-long tunnel and opens out into a nesting chamber. In northern Australia, Cane Toads take up to 50 per cent of bee-eater chicks.

The beautiful Rainbow Bee-eater, with its pointy wings and delicate streamer tail feathers, is aerodynamically built. It can chase flying insects at high speed and change direction rapidly, catching prey in its pincer-like bill. Despite the sting of European Honeybees, these are a favourite. Bee-eaters grab them carefully by the waist, bash them silly on a perch before deftly rubbing the sting out of their abdomen and downing them whole.

Pittas

Pittas (17–21cm / 7–8in) are upright, dumpy birds of subtropical and tropical forest floors. They have short tails and wings, and long, strong legs with robust feet for scratching around in the leaf litter, mostly for invertebrates and small reptiles. Snails are highly prized. To reach their soft bodies the pitta must continuously smash the shell against a rock. A scattering of smashed snail shells beside a rock on the forest floor is a sure sign of pitta activity.

Three of these bright-coloured birds occur in Australia. The Rainbow Pitta is endemic to the Kimberley and the Top End, where it is reasonably common in dense vine thickets, monsoonal forests and native bamboo grasses. The Noisy Pitta is a bird of east-coast rainforests from the tip of Queensland to just north of Sydney in New South Wales. It is indeed noisy, especially during the breeding season (October to January in the south; January to April in more tropical forests), its loud three-note whistle having a rising intonation. The Red-bellied Pitta is a Wet-season migrant from New Guinea that breeds in the monsoonal forests at the tip of Cape York.

Despite being large and bulky, pitta nests are easily overlooked as a pile of twigs and leaves, with a thatch of moss. Domed, and sometimes with a ramp to the entrance, nests are often constructed between the buttressed roots of large rainforest trees or in tangles of vines off the ground.

For most of the year the Rainbow Pitta lives a quiet, solitary life in the gloom of the vine forest floor, but just before the monsoonal rains break the male begins whistling loudly from tree branches to declare his breeding territory and attract female attention.

Lyrebirds

It is the ambition of many Australians to see, or at least hear, a lyrebird. These large birds are endemic to Australia's forest floors. They are remarkable singers and the male's spellbinding courtship display is the best performance you will ever see in the country's temperate forests.

A rare and wonderful sight: a male Superb Lyrebird singing and displaying to woo a female. His central tail feathers are filamentous and pale, while the two outside ones are lyre-shaped 'ribbons', delicately barred with white, chestnut and black. Although rarely seen, this species is quite common for those prepared to venture into its habitat.

There are two species: Albert's Lyrebird (65–90cm/26–35in) lives isolated in the ranges that span the New South Wales–Queensland border; and the larger, more widespread Superb Lyrebird (80–95cm/31–37in) lives throughout the wet forests of Australia's east coast from southern Queensland to just beyond Melbourne in Victoria, and it has been introduced into Tasmania.

The chestnut-coloured Albert's Lyrebird and the greyer Superb Lyrebird blend into their respective forest floors. Their tails, held graciously out of the dirt, are longer than their bodies and those of the larger males are especially beautiful. That of the Superb is the longer, more impressive one.

Lyrebirds use their strong legs and toes to fossick through the thick leaf litter for worms, insects and snails. They sing like no other bird. Clear and loud, their songs cut the forest air with a medley of mimicked sounds from their world: kookaburras, whipbirds and Eastern Robins but also mechanical sounds, like chainsaws and farm machinery. Of the two species, the Superb has the wider repertoire.

In preparation for the winter breeding season male lyrebirds scratch up soil and litter to form large mounds about a metre (39in) high. They attract the attention of females by standing on the top and spreading out their magnificent tail feathers, lifting them up and over their body and head so both are veiled. In this contorted position they then softly shake and pivot on the mound, singing all the while.

After mating, females are left to construct bulky stick nests on, or up to a metre (39in) off, the ground. Here they incubate the single egg and care for the chick.

Bristlebirds and Scrub-birds

Bristlebirds and scrub-birds are rarely seen. Although unrelated, they share similar discreet and unassuming appearances and spend much of their lives skulking about in leaf litter and dense undergrowth.

Bristlebirds

Bristlebirds (18–25cm/7–10in) favour the dense undergrowth of heathlands. Their clear lilting songs are distinct, although they are notoriously hard to see.

All three species are rare. Ironically Two People's Bay in south-western Australia doubles as a stronghold for the Noisy Scrub-bird and the Western Bristlebird. Just as the Western Bristlebird had the misfortune to live where Perth now stands, the Eastern Bristlebird lost a sizeable chunk of its habitat to Sydney. There are, however, scattered populations up and down the east coast.

Bristlebirds are endemic to Australia. Brown, rufous, grey and pale, little distinguishes them from scrub-birds but the whiskers around their mouth (for which they were presumably named) and their red, rather than dark, eyes.

From Anglesea in Victoria to the Coorong in South Australia, the Rufous Bristlebird stalks through coastal heaths and dense gullies of forested areas. Having such a restricted habitat and distribution, this species is especially vulnerable to the dangers of fire.

Scrub-birds

Endemic to Australia are a pair of furtive little birds that ferret about in thick leaf litter or dense vegetation. Almost impossible to see but ear-splittingly loud, the Noisy and Rufous Scrub-birds are extremely rare.

The Noisy Scrub-bird (21–23cm/8–9in) was rediscovered in 1961 in a patch of scrubby coastal forest at Two People's Bay in south-western Australia. The Rufous Scrub-bird (17–19cm/7in) frequents the edges of temperate and subtropical highland rainforest from Barrington Tops in New South Wales to the Macpherson Ranges in southern Queensland.

Thanks to special protection programs the Noisy Scrub-bird has been introduced to new sites and re-introduced into localities from which it had long ago disappeared. The lower-altitude habitat of the Rufous Scrub-bird has been largely cleared, but populations of this species appear healthy.

A Noisy Scrub-bird sings with gusto but despite its loud and prolonged songs it is notoriously difficult to track down. Australia's two rare scrub-birds have long tails, small wings and cryptic plumage. They run through the undergrowth like small mammals and are reluctant to fly, which severely hampers their escape from bushfires.

Treecreepers and Sittellas

Treecreepers and sittellas are insectivorous birds of timbered areas. Although not genetically related, they forage in a similar way, climbing up or down tree trunks and branches without the aid of tail props as seen in other climbing birds outside Australia. Curiously, none of these birds are found in Tasmania.

Treecreepers

All seven species of these 14–19cm (5–7in)-long birds evolved in Australia or New Guinea, six are endemic to Australia. Generally brown above with paler streaked underparts, they have powerful long toes and claws, and slightly downward-turned bills with which to probe for insects and glean from bark surfaces.

Treecreepers inhabit wet coastal forests, open woodlands and arid inland scrubs. Unlike sittellas, they ascend in a gentle spiral from the bottom of a tree. They can hop upside down along a horizontal branch but they cannot descend head-first.

Treecreepers nest in tree hollows or spouts, forming a cup-shaped nest of soft materials in the base. Family members sometimes help to raise the young and two broods may be successful in good years.

White-throated and Red-browed Treecreepers feed in the eucalypt forests of the south-east. The White-throated concentrates on fibrous-barked eucalypts, while the Red-browed prefers smooth-barked eucalypts with patches of peeling bark. The White-throated tends to be solitary and is the only species to inhabit rainforests; Red-broweds travel in pairs or small groups.

ANTY ACID

Treecreepers are one of the few birds that eat ants and seem able to withstand the effects of their formic acid.

The Rufous Treecreeper occupies a range of habitats from the karri and jarrah forests of south-western Australia east across the salmon gum and wandoo woodlands and the desolate Nullarbor to the mallee of the Eyre Peninsula in South Australia.

A Varied Sittella feeds its chicks. The nests of sittellas are skilfully camouflaged in the fork of trees up to 25m (27yd) above the ground. Family members gather bark fibres, which are bound with cobwebs and finished with a shingle of bark and lichen pieces to match the nesting tree.

Sittellas

Sittellas travel in noisy cohesive groups of up to eight birds, usually fanning out as they land in a tree. They travel downwards from the canopy looking for prey in the fissures and furrows of the trunk and branches, sliding their slightly up-tilted bills under the bark. Agile and confident, they can move in any direction on tree trunks.

Sittellas are small; only 11–13cm (4–5in) long. They are dark above, pale below, with a short tail, a yellow bill and eye-ring and, usually, a black crown. In flight a band of white (in the north) or cinnamon (in the south) is conspicuous in the wings. The sole Australian species, the endemic Varied Sittella, is split into many regional races that, between them, occupy all but the treeless deserts of mainland Australia and the rainforests of the east coast.

Fairy-Wrens, Emu-wrens and Grasswrens

These small birds were named by nostalgic colonists who, noting their cocked tails, assumed they were related to the little brown wrens of their homeland, the British Isles. In fact they are members of an entirely Australian–New Guinean family of birds that has evolved to fill virtually every Australian terrestrial habitat.

Being small birds, wrens avoid the attention of predators by keeping to thick undergrowth and low, dense vegetation. They live in extended families and when they venture out into open ground to forage for insects they twitter among themselves, keeping in touch with the group and alerting one another to any danger.

Fairy-wrens

Fairy-wrens are delightful plump little birds with long tails. While females are usually shades of brown, the bright plumage of breeding males in all nine species is striking and looks almost velvety.

With the exception of the little dapper black-and-red Red-backed Fairy-wren (10cm/4in) of subtropical and tropical grasslands, the breeding males of all fairy-wrens have at least some blue plumage. Splendid Fairy-wrens (11–13cm/4–5in) occupy dry southern inland areas. Their handsome breeding males are almost entirely cobalt blue and black. Breeding males of White-winged Fairy-wrens (12–13cm/5in), a species that lives mostly among the saltbushes,

A male Lovely Fairy-wren perched at the side entrance to his dome-shaped nest, which is discreetly tucked into a dense bush. While the outside of the nest is well camouflaged with coarse dead leaves and grass bound with spider webs, the interior is cosily lined with feathers, down or mammal fur. These little birds may nest at any time of year since they live around tropical rainforests where there is little seasonal fluctuation in temperature.

MIXED FLOCKS OF TRAVELLING BIRDS

When not breeding, fairy-wrens often travel in mixed flocks of other small birds, like thornbills and pardalotes, for extra protection.

A male Mallee Emu-wren risks exposure in order to defend his territory of spinifex clumps. Note the long spiny tail feathers that blend so perfectly with the surrounding blades of grass. This species is restricted to small fragments of mallee across south-eastern South Australia and south-western Victoria.

THE CUTE AND THE CUCKOLD

Extensive studies of Superb Fairy-wrens reveal a remarkable family life. In areas where territories with nesting sites and food are scarce, last year's siblings often stay on, earning their keep by defending their parents' territory and helping to raise the next generation. In these extended families only one pair breeds each year. Should a breeding partner die, a father–daughter or mother–son sexual bond may occur. To overcome the genetic hazards of in-breeding, however, mating often occurs outside of the family group.

Usually, males replace their brown winter feathers with their sleek colourful breeding plumage in early spring but a few individuals with high levels of testosterone may turn iridescent blue and velvet black in winter. These reckless birds stand out like beacons to predators but they also turn the heads of females in neighbouring family groups. It is from these males, with their sturdy genes, that the females often select a mate. The cuckolded male in the family group receives just enough sexual attention to keep him providing for the family but most of the eggs will be fertilised by the daring early moulter.

bluebushes and samphire bushes of the inland, also sport cobalt blue plumage, with only their wings white or grey. (Curiously, the males of two Western Australian island races of this species moult to black, not blue, and white plumage.)

Best known in south-eastern Australia and Tasmania are the Superb Fairy-wrens (13–14cm / 5–6in). The heads and necks of breeding males of this species are bright blue and black. Purple-crowned Fairy-wrens (13–15cm / 5–6in) live among clumps of cane grass and pandanus lining the rivers of the Kimberley and the Gulf of Carpentaria. They are mostly brown but in the breeding season males acquire blue tails, violet crowns and a black mask that runs through the eyes. These fairy-wrens are becoming rare.

Orange or red shoulder patches in breeding males are another useful identification feature. These are to be found in the common and widespread Variegated Fairy-wrens (15cm/6in), the Lovely Fairy-wrens (13cm/5in) that lives on the coastal edges of Cape York's rainforests, the Blue-breasted Fairy-wrens (12–15cm/5–6in) that occur in the south-west and on the Eyre Peninsula in South Australia and the Red-winged Fairy-wren (12–13cm/5in) of south-western Australia.

GRASS FEVER

Some birdwatchers find the challenge of seeing all ten species of grasswrens so compelling they join grasswren-spotting tours; the perfect excuse for travelling to outback Australia.

Emu-wrens

These tiny elusive birds are recognised easily by their filamentous emu-like tail feathers. The three species are quite heavily streaked, most with blue around the eyes, and breeding males have blue breasts. The Southern Emu-wren of Tasmania and south-eastern and south-western Australia lives in the thickets of coastal, alpine and swampy heaths, in buttongrass and sedges. The Rufous-crowned Emu-wren is a bird of spinifex country right across the arid inland.

Grasswrens

Most grasswrens are heavily streaked brown birds endemic to Australia. Larger than fairy-wrens, many of the ten species are rare or at least rarely seen as they live in remote areas of the inland, often within limited ranges. Most live and nest in clumps of spinifex, although the Grey Grasswren inhabits the dense lignum-vegetated edges of inland lagoons and swamps and the nest of the Black Grasswren of the Kimberley is yet to be found. These birds hop out onto open ground to pick at insects and seeds, only flying short distances.

A pair of Striated Grasswrens rest at the base of a clump of spinifex grass. Grasswrens are not strong fliers, preferring to flit, run and hop from cover to cover. Their inability to fly far from harm's way puts them at risk from bushfires and land clearing.

The Australasian Warblers

This large family of small inconspicuous birds is known only from New Guinea, Australia, New Zealand, South-east Asia and neighbouring islands. The 60-odd species mostly feed and nest in trees and shrubs but a few have taken to dense ground cover. They are highly active, largely insectivorous foragers.

The White-browed Scrubwren hops, alone or in pairs, through the dense shrub layer of forests, woodlands and sandy heaths. It is common across a broad coastal area from north-eastern Queensland clockwise to south-western Australia, including Tasmania. The white streak below and above its bill gives it a rather cross look that matches its persistent harsh scalding call which it utters when disturbed.

Identifying these plain-looking birds is a challenge. Not only do many species look alike but females look only slightly duller than males and loose flocks of different species often forage together. As the name 'warbler' suggests, many of them sing with lovely liquid voices and you can sometimes attract their attention by making soft squeaking noises.

Members of this family build dome-shaped nests constructed from plant material and woven together with spider webs. Females do most of the incubating of the eggs but males, and sometimes a couple of helpers, assist in raising the young.

Scrubwrens, Heathwrens and Fieldwrens

Scrubwrens (11–15cm / 4–6in) are elusive but inquisitive little birds that hop around in thick scrub searching for invertebrates, which they grab with their robust slightly down-curved bill. Some, like the widespread White-browed Scrubwren, can be recognised by a prominent white 'eyebrow'. Many scrubwrens are forest birds but some are confined to rainforest where they forage in leaf litter or flit around the leaves of vines and trees.

The Shy Heathwren hops along the ground, and upon low vegetation, searching for small invertebrates and sometimes seeds, often in pairs or as a small group. It lives mostly in the low dense mallee country of southern Australia but also frequents coastal heaths and scrub among dunes in the south-west. It is one of two elusive little heathwrens, both with little cocked tails and chestnut rumps—only a white patch in the shoulder differentiates it from the Chestnut-rumped Heathwren.

Heathwrens and fieldwrens have streaky breasts and most have cocked tails that are shorter and broader than the fairy-, emu- and grasswrens. They generally inhabit drier country, although the heavily streaked Striated Fieldwren lives on buttongrass plains and in swampy heaths.

Some scrubwrens utter harsh scolding alarm calls but many also produce melodious fluting calls. The heathwrens and fieldwrens are particularly musical songsters and very fine mimics.

The nests of these birds are well hidden, usually in low vegetation or on the ground. The large, bulky nest of the Yellow-throated Scrubwren that lives in gullies of dense vegetation, however, is suspended from a branch overhanging water. Although conspicuous, it looks like floodwater debris and therefore rarely draws attention.

Gerygones

The plain little gerygones (9–12cm / 4–5in) commonly live in tropical and subtropical rainforests, mangroves and estuarine vegetation. They flutter about foliage, flushing out invertebrates, hovering, snatching and gleaning. Gerygones are usually brown–grey above, with a buff or yellow underside, often with red eyes and white on the forehead,

> ### SMALL-BIRD HAZARDS
> Life for a small bird is tenuous. Many larger birds like currawongs eat small birds if they can and cuckoos often parasitise them. The larger reptiles are partial to their nestlings and eggs, and their frail nests are often swept away in storms.

The White-throated Gerygone feeds, often in pairs or small groups, in the canopy of eucalypts in woodlands and dry forests. It scours leaves and branches for small invertebrates and snaps them up in mid-air as it flushes them from cover. During the breeding season males trill loudly and sweetly. The Shining and Horsfield's Bronze-cuckoo often lay their eggs in the nest of these little birds.

eyebrow and/or tail. Sometimes known as fairy warblers or bush canaries, they have wavering, downward tumbling calls.

Perhaps the most common of the nine Australian species is the White-throated Gerygone that occurs widely from the Kimberley clockwise to south-eastern Australia, although southern populations migrate north during the colder months. It has a lemon belly, white throat and a delicious trickling song. The Western Gerygone is unusual in that it ranges over the dry mallee, mulga and open woodlands of central and south-western Australia.

The spherical nests of gerygones hang from foliage; they have a 'tail' of hanging vegetation and often a 'porch' over the side entrance.

The Chestnut-rumped Thornbill is a nomadic thornbill of the southern inland. In response to the relative scarcity of food in its habitat, it is highly resourceful and searches for food from the canopy to the ground. The chestnut rump and tail are out of view but the striated or speckled appearance around its face is typical of thornbills and its pale iris is another helpful diagnostic feature.

Thornbills

Thornbills (9–11cm/4–5in) largely replace gerygones in southern temperate Australia. Generally birds of eucalypt forests and woodlands, they have thin pointed bills for snatching up tiny insects. Their markings are more distinctive than in gerygones with fine dots or streaks on faces and throats and they often have yellow or chestnut rumps.

Thornbills are gregarious and move around in twittering flocks. Different species feed at different levels of vegetation; some, like the widespread Yellow-rumped Thornbill, feed on the ground.

In addition to the thornbills, there are three species of so-called 'whitefaces': chestnut or pinkish brown birds with a broad white stripe above the bill. Their diet largely consists of seeds. Confined mostly to the inland, the Banded and Chestnut-breasted Whitefaces live in arid mulga, saltbush and spinifex country but the range of Southern Whitefaces extends into fertile woodlands.

The dumpy little Weebill (9cm/4in) is a pale yellowy brown bird that is found throughout Australia in all but the wettest and driest of places. It is a specialist in prising lerps off eucalypt leaves with its short stout bill which is unlike that of other thornbills. It also hovers and snatches prey from foliage. Its call is often heard before the bird is seen.

OTHER BIRDS TO LOOK OUT FOR

Of interest are two reddish brown ground-dwelling warblers of south-eastern Australia. The Pilotbird (17cm/7in) runs across the rainforest floor and is known to follow in the wake of the Superb Lyrebird, pecking up leftovers from its scrapings. The Rock Warbler (14cm/6in), lives only in the sandstone country around Sydney and the Blue Mountains. It bounces along rock-strewn watercourses, investigating crevices for food and builds its nest suspended from the roof of a cave, often behind a waterfall: the limestone caves of Jenolan and Wombeyan are well-known nesting haunts. Both birds have a horizontal stance and flick their tails: up and down in the case of the Pilotbird and sideways in the Rock Warbler.

Pardalotes

It is worth learning the peeping calls of the pardalotes as they are a common sound in eucalypt forests and woodlands. All four species are tiny birds that forage high in the canopy. They have developed a special relationship with gum trees and service them well by feeding on minute insects called psyllids that infest the undersides of leaves where they suck out plant juices, reducing the vigour of trees.

These delightful dumpy birds (8–12cm/3–5in) are all brightly coloured. They have short tails, strong legs and stout little bills. The legs must be powerful as the birds hang upside down on the outer branches of the canopy while they tear away the sticky sugary domes called lerps that house the psyllids beneath.

The legs also are employed to excavate nests. Surprisingly, these canopy dwellers often nest in a chamber at the end of a tunnel dug into a muddy or sandy bank. Nesting pairs, and sometimes helpers, make the chamber cosy with strips of bark and grass. Only the Striated Pardalote nests regularly in a tree hollow or crevice.

Striated Pardalotes are widespread among eucalypts from the wet forests to the dry woodlands of the inland. The more coastal Spotted Pardalote sometimes threads its way up rivers into dry woodlands and mallee. The Red-browed Pardalote is best known from the dry open woodlands of central and northern Australia. Tasmania is blessed with its own rare Forty-spotted Pardalote, which is confined to patches of dry forest in the south-east and Bruny, Maria and Flinders islands.

There's no mistaking the brilliant white spots on the black crown and dark wings of the male Spotted Pardalote, nor its bright throat and undertail. The plainer Striated Pardalote also features yellow, black and white plumage but set against soft grey or brown and often with a red spot in its wings. The crown of the Red-browed is similar to that of the Spotted but a red spot forms part of its buff to yellow eyebrow. Only in the Forty-spotted Pardalote is red absent, as is a spotted or streaked crown; rather it is a yellowish green bird with tiny white spots in its dark wings.

Honeyeaters

The honeyeaters are Australia's quintessential bush birds. While some species are common in woodlands and forests, others are often found in deserts, rainforests, mangroves or on islands. On a short bushwalk—no matter where you are—you are likely to encounter several different species, and some of the bolder ones inhabit parks and city gardens.

The New Holland Honeyeater (16–18cm/6–7in) is a common species in the heaths and dense shrubby understoreys of forested parts of the south-west, Tasmania and south-eastern Australia. It visits a succession of seasonal flowers and is an important pollinator of many native plants. Small groups jealously guard feeding territories with aggressive chatterings and aerial swoops in and out of bushes.

Most of the world's 173 known species of honeyeaters live in Australia and New Guinea; others inhabit islands to the north-west, in the Pacific and New Zealand. Over tens of millions of years Australia's honeyeaters have lived in isolation, adapting to an increasingly arid continent and diversifying into one of its most widespread and dominant families.

Most honeyeaters are small- to medium-sized slender birds. Perhaps the smallest is the unobtrusive Brown-headed Honeyeater (13cm/5in), while Tasmania's endemic Yellow Wattlebird (48cm/19in) is the largest. Many of the small honeyeaters are olive green or brown above, paler beneath and with very distinct head markings, such as ear patches, eyebrows or neck plumes; attention to such features will lead to successful identification of many species. Larger honeyeaters are often dark brown, sometimes heavily streaked as in the wattlebirds, and occasionally black and white as in the Blue-faced Honeyeater, the New Holland Honeyeater and the White-cheeked Honeyeater.

Honeyeaters tend to specialise in certain foods, although all take a proportion of insects and nectar. Some are mainly fruit eaters, some eat mostly insects and many rely heavily on nectar from flowering eucalypts and other native plants, which they pollinate as they go. They have a special brush-tipped tongue for mopping up nectar and a slightly downward-curved bill for reaching into nectaries seated deep within flowers.

Nectar is a carbohydrate. It provides honeyeaters with an energy rich diet. It can be highly concentrated but supply is unpredictable and cannot be wholly relied upon. Many honeyeaters therefore collect carbohydrate rich manna, honeydew and lerps from the bark and foliage of eucalypts and all take invertebrates, which provide protein.

The Movements of Honeyeaters

Fuelled on an energy rich diet, honeyeaters are very active foragers and flocks often converge on flowering eucalypts to gorge themselves. The fluctuating availability of nectar dictates how they live. Some are sedentary and able to defend a constantly nectar-rich patch but most of these birds, including many of the desert honeyeaters, are highly mobile and they probably follow the mass flower-ings of eucalypts and other plants. There are also honeyeaters that migrate regularly. For example, the Yellow-faced Honeyeater, commonly found in eucalypt forests and adjoining woodland along the east coast, travels north after breeding to over-winter. Still other honeyeaters are nomadic, like the Painted Honeyeater, a mistletoe specialist that roams the woodlands of the eastern half of the continent in search of mistletoes in flower or fruit. The elusive and endangered Regent Honeyeater is also nomadic. The movements of many honeyeaters are still very poorly understood and require further study.

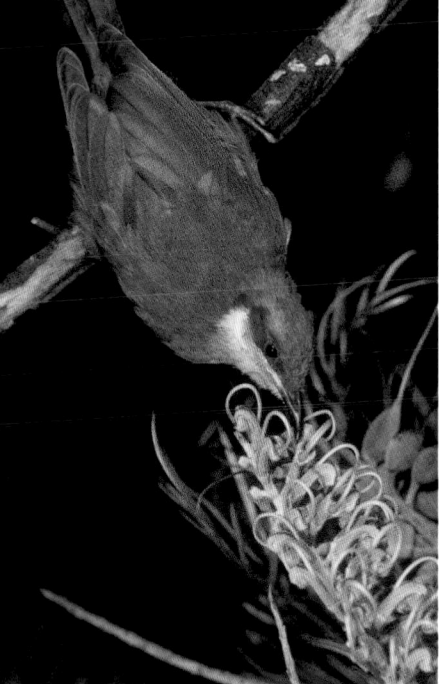

Despite being a stranger to the east coast, the Singing Honeyeater (17–21cm / 7–8in) is one of the most wide-spread of all Australian honeyeaters. Its subtle colouring and face markings are typical of many honeyeaters. It sings out across the coastal heaths, shrubs and low trees, uttering several distinctive whis-tles and trills, sometimes as a duet with another bird.

Protecting Food Sources

Many honeyeaters defend plants with high nectar yields aggressively. For example, the quarrelsome friarbirds chase away smaller birds with harsh cackling cries. Despite appearances, these large gothic-looking birds, with their black faces of bare skin and sinister humps on their bills (except in the Little Friarbird), are honeyeaters. Some species have a ruff of feathers on their hind neck. Friarbirds are generalists, taking a broad diet that includes insects and nectar. They are absent from Tasmania and all of Western Australia except for the Kimberley.

The loud, hoarse calls of wattlebirds are unmistakable declarations of nectar rights. The wattlebirds are so named for the fleshy wattle of skin that hangs from the side of their face: red in the case of the Red Wattlebird of south-eastern and south-western Australia and yellow in

> ### NECTAR PRESS
> Honeyeaters feed on nectar with rapid flicks of the tongue into the throats of flowers. Equally rapidly the nectar is squeezed out of the brush-tipped tongue by being pressed against the roof of the upper mandible when the bill is shut.

The Little Friarbird (25–29cm / 10–11in) is always on the move across the open woodlands of northern and eastern Australia, looking for blossoms upon which to feed. Its harsh, raucous call often draws attention as squabble breaks out among the blossoms. Look up and you may recognise the bare black heads that give these birds their name.

Tasmania's Yellow Wattlebird. The Little Wattlebird (26–33cm / 10–13in) is a heathland inhabitant that is especially partial to banksias in the south-east and dryandras in the south-west. Unusually, it does not have a wattle like its larger cousins.

Other smaller birds get their share of food by banding together. The Noisy Miners operate like members of a gang: they depend heavily on insects in their diet but territories are still heavily guarded, with intruders being subjected to collective screechings and aerial bombardments. These birds are dominating the gardens of eastern and southern Australia and the eastern half of Tasmania. At home in the wide open spaces we have created, they are excluding Australia's smaller birds, including other honeyeaters.

The Bellbirds or Bell Miners adopt a similar strategy and are an out-competing threat to Victoria's avian emblem, the Helmeted Honeyeater. Colonies have invaded south-eastern Australia's wet eucalypt forests, where trees are infested with sap-sucking psyllids upon which they feed. They keep in contact with one another with deafening high-pitch pinging calls that ring out through the forest.

The Red Wattlebird (32–35cm / 13–14in), like all honeyeaters, has a brush-like tongue for mopping up nectar from flowers. It is a common inhabitant of southern Australia. Wattlebirds defend their feeding territories of flowering trees and shrubs with loud staccato crowings and clucks, and by chasing competitors away.

Clever Adaptations

Some small honeyeaters have especially fine, long curved bills that can reach into deep-throated flowers that others cannot reach. The Eastern and Western Spinebills are just such birds. They are light enough to hover as they collect nectar from flowers and are important pollinators of many native plants such as grevilleas and kangaroo paws.

The small Strong-billed Honeyeater (15–17cm/6–7in) has learned to exploit a niche in its native Tasmania that is occupied by treecreepers and sittellas on the mainland. It uses its bill to probe into and under the bark of trees; occasionally it even feeds on the ground. Miners and the Tawny-crowned Honeyeater also feed on the ground sometimes.

Nesting and Young

Honeyeaters build cup-shaped nests of woven plant material bound with spider webs and often lined with soft material. Supported in the forks of shrubs or trees or suspended from vegetation, they may occur from the canopy to just above the ground, depending on the species.

While males defend territories females construct the nest and

CLEVER LAND USE

Australia's native people knew the value of nectar. Early settlers reported how they sucked the 'honey' from banksias and soaked the flowers in water to make a sweet drink.

The Yellow-throated Miner (25–28cm/10–11in) is a widespread species of inland wooded areas and banksia scrub. It is closely related to the more familiar Noisy Miner (25–29cm/10–11in) and the Bell Miner (25–28cm/10–11in). Australian miners are grey-brown or dull green honeyeaters with yellow bills, black face markings and bare patches of skin behind the eyes. Noisy, industrious and gregarious birds, they mostly eat insects, diligently searching for them on the ground and in vegetation. By clinging to the flexible ends of branches with their sharp claws and hanging upside down on their strong legs they reach awkward places. Miners are co-operative breeders; that is several birds help to raise the chicks of a single pair.

The Western Spinebill (14–15cm/6in) is a little honeyeater from the south-west. Like the Eastern Spinebill, its counterpart from eastern Australia, the south-east and Tasmania, it is a highly active bird that flits among flowers a metre or two (39–79in) above the ground, clinging to stems or hovering briefly to insert its long, narrow, curved bill into the throats of flowers. Spinebills are major pollinators of native plants with tubular flowers, such as the kangaroo paw.

The small Brown Honeyeater (11–15cm/4–6in) is a nomadic bird that chases the blossoms. A common bird in Darwin gardens and mostly an inhabitant of northern Australia, it is also found in warmer areas of the south. Alert and chirpy, Brown Honeyeaters work their way through flowering shrubs and paperbarks along creeks and at the edges of rainforests and mangroves. Sometimes they flush insects from the foliage and snatch them in mid-air.

THE NECTAR–POLLEN EXCHANGE

Many plants in Australia are pollinated by birds. Not a single bird in Europe is known to act as a pollinator, yet in Western Australia alone the flowers of 600 species are visited by birds for their nectar, picking up pollen on their way. The outstanding diversity of Australia's eucalypts, grevilleas, banksias, melaleucas, grasstrees, hakeas and dryandras comes courtesy of the honeyeaters and the lorikeets.

The call of Lewin's Honeyeater (19–21cm/7–8in) rings through the forest gullies and rainforests of eastern Australia like automatic gun fire. Mostly sedentary and usually solitary or in a pair, it defends it territory aggressively. It feeds on nectar and fruits and gleans invertebrates from bark.

incubate the eggs. Both parents feed the young and some species have extra helpers. All young honeyeaters are fed on a protein-rich diet of insects. Cuckoos sometimes lay their eggs in the nests of these birds.

Rare Birds

There are a number of honeyeaters that are known to be disappearing. Among them is the pretty Helmeted Honeyeater, a larger, brighter subspecies of the Yellow-tufted Honeyeater with a striking yellow crest. It is endangered and restricted to narrow patches of tall forest along streams or in swamps near the Yellingbo area, east of Melbourne in Victoria. This sedentary species forages for insects, honeydew and nectar in dense trees and shrubs and was once found throughout the forests of south-eastern Victoria. Extensive clearing has left remaining trees stressed and infested with psyllids, which has drawn in the highly territorial Bell Miners. Healesville Sanctuary has been at the centre of a captive-breeding program since 1989, when it was estimated that no more than 50 birds were left in the wild.

The distinctive Regent Honeyeater is a black, white and yellow bird with yellow or pinkish skin around the eye. Before the extensive clearing of box–ironbark eucalypt woodlands in eastern Australia it roamed across a 300km (190mile)-coastal band from Brisbane to Adelaide. Today maybe 1500 birds are found in fragments of north-eastern Victoria and central New South Wales. Recent awareness of its plight has lead to a captive-breeding program and restoration of some of its former habitat by many volunteers.

Chats

Chats are a small group of mostly ground-dwelling birds that live in the arid and semi-arid inland, as well as coastal areas. They are small but colourful birds (11–13cm/4–5in), closely related to honeyeaters. They have the same brush-tipped tongue suitable for nectar feeding but they mostly eat small insects pecked off the ground and from low vegetation. All five species are endemic to Australia.

The males of four of the five chat species have bright plumage, especially on their underside. Even the fifth, the Gibberbird, has a distinctly pale orange underside. The tails of chats are shorter than those of honeyeaters and, rather than hop, they walk and run, their heads bobbing back and forth. They take to the air with a bouncy undulating flight.

Chats live a nomadic existence, often appearing suddenly at bores and dams or where recent rains have lead to an outbreak of insects, and just as suddenly disappearing. They travel in large and often mixed flocks.

In the southern half of the continent, including Tasmania, White-fronted Chats patrol coastal swamps and chenopod shrublands around ephemeral lakes. Scattered along northern floodplains and remote natural springs are populations of Yellow Chats. Widespread and common inland, although unpredictable, are the gregarious Crimson Chats, the brilliant scarlet breast, rump and crown of males catching the eye in a parched landscape. Orange Chats inhabit saltbush plains and spinifex grasslands and remarkably the Gibberbird has adapted to the desolate, waterless plains of gibber desert.

Chats nest after rain when insects are plentiful. They build cup-shaped nests of stems or small twigs with grass, tucked discreetly into low dense vegetation. The Gibberbird's nest is no more than a depression on the ground, shaded and sheltered by a tuft of vegetation.

The dapper black and white plumage of the male White-fronted Chat is unmistakable, that of the female is a discreet grey-brown. These chats nest in loose colonies. Females build the nest while males guard the territory. The pair share the duties of incubating the eggs and feeding the young. White-fronted Chats declare their territories and keep in touch with one another with repetitious 'tang' notes.

OH, MY WING!

When predators lurk, nesting chats employ the old birdy trick of pretending to have a broken wing. By hobbling away from the nest looking pathetic and vulnerable they entice the predator away from their chicks.

Robins

The similarity between northern and southern hemisphere robins is striking, but superficial. The small- to medium-sized Australasian 'robins' are part of a separate assemblage of birds found only in Australia, New Guinea, New Zealand, New Caledonia and many Pacific islands.

The bright yellow breast of an adult Eastern Yellow Robin is unmistakable. This bird perches a metre (39in) or so off the ground and pounces on unsuspecting prey. It is a common inhabitant of wet eucalypt forests in eastern Australia. The very similar Western Yellow Robin is a common inhabitant of woodlands, shrublands and coastal scrubs from south-western Australia to the Eyre Peninsula in South Australia. Sexes are similar in both species and they all have a plaintive piping call.

There are 22 Australian species, most varying in length from 11 to 17cm (4 to 7in). While female plumage is often subdued, most male robins have brightly coloured breasts and are named for these. There are, however, several common plain, soft-brown robins. The Jacky Winter that sallies out to catch flying insects from fence posts is one. Another is the Dusky Robin (16–17cm/6–7in), endemic to Tasmania and the Bass Strait islands, which frequents forest edges, woodlands and gardens.

Robins are insectivorous. Most catch food with perch-and-pounce tactics but some are flycatchers and two 'scrub-robins' are largely terrestrial. Many robins are woodland birds. In any eucalypt woodland in south-eastern Australia you might see a Flame, Scarlet, Hooded or Red-capped Robin. Drop into a moist fern gully and you might find a little Rose or Eastern Yellow Robin.

Jacky Winters and the Red-capped and Hooded Robins are the most widespread and these three have penetrated deepest into the arid centre. The Red-capped's ability to undergo torpor during freezing night-time temperatures and its tendency to breed after rain demonstrate adaptations to the dry inland conditions. At the other end of the scale the Flame Robin inhabits snow country in summer, although it moves down into open woodland, heath and grassland in the coldest months.

Some robins are sedentary but many disperse to varying degrees after the breeding season. Some Flame Robins, for example, are said to migrate from Tasmania to the mainland for winter and Pink Robins (11.5–13cm/ 5in), common in Tasmania but less so on the

mainland, move into more open forest after nesting in the thickets of tree-fern gullies and wet forest. The Rose Robin, too, spreads out into more open habitat after breeding in wet forests.

Tropical Robins

There are several tropical robins. Most are brownish grey. In northern Australia the Mangrove Robin hops between the roots on mangrove mudflats pecking up invertebrates at low tide. The Lemon-bellied Flycatcher snatches insects from the air around the edge of the mangroves, alongside river vegetation and in woodlands and swamps. The Grey-headed Robin (16–18cm / 6–7in), known only from a restricted patch of highland rainforest, is a rather beautifully marked chestnut, white, grey and black robin that is often flushed from bush tracks and roads.

Scrub-robins

There are two species of so-called scrub-robins. They are large ground-living robins (20–23cm / 8–9in) with long tails and long legs. Both hop about leaf litter searching for invertebrates. The little-known Northern

Males of the sedentary Scarlet Robin (12–13cm / 5in) (above) and migratory Flame Robin (12.5–14cm / 5–6in) (below) are both red-breasted with a tuft of white feathers on their forehead. Both, too, may nest in the same open wood-lands of south-eastern Australia. The breasts of Flame Robins, however, are more orange and they have dark grey backs, while the breasts of Scarlet Robins are indeed scarlet and their backs and throats are black. Scarlet Robins are also found in south-western Australia.

TAIL FLICKING

Some Australian robins flick their tails and sometimes their wings. We have yet to discover why but perhaps this behaviour indicates agitation or it may be a strategy for flushing out prey.

Scrub-robin lives in the rainforest of Cape York's northern-most tip and New Guinea, while the Southern Scrub-robin forages widely across southern Australia through mallee, broombush and acacia shrublands.

Raising Young

Although Jacky Winters build shallow plate-like nests, those of many robins are deep cups bound with spiders' webs built in the forks of trees and camouflaged with lichen or moss. Only scrub-robins nest on the ground. Their scrapped depressions are lined with soft plant material and encircled by twigs designed to disguise their presence. Female robins appear to be the major nest builders and incubators, while males feed their mate and share the feeding of hatchlings.

Compare this female Flame Robin with her male counterpart (previous page). She demonstrates well the very different plumage of many female robins from those of the more showy males. Discreet plumage that blends in with the habitat is a distinct advantage to a bird sitting on eggs.

Chowchillas and Logrunners

These two sociable birds of the rainforest floor are renowned for dashing across fallen logs with surprising agility and speed. The Logrunner is endemic to Australia's central eastern rainforests, while the more northerly Chowchilla is endemic to north-east Queensland's tropical rainforests.

The spiny feathers in the tails of these birds have hard shafts and bare tips, sturdy enough to be leant upon while first one foot and then the other kicks aside leaf litter. The strong feet can dislodge heavy loads of twigs and damp litter to reveal snails, worms and insects which are quickly pecked up before the bird runs on to repeat the process elsewhere.

You can detect the presence of Logrunners and Chowchillas by their  loud dawn calls (especially the Chowchilla's) or by the rustling of leaves in the undergrowth. If alarmed, they rapidly run or, if really pressed, fly for cover but rarely do they go far.

A female Chowchilla with a beak full of grubs obtained from the damp litter of the rainforest floor. While both sexes are dark above and feature pale blue or white eye-rings, the orange chin and breast of the female is white in males. Chowchillas may breed at any time of year. The female constructs a large nest of twigs usually a metre or so above the ground. Hidden in a dense clump of lawyer vines, among fallen timber or beside epiphytic ferns, the interior is kept dry by an overhanging 'roof' of leaves and moss. The female incubates the single large white egg and brings food to the nestling while the male feeds his mate near the nest.

Chowchilla

The larger Chowchilla (25–27cm/10–11in) inhabits the rainforests of north-eastern Queensland from Mt Spec near Townsville to Cooktown, with the Atherton Tableland forming its stronghold.

Logrunner

Logrunners (18–21cm/7–8in) are brownish, beautiful, dumpy birds with white, grey, rufous and black markings. The throat and breast of females are orange while those of males are white. These colours blend into the leaf litter, as do their winter nests—a large pile of twigs with an ascending platform and a leaf-and-moss waterproof 'roof' tucked in against a fallen log between the buttress roots of a tree or into a tangle of vines.

The stronghold of the Logrunners is the McPherson and Border ranges, a World Heritage area that spans the Queensland–New South Wales border. However, their range extends as far north as the Bunya Ranges and as far south as the Illawarra district.

Babblers

Of the five Australian–Papuan babbler species, one is a forest bird of New Guinea, three are endemic to Australia, and the Grey-crowned Babbler occurs in both countries. Despite remarkable similarities to Asian scimitar babblers in appearance and behaviour, this group evolved quite independently.

A Chestnut-crowned Babbler brings home the food. Up to 15 babblers may help feed a single brood of chicks.

TOO GOOD TO WASTE

Babblers build massive constructions of sticks in which groups roost and pairs nest. In the sparse outback these roost and brood nests can be conspicuous from a distance. Other bird species, such as honeyeaters and thornbills, may use them for their own nesting purposes and bats have been found roosting in disused babbler nests.

As their name suggests, babblers are endearingly chatty birds with a distinctive appearance. Medium-sized (18–25cm/7–10in), deep-bodied, with broad, white-tipped tails and conspicuous eyebrow markings, they have long down-curved bills that come to a sharp point. Sexes are hard to tell apart but head markings distinguish species.

The highly sociable babblers live in tight-knit groups of two to 15 or more individuals. They maintain constant contact with a range of conspicuous calls. As they forage together for spiders, insects, insect larvae and small lizards, they probe under bark and bounce along the ground tossing aside leaf litter, stabbing into the ground and overturning stones and fallen timber. They depend upon undisturbed ground litter for much of their food. When alarmed they retreat to bushes and trees rapidly.

Although Australian babblers are absent from Tasmania and rainforests, they occupy a range of habitats. The White-browed Babblers inhabit the wet and dry eucalypt forests of eastern Australia and the south-west, as well as mallee, heaths and open arid country. The large Grey-crowned Babblers are generally found in open woodland; while common in the monsoonal north-west, they are declining in the south-east. Halls Babbler is largely confined to the mulga country of south-western Queensland and north-western New South Wales, and the Chestnut-crowned Babbler is endemic to the inland of south-eastern Australia.

A pair of Grey-crowned Babblers. As with all things babbler, roosting and nesting is a communal affair. Groups of Grey-crowned Babblers work together to build large untidy dome-shaped nests from sticks and other plant material. Typically positioned in a tree, these nests are used either for communal roosting or for breeding.

Whipbirds, Wedgebills and Quail-thrushes

These furtive ground-dwelling birds feed on seeds and/or invertebrates. Elusive but sometimes musical, their cryptic plumage and reluctance to fly far or high, keeps them—for the most part—under the radar of aerial predators.

Whipbirds

Eastern Whipbirds (25cm/10in) are rarely seen as they skulk about in the dense undergrowth, pecking seeds and invertebrates from low bushes and leaf litter. They find one another or declare their territories by sound rather than sight. Common, even in outer suburbs, they have benefited from the growth of dense weeds, such as lantana and privet, which provide excellent cover. Their seemingly messy large nests, built by the females off the ground and in vegetation, become increasingly neat and finely woven towards the centre.

The greyer, slightly smaller Western Whipbird is adapted to arid environments. It lives in fragments of coastal heaths, sedges, spinifex clumps and other thick vegetation along the south coast from far western Victoria to southern Western Australia. Its extremely restricted

Despite being rarely seen, the Eastern Whipbird is quite common and frequently heard. It inhabits dense gullies in forested areas all along the eastern seaboard and from such places comes the distinctive rising whistle and loud whip-crack call of the male, sometimes followed by a couple of softer toot-tooting notes from the female if she is present. Peering into the gloom of the undergrowth you may catch sight of this bird's splash of white or its pointy black head-crest, which is often raised.

The Chiming Wedgebill hops through arid mulga, scrublands, broombush and mallee. People who come in spring to visit Western Australia's wildflower spectacle are often treated to this bird's hypnotic song. Delivered from the tops of bushes, it sounds like tinkling bells. At the slightest hint of danger, wedgebills drop to the ground and disappear without trace. They run fast and fly low, only drawing attention when proclaiming their territories during the breeding season.

distribution is the result of extensive clearing and inappropriate fire regimes and it continues to thrive only in a few protected areas.

Wedgebills

More often heard than seen are the insectivorous wedgebills (19–22cm/ 7–9in) that forage among the low dense bushes of the open interior. These are rather plain brown birds, paler below, with wedge-shaped bills, white edges to their tails and distinct head crests. They are fine songsters, their clear strong bell-like notes ringing out across the dunes at dawn and dusk. The two species—the Chirruping Wedgebill and the Chiming Wedgebill—are similar but their distributions differ, as do their songs.

The Chirruping is locally common among the sparse bushes of the arid plains from Port Augusta north through the Lake Eyre region to the lower reaches of the Diamantina River and across the Corner Country. Directly to the west, lies the range of the Chiming Wedgebill, which stretches across the western deserts to the sea between Geraldton and Carnarvon.

Quail-thrushes

The four Australian species of shy ground-dwelling quail-thrushes are delicately marked in desert colours of cinnamon, chestnut, grey, white and black, each with a distinctly pale eyebrow. Of medium size (17–28cm/7–11in) and long tailed, they have the superficial appearance and shape of a thrush and, when flushed, the whirring flight of a quail. Males and females are marked differently but identifying species requires a practiced eye.

Pairs or small parties of quail-thrushes probe into crevices and toss aside leaf litter in their search for invertebrates, small lizards and seeds. When scared, they crouch low or run away. Able to do without drinking for long periods, some species have penetrated Australia's most drought-ridden environments.

All but the largest, the Spotted Quail-thrush, are inland birds. This species lives among stony ridges in the dry eucalypt forests from south-eastern Queensland to south-eastern South Australia, and in Tasmania. Exquisitely speckled on its back and flanks with a soft grey breast, males have a black throat and chin, and white cheek patches.

Populations of Cinnamon Quail-thrushes are separated by a band of dunes, isolating one subspecies in the mallee and woodlands of the Nullarbor Plain from the more northerly subspecies in the open country, chenopod shrublands and gibber plains of the Lake Eyre Basin.

Populations of Chestnut-breasted Quail-thrushes have also been divided by sandy deserts, resulting in disjunct populations: one in central Western Australia and the other in central eastern Australia.

The desert quail-thrushes breed shortly after good rains. All four species nest on the ground, beside a rock, fallen log or tuft of vegetation, in a shallow cup usually lined with bark, grass and leaves.

A male Chestnut-backed Quail-thrush. Most quail-thrushes prefer stony ground, often on ridges, but this species is at home on soft, sandy ground. From south-eastern Australia to the west it occurs in semi-arid woodlands of mallee and native pines, arid sandplains and dunes and along coastal dunes. The chestnut colour on the lower back is especially obvious in males and more so in desert-living birds.

The Whistler Family

This family of fine songsters originated in the southern hemisphere and members are now widespread throughout the Australia–New Guinean region, reaching to the Philippines, Indonesia, South Pacific islands and New Zealand. Established in Australia are 14 of the 54 or so species.

The chunky bill of the Crested Shrike-tit is its most valuable asset. As shrike-tits glean from bark and leaves, they use this powerful tool to snap open hard leaf galls and tear bark from tree trunks to expose the spiders, centipedes and insects beneath. They also peel strips of bark off for nesting material and prune obstructive twigs around their nest. Shown here is a male; females look similar but their throats are olive green rather than black.

These small- to medium-sized insectivorous birds are full-bodied and round headed; they are sometimes referred to, unglamorously, as thick-heads. As their name suggests, whistlers are a tuneful mob, especially during the breeding season when they sing at full throttle to attract mates and defend territories. Females and even young birds sing. At other times of the year, whistlers are unobtrusive and often solitary, making them hard to find. Although insects and other invertebrates are their staple diet, they may take small mammals, frogs and reptiles as well as nestlings and plant material such as fruit and seeds.

Crested Shrike-tit

There are three regional races of the Crested Shrike-tit (15–19cm/ 6–7½in), an inhabitant of eucalypt woodlands and forests. One is in the Top End and the Kimberley, another in the wandoo and jarrah–karri forests of Western Australia and the last in the south-east, although absent from Tasmania. Nowhere is it common, so spotting this colourful little bird with its thick black crest, black and white face and oversized laterally compressed bill is a treat. Sometimes a forlorn rising or falling whistle gives away its presence.

Shrike-tits are sociable birds. They often feed together and help breeding birds in their group to raise their young. Between the upright branches of saplings they build finely woven deep cups of shredded bark, bound with spider webs, lined with grass and thin strips of bark and camouflaged with lichen.

Crested Bellbird

The liquid bell-like notes of Crested Bellbirds (20–22cm / 8–9in) ring throughout most of the dry inland. They are essentially olive brown birds with golden eyes and a short head-crest that is often raised when singing. The white face and throat of the male contrasts with its black breast and a narrow black crest; the female has a grey head with a dark streak on her crown.

Found throughout dry woodlands, farmlands and scrub, this bird spends much of its time hopping around on the ground. Its song, often delivered from the top of a bush, is hard to track down to its source because, as it sings, the bird turns its head in one direction and then the other.

If you live in Melbourne, Sydney, Coffs Harbour or Mackay you may have noticed a slender bird with a black and white face, a dab of scarlet beside the eyes and under the tail, and a pointy black crest. Although not a member of the whistler family, the Red-whiskered Bulbul sings sweetly. An inoffensive introduced bird from South-east Asia, it often perches on telegraph wires or exposed branches beside open ground, from where it hawks for flying insects.

HAIRY PROTECTION

Crested Bellbirds nest a metre (39in) or so above the ground. They have the curious habit of placing live but paralysed hairy caterpillars around the rim of their nest during incubation. These furry wrigglers cause itchiness and inflammation, so perhaps they are to protect the eggs.

Whistlers

Within the whistler family is a group specifically referred to as whistlers, eight species of which inhabit Australia. Their songs are melodious, high-pitched, loud and complex and males are more brightly coloured than females.

The males of several species have white throats encircled by a black band. Perhaps most spectacular and best known of these is the black-headed, yellow-bellied Golden Whistler that inhabits densely wooded areas from the rainforests of northern Queensland to the mallee in southern Australia, as well as the south-west and Tasmania. The slightly smaller Mangrove

Golden Whistler looks very similar but it is confined to the mangroves of the north. Another mangrove specialist is the White-breasted Whistler, with its diet of molluscs, crustaceans and insects, while the Rufous Whistler inhabits a wide variety of forests and woodlands.

The whistlers methodically search leaves and branches for prey. When something comes to light, they quickly pounce or snatch it up. Although most whistlers forage among the middle and upper canopy, the Olive Whistler, commonly found in the wet forests and heaths of Tasmania and less commonly in the highlands of the mainland, often feeds in low, dense understorey and on the ground. So, too, does the small tropical Grey Whistler in the monsoonal forests and woodlands of the Top End and north-eastern Queensland.

Gilbert's Whistler is found across the southern mallee, as is the rare Red-lored Whistler, much of whose very limited habitat in the south-eastern inland has been cleared and burned.

The handsome male Rufous Whistler forages mostly in trees and shrubs. The brown-grey female is heavily streaked on her paler underside. Found in every mainland state, this is a common whistler that sings lustily in spring throughout woodlands, forests and mallee. In winter it migrates inland and northwards.

The subdued colouring of the female White-breasted Whistler is typical of female whistlers. This species is a mangrove specialist of northern and western coastlines. It sits quietly in the gloom beneath the canopy watching and waiting for prey. With its broad strong bill it has no problem in despatching small crabs and molluscs.

Shrike-thrushes

The shrike-thrushes are large whistlers (17–26cm / 7–10in) with robust bills, hooked at their tip. Despite their name, they are not related to shrikes, nor are they thrushes, although they do commonly hop along the ground in a thrush-like manner. Their subdued brown, grey and rufous plumage provides them with a degree of camouflage. Given their size and bill, their menu extends to small vertebrates, such as baby birds and small lizards. They also take other bird's eggs. Of the entire family, shrike-thrushes are the most melodious singers.

The Grey Shrike-thrush is the best known of Australia's four species. Although quite a common and even companionable bird, it is often overlooked due to its pale grey plumage and quiet disposition. Its lovely deep rich song, however, is one of the most beautiful sounds of the bush.

The smaller Little Shrike-thrush inhabits the rainforests, mangroves and paperbark swamps of eastern and northern Australia. It forages in the upper and middle levels of the

canopy but it also rifles through leaf litter on the ground. Between Cooktown and Townsville, in a restricted area of mostly high-altitude rainforest, the short-tailed, big-headed Bower's Shrike-thrush is quite common. Ringing out from the rugged sandstone escarpments and dissected gorges of the Kimberley and the Top End is the rich song of the Sandstone Shrike-thrush. Undertaking short low flights, this mostly terrestrial bird is quite common within its habitat.

A male Grey Shrike-thrush (22–25cm/9–10in). This widespread species is found in every state in all wooded areas including mulga and mallee country but excluding rainforest. It forages at every level from ground to canopy, and can be quite tame around parks and gardens.

SOUND-SENSITIVE BIRDS

Perhaps unsurprisingly the singing whistlers appear to be highly sensitive to all sounds. The slamming of a car door or a crack of thunder is enough to launch some members of this family into a volley of singing. Some, too, are attracted by squeaking, so if you hear what you suspect is a whistler, why not try 'squeaking it up'.

The Little Shrike-thrush builds a deep nest of twigs, leaves and bark, bound with vine tendrils and spider webs, well hidden among dense foliage. It is likely this species follows the domestic trend among members of the whistler family of monogamy and care of the young by both parents.

Flycatchers

These are alert and active small- to medium-sized birds that mostly catch their food on the wing. Many have strong affiliations with subtropical and tropical rainforests and are found throughout Africa, India, South-east Asia and the islands of the Pacific Ocean but their ancestors appear to have evolved in Australasia.

Rarely do Willie Wagtails stay still for long. Alert and lively, they perch on the ground, branches or fence posts, swivelling their bodies from side to side and scouring the air for small aerial insects. Throughout mainland Australia they are a common sight, even in the open grassy areas of our cities. When approached, they may utter loud, distracted alarm calls but in spring and summer they often sing sweetly, especially early in the morning and often through the night.

Flycatchers are a large family of birds that encompass the crested flycatchers, monarchs and mud-nest builders, the fantails and the drongos. With the exception of the fantails, males and females rarely look alike but females are often as colourful as their male counterparts.

Australia's flycatchers are typically forest birds that hawk from mid-level perches for aerial insects or glean from the outer foliage and branches of trees. Their wide gape and grey flattened bills help to funnel prey into their mouths. Aiding capture further are the modified feathers that form bristles around their mouths and are sensitive to touch. Tail swinging and fanning is quite a common behavioural quirk and, in the case of some species, serves to flush out prey.

Some Australian flycatchers are confined to the rainforests and mangroves of northern and eastern Australia but others have adapted to drier and more open habitats. There is a tendency among some to shift northwards in winter along the east coast and ranges and several species winter in New Guinea. They then return south to breed.

Most widespread are the Grey Fantails that inhabit the forests and woodlands of every state and the familiar and plucky Willie Wagtails that have adapted to man-made open spaces, such as playing fields and golf courses.

Many flycatchers' nests are tiny, deep cups of firmly woven natural fibres bound with spider webs and camouflaged with moss or lichens, fastened to a branch or in the horizontal fork of a tree. Some have 'tails' of woven vegetation dangling from their base. In most species, males and females incubate the eggs, which hatch after about 14 days.

A female Leaden Flycatcher. The male has a distinctive dark, leaden grey head, throat and upper breast. Both sexes have a slight crest, which is not apparent here but is raised when the bird is aroused. This is a feature that is shared with the Restless, Shining, Satin and Broad-billed Flycatchers.

Crested Flycatchers

The squarish heads of crested flycatchers (15–21cm / 6–8in) is due to a thick crest of feathers on their crown which lifts when they are excited. Their tail-quivering habits, too, assist in their identification. Glossy blue-black plumage is a common feature of these birds. Satin Flycatchers inhabit tall eucalypt forests while the very similar but less bright Leaden Flycatchers inhabit more open drier forests. Restless Flycatchers forage among the understorey and leaf litter of open eucalypt woodlands from low perches, often hovering just above the ground. The Shining Flycatcher hunts for invertebrates in the mud of mangroves and tropical waterways, as does the small Broad-billed Flycatcher, with its black, exaggeratedly broad bill.

Monarchs

Monarchs (14–20cm / 6–8in) have a distinct preference for wet gullies and the edges and interiors of rainforests. The six species in Australia are strikingly marked, especially on the head. Three are pied as in the White-eared, Frill-necked and Pied Monarchs, the latter two having blue eye-rings, while the Black-faced, Black-winged and Spectacled Monarchs are slate grey with orange breasts or bellies and black patches on their faces.

Best known are the Black-faced and Spectacled Monarchs, which migrate up and down the east coast. These birds flutter about the middle and lower layers of the forest seeking out invertebrates among the branches, trunks and leaves of trees. The rarer Black-winged Monarch is confined to eastern Cape York Peninsula. High in the canopy of the east-coast wet forests nests and feeds the White-eared Monarch.

The black mask around the eyes of the Spectacled Monarch distinguishes it from the similar-looking Black-faced and Black-winged Monarchs. The cup-shaped nest, camouflaged with moss and spider egg sacs and hidden in dense vegetation, is typical of monarchs, although this species choses especially vertical forks into which to lash its nest, resulting in a deeper cup.

The Frill-necked and Pied Monarchs live in restricted areas of Cape York Peninsula where they work the trunks of trees for invertebrates, flushing them out with spread out flapping wings and fanned tails. Despite their similar appearance, they are easily told apart as they do not overlap in distribution, the Frill-necked being confined to the Cape's northern-most tip.

The Yellow-breasted Boatbill (11–15cm / 4–6in) is a small but eye-catching bird that has a bright yellow breast and eyebrow and its flattened bill is shaped like the prow of a boat when seen from above or below. It forages, often in small parties, deep in the rainforests of eastern Cape York Peninsula where it also builds its nests.

Fantails

The busy fantails (15–20cm/6–8in) often catch our attention as they zip around the edges of forest foliage, their wings and tails fanned out and their bodies twisting and turning in pursuit of flying insects. The Rufous Fantail inhabits wetter areas of northern and eastern Australia to Victoria. It breeds in the more southerly part of its range. The Grey Fantail prefers more open areas.

Northern mangroves are the denizens of the Mangrove Grey Fantail and the Northern Fantail, which also commonly frequents tropical open woodland. The bold Willie Wagtail is well-known to most Australians, even in cities where it may live in parks and gardens.

Magpie-lark

Although it is far from obvious, DNA studies reveal that the common Magpie-lark (25–28cm/10–11in) is in effect a monarch that has taken to feeding on the ground. Typically an inhabitant of open woodlands, it has adapted to the well-spaced eucalypts and extensive lawns of many outer suburbs and is a frequent sight on the sides of roads where mown grass makes pecking up ground-dwelling insects, worms and snails easy. These birds also live in the drier plains of the interior provided there is water nearby.

Magpie-larks are sometimes called mudlarks as they build thick mud nests mixed with grass. It is for these they require water and why inland birds

The Grey Fantail is quite a common bird that actively forages from a mid-storey perch in forests and woodlands throughout Australia, including Tasmania. It hawks for aerial insects with deft manoeuvres, using its fanned-out tail and wing feathers to net its prey. It also flutters among leafy branches in an effort to flush out prey.

A white eyebrow and a black throat identify this Magpie-lark as a male. These birds are rare in Tasmania but they are otherwise widespread and large numbers migrate north during winter. They are also known as pee-wees, which describes their high-pitched rather anxious calls, often sung as a duet between pairs.

FARMER'S FRIEND

The miserable liver-fluke that infests sheep spends part of its life cycle in land snails. Magpie-larks perform a valuable service to farmers by including such snails and other invertebrate pests in their diet.

usually nest after rain. Both partners laboriously fly hundreds of beakfuls of mud from the edges of coastal or fresh water up into trees. Both male and female birds incubate and feed the young. When these birds leave home they may form large nomadic flocks. In adult plumage males are differentiated from females by their white 'eyebrows'.

Spangled Drongo

Drongos are found as far afield as Africa but Australia's Spangled Drongo is the country's sole representative. It is a large, glossy black bird (28–33cm / 11–13in), with wonderful iridescent spangles of blue-green on its breast, head and neck, blood-red eyes and a distinctly fish-shaped tail. It lives in the wetter regions of northern and eastern Australia. Drongos are migratory and more common in the north than the south. After breeding most birds head north.

The drongo is an acrobatic flyer, adept at catching fast-flying insects and even small birds. It has an exceptionally strong bill that is able to crack the hard cases of cicadas, beetles and dragonflies. It watches quietly from an exposed branch before sallying out in hot pursuit. Drongos also eat fruit and nectar, and root out invertebrates from beneath bark and foliage.

Unlike the tightly woven deep cup-shaped nests of most flycatchers, the nest of the Spangled Drongo is a wide bowl of woven vine tendrils built into the horizontal fork of branches in the canopy. Both sexes contribute to its construction and share incubation and care of the young.

> ### MIXED SPECIES FEEDING FLOCKS
>
> Outside of the breeding season many small woodland and forest birds of different species join up to feed together in flocks. Most are insectivores but there are also seed eaters, nectar feeders and fruit feeders. Mixed flocks reduce the risk of being taken by predators and increase foraging efficiency. Gerygones are often accompanied by flycatchers and monarchs. In New Guinea babblers are often accompanied by Spangled Drongos. The drongos act as sentinels, watching for predators and alerting the flock with calls that are quickly heeded. They benefit by snatching up prey flushed out or exposed by the foraging mob.

Both sexes of the Spangled Drongo share with male Koels the characteristics of blood-red eyes and shimmering black plumage but the drongo's fish-shaped tail is a distinctive trademark. Its grating chatterings can be heard at dawn and dusk. When defending territories these birds are noisy and quarrelsome, chasing other birds as large as crows and raptors away from their nests.

Cuckoo-shrikes and Trillers

There are 70-odd species of cuckoo-shrikes and trillers from Africa eastwards to New Guinea and Australia. These largely insectivorous and mostly arboreal birds fly with sweeping shallow dips and glides on long pointed wings and long tails. Five cuckoo-shrikes and a couple of trillers reside in Australia.

Cuckoo-shrikes

These birds (24–26cm/9–10in) are related to neither cuckoos nor shrikes but their large, hooked bills resemble those of shrikes and some species have heavily barred bellies like cuckoos. Their black faces and throats often contrast strikingly with their plain soft grey or brown plumage. A habit of cuckoo-shrikes is to shuffle their wings when they alight upon a perch.

The large tree-dwelling Black-faced Cuckoo-shrike is commonly seen throughout Australia. The similar but smaller White-bellied Cuckoo-shrike frequents northern Australia, its occurrence diminishing towards the south. The terrestrial Ground Cuckoo-shrike struts around the dry inland and drier parts of the coast in pairs or small parties, its head nodding back and forth like a pigeon. Large, elegant and grey, it has strong, long legs, black wings, dark bars on its underside and a forked tail that is more easily seen in flight. The dark-grey Barred Cuckoo-shrikes of the east-coast rainforests supplement their penchant for small fruits with invertebrates such as stick insects.

Unlike most cuckoo-shrikes, male and female Cicadabirds look different from one another: the male is a soft dark grey and black; the female, dark brown with a heavily barred cream and brown underside. These birds live in the canopy of rain-forest, wet eucalypt forest, mangroves and paperbark swamps throughout northern and eastern Australia. The name alludes to the loud buzzing calls of breeding males.

> ### KEEPING YOUR POWDER DRY
> Cuckoo-shrikes have powder down. Powder down comes from especially fine feathers beneath the outer feathers, the base of which gradually disintegrates into a fine powder. The birds spread this powder through their outer feathers to condition and waterproof them. Many birds work oil from oil glands through their plumage but powder is less common.

The Black-faced Cuckoo-shrike has a rolling chur-ring call. Originally an inhabitant of forests, woodlands, mangroves and grasslands, this highly adaptable species nowadays lives on farmlands, plantations, towns and cities.

Trillers are small cuckoo-shrikes (16–19cm/6–7in). Breeding males sing prolonged songs that terminate in a trill. The plumage of this non-breeding male White-winged Triller is similar to the female's but it will moult into a dashing black and white plumage for the breeding season. This species is quite common throughout the dry mainland, while the pied Varied Triller prefers the wetter areas of northern and eastern Australia.

Figbird and Orioles

All three representatives of the oriole family established in Australia are also known from New Guinea. Another 22 species are spread from Asia through Africa to Europe. These forest birds feed in the canopy on fruit and insects.

A male Australasian Figbird (27–29in/11–11½in) on the nest. Males share incubation with their partners and pairs are often assisted by other figbirds in raising the young. Typical of the oriole family, the cup-shaped nest, constructed from lengths of vine tendrils or bark strips, is lashed to the horizontal branches of a leafy tree.

Figbird

This member of the oriole family is a fig specialist. Slightly dumpier than the other two species and with a stouter, dark bill, it is a gregarious and noisy bird that often gathers to feed in fruiting trees. It can frequently be seen in the parks and gardens of tropical and subtropical cities and towns. There are two races, the plumage of which is easily distinguished in males. Across the north the breast and belly of males is bright yellow but down the east coast males have olive undersides. In both races, the black head is studded with scarlet eye patches. Females of both races are streaky brown.

Orioles

The other two orioles are slender birds (25–30cm / 10–12in) with long, slightly downward-curved bills. In adults the eyes are red and the bill is orange. While the plumage of the Olive-backed Oriole is a subtle olive green, the Yellow Oriole is much brighter, tending towards yellow. Both species are heavily streaked with grey-brown on the wings, back and breast.

Orioles sing with beautiful fluting notes. Mostly unobtrusive, solitary birds, they are often obscured by leaves as they feed singly, in pairs or occasionally in small flocks. While the Yellow Oriole favours the fruits of the dense rainforest, the Olive-backed Oriole feeds in more open forest, woodland and even inland scrub from the Kimberley, across the Top End to Cape York and down the east coast, through Victoria and into eastern South Australia.

A Yellow Oriole feeds its chick. Orioles are monogamous. While females are the primary nest builders and carers of the young, males protect the territory. The Yellow Oriole is confined to the Kimberley, Top End and Cape York.

Woodswallows

There's something endearing about woodswallows. They are sociable little birds that often huddle together. Of the 11 species, six reside in Australia. Like many of Australia's songbirds, they are believed to have ancient Gondwanan ancestors.

A courting pair of White-browed Woodswallows bond in a round of tail swivelling and wing lifting. The male is on the right. This species is widespread throughout the drier areas of Australia.

These rounded, soft brown and grey birds (12–18cm / 5–7in), usually bear patches of white. Their blue-grey conical bills have black tips and their tails have white tips. Primarily insectivorous, they mostly catch their food on the wing but they have a brush-tipped tongue with which they take nectar and pollen. On their sickle-shaped wings with pointed tips they fly with bursts of wingbeats followed by glides, and even soar on air currents, a rarity among small songbirds.

These gregarious birds feed in flocks, often rearing their young in groups and forming mobs to harass predators. They chirrup, flick and wag their tails as they launch from branches on aerial sorties. They swarm and cluster together for warmth in crevices and huddle up, side by side, on low branches of trees, even in mixed species and during the day.

Mostly birds of grassy woodlands, some species are sedentary, like the Black-faced Woodswallow. Others are nomadic like the Little, Masked and White-browed Woodswallows. In the summer White-breasted Woodswallows may migrate as far south as Sydney and Dusky Woodswallows to Tasmania.

Woodswallows build untidy twig nests in the forks and spouts of trees, in hollows of old stumps and fence posts, bark cavities and low prickly bushes.

A WINGED SECURITY ALARM

During their breeding season Black-faced Woodswallows on Cape York Peninsula seem to provide a service to several ground-feeding birds, including the endangered Golden-shouldered Parrot. Mobs chase away potential predators from the area around their nests, affording at least a degree of protection during this crucial time of year.

Currawongs

The currawongs (40–53cm/16–21in) are among the most predatory of all Australia's songbirds. All three species eat invertebrates, small birds, nestlings, lizards and frogs, but berries, too, are a major component of their diet.

These jaunty crow-like natives are birds of the forest. Adept fliers, they chart their course through the trees with speed and precision. They have a wide repertoire of loud calls and sharp whistles, and in most parts of forested Australia they are a highly audible and visible presence.

Of the three species, the Pied Currawong lives in eastern Australia from Cape York to the Grampians in Victoria, the Grey Currawong is found across southern Australia and eastern Tasmania and the Black Currawong is a Tasmanian endemic.

All currawongs have yellow eyes, white tail tips and most have white patches in the wings and under the tail. The white rump identifies the Pied. The massive bill with its convex upper mandible is characteristic of the Black. The Grey, while definitely dark grey, is brownish in the Eyre and Yorke peninsulas of South Australia but almost black in Tasmania.

Tasmania's Black Currawong takes a small insect whose camouflage was not good enough to escape the attention of this wily predator. Currawongs have good eyesight and are incredibly curious.

Currawongs breed from August to December. Both sexes gather material but the female constructs the large stick nest high in the fork of a tree and lines it with soft material. The male feeds her as she incubates the eggs. In winter, large bands of currawongs roam the bush in search of food. In cold climates, they tend to migrate down from high altitudes.

TELLING THE DIFFERENCE

Setting currawongs apart from magpies is eye colour, bill shape and Colour, as well as their preferences for different habitats and the way currawongs hop, rather than walk or run, on the ground.

A Pied Currawong in a typically alert pose. This species is increasingly taking up year-round residence in the gardens and parks of eastern Australia, where orna-mental berries provide seasonal sustenance. They are dispersing weed seeds into bushland and may be contributing to the loss of small birds from our backyards.

Butcherbirds

At first sight butcherbirds look like their close relatives, the currawongs and magpies, but the bills of butcherbirds have a distinct hook that is absent in magpies. The heavy-duty black bills of currawongs are completely different. Four species of butcherbird inhabit Australia. The Grey Butcherbird and widespread Pied Butcherbird live only here; the others two also inhabit New Guinea.

A Grey Butcherbird (24–30cm/9–12in) snaps up a grasshopper. Common in Tasmania and widespread throughout southern Australia, the distribution of this species peters out in northern inland regions, reappearing in the Kimberley and the Top End, where it is known as the Silver-backed Butcherbird.

The name 'butcherbird' is derived from the habit of these birds of wedging their prey in the fork of a tree or impaling it on a spike, then tearing it into smaller pieces with their hooked bill. While they live and nest in trees, they often hunt ground dwellers. Insects, small birds and reptiles are subjected to wait-and-watch, pounce-and-grab tactics. Butcherbirds like timbered areas with little or no understorey and low- to mid-level perches for prospecting.

One of the delights of the Australian bush is the sound of butcherbirds singing. These usually sedentary birds are territorial and often establish themselves around homesteads and along the wooded edges of suburbia. Males declare territories with clear fluting calls and pairs sing intricate and delicate rolling duets. Butcherbirds mostly nest and raise their young as a pair, although there have been a couple of records of helpers at the nest.

The two northern butcherbirds have limited Australian distributions. The heavy-billed, large-tailed Black Butcherbird (32–44cm/13–17in) keeps to dense vegetation in the Top End and north-east Queensland. It usually hunts around waterways, especially mangroves, where it often plucks crabs from the mud. Juveniles have streaked rufous plumage. The relatively small Black-backed Butcherbird (26–28cm/10–11in) lives in the woodlands and forests of Cape York Peninsula, where its white chin and breast set it apart from the Pied Butcherbird.

The handsome Pied Butcherbird (28–32cm/11–13in) is a common and widespread species but it is absent from Tasmania, much of the coast and the arid inland of the south. Its distribution reaches up into northern Australia and overlaps that of the Grey Butcherbird but it prefers drier habitat. It is distinguished easily by its black hood, chin and breast, and its more distinct pied plumage.

Australian Magpie

The Australian Magpie is one of the most familiar large birds in the country. Found throughout Australia except in the Top End and the tip of Cape York Peninsula, this single species has many regional variations of its pied plumage. Its lovely bubbling warbles are a quintessential sound of Australia's open spaces.

Its name is misleading since its only resemblance to the unrelated European magpie is its pied plumage. This crow-like bird has sturdy black legs and a large white bill tipped with black. It finds most of its food on or just beneath the ground, using its bill to unearth and grab grubs and worms.

Magpies are often seen walking slowly and deliberately through open ground, sometimes tipping their heads to one side to listen for underground movement. Found in eucalypt woodland, mallee, mulga, semi-arid scrub and in forest clearings, it is little wonder that magpies have taken to paddocks and the lawns of parks, golf courses, game fields and gardens. When alarmed and when roosting, magpies take to trees or shrubs for safety.

They live in family groups and defend territories of 2–18ha (4–45ac), depending on the availability of food, shelter and nesting sites, as well as on competition. Usually only one pair in the group have young in a season, the female building the large stick nest in a tree and incubating the eggs. Other members help feed the brood and defend the territory. Once grown, the young birds may be firmly discouraged from staying with the group and become vulnerable loners or join packs of other roaming evictees. Eventually they may find and fill vacancies in existing territories or establish their own.

The iconic Australian Magpie also lives in New Guinea and has been introduced into New Zealand. In some areas Magpies have black backs; in others, they have white backs. Northern birds are distinctly smaller and less common but the orangey brown eyes and the white bill with a black tip distinguishes all magpies from the currawongs.

BOMBING BIRDS

Beware spring, the magpie's bombing season. Innocent walkers and cyclists unwittingly passing too close to a magpie's nest may find themselves the target of a dive-bombing 'maggie' that deems the 'intruder' a risk to his or her nest. It swoops from behind and, on occasion, draws blood in the over-zealous protection of its young.

Crows and Ravens

The world's crows originated from Gondwanan ancestors here in the southern hemisphere. Having diversified and spread throughout the globe, the ancestral stock became extinct and today's five native crows and ravens are the progeny of birds that returned to their homeland about 15 million years ago.

The long throat hackles of the Australian Raven distinguish it from other Australian crows. This bird is widespread and its grating, mournful cries can be heard throughout all habitats of eastern and south-western Australia, and even across that harsh landscape that is so often a barrier to bird movements, the Nullarbor Plain.

Sharp-eyed and keenly intelligent, these large glossy black birds (48–52cm / 19–20in) are quick to seize opportunities. They are highly adaptable and able to survive in many different habitats. They feed mostly on the ground, taking a broad diet of seeds, fruit, eggs, insects and other small animals, as well as carrion. They are drawn to farms, orchards, towns and cities by food and waste. Favourite spots include abattoirs, garbage tips, markets and the sides of roads where road-kills lie. Every city has its crows or ravens: Adelaide and Melbourne have Little Ravens; Canberra, Perth and Sydney have Australian Ravens; Brisbane and Darwin have Torresian Crows, and Hobart has its own endemic subspecies of the Forest Raven.

Crows and ravens fly with a slow, almost lazy wingbeat, their outer wing feathers spread out

EYE COLOUR

For the first couple of years of an Australian crow's life, its irises are brown; as it matures they gradually turn white.

like fingers. They are often mobbed by smaller birds that fear their predatory tendencies. They are social birds, commonly forming flocks outside of the breeding season and roosting together. Some are migratory. For example, in summer the small desert-dwelling Little Crows head toward the coast in large nomadic groups, while the Little Ravens of the south-eastern mainland descend in their thousands upon the snow country to feast on Bogong Moths.

Crows are monogamous and raise one brood a year. Breeding pairs build bulky stick nests lined with grass, usually high up in a tree, although ravens sometimes nest on the top of buildings and steel towers. Only the female incubates the eggs but both sexes feed the young.

A NEW PLAYER
The odd House Crow from southern Asia has hopped on board a ship and disembarked in Australia. With a reputation as a crop raider, authorities are keen to prevent its establishment.

NO DUMMIES
These smart birds have learned how to avoid the poisonous shoulder glands of Cane Toads by flipping them over and safely devouring only parts from the stomach region.

A pair of sleek Torresian Crows tuck into a carcass on the flood-plains of the Top End. These crows have a northerly distribution in Australia that extends into New Guinea and the Molluca Islands.

White-winged Chough and Apostlebird

These two rather unusual birds are the only members of a uniquely Australian family. Despite their different appearances, the two species have much in common.

A mature White-winged Chough displaying. Social interactions between these gregarious birds are highly complex. Adults often spread out and waggle their wings and tail when bringing food to nestlings.

PINING FOR FOOD

The White-winged Chough is one of very few bird species that has adapted to transformation of its native habitat into pine plantations.

These are ground dwellers of eastern and south-eastern Australia's woodlands, mallee and farmlands. They live in family groups; about four to ten in the case of the White-winged Chough and six to 16 in the case of Apostlebirds. Both species fossick through leaf litter and investigate logs, crevices and bark looking for food. They eat invertebrates and plant material, including seeds. Choughs dig deeply into the ground and may take small vertebrates, while Apostlebirds eat a lot of seeds.

The White-winged Chough (37–43cm / 15–17in) looks a little like a currawong, being about the same size and entirely black—except for white panels in the wings that

are usually visible only when it flies. However, the more slender, downward-curved bill and the red eyes of sexually mature birds are distinct. The Apostlebird (29–33cm / 11–13in) is mostly grey with brown wings, a long black tail, dark eyes and a stubby, finch-like bill.

There's something touching and comical about choughs and Apostlebirds. They are highly companionable, keeping in touch with one another through constant vocalisations: high-pitched squawks in the case of the Apostlebirds and mournful clear whistles, soft snorts and wheezes in the choughs. They become quite tame around homesteads and fearlessly feed at the sides of roads.

An Apostlebird family gathers at a puddle. For these birds, and for choughs, fresh water is essential since both are mud nesters. In both species, family members collect mud and construct a solid bowl-shaped nest, reinforced with plant material and secured to the horizontal branch of a tree. Apostlebirds and choughs never travel far from water and rain often triggers breeding.

Family arrangements

Both species of birds breed co-operatively with the dominant pair being assisted by helpers to build the nest and raise the chicks. In the dry habitats that choughs occupy pickings are often lean and breeding birds and their helpers have been known to 'kidnap' a juvenile bird from a neighbouring group to enlist its assistance in finding extra food to raise their chicks. Fledgling choughs have brown plumage and orange irises, which gradually turn red over the next four years.

A CHRISTIAN PERSPECTIVE

The Apostlebirds appear to have derived their name from the fact that they occur in twelves. While this is a good average number, group sizes are much more variable.

Birds of Paradise

One of the world's most spellbinding natural sights is the courtship display of a male bird of paradise. New Guinea is home to most of these birds but, of the 40 species, Australia has four living in its rainforests, two of which live nowhere else.

A female Victoria's Riflebird stands framed in the fanned out wings of a performing male. Males select their display perches for high visibility, good acoustics and dramatic light to illuminate their iridescent plumage to its best advantage. The courtship ritual begins with the male throwing back his head and opening his mouth wide to reveal a bright yellow gape. Swaying and calling loudly he fluffs out his shimmering breast plumage and raises his rounded wings, spreading the feathers out in a semi-circle and then folding and unfolding them like a fan before the mesmerised female.

The adult male plumage of the Magnificent, Paradise and Victoria's Riflebirds (23–33cm/10–13in) is glossy black with iridescent green, blue and purple breastplates that shimmer in sunlight. Females are grey, brown or cinnamon with dark streaks or bars on paler underparts. These three deep-bodied birds with their long, down-curved bills and short squared-off tails look utterly different from the short-billed, long-tailed glossy black Trumpet Manucode (28–32cm/11–13in), with its red eyes and fine long iridescent blue neck plumes.

The Manucode and Magnificent Riflebird share the same tropical forests at the tip of Cape York Peninsula and in New Guinea. Victoria's Riflebird is endemic to the rainforests of north-east Queensland, while the Paradise Riflebird is endemic to the rainforest areas from Barrington Tops in New South Wales to the Bunya Mountains in Queensland.

Birds of paradise feed upon rainforest fruits and insects. While the short thick Manucode bill is perfect for plucking fruits from the canopy, riflebirds have the ideal bill for probing into crevices. Their strong feet cling to tree trunks as they investigate bark like large treecreepers do and rifle through the leaf litter in epiphytes.

Male birds devote their time and energy to courtship. After mating, the female departs to build a nest, incubate the eggs and raise the young alone. He will pursue his playboy career, wooing as many females as he can with his acrobatic contortions.

Sunbird and Flowerpecker

Two tiny colourful birds from separate Asian families have developed special ways of feeding and building nests in Australia.

Sunbird

The Yellow-bellied or Olive-backed Sunbird (10–12cm/4–5in) is a gorgeous little bird that inhabits Queensland's tropical coast and islands. Both names describe it well, although the male has an iridescent blue-black 'shield' of feathers on its chin and breast that is especially vibrant during the breeding season.

Like a hummingbird, this bird can hover on the spot as it pokes its long thin downward-curved bill deep into the throats of flowers, extracting nectar through a tube-like tongue. No other Australian bird can achieve such a measure of control while in flight.

Spiders are an essential part of the sunbird's ecology. In the deep, heavily vegetated gullies in which these birds like to feed and nest, spiders are plentiful and provide valuable protein as well as indispensable material for nest building.

A female Yellow-bellied Sunbird feeds her chick at the nest. The female skilfully binds the long dangling nest of bark, twigs and leaves with spider thread, suspending it from an overhanging branch. Sunbirds sometimes nest in tropical gardens. They are members of a family that occurs across Asia and Africa and is renowned for its nest-building skills.

Mistletoebird

The Mistletoebird (10–11cm/4in) is the only member of the flower-pecker family to breed in Australia. Short-billed and stumpy-tailed, it lives in New Guinea and throughout mainland Australia but is absent from Tasmania, as indeed is mistletoe upon which it primarily feeds. Widespread and common, these nomadic birds range across almost all habitats searching for berries, insects and, most particularly, mistletoe fruits.

The Mistletoebird is a major disperser of mistletoe. It wipes its rear on a twig, leaving an undigested gluggy seed attached. Suckers that then sprout from the seed attach it still more firmly. Then enzymes eat into the wood allowing roots to penetrate and a new clump of mistletoe to grow. This ancient association between bird and plant probably evolved in the southern hemisphere.

The female Mistletoebird builds a domed nest of soft plant material heavily woven with spider webs and suspended from a twig hidden in the foliage of trees or bushes.

Although small, the male Mistletoebird is easily recognised by its bright plumage: iridescent blue-black above, with scarlet on the throat, upper breast and undertail and a white abdomen divided by a dull black band. The female is a subdued grey above, pale below with a pink undertail. Mistletoebirds are often detected by their spirited song.

Bowerbirds

Members of this fascinating family live in Australia, New Guinea and nearby islands. Ten of the 20 species live solely in Australia. The name bowerbird comes from the 'bowers' constructed by males. These complex twig or grass structures, decorated with coloured objects and sometimes even painted, act as stages upon which males call and display to entice females.

A pair of Great Bowerbirds. Drawn into the avenue of twigs a curious female watches as the male displays his showy headdress. He has carefully arranged a selection of shells, bones, tinfoil and frosted glass fragments designed to show himself and his bower off in the best possible light.

Bowerbirds (23–38cm/9–15in) are well-built birds with sturdy bills. The adult male plumage of rainforest bowerbirds is often bright and spectacular, as in the black and golden Regent Bowerbird, but females are usually quite inconspicuous, as are immature males. Australian bowerbirds that have adapted to drier conditions, however, are speckled grey to brown birds in both sexes, although males have a patch of pink feathers on the nape that is raised into a fetching crest during courtship.

Most bowerbirds prefer rainforests but the Western, Spotted and Great Bowerbirds have adapted to woodlands, savanna and even semi-arid regions. The Spotted remains close to the watercourses of the

A male Satin Bowerbird undertaking his daily routine of sprucing up his bower. This bird constructs smooth 'U'-shaped avenues of dried twigs set into a platform of other twigs and decorates the surrounding ground with blue objects to complement his own beautiful glossy plumage and the unusual mauve of his eyes.

Murray–Darling river system in the east, while the Western mostly inhabits the gullies and rocky ravines of Central and Western Australia where it feeds on native figs.

Bowerbirds are mostly fruit eaters but they also take small invertebrates, seeds, leaves and flowers, foraging from the canopy to the ground. The Regent Bowerbird takes an abundance of nectar and the Tooth-billed Bowerbird eats mostly leaves in winter.

Bowers may be shaped avenues of vegetation or decorated columns of twigs carefully piled metres high called 'maypoles'. As a rule, the plainer the adult male bird, the more elaborate the bower. Some birds go so far as to chew up charcoal or fruit with saliva and paint the mixture on to their bowers. The surrounding ground is decorated with objects. While flowers, moss, feathers, shells, pebbles and bones are gathered from the bush, man-made objects like pieces of coloured paper and plastic drinking straws, foil and clothes pegs may appear. Sometimes thousands of objects are collected, each species choosing a colour that sets off its plumage and bower to its best advantage.

The Tooth-billed Bowerbird does not build a bower but he clears a 'court' for his performance and meticulously lays freshly plucked leaves upside down upon the ground. Older leaves are continuously replaced. Male

TRASH AND TREASURE

Several bowerbirds seem happy to make their bowers in reasonable proximity to humans. Parks and gardens may host Satin Bowerbirds in the south-east and Great Bowerbirds in the north. Perhaps our untidiness is part of the attraction, our trash being their treasure.

bowerbirds tend their bowers with constant care, always adding, refining and replacing sticks and objects. Young males practice the art of bower-building and performing from an early age.

Competition between males is fierce and a considerable amount of pilfering and even wilful destruction occurs at rivals' bowers. When displaying, bowerbirds whistle, make loud buzzing and hissing sounds and imitate the calls of other birds as well as a variety of everyday sounds. These calls are part of a male's rumbustious performance as he picks up and throws down objects, struts, bows and twirls, opens his mouth to show off a bright gape and jumps up and down.

Most male bower-builders attempt to mate with as many females as possible so females must build their own nests, incubate the eggs and raise the young alone. Only the Spotted and Green Catbirds of the east-coast rainforests, which do not clear or build any kind of display areas, are monogamous. They live as pairs in permanent territories, which they defend with loud rasping cries.

It takes seven years for a male Regent Bowerbird to acquire its brilliant adult plumage. The highest concentration of these birds occurs in the subtropical rainforests of the Border–McPherson Ranges on the Queensland–New South Wales border. Bowers are rarely found as males regularly destroy them and relocate to build another.

A male Golden Bowerbird dwarfed by his enormous 'maypole' construction. The skeleton of the bower is two saplings about a metre (39in) apart crossed by a high horizontal branch. The bowerbird painstakingly builds a tower of small twigs up each sapling to about 3m (10ft) and secures more across the horizontal branch, which becomes his display platform. All year round he tends his bower, decorating it with lichen, fruit and green and white flowers. Golden Bowerbirds live only in the high-altitude rainforests of far north Queensland.

Larks, Pipits, Wagtails and Old World Warblers

Although not part of the ancient Gondwanan assemblage, most of these birds are native to Australia, a few, however, are migrants, vagrants or introduced species. All these birds sing extensively, males calling heartily from the tops of vegetation during the breeding season and many performing musical aerial displays.

With the exception of the wagtails, these are slender well-camouflaged brown birds, usually plain or streaked above and paler below, and with males and females similar. They are either ground dwellers of open country that run rather than hop on strong legs and feet or furtive inhabitants of grasslands or reed beds that make short, low dashes for cover.

Larks, Pipits and Wagtails

Streaked breasts and white edges to tails identify Australia's two larks and one pipit. The larks' head feathers are raised during territorial or courtship displays, or while singing. These are especially pronounced in the Eurasian Skylark (17–19cm/7in) whose song has enraptured so many poets.

Introduced in the early 1800s, this bird is established in Tasmania and the south-east mainland. It has the remarkable habit of rising up vertically from the ground on fluttering wings, twittering loudly with a high-pitched continuous song, until it disappears up into the sky but the song remains.

The smaller, more rufous native Horsfield's Bushlark (12–15cm/5–6in) performs a similar vanishing act. It has a tinkling song, full of mimicry. It is quite widespread, although absent from Tasmania, the south-west and the western deserts.

Larks have stout bills and feed mostly on seeds, while the slender bill of Richard's Pipit (17–18cm/7in) indicates an insectivorous diet. It has a paler belly and eyebrows, a longer tail and it runs quickly for several steps, then stops and bobs its tail up and down.

Similar in shape are the wagtails and they, too, bob their tails up and down. Wagtails are colourful and, depending on the species, feature large patches of black, white, grey and/or yellow, especially bright during the breeding season. Females are duller. Most wagtails are either over-wintering visitors to the north, or vagrants.

A male Golden-headed Cisticola (9–11cm/4in) acquires its golden head in the breeding season. This tiny bird's claim to fame is its nest: a soft construction of fluffy seed heads and fine grass bound with cobwebs and reinforced with fresh leaves literally stitched together with spiders' silk. The equally tiny Zitting Cisticola has a more northerly and limited distribution. Cisticolas inhabit a variety of freshwater and saltwater habitats and are in the same family as songlarks and reed-warblers.

FLOCK OR NOT

Pipits gather in winter flocks, but songlarks are solitary birds. Horsfield's Bushlarks may travel alone or in flocks.

The streaked breast of Richard's Pipit is typical of the larks and pipits. An early coloniser of cleared land, this cosmopolitan bird is found throughout Australia, among grasslands and the hind dunes of beaches. Typically this courting male has chosen a top spot from which to advertise his presence with his loud trilling song.

Old World Warblers

Australian members of this huge cosmopolitan family include the Brown Songlark, a desert nomad that follows the rains, and the paler, rufous-rumped Rufous Songlark (16–19cm/6–7in) that migrates south to breed. Despite their names, neither are strictly larks, although both are fine songsters. They are common birds, most noticeable when males sing lustily from bush-tops or engaged in display flights. The male Brown Songlark (25cm/10in) is larger than the female (18cm/7in) and dark brown in breeding plumage.

Spinifexbirds (14–16cm/6in) live in arid spinifex grasslands from the Barrow Island in the west across the Tropic of Capricorn to Mt Isa in Queensland. Sometimes seen singing from clumps, their long, broad tail, drooped or cocked, may distinguish them.

Reed-warblers and grassbirds feed and nest in reed beds. The Oriental Reed-warbler (19–20cm/7–8in) is a rare summer visitor but the Clamorous Reed-warbler (16–17cm/6–7in) is a common and widespread bird of wetlands.

The lively, insectivorous Tawny and Little Grassbirds are often distinguished in the reed beds by their dark-streaked backs. The larger Tawny (17–19cm/7in), found in near-coastal areas of eastern and northern Australia, has a long tail, rufous plumage and a pale underside, while the Little (14cm/6in), which has penetrated inland and is present in Tasmania and the south-west, has dark streaks on its underside and crown.

A pair of Clamorous Reed-warblers tend their brood in the relative safety of the reed beds. Such places are fairly inaccessible to predators and provide good cover, making them attractive to a number of warblers, grassbirds and cisticolas. The Clamorous Reed-warbler feeds on aquatic insects, supplemented by shrimps and creatures picked from the water's edge. During the spring breeding season males cling to long stalks singing with gusto but throughout much of the year they remain hidden quietly in the reed beds and in winter they migrate northwards.

Finches

There are over 20 species of finches in Australia. The sparrows, Common Greenfinches and Goldfinches were introduced during the 1860s and 1870s in a fit of nostalgia for birds of the old country, whereas the native grassfinches and mannikins arrived several millions of years ago, probably from Asia. Most finches are associated with grasses and it is believed that they originated in Africa as its forests gave way to grasslands about six million years ago.

A flock of Zebra Finches. These birds are widespread throughout the drier parts of the mainland. Their black and white 'zebra' stripes are on their rumps and tails. The adult males and females can be distinguished by their red bills; those of the juveniles are still dark.

The small dumpy bodies, relatively short tails and thick, strong bills of finches are distinctive. While introduced finches are 12–16cm (5–6in) long, most native finches are smaller, about 10–13cm (4–5in) long. Brightly coloured and boldly marked, often with bars and dots, the native finches frequently feature rich red, orange and yellow plumage, legs and bills.

Food, Drink and Travel

Seeds are the staple diet of all finches and the bill is designed for picking them from stalks and plucking them from the ground. Some insects are also taken, especially during the breeding season when termites swarm, and insects are fed to the young. Many grassfinches are able to suck water, rather than tip it down their throats as is usual in

Like all finches, House Sparrows traditionally feed on grasses but since their introduction to Australia they have expanded their menu to plant buds, fruit and human scraps. Populations are now well established across eastern Australia but Western Australian authorities are trying to prevent invasion into their state.

other songbirds. As finches must drink every day and are vulnerable to predators patrolling waterholes, being able to quench their thirst quickly is a useful ability.

Finches travel around in large flocks, keeping together even when fast changes of direction are required. Being small, they find safety in numbers and keep in touch with one another through soft pipping calls, both in the air and while feeding. They may also roost together and some are communal nesters.

Most finches live in open woodlands and grasslands, often on agricultural and pastoral land, but Painted and Zebra Finches are found throughout much of the semi-arid inland, although never far from water. Also in Australia's north-eastern rainforest, mangroves and forest clearings there are the highly sought-after Blue-faced Parrot-finches. These are likely to be a remnant population of a larger one that once lived in the north-east and the highlands of New Guinea.

Domestic Life

Finches are monogamous and may pair for life. Males initiate courtship by bobbing up and down, sometimes proffering a long grass stalk in their bill. The female responds with tail quivering and pairs bow to one another and wipe their bills against their perches. Males make solitary expeditions to find suitable nesting sites that are frequently rejected on inspection by the female. Given their need for

Star Finches are found across northern Australia. While still quite common in the west, their distribution is shrinking from the south and east. These birds nest among the rank grasses of the floodplains and around waterholes in the drier southern part of their range. Grazing cattle are trampling the waterhole grasses, reducing the finch's habitat but sugarcane is providing new nesting habitat, with irrigation channels and surrounding grasses for water and food.

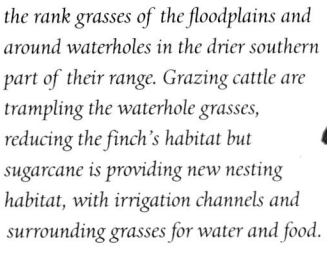

SAVING A COLOURFUL LITTLE NATIVE

The vibrantly coloured Gouldian Finch (11–13cm/4–5in) is the focus of a major conservation effort. A highly desirable specimen for aviary collectors, it has a lilac breast, bright yellow belly, bright-green back with a blue and black tail. Curiously, its head may be black, red or, more rarely, yellow. Found only in the woodlands of northern Australia, it feeds on native spear grass and, during the breeding season, almost exclusively upon insects. It nests in small but deep tree hollows. Trapping, pastoralism, limited nesting sites, lack of suitable grasses and inappropriate fire regimes are all likely pressures on these birds but another welfare factor is their frequent infestation with air-sac mites which, in severe cases, prevent birds travelling to find food. With only 2500 birds left in the wild, the World Wide Fund for Nature is working with several agencies on a raft of strategies to save this gorgeous little bird.

Those seeking to find Painted Finches may need to venture into the rocky spinifex-clad gorges of the north-western inland and Central Australia. Not surprisingly, they breed after rain and nest in spinifex.

In the coastal north and north-east, clouds of Chestnut-breasted Mannikins haunt mangroves and swamps. They are sometimes seen darting into a bush that becomes suddenly alive with vibrant twittering. These highly social birds not only travel in large flocks; they also nest in colonies.

protection, predator-proof nests are often in thick thorny bushes, over water or near the nests of stinging wasps or even raptors.

Once a site is selected, the male gathers most of the nesting material while the female builds the nest, which may be a grassy dome, open cup or simply a bare cavity in a hollow branch. The pair share incubation and the feeding of the young. The tongue and lining of the mouth in some species of nestlings are marked with luminous spots. In the gloom of the darkened nest, these assist the parents to guide the food directly into the chicks' gaping mouths.

Firetails

The earliest finch ancestors in Australia are thought to be the little firetails, so-named for their scarlet rumps. Most common in the east and south-east is the Red-browed Finch that sometimes comes into public gardens and suburban open spaces. The Red-eared Firetail is endemic to the south-west and the Beautiful Firetail is the only native finch in Tasmania. Although common in the gullies there, it is much less so in the southern-most parts of the mainland. The ground-feeding Diamond Firetails live in the grasslands of south-eastern Australia's open woodlands. The Painted and Star Finches are also firetails.

Mannikins

Australia's three native mannikins have a generally northern distribution. These finches usually have pale grey or bluish grey bills set off by smart black, chestnut, grey, ochre and / or olive green plumage. The Yellow-rumped Mannikins often flock with the widespread Chestnut-breasted Mannikins, with which they also roost and hybridise. With an apparently nomadic lifestyle, Pictorella Mannikins are patchily distributed across the drier northern woodlands. They appear to be declining and ecologists are trying to find out why.

White-eyes

The white-eyes are delightful little birds that colonised Australia from Asia a few million years ago. Despite their small size, they are excellent fliers and adept island hoppers. Of the six Australian species, four are confined to islands.

A small flock of Silvereyes stop off briefly for a drink. Like most small birds, the white-eyes are forever wary of predators. They forage in flocks, darting from one bush to another, methodically scouring shrubs, canopy leaves and undergrowth and keeping in touch with one another with constant contact calls. Outside of the breeding season, they gather in large and sometimes mixed-species foraging groups.

Typically white-eyes (9.5–12cm / 4–5in) are little, plump yellowish green birds with pale undersides and a white ring of feathers around their eyes. Despite having a typical bill for insect feeding, they also have a brush-tipped tongue (like the honeyeaters) with which they often take nectar.

Most people in the south, down the east coast and in Tasmania are familiar with Silvereyes. These lively little birds have adapted to a wide range of bushland, including gardens where there is sufficient cover. Yellow White-eyes are tropical mangrove inhabitants of northern Australia.

Of the island white-eyes, the Slender-billed and White-chested White-eyes are confined to Norfolk Island, while the Christmas Island White-eye inhabits Christmas Island and the Cocos-Keeling Islands. The Pale White-eyes are widespread and common on some islands off the north-eastern tip of Cape York Peninsula.

Despite their small size, white-eyes are fast fliers and can cover long distances. Silvereyes undertake northward migrations up the east coast and Tasmania's Silvereyes migrate across the Bass Strait to the mainland to avoid the rigours of winter, returning in spring to nest. Tasmanian birds can be recognised by their orange flanks. In the 1850s some intrepid birds flew all the way across the Tasman Sea to New Zealand where they are now well established.

Silvereyes are known to have a very broad diet. While they feed on nectar and regularly glean insects from leaves in trees and shrubs, especially psyllids, they are also partial to figs, grapes and other fruits much to the chagrin of orchardists and viticulturists.

DISCREET NESTS

Silvereyes build deeply-slung, cup-shaped nests of grass, bound with cobwebs. These are well hidden in a dense bush or lower tree canopy.

Swallows, Martins and Swifts

Generally dark above and pale below, these small, fast-flying birds dart through the sky snapping up flying insects. Three swallows and two martins are common in Australia. Most are summer visitors from the north but at least some Welcome Swallows and Tree Martins remain in the south throughout winter.

The pretty little Welcome Swallow (15cm/6in) makes hundreds of trips from muddy puddles or the edges of fresh water with beakfuls of mud to sculpt a cup-shaped nest under a cliff overhang, bridge, culvert or eave. It is then lined with soft grass, feathers or hair. Swallows and martins are renowned for their painstaking construction of mud nests.

Swallows and Martins

Best known in Australia is the Welcome Swallow (14–15cm/6in), a little bird that often gathers with its companions on telegraph wires or on low branches over water. It is easily identified by its orange throat and forehead, although it is not dissimilar to the Barn Swallow, a northern hemisphere bird that is increasingly becoming a common summer visitor to Queensland's east coast and north-western Australia. Distinguishing it from our familiar Welcome Swallow is a blue-black breastband that divides its russet throat from its white belly.

White-backed Swallows flutter in small twittering flocks throughout the open inland areas of southern Australia. These birds nest in colonies; they excavate nesting chambers at the end of 60cm (24in)-long tunnels, usually in sandy banks. On freezing nights in the non-breeding season several birds may huddle together there in a state of torpor.

While swallows' tails are deeply forked, those of martins are shorter and only slightly forked. Australia's two martins have white rumps. The widespread dusky-headed Tree Martins (12cm/5in) are often out in force on summer evenings before roosting in trees. They nest in the spouts of trees or suitable holes, often sealing the entrance with mud to make a tight fit.

Swifts

With their torpedo-shaped glossy dark bodies and long sickle-shaped wings, few birds are better adapted for life on the wing than swifts but, once grounded, they must hobble on small, weak legs to the nearest vertical surface and clamber up to a height from which they can launch themselves back into the air. Swifts fly at much higher altitudes than swallows or martins, and at phenomenal speeds. Some are said even to mate and sleep on the wing, only touching land to nest and care for young. Even then it is usually vertical land as they build their nests on the sides of cliffs and caves. The nests are made of airborne flotsam bound with spittle.

Australia's only resident swift is the diminutive Australian Swiftlet (11cm/4in) of north-eastern Queensland. It breeds through the Wet in large colonies in caves, navigating in the pitch dark by echolocation and hawking above rainforest canopies and tropical beaches.

Australia's most common visitors, the White-throated Needletail and the Fork-tailed Swift, arrive from Asia in about October. The Fork-tailed Swifts disperse across all the continent's habitats. The larger White-throated Needletail is a common sight throughout eastern Australia; while only 20cm (8in) long, it has a wingspan of 50cm (20in). The forked tails and white throats referred to in the names of these respective species may help to distinguish them.

Rare vagrant swifts to Australia include the House Swift (15cm/6in), whose square tail when fanned distinguishes it from the very similar Forked-tailed Swift. Another vagrant, the tiny Glossy Swiftlet (10cm/4in), which can be distinguished by its pale underside, sometimes flies over the rainforest-clad ranges of north-eastern Queensland.

UNLIKELY RELATIVES

Having four forward-facing toes, swifts are classified as non-passerines and are more closely related to frogmouths and night-jars than to swallows and martins. Indeed they share the same insect-hawking habit of catching prey in their wide open mouths.

The little russet-headed Fairy Martin (11cm/4in) migrates up and down the continent but not across the Bass Strait to Tasmania. It builds architecturally impressive flask-shaped nests of mud under bridges, in caves and other sheltered places, large colonies creating a metropolis of communal living.

Thrushes

Thrushes are medium-sized birds that find food on or in the ground. Members of this family are scattered across Europe, Africa, Asia and North America. In Australia two species have been introduced from England and two are native.

A yellow bill and eye-ring sets off the glossy black plumage of this male Common Blackbird (25cm/10in). Like Australia's native thrushes, it feeds on invertebrates, especially earthworms, and fruit. Introduced to Melbourne from England in the 1850s and later into Adelaide and Tasmania, this bird has spread across the south-east and has successfully penetrated into bush-land, although it still prefers to nest in gardens. It now competes with native birds, orchardists and grape growers.

The plain-coloured Common Blackbird is an introduced thrush that is well established across south-eastern Australia. Adult males are jet black and females a plain brown. Three other Australian thrushes are brown birds with pale breasts and bellies, distinctly marked with dark spots, streaks or scallops.

The smallest is the introduced Song Thrush (23cm/9in), which has not spread far from its original release site of Melbourne. It remains a visible presence in parks and suburban gardens but it has been unable to penetrate into the bush. The dark streaks on its pale underside are a diagnostic feature of this species.

Australia's two native thrushes have dark scalloping on their undersides and fossick through the leaf litter of wet forest floors. They are rather quiet, secretive birds. Although they do not sing as beautifully as the Song Thrush, their clear notes are still distinctly thrush-like. The Bassian Thrush (26–27cm/10–12in) inhabits Tasmania, islands of the Bass Strait, the south-eastern ranges of the mainland and Queensland's Atherton Tableland. In drier South Australia, where land clearing threatens its survival, it is restricted to gullies.

The Russet-tailed Thrush (25–27cm/10–11in) is endemic to Australia. It occurs along the Great Dividing Range from the mid-east coast to north-east Queensland. Only the more subtle markings on its back, its more rufous plumage and shorter tail distinguish it visually from the Bassian Thrush, although their songs differ. Where the distribution of these two species overlaps, the two do not interbreed.

This Bassian Thrush is gathering rootlets to bind its nest of bark strips and leaves. To avoid predators it nests in trees or hollow stumps well off the ground but its discreet plumage blends well into the forest floor as it forages. Should it sense danger, it moves quickly away, then remains stock still to avoid detection.

Starlings and Mynas

Three very different-looking members of this cosmopolitan family are found in Australia. The introduced Common Starling and Common Myna have proved so adaptable that they are considered pests. The Metallic Starling is a native of tropical Australia.

Starlings and mynas are medium-sized flocking birds with strong legs and dark plumage that gleams with an iridescent sheen during the breeding season. Highly gregarious and vocal, they eat invertebrates, seeds, fruit and sometimes leftover human food.

The Common Starling (21cm/8in) is the most widespread bird in the world. It was introduced into Melbourne to control crop pests in 1850. Able to raise seven offspring in a brood and up to three broods in a year, it rapidly spread across Victoria and into neighbouring states.

Also introduced into Melbourne for similar purposes was the Common Myna (24cm/9in) in 1862. It was released elsewhere, too, including north Queensland where cane farmers hoped it would destroy sugar cane pests. Much to everyone's horror, it soon became clear that both birds not only devoured insects but seeds and fruit as well.

While Common Starlings are accomplished fliers that flock around the mudflats, stubble fields and orchards of south-eastern Australia and beyond, the Common Myna prefers to walk or hop around human food outlets. Both birds are naturally assertive and have invaded the nesting holes of native birds, thereby seriously impairing the local bird's ability to breed.

In August each year Metallic Starlings (22–24cm/9in) arrive from islands to Australia's north and New Guinea. They settle in the tropical rainforests of north-east Queensland, sometimes spilling over into parks and gardens. Highly gregarious and noisy, they feed in large flocks on rainforest fruits and insects and nest in large, dense colonies of hundreds of birds.

Metallic Starlings stare out from their apartment-style nests built high in the crowns of rainforest trees. Made from woody vine tendrils and lined with soft material, the bulky nests hang like vertical hammocks from branches, often clustered so close together it is hard to discern individual constructions.

The villainous-looking Common Myna has become Australia's public avian enemy number one because it commandeers nesting tree holes from native birds. Myna traps are being trialled for the eradication of these birds.

PUTTING ON A SHOW

The Common Starling may appear black but in the breeding season its plumage acquires a spangled green and purple iridescence and its dark bill turns yellow.

REPTILES

Australia is a land of lizards and snakes. Indeed, there are as many reptiles on this continent as there are resident and visiting birds. The country hosts the world's ten most venomous snakes and its second largest lizard. It is a prime destination for nesting sea turtles and has the greatest diversity of skinks in the world.

About 840 species or 12 per cent of the world's reptiles live in Australia and almost 90 per cent of these are found nowhere else on Earth. The continent is home to crocodiles, geckos, dragons, goannas, hundreds of species of skinks, freshwater and marine turtles and some impressive and infamous snakes.

A few Australian reptiles can withstand the rigours of a southern winter and there are many rainforest reptiles but, given that these 'cold-blooded' animals depend on external heat for an active life, it is no coincidence that they are most abundant in the centre and north of the country. Here, the vast tracts of hot, dry and mostly flat land provide a wealth of suitable places in which lizards, snakes and dragons can thrive. With no major geographical barriers, such as mountain ranges or permanent river systems, to impede their progress, there is plenty of room for populations to proliferate and expand.

Two habitats within these expanses are especially conducive to reptiles: termite mounds and spinifex. In the outback termite mounds are abundant, poking out of the landscape as irregular monsoon-washed cones of chewed soil, termite saliva and faeces. These strange towers provide shelter and accommodation for many reptiles, and for other desert animals, too. Much of the inland is sparsely vegetated, especially with spinifex. Some species form dense spiny hummocks which, with age, spread out 2 or 3m (6½ or 10ft) from their centre. With an armour of spiny foliage enclosing a humid interior these clumps offer an ideal reptile habitat which is shared with other animals that shelter, forage and nest among these grasses.

Reptiles evolved from amphibians, animals bound to water for the development of their eggs. The reptiles' great evolutionary breakthrough was the modification of their eggs so that they could withstand dry environments. While many reptiles lay eggs, many others are able to give birth to live young like most mammals do.

Reptiles came to be in Australia via various routes. The freshwater side-necked turtles are thought to have an ancient Gondwanan origin, as evidenced by their restriction to Australia, New Guinea and South America. Two families, the Flap-footed Lizards and the Pig-nosed Turtle, are confined to Australia and New Guinea and may have evolved locally. Pythons probably originated here, too, and have since spread beyond our shores to Asia and Africa. Some reptiles are more recent arrivals; tree snakes, freshwater snakes and their relatives probably migrated from Asia on land bridges during ice ages. Whatever their origins, once here the reptiles radiated out into the continent and diversified.

PREVIOUS PAGE *North-western Red-faced Turtles. These short-necked turtles are restricted to the rivers of the north-west, from the Fitzroy in Western Australia to the Daly River in the Northern Territory.* RIGHT *A pair of courting Spotted Tree Monitors.*

Crocodiles

The body plan of crocodiles has barely changed in over 200 million years. They were on Earth before the dinosaurs and they survived the mass extinction event that occurred 65 million years ago which led to the demise of the dinosaurs. Today there are 23 species of crocodile; two of them live in tropical Australia.

LIFESPAN

It is estimated that Saltwater Crocodiles can live for up to 100 years.

While the Saltwater or Estuarine Crocodile is known from as far east as Sri Lanka, the Australian Freshwater Crocodile is endemic to northern Australia. 'Salties' are the largest reptiles in the world. Males reach 7m (23ft) long and can weigh over a tonne. Females are usually about half this size. Salties inhabit a broad range of habitats: inland freshwater

waterholes and creeks, tidal rivers, floodplains, estuaries and mangrove swamps, and they may be found on coastal beaches, coral reefs and inshore and offshore islands and cays. Male 'freshies' rarely exceed 3m (10ft). They venture further inland, up rivers and into tributaries and floodwaters.

These magnificent predators house their best weaponry in their heads. Their senses are acute, with nostrils, eyes and ears all appearing above the surface when at rest, and sensory pits around the mouth able to detect the slightest ripple. The heavily ossified skull protects the brain during combat. The immense and powerful jaws can crush a pig's skull, and the conical teeth are designed to grasp and hold rather than cut and chew. A crocodile clamps large prey in its jaws and rolls with it around and around, pulling it into deep water and thrashing it until it ceases to struggle. The prey may drown but the crocodile has a valve in the back of its throat that closes, preventing water being swallowed.

Australian crocodiles hunt mostly at night. Small Salties eat crabs and prawns and move on to bigger prey as they grow. Most commonly they target prey close to the water's edge. Dropping quietly beneath the surface they swim towards it until they are within range. Just the eyes and nostrils break the surface. In a split second the crocodile lunges forward, its open jaws snapping shut on the victim. Prey swimming on the surface is also taken and the scent of a carcass may lure a Saltie a 100m (330ft) or more from the water.

Freshies eat mostly fish, shrimps and crayfish but spiders, insects, frogs, lizards, snakes, turtles, birds, rats and bats are all on the menu. They may stalk

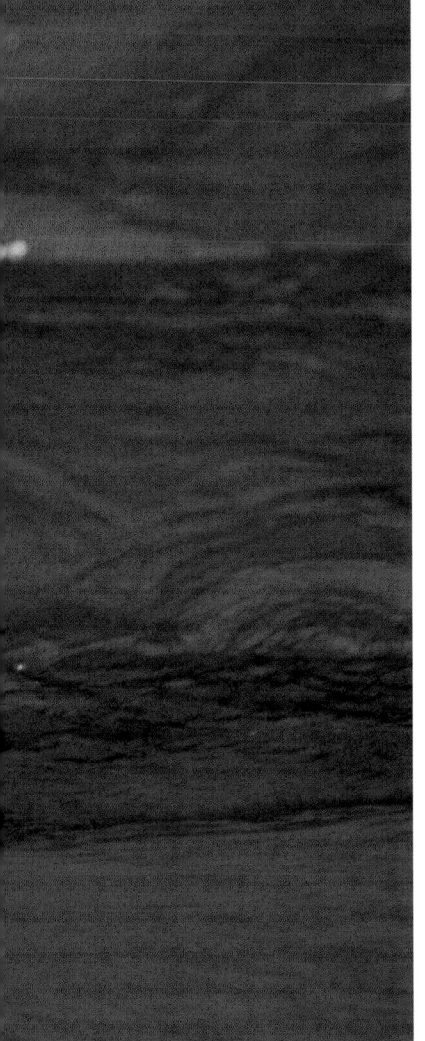

> TAKE CARE!
>
> Salties do occasionally kill people (although we have killed many more of them, than they of us). Be cautious in Saltwater Crocodile country. Do not swim, bathe or camp near the water. Keep your distance from visible animals and don't clean fish at the river's edge. A safe way to see them is on a guided river cruise. These are run in Kakadu National Park in the Northern Territory and along the Daintree River in Queensland. Freshies are generally not dangerous but don't provoke them. They, too, have sharp teeth! Geiki Gorge in Western Australia, Katherine Gorge in the Northern Territory and Lawn Hill Gorge in Queensland are good places to see them.

> STONY CARGO
>
> Crocodiles often have stones in their stomach. These can help in breaking down large chunks of food. They may also act as ballast, giving a crocodile greater stability in water.

A Saltwater Crocodile half walks, half swims through the tidal mud. During the Wet, Salties move up rivers and onto floodplains but during the Dry their movements may become restricted as waterways disappear.

Being reptiles, crocodiles alter their behaviour to keep their body temperature just right. This Freshwater Crocodile is too hot. It has sought shade and its mouth is open to increase evaporative cooling. A dip in deep cool water might also help. In the morning and on a cool day the same animal might be found sunbaking on a river bank to raise its body temperature.

prey, as salties do, or ambush them. Both species cannibalise crocodile hatchlings and salties also prey on Freshies.

Domestic Life

A male crocodile courts a number of females. Displays of submission and snout nuzzling are a prelude to mating which happens in water. Crocodiles lay eggs. Salties breed and nest during the Wet, females laying their eggs into mounds of vegetation. Freshies breed and nest in the Dry. The females lay their eggs in holes on sandy banks. The sex of hatchlings is determined by temperatures in the nests. At 30°C (86°F) the clutch consists mainly of females. A degree higher and both sexes hatch. Between 32°C (90°F) and 33°C (91°F) most hatchlings are male. During incubation, females remain close to their nests. The Saltie defends her nest fiercely. Within two to three months the young crocodiles, still within their eggs, start to call. Their mother responds by excavating the nests as the hatchlings slice their way out of the eggshell with a sharp 'egg tooth' on their snout tip. With great tenderness, mothers may transport their hatchlings in their mouth down to the water where they swim readily.

ALLIGATOR OR CROCODILE?

The main way to tell these two groups apart is to look at the snout. In alligators the broad top jaw closes over many of the teeth of the narrower lower jaw, accommodating them in sockets. The very large fourth tooth from the front in the lower jaw of both groups is partially hidden in alligators.

Freshwater Turtles

Australia has no land-dwelling tortoises but it has 25 species of freshwater turtles. All but one are 'side-necked' turtles, a family endemic to Australia, New Guinea and South America. This distribution suggests a Gondwanan origin.

Freshwater turtles are protected by a top shell (carapace) and bottom shell (plastron) joined at the sides but with openings for their legs, tail and head. Australia's largest freshwater turtle is the Pig-nosed Turtle, with a carapace length of up to 65cm (26in). The carapace of a female Western Swamp Turtle grows only 13.5cm (5in) long and that of the male, just 15cm (6in) long.

The feet of side-necked turtles are webbed and clawed. The head and neck fold under the top edge of their carapace with a sideways horizontal motion. Some side-necked turtles have exceptionally long necks; others are short. Long-necked species are carnivorous and prefer billabongs or the slow, sluggish backwaters of quiet creeks. Here they ambush and stalk yabbies, shrimps, snails and fish. Most short-necked species occupy faster-flowing creeks and rivers but some live in stagnant waters. They forage for a broader diet that includes vegetation.

There is no mistaking the pig-like snout of the big Pig-nosed Turtle (20kg/3st). This curious species is in a family all of its own. Although it was known from New Guinea and Aboriginal cave paintings, it was only discovered in Australia in 1964. Unlike other Australian species, it has flippers and a neck that retracts directly into its shell. It searches at night for snails, crustaceans, fruit, fish and water plants in the muddy bottoms of several slow-flowing river systems and lagoons of the Northern Territory.

When fully extended, the neck of the Eastern Long-necked or Snake-necked Turtle is as long as its 25cm (10in)-long carapace. It is a common species of east Australian rivers and swamps. Hidden in the debris of lakes and river bottoms, it shoots out its long neck to snap at unsuspecting passing fish. It lives about 36 years. Other common species are the Northern Long-necked Turtle in northern Australia and the Oblong Turtle in the south-west.

In turtles, teeth are replaced by horny plates. Short-necked species have powerful jaws that crush, chew and grind; those of long-necks are weaker but their reach is greater. Sometimes turtles use their feet to hold their prey.

Turtles take in oxygen from the air through their mouths but some also extract oxygen from water, which they pump through their anus into a cavity in the terminal region of their gut. This allows them to remain submerged for long periods. Above the water's surface freshwater turtles see well. No living reptiles have external ears like we do but turtles do register noise through a smooth piece of skin known as a tympanum, which is actually an eardrum.

LAYING EGGS ON A FLOODPLAIN

Until only a few years ago it was believed that all turtles had to come to dry land to lay their eggs. However, a zoologist working in the floodplains of the north was studying the Northern Long-necked Turtle and discovered what Aboriginal Australians of the area had known for centuries: this species lays its eggs in shallow water. Turtle eggs are usually porous. In water, they swell and rupture, drowning the embryo, but the eggshells of Northern Long-necked Turtles are lined with a thick membrane that prevents water reaching the embryo.

Although mainly aquatic, turtles do sometimes venture onto land. Females lay their eggs in a hole or burrow that they scoop out above the high-water mark. On hatching weeks or months later the young head straight for the water where they may remain for the rest of their lives.

If habitats dry out, some turtle species may move into bushland and hide in holes or bury themselves in the ground. Others dig themselves down into the mud of disappearing waterholes to wait out the drought. In these circumstances, turtles are said to aestivate, that is they become inactive and their metabolisms slow right down so their bodies tick over on their minimum life-force until the rains come.

> ## BUSH TUCKER
> Long-necked turtles are considered a delicacy by northern Aborigines. They are harvested by the women who feel around with their feet and toes in the mud for the turtles. The animals are cooked on fires in their shells.

The Western Swamp Turtle

The Western Swamp Turtle is Australia's smallest freshwater turtle and its most critically endangered reptile. Once thought to be extinct, it was re-discovered in 1953 in a swamp in the outer suburbs of Perth. Known only from a 3–5km (2–3mile) strip of the Swan River's coastal plain, this little turtle became the focus of a well-coordinated conservation effort. In 1962 much of its habitat was bought to create two nature reserves. Perth Zoo embarked upon a captive-breeding program. From only 30 known individuals they have now raised hundreds and returned many back into the reserves.

Western Swamp Turtles catch aquatic invertebrates and tadpoles when the swamps are full of water during winter and spring. As summer approaches and the swamps dry, they move out into the higher bushland. Here they aestivate in holes or under leaf litter through the summer, until these ephemeral swamps fill with rain once again in the late autumn.

The Western Swamp Turtle remains at risk of extinction after making it through the past 15–20 million years. Clay that underlies the swamps where these turtles live continues to be excavated for brick-making, and Foxes and Cats are a constant threat. The small reserves set aside for the conservation of this species, where local volunteers, conservation agencies and govern-ments are doing all they can, are the only hope left of saving them from extinction.

Sea Turtles

Australia has some of the world's most suitable and protected sandy beaches for the breeding of sea turtles. Six of the world's seven species nest here and one, the Flatback Turtle, nests nowhere else.

Under cover of darkness, a female Loggerhead Turtle lays her eggs in the sand of a deserted beach on the offshore island of Dirk Hartog in Shark Bay, Western Australia.

Turtles are defined by their shell, a protective armour that comes at the price of flexibility. The top shell, the carapace, is joined to the lower shell, the plastron, at the sides and the turtle's backbone and ribs are fused to its carapace. In all but the Leatherback Turtle, the shell is composed of fused bony shields and the carapace is covered by more bony plates. The carapace of an adult Flatback Turtle is further covered by thin fleshy skin.

Sea turtles are measured by the length of their carapaces. They range in size from the giant 2m (79in) long, 600kg (94st) Leatherback Turtle to the 70cm (28in)-long Pacific Ridley Turtle. Their head is non-retractable and their legs have become flippers; the longer front ones paddle, while the shorter back ones steer.

Turtle Tucker

In sea turtles, teeth are replaced by a horny beak that combines with powerful jaws to crush food or shear off vegetation. Each species has a slightly different diet. Loggerhead Turtles eat sea stars (starfish) and sea cucumbers but their exceptionally powerful beak can also crack open shellfish, even giant clams. Flatbacks eat mostly sea cucumbers, soft corals and jellyfish. Green Turtles are vegetarians, except when they are young. They have green body fat, reflecting their diet of seagrasses and algae. The

Leatherback is a jellyfish specialist but it also takes fish, squid, sea stars and sea urchins. The Hawksbill Turtle is fond of sponges but also eats soft corals, molluscs and seaweed.

Long-distance Ocean Swimmers

Sea turtles are born on land but spend their entire lives at sea except for mature females who come back onto land to lay their eggs. They undertake long-distance migrations between feeding grounds and nesting beaches. While most sea turtles prefer warm tropical waters, the Leatherback Turtle swims north of the Arctic Circle and south of New Zealand in waters as cold as 7°C (45°F). It travels further than any other species. It feeds around Australia's coast but breeds throughout the world. The Solomon Islands and islands of the Malayan Archipelago provide some of their favourite egg-laying beaches.

Turtles come to the surface to breathe air through their lungs. Since their rib cages are embedded into their shells, they cannot expand them as we do, so they use the movements of their limbs and muscles to help draw air into their lungs.

Sea turtles swim strongly, with Loggerheads covering 70km (44mile) a day during breeding migrations. They are also proficient divers. Being reptiles, turtles have slow metabolic systems. While diving, they can minimise their heartbeat and pump blood only to essential organs to reduce oxygen use. Some species have exceptionally high levels of oxygen-carrying red blood cells. Leatherbacks can dive to a depth of 1000m (3200ft) and Green Turtles can remain underwater for up to five hours.

A Brief Life on Land

Mating takes place at sea just off nesting beaches. Hawksbills may breed at only

A female Flatback Turtle (90cm/35in, 80kg/12½st) returns to the ocean exhausted by her night's digging and egg laying. Flatbacks were named for their flattish shells, up-turned at the edges. This species only breeds on Australia's tropical beaches and, while it may feed in Indonesian or New Guinean waters, it rarely wanders beyond the Australian continental shelf.

A SPECIAL TURTLE

The Leatherback Turtle is unique and is therefore placed in a family of its own. Its carapace is made of hard rubbery leather in which numerous polygonal bony plates are embedded.

A Green Turtle (2m/79in, 185kg/29st) pokes its head up to breathe. This species is commonly seen in the shallows of Great Barrier Reef islands. Not all turtle flesh is palatable but that of the Green Turtle is considered delicious and it is the basis of turtle soup. For this reason, Green Turtles have suffered the most from hunting.

WHERE TO SEE SEA TURTLES

Each year, between mid-November and early February at Mon Repos, 14km (9mile) east of Bundaberg in Queensland, you can watch female Loggerheads coming up the beach at night to nest. You may also see Flatbacks and Green Turtles.

three years of age but Loggerheads are not sexually mature for 20 years or more and Green Turtles may take still longer. Several weeks after mating, a solitary female hauls herself ashore at high tide to lay her eggs. Remarkably most turtles come ashore to lay their eggs on exactly the same tropical sandy beach on which they were born decades before. How they navigate the oceans so skilfully we do not know. Very likely their cues are the Earth's magnetic field, visual landmarks, ocean currents and the smell, taste and temperature of the seawater.

The female sea turtle drags herself up to the fore-dunes on her front flippers, and then excavates a body pit. With her hind flippers she then digs a deeper, narrower egg chamber into which she finally deposits

Three Flatback hatchlings go for their lives, literally, as they race towards the sea. There are numerous land and sea predators that relish crunchy baby turtles.

50 to 200 eggs. Round and white, they are soft shelled and covered in mucus. Having covered the nesting hole with sand, using her hind flippers and compacting it with her body, she trundles back down to the sea. Nesting usually happens during the warmer months but in northern Australia, when temperatures are hotter, turtles nest in the cooler months. A female may return to the same or another nearby beach up to nine times to repeat the process in a single season. So great is the effort, she may not nest again for another two or three years.

The buried eggs remain moist and warm. If they are not dug up by goannas, Dingoes, Pigs or Foxes, they may hatch six to ten weeks later. As with crocodiles, temperature determines the sex, cooler temperatures producing more males. Hatchlings open their shells with sharp 'egg teeth' at the end of their snout. They then swim up through the

sand to the surface. Under the cover of darkness they scramble towards the sea. Whether it is light reflected on the sea's surface or a magnetic force that orientates them towards the ocean we still do not know.

The young of most species are hardly ever seen and it is thought that most young turtles ride the ocean currents between floating masses of vegetation as cover for the first few years of their lives. Very few turtles make it to adulthood—probably only about one per cent of hatchlings—but if they survive the early years, they can live a long time. Exactly how long is still unknown but 80 years is a conservative estimate for the Green Turtle.

A female Hawksbill Turtle (85cm/33in). This species is distinguished by its hawk-like beak and the beautiful black and golden overlapping scales of its shell. Needless to say, this carapace is highly sought-after as 'tortoiseshell'.

Trials and Tribulations

All the world's sea turtles are threatened. Adults and eggs are eaten by many people. Shells are sold to tourists. Eggs are spruiked as aphrodisacs. At sea individuals are sometimes rammed by boats or damaged by propellers. Thousands drown every year in trawl nets and fishing lines, although in Australia turtle-excluder devices are proving effective. Plastic bags floating in the oceans are often mistaken for jellyfish resulting in the deaths of Leatherbacks. Beach development and human shoreline activities threaten breeding areas and hatchlings become disorientated by artificial lights.

In Australia the conservation laws pertaining to sea turtles are strict, so there is some hope for the Flatbacks that are confined to Australian waters. Awareness is growing but the battle to save the world's sea turtles is strewn with obstacles. The general public can play an important role in sea turtle conservation by obeying guidelines on nesting beaches, not driving vehicles on beaches, keeping boat speeds to a minimum in turtle-feeding areas, not discarding rubbish and not buying turtle products while overseas.

A freshly hatched Loggerhead Turtle floats briefly on the water's surface before diving and heading out to sea in a furious paddlethon that may last many hours.

Geckos

Geckos are a family of nocturnal lizards that favour the warmer parts of the world. There are over 1000 species worldwide, of which 111 are known, to date, from Australia. There is a greater diversity of species in the tropical north and arid centre than in the south of the country. Both Tasmania and the snow country of the mainland are devoid of geckos as it is too cold.

The Prickly Gecko, sometimes known as Bynoe's Gecko (5.5cm/2in SVL), is one of Australia's most common species. It occurs throughout most of Australia, often foraging around rocks and fallen tree trunks. Its skin is rough to the touch and, although patterning varies, the brown background is a constant.

SNOUT–VENT LENGTH

SVL means 'snout to vent length'. Because geckos often lose their tails, herpetologists (reptile specialists) measure their length from snout to vent (SVL). Measurements given here comply with this convention.

Most Australian geckos are endemic to the continent. They have evolved from two sub-families: one a cosmopolitan group with many species across the world; the other an entirely Australian, New Zealand and New Caledonian group. The former has undoubtedly undergone a significant diversification since arriving in Australia as many species are found nowhere else. Members of the latter are derived from stock that has lived in this part of the world for a very long time. Among these are the magnificent leaf-tailed geckos whose ancestors are believed to have lived in the rainforests of Gondwana 60 million years ago.

Geckos are generally small. Australia's largest is the Ring-tailed Gecko (16cm/6in SVL) that lives among boulders on Cape York Peninsula. Smallest is the Clawless Gecko (3.5cm/1⅜in SVL), a shy ground dweller that haunts spinifex, rocks and leaf litter in arid and semi-arid Australia. Most geckos have delicate bodies with soft skin that looks velvety although in some species it can be quite rough and bumpy. Unlike skinks and snakes, geckos have no shiny overlapping scales. In fact their bellies are sometimes so smooth and translucent that the internal organs and even forming eggs show through.

Each of a gecko's four legs bears five digits. Those inhabiting areas with rough surfaces have claws for climbing but many geckos need to climb smooth vertical, or even overhead, surfaces like cave walls and ceilings. They do this by using ridged pads on the undersides of their feet. These expand to give a larger surface area over which they can grip. The pads are covered in microscopic adhesive hairs that can catch on the slightest irregularity on the smoothest of surfaces.

The Beautiful Gecko (6cm/2in SVL) hunts on the ground among the coastal and inland dry woodlands and shrublands of central Western Australia.

Geckos may hunt on the ground, among rocks, in caves or on trees. They are lively and agile chasers and ambushers, often flicking their tail from side to side before pouncing. They have sharp teeth and powerful, wide jaws. They bite their prey and beat it against a hard surface with a sideways action of the head before swallowing it whole. Some small geckos supplement their largely insectivorous diet with nectar and fruit juices. A few are termite specialists. Large geckos may extend their invertebrate diet to small frogs and lizards.

Huge eyes and excellent vision are adaptations to a nocturnal existence but it is quite surprising that geckos have no eyelids and cannot blink. Instead, a protective transparent scale stretches over the eye and is sloughed off

DOMESTIC LIFE

There is still much to learn about the life history of geckos. Australian geckos lay eggs, typically two in a clutch but sometimes only one. These may be hard-shelled and deposited under bark or in crevices, or leathery (as in most lizards) and laid in burrows that are carefully filled in. Some geckos deposit their eggs in communal burrows, possibly where individual suitable sites are scarce. Nobody knows how long geckos live in the wild but they are suspected of being relatively long-lived for their size.

The Soft Spiny-tailed Gecko (7.5cm/3in SVL) (left) is a common night prowler of Perth's suburbs. It also occurs on dunes, in shrublands and woodlands from Shark Bay to the Great Australian Bight, excluding the south-west corner. It is one of several related geckos that may squirt a sticky musty fluid from a gland in its tail in a bid to defend itself from perceived danger.

with every moult. The eyes are kept moist by these impermeable scales and their external surface is regularly wiped clean by the gecko's fleshy tongue.

Geckos, like other reptiles, depend upon external heat to energise them and, although many live in hot climates, warm daytime shelters promote their ability to actively forage by night. Some geckos shelter under rocks and logs or in crevices, leaf litter or burrows (borrowed or self-made). Peeling rock slabs and peeling bark are other useful hideouts. Small geckos often snuggle down in disused spider holes and the Pilbara Dtella (5cm/2in SVL) tucks itself into the crevices and tunnels of termite mounds.

Gecko Tails

Geckos' tails are highly variable. Some have short fat tails in which they are able to store food during times of scarcity. These tails sometimes end in a little knob and so they are known as knob-tailed geckos. Most knob-tails live in arid areas where conditions are unpredictable, with times of plenty alternating with times when food is scarce, so a built-in food storage facility is a valuable attribute. Just a few of Australia's cave- and tree-dwelling geckos have long cylindrical tails capable of wrapping around objects to provide increased stability and greater reach. The undersides of some tails have ridged pads similar to those on the undersides of their feet, giving the animal additional support when clinging to smooth surfaces.

The leaf-tail geckos are spectacular and relatively large species that live in sub-tropical and tropical forests. They are masters of disguise as they cling upside down, stock still, on tree trunks or vertical rock surfaces. Their flattened heads, bodies and tails blend in perfectly with mottled lichen-covered surfaces. The tail, shaped like a leaf, may be mistaken for just that. Their broad, triangular head initially looks quite similar to their tail, leading to confusion for any potential predator as to which end to attack.

Many lizards, including geckos, shed their tails if threatened by predators in order to save their lives. The body-less tail continues to wriggle after the gecko has fled, leaving a bemused predator in its wake. Tails re-grow but they are never as long, nor as perfect, as the

A number of exquisitely camouflaged geckos live in Australia's rainforests, among them this Southern Leaf-tailed Gecko (13cm/5in SVL). Their markings blend into the lichen-covered trees, making them hard for predators to find and prey to notice. Leaf-tails usually hunt head downwards on the trunks of trees, where they wait and watch for unsuspecting prey to pass. They then lunge with lightning speed, clamping their jaws firmly around their quarry.

The price of beauty. All reptiles, including this Barking Gecko (10cm/4in SVL), must moult in order to grow.

NATURAL CLONING

A curious phenomenon found among reptiles is the ability of a few species to completely dispense with males. Females simply clone themselves. An example is the Mourning Gecko (5cm/2in SVL) which probably arrived in cargo from Hawaii. This species has recently established itself among the beaches and buildings of tropical Queensland and has recently colonised Heron Island and Darwin. Females lay unfertilised eggs with a full complement of their own genes and they all hatch as females. If quick colonisation is the name of the game, this is the way to go but, since the whole population is genetically identical, it is risky in the long run. A change of conditions or the arrival of a disease for which they are not adapted can wipe out a population in one sweep as there is no scope for adaptation.

A plucky Pale Knob-tailed Gecko (9cm/3½in SVL) stands its ground, opening its mouth to show its bright interior and lashing its tail from side to side. This typical defence strategy relies on bluff. Pale Knob-tailed Geckos hunt among spinifex clumps growing on the ridges of sand dunes in desert country. With their original tail intact, they are 12cm (5in) long.

original ones. Some geckos use their tails to block the entrances to their shelters; if anything must go, it's their expendable tail.

Companionable Geckos

Geckos are regular inhabitants of buildings and places where artificial light attracts insects. Best-known is the Asian House Gecko (6cm/2in SVL), which arrived in Australia from South-east Asia on cargo ships. From northern ports it has spread inland and down the east coast into northernmost New South Wales. It is a highly vocal gecko, regularly despatching a series of 'chuck, chuck, chuck' calls.

For a nocturnal creature, noise is a useful way to communicate and geckos often utter sounds in defence of their territory or in pursuit of mates. Some chirp, others produce a series of clicks, some scream. Their ears are usually visible as tiny openings behind the eyes.

Geckos and people live a mostly companionable existence. They are harmless animals, wonderful pest controllers and, for many of us, the sound of geckos conjures up images of balmy summer nights.

Legless Lizards

This is a family of lizards that is almost exclusive to Australia, although a couple of species are found in New Guinea. Sometimes referred to as pygopods or flap-footed lizards, there are 38 known species in Australia but possibly more exist. None, so far, have been found in Tasmania.

The Excitable Delma (45cm/18in) forages out from the shelter of logs and rocks into a wide range of habitats. It is widespread across much of northern Australia but prefers the drier ground. Its head markings are usually distinct.

Legless lizards vary in length from 15–85cm (6–33in). Tails may be blunt as in worms or tapered as in snakes. Unfortunately they look like snakes and, as a consequence, often suffer at the hands of humans. They are, in fact, far more closely related to geckos and, although they appear to be legless, they have tiny scaly flaps where their hind legs should be. These are often obvious and responsible for their other name of flap-footed lizards.

Another characteristic shared with geckos is their ability to lose their tails and re-grow new ones. They also sometimes squeak. While many snakes and lizards may hiss by expelling air through their throat, geckos and legless lizards actually have sound-producing organs.

Most legless lizards like dry open country. They are particularly numerous in the coastal and inland heaths of Western Australia and the spinifex country of the arid and semi-arid south and inland. Many of these lizards burrow, among them the rarely seen worm-lizards. Others live at the base of thick vegetation, virtually swimming through it.

The Western Hooded Scaly-foot (57cm/23in), a nocturnal hunter of scorpions. Scaly-foots are the largest and most robust of the legless lizards and have the most conspicuous hind flaps. The five species between them cover most of the mainland. The Southern Scaly-foot, which can grow up to 85cm (33in) and specialises in hunting spiders, is sometimes encountered by day in the dense vegetation of heathlands and woodlands across much of southern Australia.

Legless lizards are mostly insectivores but some species specialise in spiders and scorpions, others in skinks. Some hunt by day, others seek their quarry at night. They shelter beneath leaf litter, in soil, cracks, crevices, termite nests and the vacant holes of spiders. They lay eggs, usually in summer. The norm is two oblong leathery eggs but the large Burton's Legless Lizard is known to sometimes produce three eggs.

These furtive reptiles are not often seen. If they sense danger they tend to wriggle or leap away as fast as possible. Large species and members of the so-called scaly-foots may raise their head and flick out a fleshy tongue, mimicking the behaviour of an aggressive snake, a ploy presumably designed to see off predators. Some species also have head markings that look like those of young Brown Snakes.

Burton's Legless Lizard (30cm/12in) is Australia's most widespread reptile but you will not find it in the cooler parts of southern Australia, the south-west corner or on the Nullarbor Plain. The pointed wedge-shaped snout is its distinguishing feature. This lizard may be yellow, rusty red or grey and with or without stripes or dashes. It hunts by ambush during the day and night, snapping its wide, strong jaws down on the heads or throats of other lizards, suffocating them by cutting off their air supply.

TELLING A LEGLESS LIZARD FROM A SNAKE

One distinction is that snakes have a long narrow, forked tongue while the tongues of legless lizards are round and fleshy. Another is that snakes have no external ear-openings but ear slits are often visible in legless lizards, some way behind their mouth and eyes (although they are not always present). The last clue is on the underside of the reptile. The vent of a reptile is where its body ends and its tail begins. Snakes have relatively short tails but the tails of legless lizards can be up to four times their body length. (Remember, however, that lizards' regrown lost tails are often shorter than their original tails.) So, if you see a snake-like lizard with ear slits, a fleshy tongue and a long tail, you are not looking at a snake but a member of an exclusive Australian family of lizards that is completely harmless.

Skinks

The skinks form a large group of lizards that is well represented in Australia. Of over 1300 species worldwide, 378 are found on the continent. Many species occur nowhere else and more are being discovered every year.

Australian skinks vary in size from 6–60cm (2–24in) long. Many are small and rarely noticed. A rustling on the side of a sunlit bush track often suggests the scurrying departure of a sun-basking skink seeking security in the leaf litter or undergrowth. Like all reptiles, skinks need to warm up before becoming active. A good time to see them is early on a summer's morning at the edge of thick cover where they like to soak up the sun's rays.

Most skinks live on the ground, although some burrow. They may zip about on rocks and the base of tree trunks but only a very few climb far into trees. They are generally active during the day but some, especially in warmer areas, can be seen out and about at dusk and a few, like the Great Desert Skink or Tjakura (36cm/14in), are nocturnal.

Skinks mostly eat invertebrates, which they pursue or ambush, but many have a varied diet which may include berries and flowers. Large ones eat smaller lizards and the big King's Skinks (50cm/20in) living on islands off Western Australia are known to eat seabird eggs. Some of the northern skinks specialise in eating termites, Blue-tongues cherish land snails and water skinks supplement their terrestrial fare with freshwater shrimps and invertebrates.

This Red-legged Skink (15cm/6in) is a member of a large group of so-called striped or comb-eared skinks. These lively day foragers can be identified by their distinct stripes or spots and the 'ear combs': tiny fleshy lobes on their ear openings.

Skinks Here, There and Everywhere

Skinks have diversified and adapted to almost every type of terrestrial habitat in Australia. They are abundant in the inland desert regions; there are also plenty in rainforests, grasslands, tropical woodlands, eucalypt forests and agricultural lands. Some skinks are swamp dwellers that hunt and take refuge among clumps of sedges and other vegetation. There are also a number of water-loving skinks to be found along creek beds where territories are often fiercely defended for the best basking spots and shelters.

In the inner cities several skink species boldly sun themselves on doorsteps and fences. The delicate 10cm (4in)-long Garden Skink commonly fossicks for insects in even the smallest backyards of Melbourne, Brisbane and Sydney. It has five miniature toes and a dark lateral stripe with pale edges along its glossy brown to grey body. In the sunlight the bronze head scales glint and the body shimmers with iridescence. In Perth gardens you are as likely to find the Fence Skink (13cm/5in).

The Unpatterned Robust Slider (16cm/6in) has a long sinuous body, reduced limbs, smooth glossy scales and a cone-shaped snout, all adaptations for a life spent burrowing through loose soil.

There are even skinks above the snowline. The so-called snow skinks are adapted for cool conditions. The Mountain Log Skink (12cm/5in), for example, occurs at altitudes of up to 2000m (6500ft) and is active at temperatures far below what is normal for skinks. Several snow skinks are endemic to Tasmania and one, the Pedra Branca Skink (20cm/8in), lives only on one tiny guano-caked rocky island 25km (16mile) south of Tasmania. Most of these cold-adapted skinks feed on berries and nectar as well as invertebrates and they hibernate through the winter, some sheltering beneath the snow. Females give birth to live young during the warmest months and some can store sperm over winter from matings in autumn. Others limit their litters to just one every two years.

A Diversity of Body Types

Skinks are remarkably diverse. Body shapes may be elongated with tiny legs and toes or bulky with relative stubby tails. Among the heavyweights are the stout blue-tongues and some robust members of the genus *Egernia*. Among more slender groups are some smooth-scaled long skinks that 'swim' through sand. These sand-swimming skinks are common in the deserts of central and western Australia but they are rarely seen. Their long bodies are ideal for wriggling and their shovel-shaped snouts are useful for clearing a path through loose sand.

Most skinks have four limbs with five digits on each limb. Digits are well developed in those that clamber about on rocks or logs but are often lost in burrowers and sand-swimming skinks. In fact entire limbs are absent in some species where these have become more of a liability than an asset.

Most skinks have shiny overlapping scales ideal for slinking through thick vegetation and burrowing through soil, but some of the largest skinks have rough dull scales. The Gidgee and Cunningham's Skinks have prickly scales on their tails, perfect for deterring prospecting predators. Sometimes skinks use their spiny scales to wedge themselves into safe hollows or crevices where poking paws are unable to dislodge them.

Tails may be cylindrical, long and tapering or flattened top to bottom. These will break off in all but the large skinks but they do re-grow, albeit not perfectly. Sometimes the break is not complete. In such instances a second, or even a third, tail may grow from the break point.

A skink's tongue is broad and rounded, not slender and forked as in snakes and goannas. Its eardrums are usually deeply embedded and may be suited more to picking up the vibrations of scurrying insects than to sound. The eyes are protected in several ways. Skinks that live in dry climates, where there is a danger of losing moisture from the surface of their eyes, have developed a fixed lens. Other skinks have movable lower eyelids that are either completely scaly or have built-in transparent 'windows', curved to cover the irises; this permits sight even when the eyelids are closed.

> **SUBTERRANEAN CONVENIENCE**
>
> When not hunting, skinks need to find shelter. They rest and hide in crevices, cracks, hollow logs and holes, sometimes communally. The Great Desert Skinks retire with their extended family by day to subterranean tunnel complexes. They either adopt an existing one (perhaps a Mulgara's) or excavate their own at the base of vegetation. These complexes can have up to 10 entrances and even an external communal toilet.

An adult Cunningham's Skink (40cm/16in) basks with its offspring close to their rock-crevice shelter. This species belongs to a group that give birth to live young. Research on King's Skinks, a close relative of Cunningham's, has revealed that young may live under the protection of their parents for their first year or even longer.

Life History

Some skinks lay eggs while others give birth to live young. Egg clutches consist of two or more pea-sized eggs in white, leathery shells. Sometimes females of the same species lay their eggs in communal nests. Usually within a few weeks the hatchlings, which may be only 2.5cm (1in) long, are born. They are independent immediately and able

This Black Rock Skink (20cm/8in) has found the perfect fit in which to shelter. It even has a north-facing sun-trap for early morning basking.

to forage for themselves. Bearing live young is common among some of Australia's larger skinks. While the rare and endangered Adelaide Pygmy Blue-tongue (16cm/6in) bears only one to four young, the Northern Blue-tongue (60cm/24in) may produce 25 in a litter.

Some small Australian skinks may live only a year or two, having produced several clutches. Others mature more slowly and live longer. The large, slow-maturing Shingleback is estimated to live for 20 years or more.

Skinks have many enemies including larger skinks than themselves, snakes, goannas and birds. Most run for their lives but heavy-bodied skinks like blue-tongues sometimes stand up to their opponents by puffing themselves up to look big and fierce, hissing menacingly and displaying their alarming blue tongues.

This Western Blue-tongue (left) knows how to unnerve a predator. Blue-tongues stand their ground, puff themselves up and extend their alarming blue tongue; a scare tactic that must be effective or they would have abandoned it long ago (although it does not deter Foxes). There are six species of blue-tongues with one in almost every part of the country. Some come into suburban gardens to sun themselves but snail bait and Cats are bad news for these impressive creatures and for other skinks.

The tiny Bright Fire-tail Skink lives (right) among spinifex in the Gibson Desert and other arid areas of north-western and Central Australia. At no more than 9cm (4in) long and with eye-catching colourful hindquarters, this day-hunter is highly visible and so under-standably shy and quick to take cover.

Dragons

Dragons are related to iguanas and the tree-dwelling chameleons. They live in Africa, Asia, Australia and on some Pacific islands. Of the world's 350 species, 70 live in Australia. Many of these are found nowhere else in the world. Unsurprisingly, Australian dragons are particularly abundant in the dry, arid interior and in the drier woodlands and grasslands of the north.

The Eastern Water Dragon (60–70cm / 24–28in) is never far from water. Generally shy, the only indication of its presence may be the sound of a plop as it drops into the creek from its basking log or rock. Its laterally compressed tail propels its through water very effectively. This dragon is found all along the watercourses of the eastern seaboard and sometimes on coastal rocks. You may see one beside a creek even in bushy suburbs. Males in breeding colours display a bright red throat and chest.

Dragons are a flamboyant lot with many species sporting crests, frills, flaps and spikes that can be raised in a display of might. Some are remarkably colourful and able to concentrate or disperse pigment in their skin to alter the intensity of their colouring according to temperature, habitat or breeding cycle. Many males become especially colourful during the breeding season.

These lizards can be quite stout and, in those that must squeeze into rock crevices, sometimes slightly flattened. They have spiny or rough scales. Their heads are big and triangular. Tails are usually long, often longer than their bodies, and sometimes whip-like, but they cannot shed them as do geckos, legless lizards and skinks. Their four limbs are well developed, as are the five digits on each limb.

When dragons are warm, most of them are surprisingly quick and agile, and many of them can sprint on two hind legs. The frantic dash of a little Bicycle Dragon (30cm/12in) as it peddles madly away on its two hind-legs is quite a comical sight.

Hot and Cold Dragons

Dragons love to sunbathe and Australia's desert regions cater well to a reptile's need to energise itself by absorbing external heat. They soak up solar power by positioning their bodies to capture as much warmth as possible from the sun's rays.

When dragons bask in the sun they usually stay close to cover but they are territorial animals and often pick a high point in the landscape from which to view their surroundings. In flat open country, this may simply be the highest rock in the vicinity. Sometimes a fence-post or termite mound provides a good look-out.

Regulating body temperature is a constant preoccupation of lizards. Although they need to warm up each day, sometimes they get too hot. In order to cool down some retreat to burrows, some pant and others lift their entire body clear of the scalding rocks, leaving only their heels' in contact with the surface. When it becomes too cold, as happens during some nights in the desert and during winter in more temperate regions, dragons may hibernate for a time in burrows, beneath logs, in crevices or under rocks.

Some Notable Dragons

Although dragons are most abundant in dry open country, there are also rainforest dragons, aquatic dragons and dragons that live within woodlands and among rocky outcrops in temperate regions. One of the best known in the woodlands of the south-east is the slender Jacky Lizard (30cm/ 12in), a prettily patterned grey and white dragon with a bright yellow lining to its mouth, designed to scare off enemies. Jacky Lizards blend in beautifully with standing or fallen timber, on which they are regularly found. The much larger and more robust Bearded Dragon (55cm/22in) is sometimes encountered in similar country, often sunning itself on a fence-post. There is no mistaking its spiky 'beard'.

The Mountain Heath Dragon (20cm/8in) has the southern-most distribution of any dragon. It lives in the heaths and woodlands of south-east Australia, including north-eastern Tasmania. Despite its name, you will not find it at altitudes greater than 400m (1300ft).

The tail of Gilbert's Dragon (28cm/11in) tapers down to nearly three times its body length. Its elongated features and ability to change colour provide excellent camouflage while perched from a good vantage point. Part arboreal, this agile lizard lives in woodlands and around riverside vegetation across much of northern Australia. On the ground, it can run fast on its two hind legs when in pursuit of prey. Its other common name, the Ta-Ta Lizard, refers to its habit of waving its forelegs as if signaling 'good-bye'.

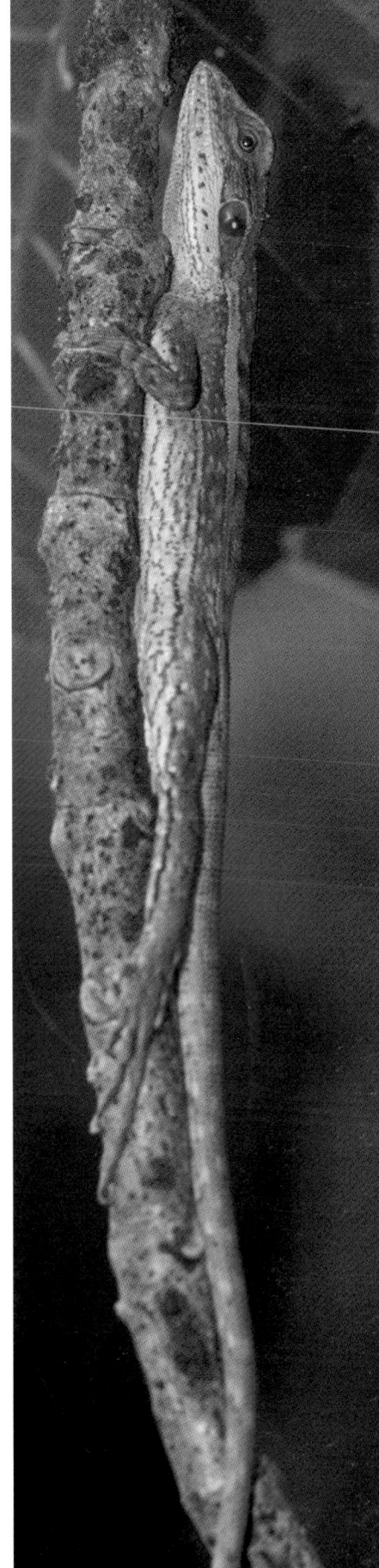

This Central Netted Dragon (20cm/8in) has just caught a huge moth as it was emerging from its pupa. A common species across the arid country of central and western Australia, its colours change to match its habitat. It catches insects and plucks and eats flower petals. At the slightest hint of danger, it nervously dashes into boltholes at the base of shrubs or clumps of grasses. During winter it becomes inactive, blocked up in its burrow.

The smallest Australian dragon is the squat 10cm (4in) Pebble Dragon. This aptly-named, tiny, rusty-red coloured dragon lives among the shiny, angular 'pebbles' of the desolate gibber plains of inland Australia. With a tail shorter than its body, its relatively round, flat shape and gibber-plain colouring, it can barely be distinguished from its surroundings, making it hard to see for even the most sharp-eyed of predators.

Among Australia's largest dragons are the Frilled Lizard, the Eastern Water Dragon and the Central Bearded Dragon. These are all impressive and plucky reptiles, any one of which may reach 60cm (24in) long, but a mature Eastern Water Dragon probably takes the record for length, courtesy of its extensive tapering tail.

Dragon Lifestyle

Dragons are active throughout the day. Most of them are terrestrial but a few live on trees and a few others are aquatic. While some dragons will eat fruits and flowers, the majority are carnivores. Insects are their main source of food. A few species specialise in termites and the diet of the Thorny Devil (15cm/6in) consists exclusively of ants. Aquatic species may take frogs and large dragons will take small mammals, other reptiles and birds. All dragons have sharp teeth and short blunt tongues.

When threatened most species beat a hasty retreat but some of the larger ones stand their ground and put up an intimidating display. The

Bearded Dragon, for example, hisses as it raises the spikes around its throat and opens its mouth to reveal serious teeth. A predator of this nasty contender may conclude that it is not worth the effort. Another ploy is cryptic colouring. Few dragons use this strategy to greater effect than Boyd's Forest Dragon (50cm/20in), an impressive tree-dwelling reptile of Queensland's northern tropical forests. When threatened, it freezes against the trunk of a tree, the spikes running along its neck and back breaking up the outline of its body, which is tinged with green so it appears to melt into the lichen on trees. In this way, although 45cm (18in) long and really quite colourful, it evades detection, even at close range.

Some dragons live in family communities with a single breeding male and several mature females. During the breeding season males are kept busy protecting females and their territory, sometimes sparring with other male competitors. Head bobbing and leg push-ups are common displays of aggression. Many dragons wave their forelimbs at one another. The relevance of this is action is poorly understood. Perhaps it is a sign of submission.

Females lay two to 35 eggs in burrows where the heat of the sun and earth

When threatened the Frilled Lizard opens its 20cm (8in)-diameter 'frill' like an umbrella. As it gapes to display its mouth's bright yellow lining, spokes in the frill, operated by muscles in its jaw, lift from its head. In this intimidating pose it hisses at its enemy. Should its opponent remain unphased, the dragon changes tactic by rising up on its hindlegs and making a bipedal dash for it.

A female Dwarf Bearded Dragon (35cm/14in) is busy excavating a nest into which she will deposit her eggs. Restricted to the sandy dry woodlands and shrublands of the western half of the continent, this species retreats into burrows during the heat of the day.

incubate them. Sometimes more than one clutch is laid in a season. The eggs take three or so months to hatch. Almost immediately the hatchlings are active and hunting. Small species of dragons may live for only one year but other large ones have been recorded living for up to 20 years.

Despite its prickly appearance, the Thorny Devil is totally harmless; its threat display is all bluff. To scare off enemies it tucks its head under its body and presents the large spikes on its neck to the opponent. A Devil's spikes fulfil another important function. These dragons live in arid country where rain is rare and the slightest moisture is valuable. Droplets that fall even from morning dew on the Devil's raised body, trickle between the spikes and are channelled into its mouth.

Goannas

If you have ever watched a large goanna nonchalantly waddling across a forest clearing, its slender forked tongue flicking in and out of its mouth as it searches for food, you might wonder whether you have travelled back in time to the age of the dinosaurs. Of the world's 50-odd species, 26 of these magnificent carnivorous lizards live in Australia, although there are none in Tasmania. A few are found in Africa; the rest in southern Asia and as far east as the Solomon Islands.

Most Australian goannas favour hot climates and many have a propensity for arid and semi-arid landscapes. The majority live in the north but the Lace Monitor (2.1m/7ft) is common in wooded areas outside of Sydney and in parts of Victoria, and the Heath Monitor (1.3m/4ft) is found as far south as Kangaroo Island off South Australia and Recherche Archipelago off Western Australia.

Goannas belong to a family of lizards known as monitors. They have long muscular tails, long necks, loose-fitting, leathery skin and wedge-shaped heads. Their short legs are powerful and their sharp, curved claws formidable. In size and weight Australia's goannas

A Bungarra (a Western Australian subspecies of the 1.4m/55in-long Yellow-spotted Monitor) in a typical alert pose: body prone but head, neck and shoulders raised. For a better view or to intimidate, it may raise its abdomen off the ground and stand on its hindlegs, using its muscular tail for support. This bipedal stance is also adopted among rival males wrestling for supremacy.

The Lace Monitor is an accomplished tree climber with a predilection for the eggs and young of hollow-nesting birds and mammals. It lives throughout wooded areas of eastern Australia. This individual is moulting. The loose scaly skin on its rear and tail will soon slough off.

range from the world's smallest—the 20cm (8in), 17g (⅝ oz) Short-tailed Pygmy Monitor, to the 2.4m (94in), 14kg (31lb) Perentie, the third largest lizard in the world. Perenties are startling enough but only about 30,000 years ago a terrifying 6m (20ft)-long giant goanna called *Megalania* was roaming through the forests and woodlands of eastern Australia.

Goannas are more active than many reptiles. This is due to the dynamics of a highly efficient respiratory and circulatory system but, like all reptiles, they need to warm up to become active. They control their body temperature in several ways. To heat up they invoke the usual reptile strategy of turning the greatest area of their body to the sun's rays. To cool down they seek shade or retire to their burrows. They also flutter their throat pouch to lose heat by evaporation from their mouth and throat.

Predatory Ways

Goannas are predators and scavengers. Most hunt by day but at least a couple of northern goannas are known to hunt after dusk on warm nights. They usually stalk their prey on the ground but they are also good climbers. Smaller species concentrate on invertebrates. Larger ones will eat mammals, birds, reptiles and frogs. Sheathed in their gums are sharp, backwardly curved teeth designed to hold prey rather than to slice through flesh. Goannas have keen eyesight and hearing but, as with snakes, they can detect hidden prey by 'tasting' the air on their forked tongue and transmitting it to an internal sensory organ on the roof of their mouth called a Jacobson's organ. Eggs are a favourite among many goannas. They also eat carrion, which they are able to tear into pieces, and cannibalism is known in several large species.

DON'T TEASE A GOANNA

Despite their threatening appearance, goannas are not venomous and do not intentionally harm people. They do, however, have powerful sharp claws and in some picnic and camping grounds they associate humans with a free feed. Under no circumstances should you feed, chase or tease a goanna. Provoked, frightened or cornered, a large individual may inflate its throat pouch, hiss, swipe its tail from side to side and even lunge with its mouth open.

Hunting in Different Habitats

Goannas are highly adaptable reptiles and they are resourceful hunters in many different types of habitat. While enormous Perenties roam along the dried creek beds and rocky places of western and Central Australia tasting the air for snakes, lizards, birds and mammals, those on Barrow Island, off the north-west coast, snap up baby turtles as they scramble to the sea. The semi-aquatic Mertens' Water Monitor (1.1m/43in) catches fishes, yabbies and snails while swimming and walking underwater along river bottoms. The Spotted Tree Monitor (60cm/24in) of northern Australia hunts in trees and the Heath Monitor (1.3m/51in) finds spiders and small skinks by sweeping aside leaf litter with its snout or digging into the ground with its claws. In the rocky terrain of the Top End and north-western Western Australia the slender Long-tailed Rock Monitor (1m/40in) hunts in the cracks for insects.

Shelters

All goannas have some sort of shelter where they sleep and retreat from danger and hot or cold temperatures. Often these are burrows dug with their sharp claws or 'borrowed' from other animals; Rabbit warrens are popular. Sometimes they are rock crevices, hollow logs, tree holes or even spaces behind lifted bark in the case of some of the

A Sand (or Gould's) Goanna investigates a clump of spinifex. These spiky grasses form impenetrable mounds that provide refuges for many small creatures of Australia's arid inland. A common inhabitant of desert environments, the Sand Goanna varies in size from 1.2–1.6m (47–63in) and is the most widely distributed goanna in Australia.

A prelude to this Pygmy Mulga Monitor's day is its early morning sunbathing routine at the entrance to its tree hollow.

Merten's Water Monitor spends most of its hunting life in the water, its laterally compressed tail providing it with excellent propulsion.

smaller species. While one goanna to a shelter is usual, Heath Monitors, especially breeding pairs, are known to share a burrow.

The Domestic Lives of Goannas

In the breeding season males follow the scent of females. Once found, they must persuade the female to come out of her burrow to mate. If successful, matings may continue over several days. Four to six weeks later the female excavates a deep hole into which she lays her leathery-shelled eggs. Egg sizes vary considerably from 5g (⅛oz) in the Pygmy Mulga Monitor (38cm/15in) to 80g (3oz) in the Perentie. Clutch sizes, too, vary. Five to 12 eggs is usual in many species but up to 35 is known in others.

Some goannas bury their eggs deep in the ground, often in the banks of creek beds, occasionally in communal burrows. They have been known to lay them in the mounds of Brush Turkeys. The Lace Monitor lays hers in a termite mound. The termites obligingly repair the evacuated hole and the eggs are then

KOMODO DRAGON

The largest lizard in the world is the 3m (10ft)-long Komodo Dragon. This monitor lives on two of Indonesia's Lesser Sunda Islands: Komodo and Flores. It has a grizzly reputation for eating people, although this is extremely rare.

cocooned in a delicately temperature-controlled environment until hatching occurs. The time it takes to incubate goanna eggs depends upon their size; it can be anything from two and a half to eight months.

Like crocodiles, hatchling goannas have a sharp little 'egg tooth' at the tip of the snout for slitting open the egg shell. Hatchlings of Heath Monitors have been well studied. They remain in the termite nest for several weeks before excavating their way out, returning frequently to the nest and resting there each night. During their early foraging days they are vulnerable to attack by birds and snakes.

Fights between rival male goannas are common and old goannas are often battle scarred. How long goannas live in the wild is still not known but they are probably long-lived.

A Perentie swallowing a Burrowing Bettong whole. Goannas have a hinged upper jaw that can move independently of the skull, allowing it greater movement, both to open wider and to slide forward for greater grip with its sharp, laterally compressed teeth. Before swallowing, the bettong will have been mortally punctured by the teeth and orientated head-first for easier consumption.

Two Perenties circle one another in a ritualised battle, probably over access to a female or territory. The far one displays his prowess by puffing himself up on all fours and strutting about. If there isn't a back-down, the two may rise up onto their back legs and lock together in combat. Wounds from claws and teeth are not uncommon.

Blind Snakes

Of the world's 150 species of blind snakes, 41 have been described from Australia. These subterranean snakes favour the warmer parts of the world, from south-western Europe across Asia to the western Pacific. None as yet have been discovered in southern Victoria or Tasmania.

The Southern Blind Snake (40cm/16in) is found across southern Australia from the west coast to inland New South Wales and western Victoria. It lives in a variety of habitats from wet eucalypt forests through the dry mallee to saltbush and bluebush shrublands.

This single slender Beaked Blind Snake lives across the northern parts of inland Australia. While over 40cm (16in) long, it is less than half a centimetre in diameter. Its matching black head and tail are intended to puzzle predators.

Blind snakes are harmless. They are sometimes known as worm-snakes because of their superficial resemblance to big worms but they are not slimy and the uniformly scaly pattern of their skin is distinctly snake-like. Australian species vary in length from 10–75cm (4–30in). While some are slender, almost thread-like, others are quite robust. Their smooth, shiny scales and blunt snouts and tails facilitate their passage through loose soil and sand but their bodies are also ideal for slipping into the galleries of termite and ant nests.

They have tiny jaws and few teeth. Some feed almost exclusively on termite eggs, nymphs and adults while others feed on the eggs, larvae and pupae of ants. The glistening smoothness of their skin leaves no projection on which these insects can get a hold to attack the snake.

Blind snakes spend most of their life underground but they do occasionally come to the surface at night, sometimes driven out by flooding. Their minute eyes barely function although they are undoubtedly light-sensitive.

Little is known about the sex lives of blind snakes. We know that several lay eggs and that Australia's only introduced species, the Flowerpot Snake, is entirely made up of females that produce clones. Its common name arose from the mode of transport in which it is believed to have arrived from South-east Asia in the 1960s.

File Snakes

These peculiar-looking aquatic snakes are non-venomous. Of the world's three species, two are found in northern Australia: the Arafura and Little File Snake.

The Arafura File Snake, which also inhabits southern New Guinea, is a large freshwater species with females growing to over 2m (79in) long while males are shorter. It is well known in the Top End, especially to Aboriginal people who eat it. Yet it was not scientifically described until 1980. Its baggy skin is an adaptation to an aquatic lifestyle. When swimming in water it flattens out to form a paddle-like shape. It also has a prehensile tail, handy for gripping submerged roots and branches while tussling with muscular prey such as barramundi.

This Arafura File Snake, lying in open water in broad daylight, runs the risk of being seized by a sea-eagle or Jabiru, despite its beautiful camouflage. The scales on the skin of file snakes are keeled and rough to the touch, like a carpenter's file. These scales are used to grip fish, while the snake constricts its prey to death.

This snake hunts by stealth. It remains quietly tucked into the edges of tropical billabongs by day but at night it slowly stalks through warm shallow water looking for sleeping fish. It probes around the roots of the pandanus palms lining the waterways and lies there in wait for passing fish. It has valves in its nostrils that close underwater and it can remain submerged for long periods. During the Wet, its range expands as the billabongs join up to form broad, flat floodplains. Males often gather around females during the breeding season and late in the Wet season females bear to up to 25 live young.

The Little File Snake grows to about 1.6m (63in) long and is mostly an estuarine species, found often in mangrove swamps and sometimes on coral reefs from the Kimberley to Cape York.

SERPENTINE BUSH TUCKER

In Kakadu Aboriginal women hunt Arafura File Snakes, often at the end of the Dry season when animals are concentrated into the shrinking billabongs. With their toes and fingers they feel around the squelchy mud beneath fallen logs and among the roots of vegetation for the distinctive rough skin. Once located, they pull it up and either throw it on the bank, where it remains too sluggish to move, or snap its neck by putting its head in their mouth and pulling down on its body. The whole animal is roasted on the fire. The eggs of pregnant females are considered a great delicacy.

Pythons

Pythons are relatives of the boas. They are found in Africa, Asia and Australasia. Of the 25 known species, 13 live in Australia, 10 of which are exclusive to the continent. Favouring the tropical north, only the widespread and adaptable Carpet Python lives as far south as northern Victoria and the south-west corner of Western Australia. None inhabit Tasmania.

Along the east coast the black and gold subspecies of the Carpet Python is often known as the Diamond Python due to the diamond-shaped patterns on its body. It is the most commonly seen python in coastal regions of south-eastern New South Wales and north-eastern Victoria. Other subspecies of Carpet Python favour woodlands and wet dense forests but they are also found in desert regions, along the Murray–Darling River Basin, in the north and the south-west. Adults are usually about 2.5m (8ft) long but can grow up to 4m (13ft).

Australia's pythons range in size from the 5m (16ft)-long Scrub or Amethyst Python from northern Queensland to Western Australia's 60cm (24in)-long Pygmy Python. While a Scrub Python can overcome a wallaby, the Pygmy Python hunts geckos in the same termite mounds it inhabits.

Pythons are not poisonous. They are muscular snakes that kill their prey by squeezing its body so tight the lungs are unable to draw breath and the heart can no longer pump blood. Rarely does the pressure crack bones. Most Australian pythons inhabit tropical rainforests and, to a lesser degree, the deserts. They are wily, mostly nocturnal, hunters that lurk around places frequented by potential prey. To help them locate warm-blooded creatures, all but two Australian species are equipped with heat-sensing pits around their mouths.

The usual tactic of pythons is to park themselves strategically, remain stock still and ambush the prey as it passes by. Once within lunging distance they open their mouth, which is lined with back-ward-curving teeth, and strike with lightning speed. The teeth grasp the victim as the python throws two or three coils around the animal's body. When the victim breathes out, the python tightens its grip. This action is repeated until the animal has no space in its lungs to draw breath.

AUSTRALIA'S LONGEST PYTHON

In 1948 a Scrub Python found in Cairns was reported to be a staggering 8.5m (28ft) long.

The python then wraps its expandable jaws around the victim's head and swallows continuously until the whole animal is no more than a bulge in its body.

The Water Python (2.5m/8ft) that relies heavily on Dusky Rats for food also waits in water for animals coming to drink. Several species stake out cave entrances, snatching flying bats from the air as the colony leaves each night to feed. Chook sheds and aviaries are easy targets, drawing some pythons close to homesteads. Womas (2.5m/8ft) are mostly desert pythons that slither into occupied burrows and squash the occupant against the walls. Tantalisingly wagging their tail tip to draw curious prey closer is another cunning Woma strategy.

Come the breeding season male pythons are hot on the scent trail of mature females. A single female may attract a coterie of males that stay curled beside her at night and bask with her by day for several weeks. Chemical cues and touch, rather than eyesight, guide the behaviour of male courtship. Depending on species, mating occurs on the ground or in branches and may last from several minutes to several hours.

A female will mate with a number of males in a season. All pythons lay eggs in well-ventilated nests. Sites may be hollows excavated by the python around the roots of a tree or bush, animal holes, burrows in termite mounds or clumps of vegetation.

It is uncharacteristic for snakes to demonstrate parental care but female pythons often coil their bodies tightly around their clutches until they hatch. They leave them periodically to bask, then return to transfer their body heat to the eggs, thereby helping to incubate them. Some species shiver, their body contractions raising the temperature of their eggs. Mothers may fiercely defend their clutches against predators. During these demanding two or three months they do not eat and may lose considerable body weight. Once the young hatch, they wriggle away to fend for themselves immediately, leaving their mothers to recover their condition.

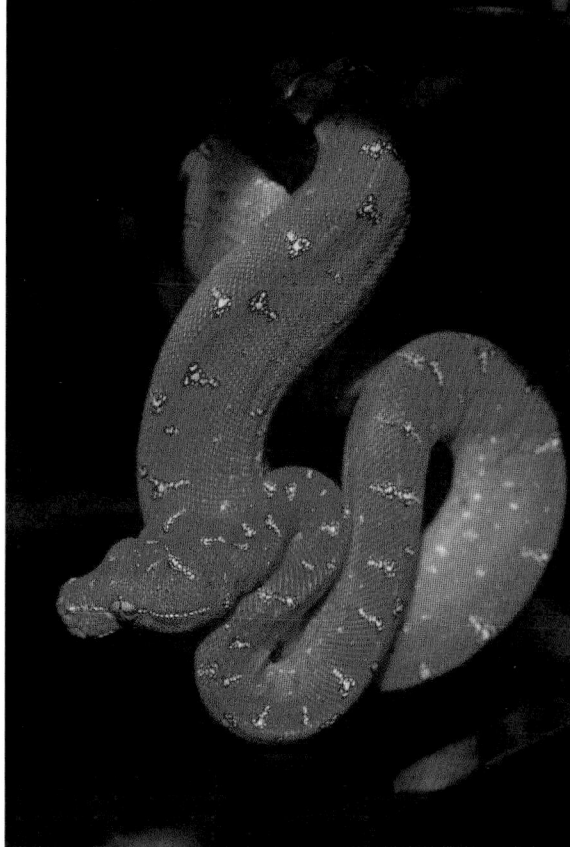

The colouring and patterning of this juvenile Green Python (1.5m/59in) will be lost in adulthood to an equally beautiful and startling emerald green. This coiled posture is typical of the tree-dwelling pythons that live hidden among the branches of rainforest trees on Cape York Peninsula's eastern seaboard. Here they mate, fight, nest and capture birds, mammals and other reptiles.

Tight in the deathly embrace of Stimson's Python (90cm/35in) this mouse has gasped its last and is being swallowed head first and whole. After a large meal pythons can go for many months without food.

Colubrids

There are 1500 species of colubrids worldwide. On most continents they are the dominant family of snakes but only 10 species are known in Australia. It is likely that most of these snakes have arrived from Asia in the relatively recent geological past.

The Common Tree Snake (1.2m/47in) slides through the prickly leaves of a pandanus palm in search of frogs, birds, bats and skinks. This species is sometimes called the Green Tree Snake but, as you see, it's not a particularly accurate description. More descriptive is the name often used by locals in the tropics for this snake: the Golden Tree Snake.

The colubrids are a diverse family of snakes. Australian members are sometimes referred to as harmless but they are nevertheless not to be provoked. Many have no fangs at all through which venom can flow; others have only small ones at the back of the mouth. If cornered or harassed colubrids will attempt to bite but, even if they do, they are unlikely to inflict harm on any human as, to be truly dangerous, the fangs must sit at the front of the mouth. That said, there are some members of this family elsewhere in the world that can kill a human.

Australian colubrids are generally tropical and sub-tropical coastal snakes, with only two species reaching as far south as Sydney. Just over half of them bear live young; the others are egg layers. Although the

Slaty-grey Snake (1.3m/4ft) hunts widely in water, trees, among rocks and along the ground, most are either aquatic or tree dwellers.

Tree Snakes

Most widespread and common are the Brown and Common Tree Snakes. Both are found across northern Australia, from the Kimberley to Cape York, and down the east coast to just south of Sydney in rainforests and eucalypt forests, especially near creeks and rivers. Brown Tree Snakes also inhabit rocky escarpments. In the tropical rainforests of northern Queensland the elegant and fast Northern Tree Snake (1m/39in) pursues a similar lifestyle. These relatively lightweight tree snakes can move out to the ends of slender branches in their search for prey, their stick-thin bodies often indistinguishable from the branches themselves. To help them balance and reach out beyond the surface of the tree, they have prehensile tails with which to grip.

> ### STINKING SNAKES
> Colubrids have few real defences against attackers. They may hiss or strike aggressively, or even bite, but the foul smell many emit when frightened can be an equally effective deterrent. Uncharacteristic of snakes, the Keelback may also drop its tail in an effort to make good its escape.

Aquatic Snakes

The wetlands and mangroves of northern Australia are abundant with prey suitable for snakes and the thicker-set aquatic colubrids are a common feature of these habitats. Macleay's Water Snakes (90cm/35in) pursue fish, tadpoles and frogs in fresh water, while in the sweltering mangroves White-bellied Mangrove Snakes (90cm/35in) twist off the legs and claws of crabs before swallowing them, and the little native Bockdams (60cm/24in) chase estuarine fishes.

The slender Brown Tree Snake is a nocturnal hunter that can grow 2m (79in) long. The bands of colour shown so clearly here explain its other name, the Night Tiger, but sometimes the bands are not so distinct and it is a more reddish brown. By day this snake sleeps in holes, crevices and hollows, sometimes in houses.

The distribution of the Keelback (90cm/35in) is very much like that of the Common Tree Snake but it is a semi-aquatic species that reaches only to the Northern Rivers of northern New South Wales along the east coast. Its name is derived from its keeled scales, which give it a rough-skinned appearance. It hunts frogs and tadpoles around wetlands and even catches fish. It is famous for being able to consume the eggs, tadpoles and newly metamorphosed young of Cane Toads, although possibly not adults, without ill effect. This introduced amphibian is wreaking havoc among Australia's native predators, many of whom die from ingesting the toxins contained in its shoulder glands.

A Roth's Tree Frog meets its end between the jaws of a Brown Tree Snake.

Elapids

Australia has some of the world's most venomous snakes and it is members of this family that gives the country its reputation. Of the 200-odd species in the family, 90 call Australia home, including a few sea snakes and sea kraits swimming in Australian waters. Although many are dangerous snakes, some of the most notorious elapids, such as the coral snakes, cobras and mambas, do not occur here.

Venom

What makes a venomous snake dangerous is the toxicity and quantity of its venom and the placement of the fangs at the front of its mouth. Venom is a product of many active ingredients produced from the secretory glands. So potent is the biochemical mix belonging to some species of this family that just a small quantity of venom can kill large animals, including humans. While some of Australia's most feared snakes have exceedingly toxic venom, certain cobras, mambas and coral snakes are just as deadly since they inject more venom.

Snakes' fangs are simply large hollow or grooved teeth through which venom is channelled from the venom gland in the roof of the

A Monk Snake (45cm/18in) 'tastes' the air for olfactory cues. It is one of the hooded snakes, distinguished by their flattened skulls and dark crowns. Hooded snakes are nocturnal lizard hunters that live in the southern half of the continent. The group is regarded as presenting little threat to humans.

snake's mouth. If they are placed at the back of the mouth, they are unlikely to make contact with human flesh but at the front of the mouth the likelihood is far greater.

Although all species in this family are venomous to some degree or another, only about 25 land-based Australian species are considered dangerous and most of these are secretive, shy and rarely encountered. Many, like the shovel-nosed snakes, are burrowers. Others are very small or nocturnal.

VENOM-LESS ATTACKS

Snakes have fangs and they may bite but that does not necessarily mean that they have injected you with their venom. Some elapid snakes just bite. Others may try to envenomate you but fail.

Australia's Ancestral Elapids

Elapids may lay eggs or bear live young. Australia's ancestral elapid was probably an egg-laying snake that came from Asia when the New Guinean/Australian landmass crashed into Asia about 15 to 25 million years ago. With a warm, wet climate and no insurmountable mountain ranges to cross, these snakes multiplied, diversified and spread across Australia. Today the variety of egg layers is considerable, from small nocturnal crowned snakes that hunt skinks to large, day-active dangerous snakes, such as the widespread brown snakes.

As a general rule, snakes in warm climates lay eggs but where the climate is too cold for the environment to incubate eggs, snakes give birth to live young. About five million years ago, as the continent began to cool with the oncoming ice ages, live-bearing elapids began to appear. The live-bearing elapids diversified rapidly and today many are among our best-known species. They include the death adders, copperheads and tigersnakes.

This little Desert Banded Snake (20cm/8in) 'swims' through sand in pursuit of small skinks and spends hot desert days underground. Note its shovel-like nose and flattened head, well-formed attributes for a burrowing lifestyle. In winter it stays in the top layer of dry sand, but in summer it goes deeper down to where the sand is moist. One of a group of harmless Western Australian burrowers, this species is common on the sand dunes of the Great and Little Sandy deserts. It also occurs in pockets of suitable habitat right to the Pilbara coast.

Bandy Bandies

One of Australia's most innocuous group of elapids is the five species of beautiful Bandy Bandies. These long thin snakes have blunt snouts and tails, and most have broad rings of black and white along their length. They are rarely seen because they spend their lives burrowing through loose sand and leaf litter in pursuit of blind snakes. If threatened, they have the curious habit of arching their bodies and contorting themselves into vertical hoops, presumably in an effort to terrify their tormentor.

Broad-headed Snakes

Most of Australia's elapids are strictly terrestrial but the broad-headed snakes of eastern Australia hunt in trees and over rocks. They do indeed have broad, flattened heads and, although mostly nocturnal, they are potentially dangerous to humans.

One beautiful black species with yellow markings lives only within a 250km (155mile) radius of Sydney. Known simply as the Broad-headed Snake, it inhabits sandstone escarpments, hunting and sheltering in the horizontal crevices between massive slabs of rock. Once common, its habitat has been disappearing to make room for ridge-top developments that afford spectacular views and to bush-rock extractors supplying the home-garden market. It has now become rare and endangered.

Whipsnakes

Whipsnakes are slender, alert daytime hunters with long, tapering tails and large eyes on which they depend to chase and catch fast-moving lizards. Most are under 1m (39in) long and present no great threat to humans, although the two largest species, both from the north, have been known to inflict painful bites.

The 1m (39in)-long Yellow-faced Whipsnake is a widespread species that is sometimes encountered even in the outer suburbs of Sydney. If threatened, it may bite but it usually dashes for cover. Although females lay up to six

The White-lipped Snake (40cm/16in) is adapted to cold temperatures and has been found at 2100m (7000ft), almost at the top of Mt Kusciuzko. It lives in the mountains of Tasmania and on the mainland among heaths, woodlands and bogs, where it chases small skinks by day. While colours vary from grey and olive to reddish brown, the thin white line along its upper lip is distinctive. Although its bite is painful, it is not dangerous.

A Greater Black Whipsnake wraps its expandable jaw around a rat which is being swallowed whole and head-first in the customary serpentine manner. At a maximum length of 1.5m (59in), this is the largest and most dangerous of the generally inoffensive whipsnake group.

An Olive Whipsnake (80cm/32in) slips gracefully into the water. The pale scales around its eye and the dark teardrop are characteristic of whipsnakes. This is a northern species of tropical woodlands. All snakes are good swimmers, even those that live in deserts.

eggs each, communal nests of this species have been discovered containing 500 eggs.

Copperheads

The copperheads of south-eastern Australia are well adapted to cool conditions. They remain active at temperatures below those at which other snakes curl up and hibernate, and they will bask in the winter sun in temperatures for which other snakes will not leave their shelters. This ability is useful since they are able to hunt around swamps and in marshes for frogs and reptiles when prey is sluggish and competitors are absent.

All the copperheads are potentially dangerous snakes. The Lowlands Copperhead (1.4m/55in) lives in Tasmania, on the islands of the Bass Strait, in southern Victoria and just into eastern South Australia, while the Highlands Copperhead (1.1m/43in) occupies the high country of New South Wales and Victoria. The Pygmy Copperhead (85cm/33in) is only found on Kangaroo Island, the nearby Fleurieu Peninsula and in the stringybark forests of the Mt Lofty Ranges behind Adelaide.

Taipans

Australia's two taipans are large and fast. The Inland Taipan (2m/79in) has the most toxic venom of any land-based snake in the world. This species is found in a restricted area of the Channel Country, mostly within the Queensland border, and in a small spot of inland South Australia; both hot and dry locations. The Coastal Taipan (2m/79in) lives in three disjunct areas of monsoonal woodland: in the Kimberley in the north-west, in the Top End of the Northern Territory, and along the Queensland coast and just into New South Wales.

These powerful snakes specialise in hunting mammals. Able to deliver a fast-acting fatal dose in a single strike, they release their prey immediately after to avoid damage in a struggle and simply wait for it to die. So remote is the habitat of the Inland Taipan it has never been

HUNTING IN THE DARK

Nocturnal hunters rely on heat and scent to locate their prey. Scent is located by the forked tongue that flicks in and out of the mouth and slots into an organ in the roof of a snake's mouth (Jacobson's organ). This organ can recognise and distinguish the scent of prey, mates and competitors.

known to kill a human, although it is certainly capable of it. You are more likely to encounter Coastal Taipans; their long fangs, combined with highly toxic venom, have resulted in several human fatalities. However, taipans are shy and fast and, given the opportunity, they will invariably avoid people.

The short but robust Bardick (60cm/24in) is known from three isolated populations along the southern edge of the continent. Inhabiting mallee and heaths, it lurks beneath vegetation where it ambushes frogs, lizards, small mammals and birds, mostly at night.

'Black' Snakes

Curiously only two of these six large, heavy-bodied snakes, with their flattened, broad heads and blunt snouts, are consistently black. They are all dangerous snakes and some are deadly to humans. Two are of particular interest.

With some individuals reaching an alarming 3m (10ft) long, the King Brown, or Mulga Snake as it is known in Western Australia, is Australia's largest venomous snake. It is also the most widespread, although it is absent from Tasmania as well as the southern and south-eastern coastal regions. The arid inland and tropical woodlands are its stronghold but it is common throughout the outback and is sometimes seen dead on roadsides. Other venomous snakes feature prominently on its menu.

The Red-bellied Black-snake (1.8m/71in) is common in south-eastern Australia and parts of coastal Queensland. Usually a hint of the red belly on this shiny black snake is visible. It is active by day and often encountered near water where frogs are a favourite prey. A generally shy species, it is likely to slink away if disturbed but it is advisable to give it a wide berth. Most black snakes lay eggs but in this species the young are born in thin-skinned sacks which burst within minutes of delivery. Up to 18 little snakes may be born in a single clutch.

> ### THE GOLDEN RULE
>
> The golden rule with snakes is to leave them alone. Snakes are not interested in hurting humans so do all you can to avoid them. Almost all snake bites occur when people try to catch or molest them.

Tiger Snakes

These dangerous snakes (90cm–2m/35–79in) live in the cooler parts of southern Australia, including Tasmania and the islands of the Bass Strait. Their colouring and size is highly variable, as is their diet. While some do have 'tiger' stripes, most of those on islands and in South Australia are entirely black; others are grey or brown.

Typical of its group, an Eastern Tiger Snake sunbathes among dead vegetation on the edge of a wetland.

Tiger snakes are most abundant in swamps with lots of frogs but island populations feast on muttonbird chicks and they will take lizards, other birds, rodents, Rabbits and even fishes. Sometimes they coil around their prey in order to hold it. Although potentially dangerous to humans, these are timid snakes that prefer to slip away when disturbed.

Death Adders

Death adders (60–70cm/24–28in) are seriously dangerous snakes. The four species are all easily identified by their distinctive squat shape, flat triangular heads and narrow tail tips. Bands of light and dark across the body vary from shades of grey to brown to burnt orange.

The well-camouflaged death adders curl up in the leaf litter and tantalisingly wriggle their tails to lure the curious closer. Although usually sluggish, they strike with frightening speed. Their fangs are exceptionally long and their venom highly toxic. While most snakes quietly disappear before we spot them, Death Adders are easily stepped upon as they hide in the leaf litter.

Brown Snakes

From a human perspective the seven species of brown snakes (50cm–2.2m / 20–87in) are probably the most dangerous as they are the most likely to be encountered. Despite having relatively small fangs, they are fast nervy snakes that do not hesitate to stand their ground. More slender than either the tiger snakes or black snakes, most species are large but not all are brown. They may be grey, black or banded with paler or spotted undersides.

Only Tasmania and the southern tips of Victoria lack brown snakes. They are generally widespread and, although traditionally they feed on lizards, frogs, native mammals and birds, the Eastern Brown Snake in particular has become common in agricultural land due to a dependable supply of introduced mice and rats.

A pair of adult Death Adders sunbathe side by side, their little tails— invaluable for catching food—rest on their heads. In all states but Tasmania and probably Victoria, these snakes are widespread though uncommon throughout forests, woodlands, grasslands and heaths. Take care in the bush to wear socks and sturdy footwear. It is easy to step on a Death Adder but, thankfully, even then it may not bite; if it does, there is an antivenom.

IDENTIFYING SNAKES BY COLOUR

You cannot rely on colour to identify a snake. Not only are individuals in a single population sometimes coloured differently, hatchlings from a single batch may be too. Snakes may also change colour with the season or with age, as they moult.

The formidable King Brown or Mulga Snake. Adults eat mostly small mammals and other venomous snakes. Although usually active during the day, in the tropics it may come out to hunt on warm balmy evenings after dark.

FROGS

Australia has over 200 native species of frogs, belonging to just four families. The notorious introduced Cane Toad represents a fifth family. All frogs need water to complete their life cycle but Australian frogs, being confined on such a dry continent, have developed a range of ingenious strategies for living independently of permanent water.

Frogs are amphibians; that is backboned creatures that live on land but breed in water. Newts and salamanders are amphibians but none live in Australia and, although only a handful of the world's 23 frog families are found on the continent, 93 per cent of these live nowhere else on Earth. This high level of endemicism suggests that there has been much evolutionary activity in this part of the world over time.

Australia's native frogs are generally small. They range from 14cm (5½in) long in the White-lipped Tree Frog from coastal north-east Queensland to 1.4cm (½in) long in the Javelin Frog, which is so tiny it could sit on your little fingernail. The dependence of frogs upon water harps back to their fishy ancestry. All stages of their life cycle are at risk of drying up. The eggs are prone to shrivelling. Almost all larvae (tadpoles) swim freely and breathe through gills and adult frogs have a permeable skin through which body fluids can be lost. They can also breathe through their skin (as well as their lungs) provided their bodies stay moist.

To avoid drying out, frogs hunt by night and rest through the day, mostly under rocks or logs or in crevices or burrows. Australia is a dry country with relatively little fresh water but frogs do not require vast bodies of water in which to breed, so the temporary swamps, creeks, soaks and ephemeral pools that form after rain serve many Australian species well enough for egg-laying.

The typical life history of a frog begins with females being called to water by males. The male clasps the female around her belly in a mating embrace known as amplexus. As the female spurts out her eggs (spawn) into the water the male covers them with sperm, effectively fertilising them. These gelatinous structures, with limited food supply for the developing embryo within, are then left unprotected from predators or the forces of nature.

Within days the free-living tadpoles hatch. Equipped with tails for swimming, they feed on microscopic plant material in the water and graze algae from rocks. They may also scavenge upon animals that have fallen into the water or simply died. As they grow, they develop legs—first the back ones, and then the front legs. Gradually the tail is absorbed and the lungs replace the gills as the tadpole undergoes its metamorphosis into a carnivorous frog.

Many Australian frogs follow this pattern of development but some fascinating variations on the traditional life cycle have arisen in response to the continent's conditions. Some curious anatomical modifications, too, have evolved in Australian species.

PREVIOUS PAGE *Cannibalism is common among tadpoles, even of the same species. Here three tadpoles of Main's Frog have mounted a vicious assault on a sibling.*
RIGHT *A Motorbike Frog from south-western Australia, so named for its call which sounds like a motorbike revving around a race track.*

Southern Frogs

The southern frogs, sometimes known as ground frogs, are ground-based and confined to the Australian region. Some live beside creeks, some in alpine areas and others in semi-arid or arid coastal or inland areas. With 120 species, they are the country's dominant frog family and have an ancient lineage that dates back to a time when Australia was part of Gondwana.

Burrowing is a smart strategy for frogs living in Australia's hot, dry areas. Here a male Western Banjo Frog (6–7cm/2–3in) emerges from his sodden subterranean burrow. As he surfaces, and in haste to find a mate, he begins calling loudly. The sound he makes has earned him another comonly used name: Pobblebonk Frog.

For these frogs living in a hot, dry land, escaping dehydration is a major concern, not just for adults but for eggs and tadpoles, too. To this end Australian southern frogs have evolved some ingenious ways of maintaining moisture at every stage of their development.

The Desert Burrowers

You might not expect to find frogs in Australia's vast deserts but they are there in surprising numbers. To avoid being shrivelled up by deadly surface temperatures they have become burrowers. These pioneers stock up with water and food before battening down the hatches under-

ground to wait out prolonged dry periods. They rest in a state of suspended animation in a moist subterranean environment, sometimes for years, wrapped in a cocoon of sloughed-off outer skin.

When heavy rains come to the desert, water seeps down and soaks the outer skin of the frog, which then revives and becomes active. Using its forelegs and feet to pull off the cocoon, it pushes it into its mouth—its first meal in a very long time. Restored by this sustenance, it then digs up to the surface to feed, mate and lay eggs in quick succession. Among these frogs, the stages of transformation from egg to adult are sped up; a necessity in a place where suitable conditions persist for only a short time.

As the land dries out, the frogs, old and new, retreat once again underground until the next major downpour. They dig deep: up to 1.2m (47in) down in the case of the widespread Trilling Frog (4–5cm/ 1½–2in). Some descend backwards at an angle but the Turtle (4cm/1½in) and Sandhill Frogs (3cm/1in) dive head first into sand; others, like the Crucifix Frog (4–7cm/1½–3in), rotate their bodies vertically down and backwards in a corkscrew fashion.

The burrowing Sandhill Frog does not even surface to have sex. Having found a partner in late winter or spring, the pair dig in about 1m (39in) down for the summer months. The female lays four to eleven large eggs, which the male fertilises. There is no tadpole stage in this frog, nor do the eggs develop in water. The yolk sustains the growing embryo for two months. Then a miniature frog hatches. Fully formed, it scrambles its way to the surface. During its brief sojourn above ground, this species walks rather than hops.

Not all of Australia's southern frogs burrow. Many small ones, like this Quacking Frog (2–4cm/¾–1½in), hide part of the year beneath logs and stones. Males emerge during winter rains to call from water. The females lay their eggs into shallow, often temporary, pools where tadpoles hatch and metamorphose within a couple of months.

These desert burrowers are usually round, rather blobby-looking creatures with short, stout legs and fleshy stubby fingers and toes. They have tubercles on the undersides of their feet that act as miniature shovels. While some survive underground without eating, the Turtle Frog that feeds on termites deliberately parks itself in the subterranean tunnels of these insects. Another little dry-forest burrower, Nicholls'

A male Lea's Frog (2.5cm/1in) remains with his eggs. Frogs' eggs are gelatinous and have no protective shell to prevent them from drying out so external moisture is essential. Sandwiched between moist leaf litter above the waterline, the tadpoles from these eggs will be washed away by winter rain into the nearby stream.

Toadlet (2cm/¾in), often does the same in rotting logs where it lives unharmed within the galleries of pugnacious bull-ants. Some frogs exude a sticky noxious fluid from their skin, perhaps as a defence against attacking insects or larger predators.

Chamber Nesters and the Soggy Burrowers

While the majority of frogs abandon their eggs freely in bodies of fresh water, many Australian species conceal their eggs in protected sites. Often they lay them at the edges of creeks and soaks, under rocks and logs, among sodden vegetation or leaf litter or in borrowed or constructed burrows.

Many of these frogs rely on seasonal flooding to flush their tadpoles out of the shallow depressions. The Red-crowned Toadlet (2.5cm/1in) that is confined to the sandstone escarpments around Sydney, and Lea's Frog (2cm/¾in), a winter breeder that lives beside creeks and swamps in south-western Australia, behave like this. The Corroboree Frog is another frog that lays its eggs in shallow 'nests'. This spectacular frog (2.5cm/1in) lives only above

NEW SCIENTIFIC BREAKTHROUGH

When developers propose construction of a building on a piece of land, they are often legally required to provide an 'audit' of what plants and animals naturally occur on the proposed site before construction can begin. Until 2002 environmental consultants employed to undertake these audits often had difficulty assessing which frogs occupied the area as daytime surveys only revealed tadpoles, but which tadpoles became which frogs was unknown. The scientific work, at least for the south-east of the country, has now been published and provides an invaluable resource for the scientists.

1000m (3200ft) in the Southern Alps. In its summer-time breeding habitat of damp sphagnum moss, the male constructs a simple nesting chamber into which the female lays 16 to 38 large eggs in a jelly that expands with the surrounding moisture. This jelly protects and confines the tadpoles over-winter beneath the snow until they hatch out of the eggs when the snow melts and spring rain washes them out of the nest into nearby pools.

Other native frogs in moist areas excavate or appropriate burrows that are well formed and deep. Best known in south-eastern Australia is the Giant Burrowing Frog (10cm/4in) that lives in

A male Corroboree Frog (3cm/1¼in) guards several batches of his fertilised eggs, often laid by a number of females. He defends his nesting chamber against other males and calls to more females to come and lay their eggs. The different stages of tadpole development can be seen through the clear swollen jelly. Eggs may hatch but development is arrested in the matrix of jelly until the melted snow and spring rains release them into a free-swimming tadpole stage.

bushland and heaths. Males call during first rains in late summer and early autumn from burrows—often those of yabbies—in creek banks. Females lay foamy egg masses into the burrows. Only when the burrows fill up and flood do the tadpoles hatch. Released into flowing water they will then take three to eleven months to become frogs.

Some Weird Brooding Strategies

Another wonderful adaptation to living in a terrestrial situation is adopted by the Pouched or Hip Pocket Frog (2cm/¾in) that lives under leaf litter or rocks in the rainforests of northern-eastern New South Wales and south-eastern Queensland. The male of this species is equipped with a tiny 'pocket' on each side of its body. To prevent his offspring from drying out, he hunkers down into the gelatinous mass of his fertilised eggs just as they are hatching. The tadpoles then wriggle all over him until they slip into his moisture-lined hip pockets. For the next few weeks he transports them in his ever-expanding brood pouches until they crawl out as miniscule frogs.

Still stranger, and unique in the world of frogs, is the brooding practice of two extremely rare, presumed extinct, gastric-brooding frogs from Queensland. These frogs are entirely aquatic, living in mountain streams. The females swallow their fertilised eggs and brood them in their stomach. All normal gastric activities, including feeding, cease in the adult frogs and the tadpoles feed on their own yolk supply. At six to eight weeks the mother regurgitates her fully formed miniature frogs one by one into the water. The first of these remarkable species was only discovered in 1973, the second in 1984. They have not been seen for 20 years, and both are likely to be gone forever.

The tadpoles of Western Australia's Spotted Burrowing Frogs (6–8cm/2–3in) must wait for winter rains to flush them free of their frothy egg masses that have lain deep in burrows. Although relatively widespread, the wheatbelt of the south-west coincides with the natural distribution of this species so transformation of its habitat and salinity have fragmented and reduced its populations.

Tree Frogs

While many of Australia's 77 species of tree frogs do live in trees, some are ground dwellers and some are even burrowers. The burrowers in this group are rotund but most other tree frogs are generally flatter than members of other frog families. What defines all tree frogs, however, is the details of their bone and muscular structure.

A couple of male Spotted-thighed Frogs (5–7cm/2–3in) attempt to mate with a female. Competition for females during prime mating conditions is often fierce, with male suitors pushing and shoving one another for a piece of the action.

Most tree frogs prefer the high rainfall areas of the north, east and south-west coasts. The greatest diversity lives in Australia's wet tropics—no less than 53 species, 21 of which are endemic to the country's tropical rainforests. In southern Australia tree frogs are less common but three species do occur, even in Tasmania. They are most commonly heard at night around wetlands after summer rain.

Many tree frogs prefer temporary water and will even breed in wheel ruts at times. In northern rainforests there are species that breed in epiphytes high up in the trees. When at rest they usually hide in tree

This Slender Tree Frog (3.5–4.5 / 1½in) never did make a successful transition from water to this twig despite several attempts. This is one of only three tree frogs from the south-west.

hollows, downpipes and rock crevices. People sometimes find them in livestock troughs, irrigation channels, farm dams, water tanks, swimming pools and even outside toilets.

Although frogs are mostly nocturnal, some tree frogs sit out on foliage over water in broad daylight. Since many are bright green or cryptically patterned, they remain well camouflaged among the plants or in the dappled shade of the forest understorey. Among the tree frogs that bask in sunlight are the Green and Golden Bell Frog (6–10cm / 2–4in) and the Dwarf Tree Frog (3cm / 1½in). They may do this to speed up digestion or, being cold-blooded, just to soak up the warmth. Those frogs that remain at large during the day ensure they do not lose water through their skin by hunching up their limbs and tucking them in close to their bodies. This reduces the area of skin exposed to the air, limiting evaporation. Remarkably, some tree frogs can alter the amount of radiant heat they absorb by lightening their colour with a waxy secretion from their skin. They spread this over their body with their front and back feet. Not only does this provide waterproofing, it may also act as a sunscreen, blocking ultraviolet light.

In order to climb slippery vertical surfaces tree-climbing frogs have developed expanded pads on their toes, the undersides of which have

NATURAL PEST CONTROLLERS

Frogs are excellent pest controllers since they pluck virtually any invertebrates from the ground, water or even air, and stuff them into their mouths. Equally, frogs fall prey to snakes, aquatic birds and freshwater turtles, and their tadpoles and eggs are often taken by fishes, birds and invertebrates such as dragonfly larvae. This prey–predator interplay makes frogs important components in many food chains.

The Dainty Tree Frog (4.5cm / 1½in) is found in permanent and temporary swampy areas, including roadside ditches all along the eastern seaboard northwards from Gosford in New South Wales. It breeds in mid-summer after heavy rain, the female laying her eggs into shallow water. The floating clumps of eggs often stick to standing vegetation.

adhesive sucker-like discs. These discs can catch hold of irregularities on surfaces as frogs clamber or leap about, and a frog can move along a smooth vertical surface, such as glass, using the discs as suction pads to grip. For greater stability they may press the underside of their bodies against the smooth surface to increase the area over which the grip is spread.

Many frogs have startlingly bright colours in their groins and armpits. We have yet to understand why this is so. Perhaps they are a means of species recognition or a warning to potential predators, or both.

Burrowing Tree Frogs

One group of tree frogs have penetrated into arid areas and are burrowers that only surface after rain. Best known of these is the Water-holding Frog (7cm/3in) that lives in the deserts of all mainland states but Victoria.

Peron's Tree Frog (5–6cm/2in) is a common species of the coastal south-east. Males usually call from a metre (39in) or so up in a shrub or tree beside water. Females are mostly seen on the ground.

This remarkable desert dweller remains in a state of suspended animation, sometimes for years, cocooned underground in a sloughed-off layer of its outer skin. When heavy rain comes to the desert the moisture penetrates down into its burrow, the cocoon softens and the frog comes to life. Tearing open the cocoon it scrambles to the surface and loses no time in finding the closest waterhole and a mate. Females lay eggs into the ephemeral pools and claypans that form after heavy rain. The whole life cycle, from egg to adult is complete within a month. As drought-like conditions once more take a grip on the land, the adult frogs dig themselves in again for the long 'sleep'.

This frog and its burrowing relatives are often the first and the fastest to breed in the desert. In a ravenous race to grow and stock up on provisions, they will eat other smaller frogs and tadpoles, including their own.

BANANA FROGS

Many tree frogs take an unscheduled journey away from home. Transported in clusters of bananas, often from northern New South Wales or Queensland, they may find themselves among the packing cases of a metropolitan supermarket. Fortunately volunteer frog rescue organisations will take these frogs, quarantine them and dispense them as pets to schools and homes.

Chytrid Fungus

As in other parts of the world, entire species of Australian frogs are disappearing at an alarming rate. The chytrid fungus seems to be the single most devastating cause. This pandemic has been in Australia since 1978 but was not recognised in Australian frogs by scientists until the 1990s. It may have come into the country via diseased axolotls imported for the pet trade, or in rainforest plants, agricultural produce and/or African Clawed Frogs that are used around the world in pregnancy testing. The highly infectious disease, which attacks the frog's skin and nervous system, is fatal in many frogs.

Curiously the frogs that are most affected by this fungus appear to be from pristine upland streams rather from lowland environments where habitats are more affected by human activity. This is especially so for frogs living in the wet tropics. In recent times three species appear to have vanished altogether, while three more have disappeared from their upland streams and now only live below altitudes of 450m (1500ft).

Other factors detrimental to the health of frogs include introduced predators and competitors, pollution, exposure to ultraviolet radiation and human disturbance. Even the chemicals from insect repellents, creams and soaps washed off our bodies into waters inhabited by frogs can be dangerous for them. Global warming, too, is undoubtedly affecting frogs as seasonal water flows alter or diminish.

The Water-holding Frog (4–7cm/1½–2¾in) is a desert burrower that stores water in its extended bladder. Desert Aborigines able to detect their burrows would dig up these frogs and squeeze them to relinquish their water.

Despite being 10.5cm (4in) long and beautifully coloured, the Magnificent Tree Frog from the Kimberley remained undiscovered until the mid 1970s. During the Dry season it shelters in caves, crevices and the crannies of buildings.

Ranids and Microhylids

Unlike the tree and ground frogs, Australia's two other native families, the ranids and microhylids, colonised Australia in the relatively recent geological past, probably via a northern land bridge. They remain confined to northern Australia and most are clustered on Cape York Peninsula.

The long, pointy-nosed Wood Frog (4–8cm/1½–3in) conforms to the appearance of a conventional frog. Another member of this family has the dubious privilege of being the focus of human culinary attention for the famous French dish of frogs' legs.

The 3cm (1in)-long Robust Frog is quite a common microhylid frog in the highland rainforests behind Townsville and Cairns. A ground-based crawler, males call from beneath rocks and fallen timber and females lay their clutches of eggs into leaf litter.

Ranids

Ranid frogs are the dominant family through-out much of the world, with members scattered across Europe, Africa, Asia, Pacific islands and the Americas. In Australia the Wood Frog (8cm/3in) is the family's sole representative in Australia. It lives in the rainforests and woodlands of Cape York Peninsula and in north-eastern Arnhem Land in the Northern Territory.

A highly active ground dweller, it hunts around permanent creeks and lagoons. Having long legs, it leaps impressively and swims well. Males call to females from dense vegetation at the water's edge. The females can lay thousands of eggs in a mass on water and the free-swimming black and gold tadpoles grow up to 6cm (2in) long.

Microhylids

Many of the tiny frogs in this large family live in New Guinea but 18 species inhabit Australia, almost exclusively in the rainforests of north-eastern Queensland. Being so small and in remote locations, they are difficult to find and much research has yet to be done.

Most appear to be ground dwellers that crawl rather than leap. However, disc pads on the toes of some species bear witness to a climbing ability. Certainly some have been found in bushes and in plants on trees. Microhylid tadpoles develop within large eggs that are deposited on the ground in small, sometimes multiple, clutches and, in some cases, they are attended by males. They hatch fully formed as adult frogs.

Cane Toad

The introduction of the Cane Toad into northern Queensland in 1935 is often cited as one of Australia's greatest human-assisted ecological blunders. The 120 individuals released at Gordonvale, near Cairns, failed to eat their proposed target, cane beetles in the sugarcane crops, and turned their attention instead to the country's other native fauna.

At 15cm (6in) long, this native South American toad is bigger and more powerful than any Australian frog. It devours lizards, small snakes, native frogs and small mammals, as well as the more usual invertebrate fare. It competes with native wildlife for food but worse, it kills its predators at every stage of its life cycle. Adults carry toxic venom in a pair of bulging shoulder glands. Dogs, goannas, large snakes, birds, quolls and even fresh-water crocodiles have died from consuming cane toads.

The toads are prolific breeders, intrepid travellers, opportunistic preda-tors and far from shy. Having penetrated the depths of the rainforests, sheltering under logs and stones by day and foraging by night, they spread north to the tip of Cape York, south down the east coast to northern - New South Wales and west into the Northern Territory. Moving at 30–60km (20–40mile) a year they reached Kakadu National Park in 2001, where they wiped out nearly all the Northern Quolls. Darwin is now ringed by thousands of frogs gathered in the surrounding bushland.

As Western Australia plans a raft of measures to prevent toads crossing their state borders, scientists at the Commonwealth Scientific and Industrial Research Organisation (CSIRO) are working on potential genetic and viral solutions, and strategies for toad-busting, and toad-mustering are being instigated in Darwin.

Come the Wet season, Cane Toads (7–25cm/3–10in) breed in night-mare proportions. Males literally fall over each other to mate. Females lay up to 35,000 eggs at a time. Their tadpoles school like fish, sometimes clogging waterways.

FRESHWATER FISHES

Compared with other continents, Australia has little fresh water and as a consequence few freshwater fishes. Only 302 species are presently known. While diversity may be low, the number of endemic species is extremely high.

Many of Australia's freshwater fishes have close evolutionary relationships with fish species living in the oceans, indicating a likely marine origin for most of them. However, the fossil record indicates that at least the Queensland Lungfish and the country's two species of saratogas were part of freshwater environments well before the continent dried out and broke away from the supercontinent of Gondwana.

Australia's most extensive drainage system is the confluence of the Murray and Darling rivers but the greatest diversity of Australian fishes is found in the tropical north. This is because aquatic invertebrates such as dragonfly and damselfly larvae, which form the staple diet of many small fishes, are more plentiful in the tropics.

Freshwater ecosystems in Australia are extremely fragile. For both fishes of the north and south seasonal flooding and rising water temperatures are

a common trigger to breeding, and many fishes migrate up and down rivers to spawn. Our purpose-built barriers, such as weirs and dams, already impede fish runs but should seasonal patterns become disrupted, by global warming for example, breeding patterns are likely to be further affected.

Australians are thirsty for fresh water. The extraction, diversion, drainage and damming of many waterways to provide irrigation for crops depletes resources for freshwater fishes and other aquatic wildlife. The Murray–Darling Basin that drains four states has borne the brunt of the nation's demands for water. With over 90 major storage facilities, it is highly regulated and some serious environmental consequences are now apparent. Lessons have been learned however, and both technology and political will are responding to these, but the race is on to save many species of freshwater fish.

PREVIOUS PAGE *A Giant Gudgeon.*
BELOW *The Western Sooty Grunter (25–45cm/10–18in) is a good sporting and eating fish, endemic to the rivers of northern Australia. It feeds during the day in relatively strong flows on fishes, crustaceans, fallen fruits and other plant material, and is taken, in turn, by barramundi. It breeds as waters rise following monsoonal rains.*

Murray–Darling Basin Fishes

The Darling River rises in the Darling Downs of Queensland and joins the Murray River, which rises in the Snowy Mountains, at Wentworth in New South Wales. This extensive river system drains southern Queensland, New South Wales west of the Great Dividing Range, much of northern Victoria and part of South Australia, eventually emptying into the Southern Ocean.

The native Murray Cod is Australia's largest freshwater fish and a celebrated food fish. It hunts by day and slopes around beneath fallen logs and snags by night. Large individuals have been known to take platypuses and ducks.

Aboriginal fishers used to make a good living by hauling large catches from the Murray–Darling Basin. The fish most highly prized was the magnificent Murray Cod, which lives in the deep waters of upland streams. Individuals are usually 50–70cm (20–28in) long and weigh 10kg (22lb) but specimens of up to 1.8m (71in) and over 100kg (220lb) have been recorded. Despite being common in the Murray River at the time of white settlement, this fish has become exceedingly rare due to overfishing and disturbance of the Murray–Darling ecosystem.

Anglers consider a number of other Murray–Darling species good eating and several have become the focus of commercial fisheries. The very similar-looking Trout Cod (40–80cm/16–31in; 5–16kg/11–35lb) is a less placid fish than the Murray Cod that searches in deep pools and fast water for smaller fishes, crustaceans and insects. Its tendency to fight when trapped in nets results in a build up of lactic acid in its muscles which may account for its tougher texture.

The solitary mottled olive brown Freshwater Catfish (40–90cm/16–35in) spends its whole life foraging along the bottom of a few kilometres of slow-flowing turbid river or lake. It uses its fleshy barbels to feel for

ABORIGINAL STORY

The Murray Cod was known as Ponde by the people of Lake Alexandrina. According to the Aboriginal story, the path Ponde took on his flight from pursuing fisherman marked the winding course of the Murray River.

Freshwater Catfish are common residents of the Murray–Darling. They are members of the eel-tailed catfish family, distinguished by the eel-like confluence of their second dorsal, tail and anal fins around their tapered posterior. Although considered tasty, the sharp spine on the lead edge of their front dorsal and pectoral fins is best avoided.

prey such as prawns, yabbies, worms, snails and smaller fishes. It constructs a nest in the gravel river bed and guards the eggs, aerating them by fanning them with its tail.

Beneath waterfalls, weirs and rapids, Silver Perch (40cm/16in) often gather near the surface. They feed chiefly on worms, molluscs, insects, smaller fishes, frogs and algae. In good flooding years they make long migrations upstream to spawn during spring but their traditional route has been blocked by dams and weirs and population numbers have dropped alarmingly in recent years. They are, however, stocked heavily in impoundments and have been translocated to other rivers.

Billabongs

Billabongs are pools that have become isolated from the winding river and only join up with it during flooding. The gentle flow of Murray–Darling billabongs suits native Flathead Galaxia, Common Carp, gudgeons, Southern Pygmy Perch and Australian Smelt.

Tolerant of high temperatures and salinity levels, the highly prized Golden Perch (40–70cm/16–28in) also inhabits these billabongs. Bronze coloured, with a yellow underside and steel grey tail, dorsal and anal fins, this small-headed but deep-bodied fish with its protruding lower jaw has been known to weigh up to 23 kg (51lb) but a specimen weighing over 5kg (11lb) is a rare catch these days. The Golden Perch stalks yabbies, shrimps, insects, molluscs and small fishes among weeds and other cover.

Unfortunately the invasion by introduced Carp, Tench, Goldfish, Redfin Perch and Mosquitofish into many of these billabongs has led to habitat disturbance, increased competition and predation of young and eggs for most of the native fishes.

WATER DEMAND

Water from the Murray–Darling has been the life-blood of local farmers. In order to meet the demand, however, the Murray has become the most heavily modified river in Australia. Dams and weirs have impeded migrating fishes and altered the seasonal flows and temperatures that trigger breeding. Major efforts are now underway to restore some of the natural flows; this should, in turn, restore at least some of the wild fish populations to the river.

The Golden Perch or Yellowbelly is a highly prized angling fish. A solitary species, it migrates upstream to spawn in creeks that fill after spring and summer flooding. Capable of moving hundreds of kilometres, its breeding activities have been severely curtailed by the human modifications to the Murray–Darling Basin.

Fishes of the North

The rivers of the monsoonal north have the greatest diversity of Australian freshwater fishes, especially those that drain into the Timor Sea and the Gulf of Carpentaria. Many of the fish species of this region are shared with southern New Guinea. There are, however, a suite of endemic species in the Kimberley region of Western Australia. These fishes take refuge during the Dry season in the deep pools that form at bottom of the area's many rugged gorges.

The Barramundi is considered Australia's number one freshwater table fish. Predatory adults lurk in upland rivers around snags, submerged logs and rock ledges, taking fishes, frogs, banana prawns, crayfish and whatever else fits their cavernous mouths. As the Dry season gets underway, they sometimes congregate at run-offs to pick off prey as they are swept back into permanent catchments.

Fishes of the north are adapted to the seasonal advance and retreat of floodwaters. Often marooned in permanent waterholes throughout the Dry, they are swept downriver by early summer torrents or spilled out across vast floodplains as rivers burst their banks. Flashes of sparkling colours from little rainbowfishes (3–14cm/1–6in) are a highly visible feature of northern rivers. So too are the related pretty little blue eyes (2.5–5cm/1–2in) with their highly decorative fins. Australia's freshwater eel-tailed and fork-tailed catfishes (8–45cm/3–18in) are mostly tropical, as are its archerfishes (15–40cm/6–16in), renowned for their breathtaking precision in dislodging insects from overhanging vegetation with a high-velocity spout of water from their mouths.

Barramundi

The Barramundi ranges widely throughout South-east Asia and is not just confined to norther Australia, although it is thought of as a tropical fish. It can grow to 1.8m (71in) long and weigh 60kg (132lb), although 70–80cm (28–31in) is a more common length.

From Shark Bay in Western Australia to the Mary River in south-eastern Queensland all 'barras' start life as males. For the first three or four years they live in

GOURMET FISH WITH ATTITUDE

Barramundis fetch high prices on restaurant menus. These fish are either harvested commercially in northern Australian coastal waters or farmed. They are extremely popular recreational species in fresh and estuarine waters, commanding respect for their spectacular leaps and as challenging fighting fish.

warm, slow-flowing upland rivers. At the onset of sexual maturity they move downstream in rivers swollen by summer storms to spawn in estuaries and coastal waters, returning after each breeding season.

At around 70cm (28 in) long, barras change sex, so small fish are usually male while females continue to grow. The females spawn vast numbers of little eggs which hatch within a day. Larvae sprout fins as they feed on their yolk sac. Juveniles take invertebrates. As they grow they change colour from motley brown to silver. After several months they begin moving upstream, migrating into fresher water and dispersing over inundated floodplains.

Saratogas

Two other large predators in tropical waters are the ancient saratogas. Closely related to one another, the so-called Saratoga or Spotted Barramundi (up to 90cm/35in) is native to the Fitzroy River system of central-eastern Queensland (but has been translocated to several other rivers in the region), while the more widespread but similar-sized Gulf Saratoga is found from the Adelaide River in the Northern Territory to the Olive River at the tip of Cape York Peninsula.

Both are solitary, highly territorial surface predators with good eyesight; they feed on terrestrial insects, small fishes, frogs, shrimps and yabbies. They loaf about beneath waterlilies in billabongs and over-hanging vegetation in slow-flowing rivers waiting for prey to pass.

While saratogas are considered too bony to be good table fish, they are exciting targets for freshwater fly fishers, fighting hard and jumping high. Their laterally compressed, scaly bodies often bare battle scars from fishes that had the temerity to encroach upon their territory.

Banded Rainbowfishes (8cm/3in) live in the small creeks and water-holes of Cape York Peninsula. Rainbowfishes are known only from New Guinea and northern Australia. Given their sparkling jewel-like colours and the ease with which they can be bred in captivity, it is little wonder that they have become popular aquarium fishes.

The Saratoga or Spotted Barramundi (right) and the Gulf Saratoga (bottom), although closely related, live in different river systems of Australia. Towards the end of the Dry season, these fishes begin to breed. Large fertilised eggs are brooded within the mouth of the mother and even after hatching juveniles take refuge there when not feeding. Only at about 4cm (1½in) long do they become independent. They then grow fast, reaching adulthood at about four or five years of age.

Other Coastal River Fishes

Rivers flow to the sea from the eastern and southern slopes of the Great Dividing Range, from the central highlands and upland areas of Tasmania and from the Darling Escarpment and Stirling Ranges in the south-west. The fishes in these river systems generally have restricted distributions and often live nowhere else in the world.

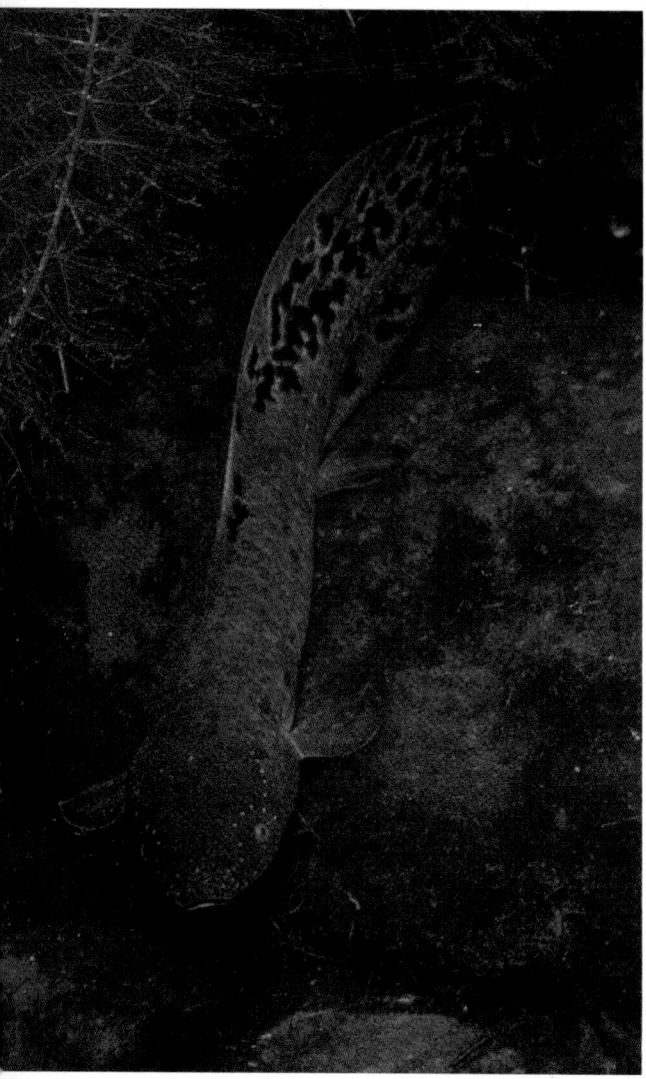

The Queensland Lungfish (up to 1.5m/59in long) is a living fossil. Scaly and plump, it resembles a bulky eel and has the same confluence of dorsal, tail and anal fins. Its pelvic and pectoral fins form fleshy lobes. It is a survivor of an ancient group of fishes that made the remarkable transition from life in water to life on land.

Lungfish

The Mary and Burnett rivers of south-east Queensland host one of the most curious fish in the world: the Queensland Lungfish. Around 150 million years ago, when dinosaurs ruled the Earth, this fish was already swimming in the rivers of the supercontinent Gondwana, of which Australia was a part.

The anatomy of this ancient fish provides clues as to how animals were able to move out of water and onto land. Although it mostly extracts oxygen from water through its gills, its swim bladder is richly supplied with blood by a network of capillaries and effectively functions as a lung. During high activity or when water becomes depleted of oxygen, the Australian Lungfish comes to the surface to gulp air.

The first animals with backbones were fishes that swam in water. They extracted oxygen from water through their gills and could not breathe air, but 370 million years ago a fish-like creature did haul out onto the land and took in air for the first time. This momentous feat led to the colonisation of the land by four-legged animals. The Queensland Lungfish is a distant relative of that lobe-finned, air-breathing fish.

Today, it forages for mussels and snails in slow-flowing rivers or still reservoirs (to which some have been transferred). In spring it spawns among aquatic weed. Tiny tadpole-like juveniles hatch and lay inert on their sides along the bottom for several weeks before commencing to feed on small invertebrates. Lungfishes grow very slowly and the large specimens can be in excess of 50 years old.

Galaxias

The largest family of fishes in the south-eastern rivers and lakes are the small trout-like galaxias. Attributed with an ancient history in Australia, they are especially widespread in Tasmania. Varying in size from 3–27cm (1–11in), species occupy a variety of habitats. Mountain Galaxias can live above the snowline in the Snowy and Victorian Alps. Hatched larvae are frequently washed out of rivers and spend their first five or six months in the sea before valiantly making their way upstream.

The Climbing Galaxia (27cm/11in) is found in coastal streams from Sydney to Adelaide and is widespread in Tasmania. Persistent young adults returning from the sea scale high waterfalls by wriggling up wet boulders.

Migrating Wrigglers

Swarms of freshwater eels and primitive lampreys gather at waterfalls and weirs on southern rivers. In their determination to complete their long-distance migrations and their life cycles, they overcome these impediments by slithering up moist rocks or across land.

Australian lampreys spawn in the headwaters of rivers. Their small blind larvae filter feed in the silt of slow-flowing waters for several years before changing into eel-like adults (35–55cm/14–22in long) with eyes, dorsal fins and sucker-like mouths armed with teeth. They migrate downstream to estuaries or the sea. Two species are parasitic, latching onto fish by their oral disc and feeding on body fluids and muscular tissue. Eventually they swim alone upstream to spawn.

Short-finned Eels live in fresh water but once sexually mature (14 years in males; 18–24 in females) they swim downstream and out to sea, spawning in deep oceanic waters up to 2000km (1200mile) off Australia where the adults are thought to die. The larvae then drift on currents and are eventually swept into bays and estuaries as semi-transparent 'glass eels'. They head upstream and, as they feed, they darken, becoming 'elvers' before adulthood.

Should weirs or waterfalls impede its progress, the muscular Short-finned Eel (90cm/35in) can slither across wet ground to reach water upstream. It can also travel long distances over land at night to other suitable habitats, such as dams, to establish a new home if overcrowding or drought threaten its old one.

Inland Fishes

Because the inland of Australia is so dry and rainfall so unpredictable, there is limited habitat for freshwater fishes. Indeed, there are only 33 native species known from this vast area. Highly localised and endemic, many are small and demonstrate adaptations to desert life.

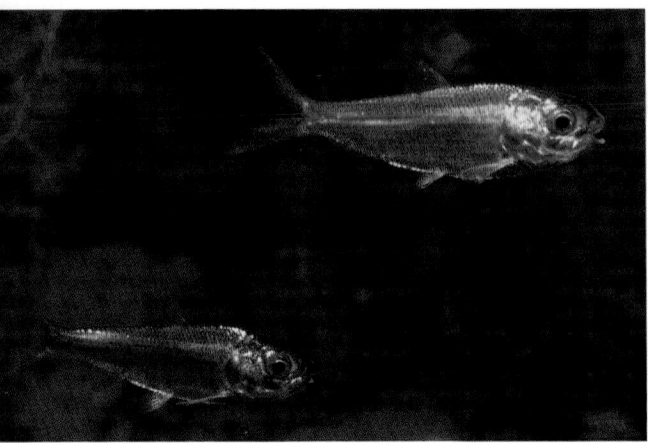

Although sensitive to oxygen depletion, the adaptable Bony Bream (15–20cm/6–8in) can withstand wide fluctuations in pH levels, turbidity and temperature in the bores and salt lakes of the inland. This widespread silvery, forked-tailed freshwater herring schools in the waterways of every state but Tasmania, bottom feeding on algae, crustaceans and insects in still or slow-flowing waters. It lays thousands of eggs on the water's surface in late spring in the south or multiple times in the north, especially during the Wet.

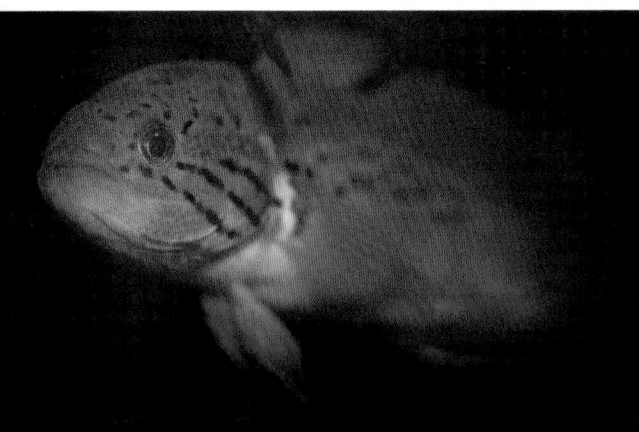

The Desert Mogurnda (12cm/5in) is known only from the Finke River system that rises in the West Macdonnell Ranges, 150km (93mile) west of Alice Springs in the Northern Territory. In the deep permanent waterholes of this ancient river course this species is one of nine that lives nowhere else.

Inland fishes must respond quickly to good rains and local flooding. Adaptations include rapid life cycles and a tolerance of oxygen depletion, temperature extremes and salinity in evaporating saltpans. The ability to leave rigorous conditions is a valuable asset. This may occur when fish eggs are transported on the feet of waterbirds from one drying riverbed or billabong to a water-filled one, ensuring the survival of the next generation.

One of Australia's most resilient inhabitants of the arid inland is the Desert Goby (6cm/2⅜in). Another is the Lake Eyre Hardyhead (7cm/3in), which can tolerate salinity three times greater than seawater. To avoid dessication in the fierce summer heat the remarkable Salamanderfish (5cm/2in) of south-western Australia digs itself down 60cm (24in) into a sandy peaty bottom where moisture persists. Secreting and sealing itself in a mucous sheath, it slows its metabolism, breathes through its skin and remains torpid until the winter rains come.

Mound Springs

In a parched forbidding landscape west of Lake Eyre a string of freshwater springs bubble to the surface from the underground aquifer that forms the Great Artesian Basin. These oases, known as mound springs, support entire ecosystems that include fishes, many of which live nowhere else on Earth. The Dalhousie Spring complex alone, which covers an areas of 7000ha (17,000ac), contains five endemic species: a catfish, a gudgeon, a goby and two endemic hardyheads. Only the widespread and hardy Spangled Perch has managed to muscle in on this highly exclusive club.

Estuarine Fishes

The calm tidal waters of estuaries are often described as fish nurseries. They provide food and shelter for juvenile fishes and spawning grounds for both marine and freshwater species.

The Bridled Goby (10cm/4in) is a common fish of southern estuaries, including those of Tasmania, and a favourite food item of cormorants and other estuarine birds.

Heavily laden female Freshwater Mullets (40cm/16in long) swim down the east-flowing rivers of northern New South Wales and southern Queensland in late summer to spawn up to three million eggs in estuarine waters. The more widespread Australian Bass, found in rivers as far east and south as Victoria and northern Tasmania, undertake spawning runs triggered by winter rain upstream. A resident of coastal lakes and rivers, the Estuary Perch (40–79cm/16–31in) is another frequently found freshwater species in estuaries. All three are considered good eating fish.

Gobies and Mudskippers

This huge cosmopolitan family is mostly marine, but in Australia gobies are features of many mangroves and estuaries, as well as some upland streams. They are small hardy fishes, almost cylindrical with large blunt-nosed heads and often lacking scales. In most species their pelvic fins are fused together to support them when resting on the water's bottom where they spend most of their time.

Mudskippers are amphibious bug-eyed gobies that hop and slither about the mud of mangrove creeks and mudflats in northern Australia. A surface network of blood vessels allows them to breathe air through their skin so they can spend much of their time out of water. This gives them the advantage over other fish of finding terrestrial food but they retreat to burrows in mudflats at the slightest sign of danger.

GOBIES HERE, THERE AND EVERYWHERE

With currently about 2000 known goby species, they are second only to the goldfish family Cyprinidae in terms of number of species. In fact, once the taxonomic work is completed, gobies may prove to be the world's largest family of fishes.

Introduced Fishes

Before white settlement, Australia lacked many of the world's dominant freshwater fish families. Twenty-two non-native species have since been introduced. As is often the case with introduced organisms, with their usual competitors and predators absent, many of these exotic fishes have run amok, disrupting the balance of natural freshwater ecosystems and endangering native species.

In its search for food, the muscular Common Carp burrows through the sediments, sucking up mud from the bottom and expelling the waste as it filters out the organic components. This activity uproots aquatic vegetation, erodes the banks (preventing establishment of young plants) and muddies the water, destroying its clarity. In some waterways 90 per cent of the fishes are now introduced carp.

The Goldfish Family

This is the largest freshwater family in the world. At least five species have been introduced into Australia for either aquariums, angling or ornamental purposes. These fishes live in slow-flowing or still water.

Largest of all is the Common Carp (30–40cm / 12–16in). While this fish was introduced in the 1860s, it seems it was the release of a new strain in the 1960s in Victoria that lead to its sudden proliferation and rapid spread throughout the slow-flowing rivers of southern Australia. Today, adult carp are wreaking havoc in many of Australia's freshwater ecosystems.

Aquarium Goldfish (up to 20cm / 8in) have entered Australian waters as live bait or discarded pets. While they compete for food with small native fishes and gobble up their eggs, some larger natives eat them. Their ability to hybridise with the Common Carp, though, is a concern.

Less common and widespread are Tench (10–30cm / 4–12in) and Roach (15–20cm / 6–8in), introduced for angling around the 1870s. While Tench inhabit the lower reaches of the Murray–Darling system,

Tasmania's Derwent River and a few other locations, the Roach appears not to have strayed far from its release sites in Victorian rivers, including the Yarra. Both are possibly being out-competed by the Common Carp.

The Trout and Salmon Family

Five members of this family have been imported into the cool streams, lakes and reservoirs of Tasmania and southern Australia. All are popular with recreational anglers and considered fine eating. The Rainbow and Brown Trouts have established wild populations, especially in Tasmania. The smaller Brook Trout has a few wild populations but is regularly re-stocked for the pleasure of anglers, as is the Quinnat Salmon in Victoria. Atlantic Salmon is farmed.

These relatively large fishes prey on small native fish, their young and eggs, and they compete for space and food. The highly successful Brown Trout in Tasmania is especially considered responsible for the steep decline of four native galaxia species and the Spotted Tree Frog.

Under no circumstances should even the most ornamental Goldfish be released into Australia's waterways. They have proved tolerant of high temperatures and oxygen-depleted waters, characteristics suitable for Australian conditions, but in the wild they are considered pests and are infesting the lower reaches of many of Australia's south-eastern rivers, including the Murray–Darling system.

Redfin

The Redfin (35cm / 14in), a true perch, was introduced for anglers and as a good table fish in the 1860s. It is now established in many southern rivers. It breeds prolifically and tolerates oxygen-depleted water (often resulting from algal blooms), giving it an advantage over the many native fishes on which it may feed. It also consumes native frogs, tadpoles, worms, snails and crustaceans. However, some decline, possibly due to carp, may be underway.

Mosquitofish

Mosquitofish, also known as Gambusia, were introduced to control mosquito larvae in the 1920s but they are more effective at eradicating tadpoles, small native fishes and their eggs. Known also as Plague Minnows, they school in vast numbers in still or slow-flowing water. They have spread rapidly through the lakes, reservoirs and rivers of south-eastern Australia, into the south west and the coastal rivers of Queensland. Now in the Channel Country, isolated bore drains and remote mound springs, they have probably established in Tasmania, despite all efforts at preventing their spread.

Mosquitofish (3–6cm / 1–2in) are a major pest in Australia's fragile freshwater environments and a serious threat to both native fishes and frog populations. Prolific breeders, they bear live young that grow fast and are able to withstand high temperatures and salinity. They aggressively harass and nip the fins of other small fishes, fry and tadpoles and out-compete them, especially in degraded systems.

INVERTEBRATES

Animals without backbones are known as invertebrates. Those living on dry land are usually small. Just under a quarter of a million species of land invertebrates have been described for Australia and there will be many more to come. Their diversity is at its greatest in the tropical forests of north Queensland.

Many invertebrates that live in Australia are found nowhere else. For example, four entire families of land snails are exclusively Australian. There are also three families of Australian beetles, three of wasps, three of bugs and cicadas, and one of termites.

Over tens of millions of years Australian invertebrates have been diversifying and expanding into different habitats. They have interacted closely with the native plants, often evolving in response to the shelter or food they had to offer. The wattles and the family to which eucalypts belong have been especially influential in their development.

Invertebrates that live in Australia contend with some very extreme conditions. Nearly 70 per cent of the land is arid or semi-arid; in these areas rain is rare and intermittent. Soils throughout the continent are poor and fires from lightning strikes are a natural and common occurrence. Despite these limitations, most of Australia's terrestrial ecosystems support invertebrates in abundance.

A number of ancient lineages have persisted in Australia. Some provide clues as to how primitive forms developed into more modern ones. The velvet worms, for example, which are believed by zoologists to be the missing evolutionary link between segmented worms and arthropods, may well have originated from a marine form on this continent. In another instance, a spider species sheltering in the caves of Tasmania displays transitional characteristics between the ancient ground-dwelling, nocturnal spiders and the modern ones that adapted their breathing systems and uses for silk to reach up into the trees in pursuit of new sources of food.

People often despise invertebrates, especially insects, yet only one per cent of insects are considered pests and many actually kill pests and carriers of disease. The invertebrates are integral parts of the many food webs on which we rely. They pollinate our flowers and disperse seeds. They free up the nutrients in our soil and water, and they feed our fishes, reptiles, frogs, birds and mammals. With so many intricacies of their lives still poorly understood and new species being discovered all the time, further study of such animals is bound to break new ground.

PREVIOUS PAGE *A female parasitic wasp. This wasp lays its eggs inside the cells of solitary bees and wasps nesting in plant stems or in underground nests, with the subsequent larvae developing on the food stores and/or nest inhabitants.*
RIGHT *A lacewing from the antlion family.*

Worms

When we think of worms we usually think first of the common garden earthworms we find in our compost and soil. Most of these ravenous wrigglers are introduced but Australia has a surprising number of native earthworms, some of them impressively large. It also has flatworms as well as those little hazards of wet forests, bloodsucking leeches.

This distinctive flatworm is only found between Gympie in Queensland and the Border Ranges of north-eastern New South Wales. It has no common name as yet but scientists have given it a scientific name: Caenoplana bicolor.

Earthworms and leeches are restricted to damp places where they can breathe through their skin, which must be kept moist. They are hermaphrodites, each individual having both male and female sex organs. Pairs sidle up to one another and exchange sperm. They then separate and in each animal a swollen area called the clitellum secretes a ring of mucus that travels forwards along its body, first receiving eggs and albumen from the worm's oviducts and then the recently deposited sperm from storage organs. The clitellum slips over the head and onto the ground, where it dries and seals in the developing eggs. Young worms hatch, consume the albumen and break free of the cocoon to start an independent life.

Earthworms

Australia is surprisingly well endowed with native earthworms. About 350 species have been described but there are probably hundreds more waiting to be discovered. There are also at least 66 introduced species. These are often widespread and, in

---

REJUVENATING WORMS

Earthworms have remarkable powers of regeneration. They can regrow parts of their body after a severe attack by, say, a bird, but they cannot clone themselves by simply splitting into two or more fragments, as flatworms can.

paddocks and gardens, they have largely displaced native species. Native species tend to be confined to certain localities. Some occur in the soils of forests, including rainforests; others live in arid Australia.

Some of Australia's native worms are incredibly long. There's a 60cm (24in)-long Tasmanian worm, a 1m (39in)-long worm from Burrawang in New South Wales, and another from northern New South Wales that is as thick as a man's finger and grows to 1.5m (60in). Vying for a world record, however, is the fragile and protected Giant Gippsland Worm from southern Victoria, which can grow to a staggering 2–3m (6½–10ft) long and 2cm (1in) thick.

A velvet worm or peripatus from south-western Australia. These 'walking worms' are not strictly worms as they have legs and antennae. Velvet worms are of great interest in evolutionary studies because they are believed to represent an early stage in the evolution of the largest group of animals alive today, the arthropods, which include insects, spiders and their kin. Although rarely encountered because they live in moist, dark places, such as rotting logs and leaf litter, velvet worms are particularly plentiful and diverse in Australia.

Flatworms

In wet places such as moist soils, under stones or rotten logs, you may find another sort of worm. Its long glistening body is flattened and it lacks the concentric rings of the segmented earthworm. It is a flatworm. Often exquisitely coloured and reasonably common in high rainfall areas, some Australian species grow to 30cm (12in). Flatworms are carnivorous creatures that ensnare slugs, earthworms and other small prey with mucus. They sometimes feed on carrion, too.

Leeches

Many types of leeches live in water but those in wet forests and gullies are more noticeable. Here they forage for warm-blooded prey. They are like earthworms but with suckers at each end of their body. The large sucker at the back acts like a foot on which the leech stands up from a leaf or the ground, extends itself and waves about feeling for stimuli. Its skin is highly sensitive to variations in light, heat and vibration.

A leech can go without a meal for months but once it locates a host its front end latches on and it loops its way to a suitable place where it can slit its host's skin open with its jaws. It then secretes mucus to secure its sucker and pumps an anti-coagulant into the victim to prevent clotting. When it is full, it drops off. The wound may continue to bleed for a while and itch for days but it is rarely a serious concern.

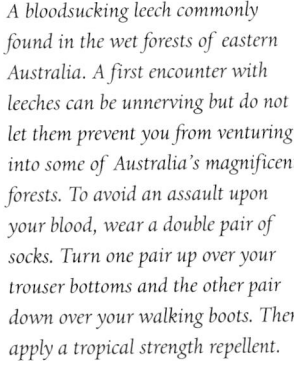

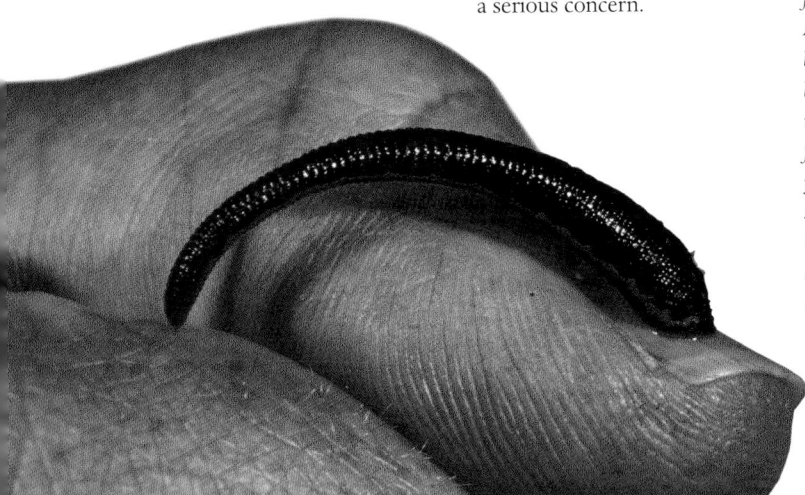

A bloodsucking leech commonly found in the wet forests of eastern Australia. A first encounter with leeches can be unnerving but do not let them prevent you from venturing into some of Australia's magnificent forests. To avoid an assault upon your blood, wear a double pair of socks. Turn one pair up over your trouser bottoms and the other pair down over your walking boots. Then apply a tropical strength repellent.

Land Snails and Slugs

Unless you get out into the bush in wet weather you could be forgiven for thinking there were no native snails or slugs but in fact there are at least 1000 recognised native land snail species. The reason you hardly ever see them is because land molluscs prefer to shelter during the day and move around only at night or during wet weather.

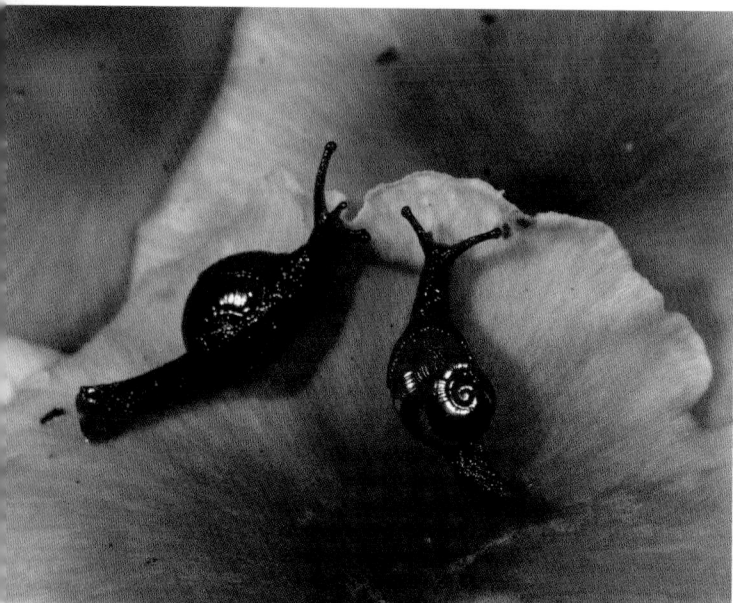

A pair of rainforest-dwelling, fungus-grazing semi-slugs. These little helicarionid snails are called semi-slugs because their shallow little shell is too small to accommodate their body.

Although the ancestors of land molluscs left watery realms millions of years ago, snails and slugs have not made substantial physiological adaptations to life on dry land apart from evolving to breathe air. They remain moisture dependent and prolonged dryness is fatal to them.

In the Rainforest

Most Australian snails and slugs live in rainforest. Forever at risk of drying out, they like dark, dank leaf litter and the crevices and cracks of the roots of giant trees or fallen logs. Here you may find Australia's largest snail, the Giant Panda Snail. Its shell is the size of a small apple and its eggs the size of marbles. The beautiful Red Triangle Slug (up to 14cm/6in) may be spotted up a tree scraping minute fungi, algae and lichen off the trunk for food. In the Sydney region this slug is usually a sandstone colour with a red edge and a red triangle on its back but there are many regional variations. Just within the triangle it is easy to see its breathing pore, which connects to its single lung; all terrestrial snails and slugs are air-breathers. It only has one pair of antennae, which is unusual as most snails and slugs have two.

Snails have many predators, among them subtropical and tropical pittas, birds that extract snail bodies from their shells by bashing them against a rock. When walking through a rainforest, you may come across a telltale pile of shells beside a favoured stone 'anvil'.

While most land molluscs are vegetarians, the Otway Range Black Snail, with its 2.5cm (1in) shell, is carnivorous. Known only from the cool temperate rainforests of Victoria's Otway Ranges, this endangered snail impales the soft bodies of worms and other snails upon its sharp teeth.

In the Arid Region

Given the need for moisture, you might expect that no snail would venture into Australia's arid regions but 80 species have been discovered from Central Australia alone and there are probably many more. The ancestors of these snails have been there a very long time, long before the continent dried out. They have adapted to the dry spells by hibernating under rocks.

Species of Australian molluscs are often restricted to very limited areas, espe-

These snails generally inhabit The saline lakes or coastal saltmarshes of western and southern Australia. To prevent themselves from drying out they have a horny lid, an operculum, on their muscular foot that they can draw in to plug their shell.

cially in desert regions where suitable conditions may prevail only in small refuges. There is, for example, a tiny snail that lives solely among the leaf litter of native fig trees in a few gorges near Alice Springs. This habitat occurs over less than 2000ha (5000ac). Should anything happen to the figs within this area, the entire species will become extinct.

Even more surprising is the number of freshwater snails that are living in arid regions. Some tough it out at the edges of salt lakes, while others are restricted to remote mound springs; the Dalhousie Springs complex in South Australia alone is a refuge to six species found nowhere else.

In the Garden and On the Farm

The garden snails that munch their way through your leafy vegetables and flowers are almost certainly the introduced Common Garden Snail. In its European homeland, cold winters and natural predators, such as thrushes, keep populations in check but in Australia these irrepressible snails wreak havoc wherever they become established. Introduced Leopard Slugs also favour gardens, while White Italian Snails are a serious pest of cereal crops. They climb to the top of stalks and glue themselves down, spoiling the harvest and gumming up the harvester.

CULINARY MOLLUSCS

It is illegal to import the European edible snail into Australia, so fans of culinary snails must eat the Common Garden Snail or do without. There have been moves to explore the potential of native species for culinary purposes but this has yet to be fully investigated.

The shell of a Giant Panda Snail can grow up to 10cm (4in) in diameter. This impressive invertebrate occurs in the rainforests of north-eastern New South Wales and south-eastern Queensland.

Slaters, Shield Shrimps and Freshwater Shrimps

These creatures are crustaceans, a group more commonly associated with the sea, but there are many freshwater and a few terrestrial crustaceans in Australia. Crustaceans typically have gills that extract oxygen from water so even the terrestrial species need moisture to breathe. The young are usually kept moist in their mothers' brood pouches but, for adult Australian species, desiccation is a constant threat.

Slaters (0.2–2cm/¹⁄₁₀–⁴⁄₅in) are most at home in amongst the moist leaf litter of forests where they are unlikely to dry out. There are, however, native species surviving in almost all habitats of Australia, including the semi-arid and arid inland.

Slaters

The most visible and best-known land crustacean is probably the slater, sometimes known as the sowbug or woodlouse. These little grey or brown creatures hide by day in damp places under rocks, logs and in leaf litter. They swim well and often crawl around the bottom of pools. On land they trundle out at night like miniature armoured trucks to feed on decaying vegetable or animal matter. Those found in the compost heaps of suburban gardens, and pillbugs that roll up into a ball, are introduced species but Australia has many native species; some even inhabit salt lakes. They survive long, dry periods by sheltering in refuges, such as under stones.

Shield Shrimps

Shield shrimps or tadpole shrimps are prehistoric animals that have altered little in 300 million years. They live in temporary pools of clear or murky water throughout Australia. Their life cycles are rapid and their minute, lightweight eggs are drought-proof. They may lie

Shield shrimps (9cm/3½in) are well adapted to life in temporary pools despite having evolved hundreds of millions of years ago. This photo depicts their primitive features clearly. Above is a pair of compound eyes and a translucent hard shield cut away to allow movement of the segmented abdomen. Underneath is a mass of feathery legs that beat the water to create a current over the gills at their base and filter small aquatic animals, plants and detritus out of the water for food.

dormant for years, hatching only after heavy rain. In just seven to ten days, after a series of rapid moults, the young shrimps can grow to 5cm (2in) long and reach sexual maturity. Having mated, they usually lay fertilised eggs but some shield shrimps can clone themselves. Some, too, are hermaphrodites so they can either fertilise themselves or cross-fertilise; for water-dependent animals living in hot, arid conditions, these are valuable survival mechanisms. As waterholes dry out, the adults perish. Eggs will remain like time capsules, some blown into other depressions, ready to spring into life when the next big rains come.

Freshwater Shrimps

Anyone trawling a net through healthy fresh water in Australia is likely to find some freshwater shrimps. In eastern Australia and Tasmania, this is very likely to be the 3cm (1in)-long translucent Common Freshwater Shrimp. Other shrimps in the same family of a similar size but with an aquamarine tinge are to be found in slow-moving fresh water and billabongs throughout mainland Australia.

In the food webs of Australia's temporary water bodies, fairy shrimps are important players. These small shrimps swim on their backs, beating their paddle-like, gill-carrying appendages as they trap food and oxygen. When heavy rain comes to the inland, populations explode as larvae hatch from their drought-resistant eggs. Before the water seeps back into the ground and evaporates into the air they will moult many times and mate. Hardiest of them all are the little brine shrimps that live in water 10 times saltier than seawater. Endemic to Australia's salt lakes, brine shrimps nourish fish like the Lake Eyre Hardyhead and inland breeding birds like the Banded Stilt.

Of greater economic significance are the larger freshwater prawns, some of which are endemic to Australia. The largest, known as Cherabin in Western Australia, grows to 11cm (4in) long. Already successfully farmed in South-east Asia, this species is currently the focus of a possible aquaculture industry in Australia.

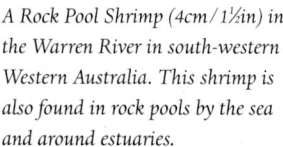

A Rock Pool Shrimp (4cm / 1½in) in the Warren River in south-western Western Australia. This shrimp is also found in rock pools by the sea and around estuaries.

In the mountain streams of Tasmania, Victoria and New South Wales live some small primitive shrimps known as anaspids. These ancient crustaceans are believed to be the ancestors from which today's prawns, crabs and lobsters have evolved. The segments of their thorax and abdomen look the same but they lack a carapace or brood pouches.

Crayfish and Freshwater Crabs

Crabs and crayfish are crustaceans whose first pair of legs have become enlarged and modified to form robust claws. Crayfish inhabit healthy fresh water throughout Australia. There are over 100 species. Most are endemic to a relatively small area. Among them are the world's largest and the world's smallest crayfish. Less diverse are the freshwater crabs commonly found in tropical Australia.

Crayfish

Most people know the dominant crayfish in their area. In New South Wales and Victoria, Yabbies are the common species, while Redclaws are best known in Queensland, and Koonacs, Giglies and Marrons are all familiar Western Australian species.

Crayfish live in streams and swamps. They are nocturnal and mostly vegetarian. They trawl for food walking along the bottom of pools, swimming close to banks or clinging to rocks. They have a suite of feeding appendages that sift, hold, push and tear food. To make a rapid escape crayfish can propel themselves backwards with a flip of their tail fan. Their claws are mainly for defence and burrowing.

The Yabbie is a widespread and hardy freshwater crayfish whose smooth carapace grows to a length of 7cm (3in). It eats organic detritus at the bottom of rivers, creeks and floodwaters, and can withstand drought conditions by digging itself a burrow in a soft bank or billabong bed.

Crayfish are often colourful. This beautiful Lamington Spiny Crayfish (with a carapace of 8cm/3in) lives only in the rainforest creeks of the Lamington Plateau in south-eastern Queensland. During winter it stays close to its burrow but on wet summer evenings it is sometimes found crossing muddy tracks.

Male crayfish fertilise females internally. The female then lays up to a 1000 eggs, which she secures to the underside of her abdomen with sticky threads that wrap around the hairs of her swimming legs. She is then said to be 'in berry'. When the eggs hatch, the young, which look like miniature adults, cling to her leg hairs until they are ready to drop off and forage for themselves.

The Giant Freshwater Crayfish from northern Tasmania is the largest crayfish in the world. Specimens up to 6kg (13lb) and 40cm (16in) long have been recorded but are rare. Other large crayfish include the Marron (38cm/15in) from the south-west of Western Australia, the

Murray River Crayfish (15cm/6in) from the Murray–Darling River system and the Large Gippsland Crayfish (15cm/6in).

Most 'crays' dig burrows into which they retreat when danger threatens or conditions become unfavourable but the most adept burrowers are small crayfish (4.5cm/2in). Members of the genus *Engaeus* from Tasmania, Victoria and New South Wales and those of *Engaewa* from the south-west of Western Australia are powerfully built; their deep, laterally compressed carapaces and downward articulated claws are designed for digging and subterranean life. Burrows may reach 1m (39in) down. The only conspicuous sign of life may be turrets of mud, known as chimneys, rising up to 40cm (16in) above the ground.

Freshwater Crabs

There are a few freshwater crabs that live in tropical Australia and at least one species, called only by its scientific name *Austrothelphusa transversa*, is known from the inland. When the rivers, creeks, springs, swamps and dams in which it lives dry up during summer this inland crab excavates a burrow up to 1m (39in) long in a clay bank and seals itself in with a plug of mud. It waits out the dry conditions in the humidity of its burrow. When floodwaters arrive, it digs its way out, feeds and mates.

Female freshwater crabs carry their eggs under their body, and when hatched the young cling to the mother's hairy legs in the same way as crayfish young do. Marine crabs produce free-swimming larvae but land crabs produce juveniles that look like miniature crabs. These baby crabs grow and moult until they reach adulthood when their carapace becomes about 5cm (2in) wide.

> ### YUMMY YABBIES
> Redclaws, Yabbies and Marrons are commercially raised in Australia for the restaurant trade, both local and overseas.

The Inland Freshwater Crab (5cm/2in wide) feeds mostly at night, nimbly picking its way through organic detritus. It survives long droughts by sealing itself into a deep burrow in which humid air is retained. Here it falls into a state of suspended animation until the floodwaters trigger it back to life.

Mites and Ticks

While there are mites that have been inadvertently introduced into Australia, there are also thousands of native species. Many of these are free-living; others are parasitic, among them the ticks, of which 75 species are recognised.

A tick preparing to puncture human skin in order to take a blood meal.

TICK PREVENTION AND EXTRACTION

Ticks can kill dogs so talk to your vet about protection. To protect yourself, spray insect repellent containing DEET before venturing out into tick country. Ticks are difficult to remove due to hooks around their mouth. If attached to the skin, spray them with a repellent containing pyrethrin or a pyrethroid to intoxicate them; spray again after one minute. Within 24 hours the ticks should drop off or you can be gently remove it with tweezers. Itchiness may continue for several weeks; if more serious symptoms develop, consult your doctor.

Mites

Mites are widespread and mostly harmless, although some are serious pests of crops. One group bothersome to humans living in tropical forests is the chiggers, which are a larval stage of some predatory mites. You need a magnifying glass to see chiggers. They feed on skin tissue and leave their hosts itching madly from the digestive juices they inject into the skin to break up the tissue.

Ticks

The notorious Paralysis Tick is found in forested regions of the east coast from northern Queensland to Victoria in a 20km (12mile) band from the coast. In late summer six-legged larvae hang from vegetation waving their forelegs, which are fitted with sensors for heat, pheromones and carbon dioxide emitted by animals such as ourselves or their favourite hosts, the bandicoots.

Having dropped onto their host they secure a moist dark spot, puncture the skin, pump in an anti-coagulant to keep the blood flowing and begin to suck. Several days later, engorged and ten times the size, they drop off. Having moulted into an eight-legged nymph, they repeat the process, this time metamorphosing into an adult. While female adults seek another blood meal, males mate with them. Enlarged to maybe a hundred-fold, females then drop off the host, lay up to 3000 eggs and die.

Scorpions

At the last count, Australia had 41 species of scorpions. None of these are seriously dangerous and, since they are nocturnal, they are rarely encountered. They can, however, pinch fiercely with their pincers and cause intense pain for several hours with the sting in their tail.

Scorpions are not awfully energetic and they cannot jump. They reserve their energy for capturing cockroaches, beetles, millipedes, centipedes, spiders and, occasionally, earthworms, which they mostly ambush rather than chase. Prey is captured in their formidable pincers. If it struggles, the scorpion swings the tip of its flexible tail over its body, sometimes flipping its victim over before stabbing it to death with its deadly toxin-laden sting.

Scorpions are highly successful predators that have roamed the Earth for at least 420 million years. Australian species vary in size from about 2.5 to 12cm (1 to 5in) long. While many live in dry habitats, their simple 'book' lungs, like those of primitive spiders, need humidity to breathe, which is why they spend their days under rocks and logs. In the deserts, where rocks are few and far between, scorpions have become burrowers. Some, like the spider-hunting scorpions, appropriate the holes of wolf and trapdoor spiders, while others construct their own. That of the widespread Inland Robust Scorpion (7cm / 3in) spirals down to where the sand is moist and the temperature cool.

Among forest scorpions the Queensland's Rainforest Scorpion (6cm / 2⅓in) squeezes its compressed body under peeling bark by day, while the little gum-tree hunting Marbled Scorpion (2.5–3.5cm / 1–1⅓in) hides in leaf litter. Occasionally teh Marbled Scorpion wanders into houses, as does the more thick-set Wood or Forest Scorpion (4cm / 2in).

> ### CANNIBALISM IN THE FAMILY
>
> Among scorpions, the rearing of young may be tantamount to storing food, as these creatures are known to turn on their own in times of starvation.

The resourceful Inland Robust Scorpion avoids desert heat and aridity by sleeping, moulting and caring for its young 1m (39in) underground where subterranean living is comfortable. At night it ascends its spiralling burrow to sit and wait for unwitting travellers to pass by. If of appropriate size, they are instantly grabbed, dispatched and consumed.

Primitive Spiders

Spiders evolved 300 million years ago. The earliest forms were ground dwellers that lived in burrows in humid forests. They ambushed crawling prey, stabbing it with jaws that moved up and down like pick axes. Australia's notorious funnel-web spiders are descendants of this group but there are many harmless and delightful spiders in Australia, too.

Large trapdoor and funnel-web spiders (1.5–4.5cm/1–2in) react to danger by standing their ground and raising their front legs and jaws in readiness to attack. They cannot jump but this threatening pose is no bluff. If you encounter a spider behaving like this, move away.

Funnel-web Spiders

If a funnel-web spider bites a human it can be fatal. Fortunately funnel-webs are rarely encountered in the bush, preferring life in and under logs or rocks in the cool, wet forests of the east coast. They spin a long flat tube of silk that divides in two, one providing a getaway exit, and their tripwires of silk radiate a long way out from the entrances. The spiders shelter at the bottom of the tubes and rarely venture far from their home, except on spring nights, when males go searching for females. Sometimes they tumble into swimming pools where they can survive for several hours before drowning.

Trapdoor, Mouse and Brush-footed Spiders

Trapdoor, mouse and brush-footed spiders belong to the same ancient group as funnel-webs. Generally large and hairy, with fangs that stab prey with a downward stroke, these solitary creatures shun the drying conditions of daylight, remaining hidden in humid holes, usually lined with silk, until nightfall. They capture prey with tripwires of silk that radiate out from their burrows. Sitting at the burrow entrances, they wait for a passing creature to stumble upon a thread, and then rush out, pounce, crush and pierce their victims before dragging them down into their holes for consumption.

Although robust and with a body length of about 2.5cm (1in), trapdoor spiders are generally timid, curling their legs up under their body and freezing when encountered. Most species are dark brown or black, often with some faint patterning.

As the name suggests, many (but not all) trapdoor spiders construct earthen 'doors', sometimes neatly bevelled and hinged at one side with silken web. These plug their burrows to deter predators and prevent debris falling in. Burrows may be shallow or up to a metre (39in) deep; they may drop directly down, incline or meander.

Most funnel-webs are restricted to the coastal and eastern slopes of the Great Dividing Range, but this Tree Funnel-web Spider, an inhabitant of crevices in fallen logs, stumps and tree ferns, was photographed near Canberra. A large species with equally large fangs, it can kill well-armoured prey like scarab beetles.

Sometimes they are forked or they lead into cells or down blind alleys.

Mouse-spiders are a family of primitive spider that earned their name for the holes they live in. Females are similar to trapdoor spiders in size and colour. Shiny except for a velvety abdomen, their

In the Border Ranges of north-eastern New South Wales a trapdoor spider sits and waits for prey to amble by. Note the trip-lines of silken thread around its burrow entrance over which its feet are splayed. Having poor eyesight, it is the tug of a thread that alerts the spider to the presence of passers-by.

VENOM

All spiders carry venom in the base of their jaws. It runs through a channel to the tip of their hard, sharp fangs and is designed for killing prey. Most spider venom, however, will not harm big animals because either the quantity is insufficient, or the fangs are too small, or the venom is not toxic enough.

huge swollen jaw bases are clearly visible. Males are smaller and those of some species have startling red jaw bases and heads with metallic blue abdomens.

The velvety brush-footed spiders have pioneered open habitats. The tufts of hairs around their claws enable them to scale smooth, vertical surfaces. While some burrow into coastal sandy soils beneath leaf litter, others, like Australia's largest spiders, the Whistling or Barking Spiders, have ventured inland. Up to 16cm (6in) long, if you count their legs, the burrows of Barking Spiders are the size of golf balls and fitted out with a side chamber, where they shelter when burrows flood and females raise their young. These resourceful spiders chase prey at night. They are usually silent but sometimes, as their name suggests, they make a sound, perhaps in courtship or in defence of their territories. This they do by rubbing their palps against pegs at the base of their jaw.

A trapdoor spider out and about. It is rare to encounter these spiders as they are nocturnal and even at night they spend most of their time catching prey close to their burrow entrances.

STAYING ALIVE TACTICS

The big hairy nocturnal spiders are sometimes hard to tell apart and, since some are deadly to humans, you cannot afford to take chances. Do not leave gloves and shoes outside. Always wear socks and walking shoes in the bush and gloves in the garden. Never handle a spider, even if it appears to be dead. Simply leave it alone.

Roaming Spiders

With the evolution of a better breathing system via a trachea, spiders were released from a life of darkness and dankness. They became energetic and able to roam freely and for sustained periods. They developed good eyesight and jaws that were hinged like pincers. Some experimented with high-rise living in pursuit of flying insects. Others, like the huntsmen and wolf spiders, took to the chase.

Huntsmen Spiders

Huntsmen are common and instantly recognisable brown, flattish spiders with long sprawling legs. Some specimens measure 16cm (6in) from leg tip to leg tip but most are not so large. Males, which are smaller than females, have bulbous palps for storing sperm.

Rather than building snares, huntsmen catch their prey by running it down, grasping it in their long legs and biting it with their fangs. These spiders mostly live in forests and woodlands on trees and decaying logs. They hunt at night for moths, insect larvae and beetles, sidling into narrow crevices by day to rest, lay eggs and moult. It is not unusual to find their cast-off skin dangling from bark.

While Huntsmen traditionally hide beneath peeling bark and hunt around tree trunks and rocks, they sometimes come into outbuildings and houses, especially after rain. They scuttle up and down walls, ceilings and curtains and can manoeuvre sideways, too. Being large and fast, they raise the heart-rate of some people and have been known to cause traffic accidents after popping up on the windscreen of cars.

A female Huntsmen Spider wraps her legs defensively around her egg sac.

HOME HUNTSMAN REMOVAL TECHNIQUE

Open the door to your house. Take a sheet of paper and a tumbler. Persuade your spider to move to a place where you can move freely. Gently invert the tumbler over the spider. Then slide the sheet of paper under the tumbler. Carefully lift both together. Turn over the tumbler and keep the sheet of paper over it until you are outside. Then release your spider away from you and the house. Easy!

Wolf Spiders

Wolf spiders are ground dwellers. More compact than huntsmen and often with handsome brown and black markings, they, too, are agile hunters, stalking and pursuing prey at speed and over considerable distances. Often found in gardens, you may catch a glimpse of one as it rushes from cover to cover in an effort to escape detection.

Some wolf spiders excavate burrows. Others live a peripatetic existence, taking advantage of shelter in other animals' holes, such as those of cicada nymphs, or just crouching in crevices.

Quite different to other roaming spiders are the comical jumping spiders. Small, colourful and often iridescent, they are plucky, agile daytime hunters with keen eyesight. On flat surfaces they move jerkily, waving their palps and pouncing on prey from a distance.

Maternal Instincts

Both huntsmen and wolf spiders have strong maternal instincts. They carefully spin a silken bowl into which they deposit their fertilised eggs. With the help of legs and jaws, they then fold and sew it together into a clean white egg sac.

Most huntsmen mothers spin a silken brood chamber, which they attach to the sides of rocky or wooden crevices. Here they deposit the egg sac, remaining on guard until the spiderlings hatch. Mothers remain with their young for some time, usually sheltering behind bark or exfoliating rocks.

Welcome aboard. Hundreds of young wolf spiders have clambered onto their mother to ride piggyback. Knobbly hairs on her abdomen help them cling on as she forages through the bush but some are inevitably swept off.

SPIDER TIP

A spider that sometimes comes into homes is the White-tailed Spider: a slender, 2.5cm (1in)-long dark spider with a white tip on its abdomen. This spider has long been accused of giving people a bite that results in a long-lasting necrotic sore but, while its bite certainly hurts, it has now been cleared of the greater crime, putting to bed a recent Australian urban myth.

Wolf spiders always carry their cumbersome egg sacs with them, attached to the spinnerets at the end of their abdomen. Once hatched the mother transports her offspring on her back for up to six months. Those that survive this trecherous mode of transporation eventually clamber to the top of a blade of grass, spin out a thread and lift off into the breeze for destinations unknown. This behaviour, known as ballooning, is a common way of dispersing among spiders.

An ant's view of a Garden Wolf Spider (1.5–2.2cm/¾–1in). Being the focus of six (of its eight) shiny eyes, and with bulging golden jaw bases at the ready, it is enough to turn a small insect to trembling jelly. This is a very successful species that has adapted to living in suburban gardens and the most common and widespread ground-dwelling spider of temperate Australia, occurring in all capital cities except Darwin.

Sit-and-Wait Spiders

These spiders have adopted a gamut of cunning strategies for capturing prey and in so doing they have exploited new habitats. Many build snares with their silk; others have honed their skills of deception and subterfuge.

The Ambushers

You might have noticed tiny, brightly coloured spiders, maybe little more than 1cm (⅓in) long, lurking in flowers or leaves. These are the flower spiders and their colours blend in with the plants they inhabit. These daytime hunters are members of a family also known as crab spiders, because they can move sideways like crabs and have two spiky front pairs of legs that they hold like crab pincers. Perfectly still with front legs at the ready, they wait for passing flies, bees, beetles and butterflies to alight on their plant. Once within range they pounce on the prey, clench it in their clawed front legs and administer a dose of venom.

Lurking around the bark of trees you may also come across their relatives: well-camouflaged little spiders with knobbly brownish bodies that can also move sideways. These are crab spiders. You can chase them around a trunk without touching them, watching them sidle around to avoid you. They hunt like flower spiders, but on bark.

For spiders that sit and wait for prey in broad daylight, camouflage not only helps them catch food; it hides them from predators. Some spiders have taken camouflage a

This small flower spider has caught a Green-blotched Moth on the blossom of a paperbark.

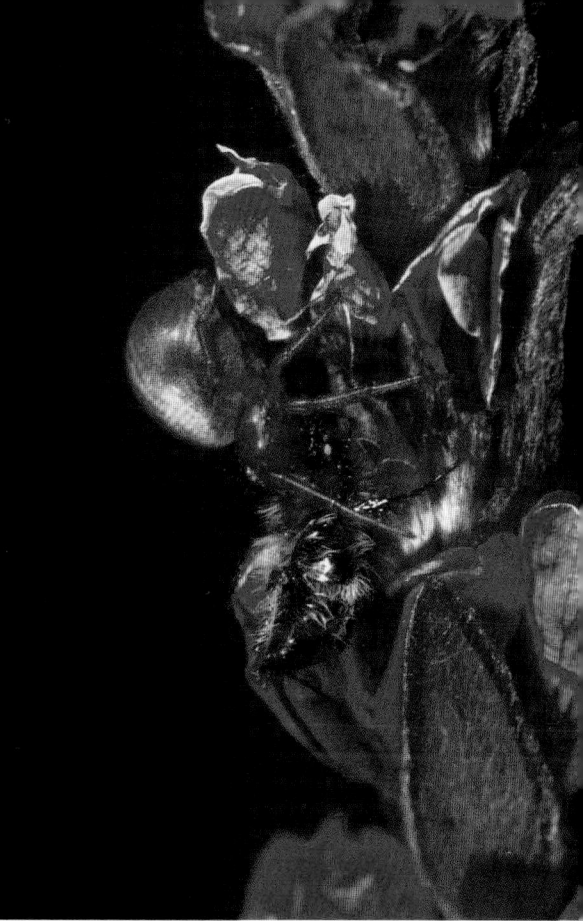

This flower spider, decked out in the colours of a native pea flower, has a wingless female flower wasp in its deadly embrace.

step further: to mimicry. For example, the small bird-dropping spiders are well nigh impossible to distinguish from, well, bird droppings when they sit, as they do, with their legs tucked in.

All ambushers use silk to weave their egg sacs and for escape lines but others have developed ingenious silken lures for catching prey.

Silken Lures

The nocturnal bolas spiders use scent as a lure and a lasso to haul in their quarry. The scent they exude mimics the perfume used by certain female moths to attract a mate. Hanging from a horizontal thread of silk, the bolas spider plays out a second, vertical 5–7cm (2–3in)-long thread. The spider deposits several smaller blobs evenly down its length and a large sticky globule at its end acts as a weight. The dangling thread and the spider remain absolutely still. The scent works its magic and the male moth arrives. As it flutters closer and closer to the lure, the spider sets the hanging thread into a circular motion. It swings around and around until the sticky blobs along the thread's length catch the confused moth. Once ensnared, the spider pulls in the line and despatches the moth with its jaws.

The nocturnal net-casting spiders have put their silk-making skills into weaving expandable nets. By day, the long, thin bodies of these brown and grey spiders hang among vegetation looking like twigs. After sunset, they commence building a rectangular framework of silk, reinforced with supporting threads and then inlaid with sticky, finely combed woolly silk that gives the structure its elasticity. Hanging by the back legs from vegetation, the spider spreads out the rectangular web with its other legs as it hovers just above the ground. When a suitable victim crawls into range, the spider snaps into action, dropping the net of silk over the victim, wrapping it and biting it until it is motionless.

One of the great engineering feats of the invertebrate world is the elaborate silken net of the net-casting spiders.

Snare-building Spiders

As insects evolved from crawling creatures to flying ones, the predatory spiders moved up into more aerial habitats in pursuit of them. Their greatest asset, silk, now became an indispensable tool for snaring prey on the wing and a multiplicity of web designs were devised.

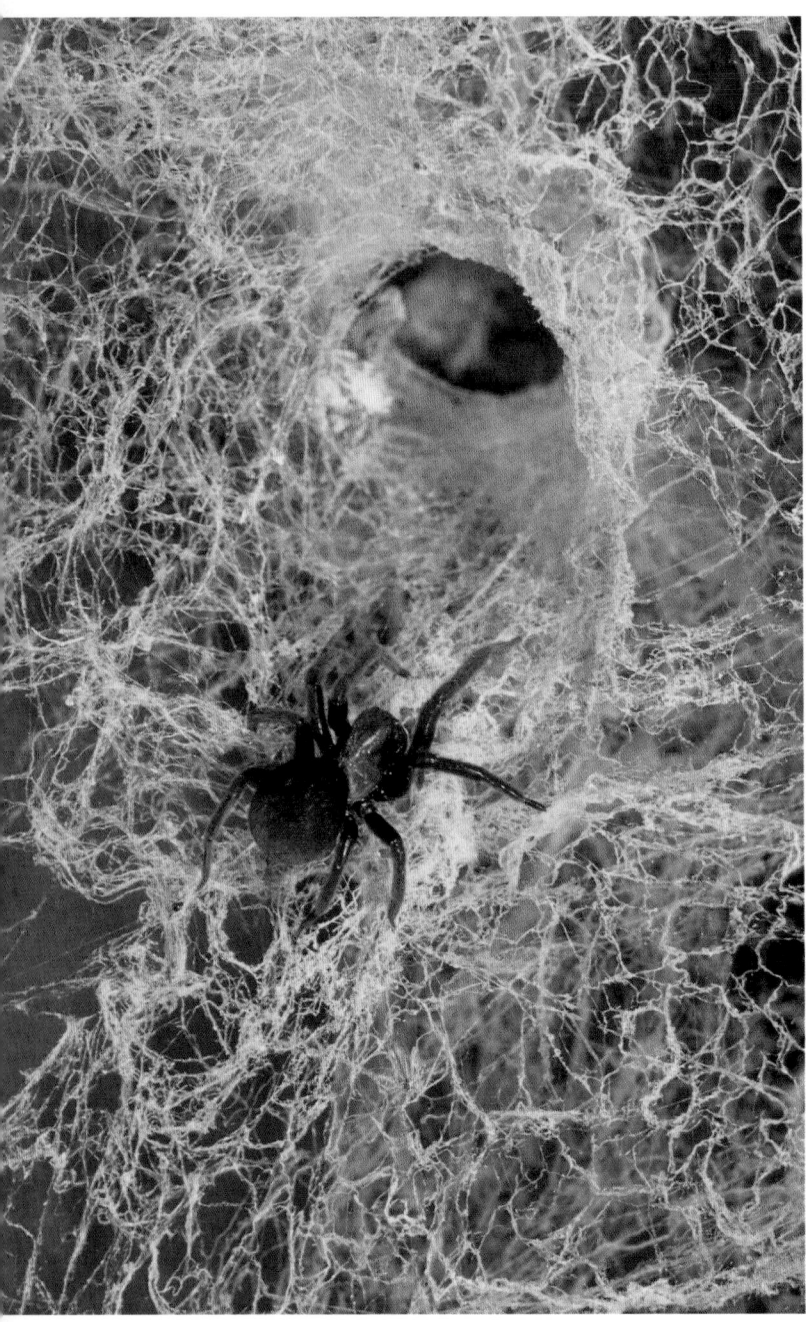

Spiders can produce dry, sticky or woolly silk from their elaborate spinning equipment on the underside of their abdomen (spinnerets) and many have combs on their legs that control the flow of silk. While the webs of some spiders may look like a chaotic jumble of threads, closer inspection will reveal some devilishly clever constructions.

Some Snare Models

One of the most conspicuous snare-building spiders is the Black House Spider that likes to build its lacy asymmetrical web in the neglected parts of buildings, especially the corners of window panes to which insects are attracted by the light. As with most snare-builders, the web of this

A Black House Spider returns to her retreat through the funnel of soft lacy webbing. These spiders are sometimes mistaken for funnel-web spiders but, with females less than 2cm (1in) long and males half this size, they are much smaller and the hole in their lacy web bears little resemblance to the thick sock-like funnel of Australia's deadliest spider.

species doubles as a hide and there is a distinct hole into which the spider retreats by day. After dark, the spider moves up to its entrance. If it detects the vibrations of an entangled insect in the web, it hauls it up into its retreat quickly, binds it up in silk and bites it into submission. This spider is not deadly to humans but its bite may cause severe pain and there is sometimes a bad reaction.

Another type of web is the work of the Crinoline or Sombrero Spider. Often slung from the underside of cliffs, the web is a horizontal opaque sheet hoisted up at its centre, where the spider sits waiting. When an insect falls onto the sheet, the spider rushes around to the underside and bites it through the thin webbing. It then wraps it up, pulls it through the sheet and consumes it in its retreat.

Perhaps the most commonly seen spider in houses is the cosmopolitan Daddy-long-legs. This gangly spider is harmless to humans. Its flimsy web is little more than a shelter but with lashings of silken bonds, effective venom and long legs to encompass struggling victims it has become one of the most successful spiders in the world.

A female Daddy-long-legs tends her freshly laid eggs. She will bundle them up in silk and hold them in her jaws while she hangs upside down in her web. With such a high degree of protection, survival rates are high and so she needs to lay only a relatively small number of eggs.

Gum-footed Spiders and the Notorious Red-back

A scaffolding of taut threads supports the seemingly chaotic webbed snares of gum-footed spiders. Above, and integrated into the web, is the spider's refuge. At its base the web is attached to the surface below by a number of sticky threads. When an insect stumbles into one of these sticky threads, it instantly breaks from its base, bouncing the glued insect up into the air. As it struggles, it knocks into another such thread. Airborne and helpless, it quickly finds itself being enthusiastically wrapped up and bitten to death by a spider.

A female Red-back Spider guards her egg sac. It is she, rather than her male counterpart, that has been responsible for some human deaths. She rates as Australia's second deadliest spider, after the Sydney Funnel-web Spider. Fortunately her venom, which attacks the nervous system, is slow acting and, since the development of an antivenom in 1956, no deaths have been reported.

This is the strategy of the notorious Red-back Spider that is widespread throughout Australia and often found in dry areas of outbuildings and piles of vegetation. While the male, at 3mm (⅒ in) long, is rarely noticed, the female is a danger to humans. Closely related to the Black Widow Spider of America and the Katipo Spider of New Zealand, it has a shiny black body with an abdomen the size and shape of a pea upon which there is a striking splash of red.

Wheel-web Weavers

As insects evolved and took to the air in increasing numbers, the predatory spiders kept pace by developing new engineering skills. The wheel-shaped gossamer webs slung between stalks of vegetation are the work of skilful master weavers. Their webs display a level of sophistication that has resulted from constant revision and modification of silken snares.

Construction Techniques

The framework of these webs begins with the spider playing out a single thread of silk with a sticky end that lifts on the breeze and catches on a rock or vegetation. The spider travels up and down the horizontal thread releasing more reinforcing silk until it drops from the halfway point, pulling a strand down with it. Halfway to the ground, at what will be the hub, it drops again on a single vertical thread and secures it to the ground or a twig. From here, two more radial lines, attached left and right to vegetation or rock, form the main structure.

The spider then lays spokes radiating out from the hub and spins out an ever-increasing spiral of dry silk around it. Eventually the spider turns and retraces its path, eating the dry silk and replacing it with wet sticky silk. It

The Garden Orb-weaving Spider (1.5–3cm/¼–1¼in) hangs upside down in the centre of its web, its legs outstretched to touch separate radiating spokes. A common spider in parks and gardens throughout Australia, this species is the architect of one of the most refined wheel webs. Each night it will rebuild its web, strategically locating it across the flight path of winged insects.

Female St Andrew's Cross Spiders (4cm/2in) are recognised by the bands of black, white and yellow across their abdomen. The 'cross' that gives them their name comes from the four zigzag lines of silk that are often built into the spokes of the web. These daytime weavers catch flies, grasshoppers, bees and butterflies. When threatened, they vibrate the web violently, becoming a blur—presumably to confound the predator. The cross reinforces the web during such activity.

ties each strand at its spoke and twangs it to space the sticky beads evenly across its length. Having paintakingly completed the return spiral, it sits at the hub and waits.

There are many variations. Not all webs are complete and some are only made of dry silk. Some have platforms, retreats and mazes off to the side. Some are horizontal or inclined rather than vertical. For example, the horizontal wheel webs of long-jawed spiders are constructed between reeds just above the water to catch gnats as they rise from its surface.

Golden Orb-weavers

In summer all the way down the east and west coasts shrubs and small trees in woodlands, forests and gardens are festooned with shimmering golden webs that catch the light of the early morning sun. These belong to female golden orb-weavers. Large, silvery grey and long-legged, these spiders build more-or-less permanent wheel webs with 1m (39in)-wide spans and sufficient strength to withstand the energetic struggles of large prey, such as cicadas.

The female stays in her web day and night, mending tears when necessary. There is a tangle of webs off to each side of the main web and waste products and remnants of meals are suspended from an upper strut of silk, forming handy decoys to potential predators. Tiny males hang around the edges, consumed with lust and fear, eeking out a living on scraps she discards from her meals. These spiders die in the colder

LOVE BITES

For a male spider, mating is often a suicidal mission as female spiders sometimes conclude the mating event by eating their partner. The best way for the miniscule male golden orb-weaver (6mm/¼in) to safely inseminate the large female (4cm/2in) is to do so while she is preoccupied with eating or wrapping food. Chances are she won't even notice.

months, having deposited eggs wrapped in golden silk into bark and rock crevices.

The Australian spiders that weave these magnificent wheel webs are generally harmless but will give a painful bite if severely provoked. Should you accidentally bump into one, do not panic. The spider will almost definitely bale out immediately, escaping on a silken safety line.

Spider Paralysis

Spiders have many enemies. Mammals, birds, reptiles and insects all eat spiders, and birds steal strands of silk from webs to build their nests. Spiders also frequently feed on other spiders. The White-tailed Spider, for example, is a spider specialist. Perhaps the worst enemy of spiders, however, are the wasps. These insects seek out spiders assiduously, slipping in behind bark, venturing down trapdoor burrows and snatching the living centrepieces from their wheel webs. They sting the spider, causing paralysis but not death. They then stuff its limp body inside a prepared cell and inject an egg into its living flesh before sealing the cell and leaving the spider to be consumed alive once the larva hatches.

> ### LEAFY RETREAT
> The asymmetrical wheel web of the Leaf-curling Spider may be untidy but its retreat is a clever piece of engineering. It hoists a leaf up from the ground into its web on a thread of silk and rolls it up with more silk. Tucked snugly within its leafy lair, it remains protected from the elements and predators, and virtually invisible to potential prey.

The jewel-like spiny spiders are found in subtropical and tropical regions of the world and several species inhabit Australia. They all construct vertical wheel webs and the most widespread and common Australian species can occur in large congregations of individual webs. Although small, they are well protected with six sharp spikes and a hard chitinous abdomen.

Centipedes and Millipedes

So far, 147 species of native centipedes and more that 300 species of native millipedes have been described for Australia, and it is likely that more are yet to be discovered.

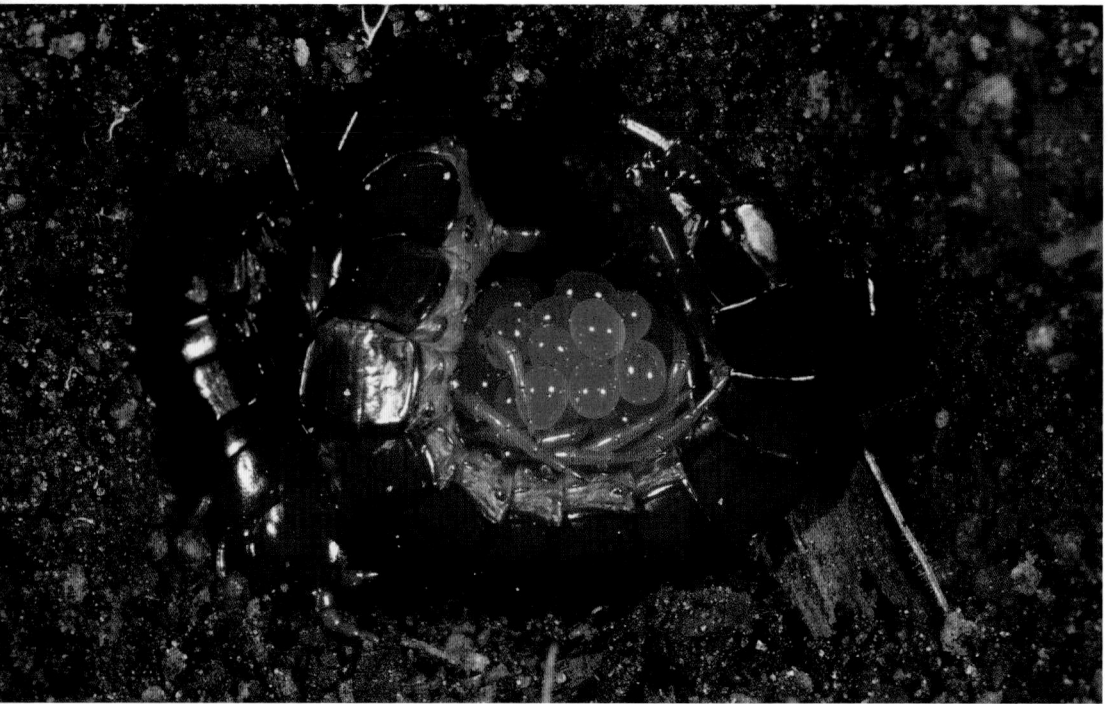

A female scolopendrid centipede curls herself defensively around her cluster of eggs. When these young hatch they will have their full complement of body segments and legs, but young that lack parental care acquire more segments and legs as they moult and grow. If young centipedes fail to disperse after their second moult, their ravenous mother may give way to temptation and eat them. Only after a further eight moults will they attain sexual maturity.

TASSIE BIODIVERSITY

In Tasmania alone 160 species of millipedes have been identified.

Centipedes and millipedes spend their days beneath rocks, logs and bark or in leaf litter and soil. Both animals have a head with a single pair of antennae and a long segmented shiny body with many pairs of legs. Both, too, employ the same system of breathing (via spiracles and trachea) and waste disposal as insects. Despite these similarities, they are very different from one another.

Predators and Vegetarians

Centipedes have flexible, flattened bodies so they can squeeze into narrow spaces. Their legs—one pair for each body segment—splay out from either side. They are carnivores whose first pair of legs has become modified to form claws containing venom glands. With these they stab and inject other invertebrates and defend themselves from predators. The last trailing pair of legs, often long and curved, may serve as pincers for grasping and holding prey, or as sensory structures. Centipedes can run fast and, while most hunt small invertebrates, Australia's largest and most aggressive centipedes, like the Giant Centipede that grows to 14cm (5½in) long, can kill geckos and mice.

The slower, less flexible millipedes have flattened or round bodies with a harder exoskeleton and generally two pairs of legs that arise from beneath each body segment, at least in adults. They are vegetarians that chew decomposing vegetable matter. Although mostly ground dwellers, they sometimes move into the lower branches of trees. They have no venom. Instead they protect themselves from predators by rolling up into a spiral and secreting irritant and foul-smelling chemicals. One group, the stout pill millipedes, roll themselves up into a round ball presenting only their hard, shiny exoskeleton.

Long-legged 'house' centipedes have 15 pairs of multi-jointed legs, whip-like antennae, large eyes and a front pair of legs that look like long antennae. They see well, run fast and hunt in more open spaces than most centipedes. Although they sometimes venture into houses, they are harmless and will keep your spiders, flies and silverfish under control.

Mating and Maternal Care

The aggressive centipedes prefer to mate at a distance, the male laying a packet of sperm on the ground, which the female then takes up into her reproductive tract. The vegetarian millipedes, on the other hand, mate in a tight embrace and face to face as the male transfers a bundle of his sperm firstly from the base near his second legs to his seventh segment and from there to the female's sexual pouch in a similar position.

While some centipedes care for their young, many abandon their eggs in soil or leaf litter. The females of several species, including some forest centipedes from an ancient Gondwanan group known as stone centipedes, have special appendages behind and between their last pair of walking legs for rolling their eggs in soil to camouflage them before hiding them beneath stones or vegetation to incubate. Some millipede eggs receive parental protection after being laid into soil, leaf litter, fashioned chambers or nests.

ANCIENT GIANTS

Four hundred million years ago millipedes up to 2m (78in) long were crawling on the Earth. Among some of the earliest pioneers of land, they crept out of fresh water and into blankets of moist ferns. Predators, such as centipedes, rapidly followed in their wake.

Nothing to Fear

Millipedes are harmless to humans although some stain soft furnishings and skin and the notorious introduced Black Portuguese Millipede that sometimes reaches plague proportions in southern Australia will destroy fruit and vegetable crops. It is inadvisable to handle centipedes. A bite from a large one can be painful and cause localised swelling but no deaths have been recorded in Australia.

HOW MANY LEGS?

Despite their names, millipedes do not have a thousand legs, nor do centipedes have a hundred. Many centipedes have only 15 pairs, although more is common. Millipedes generally have more than centipedes; up to 375 pairs have been recorded but as few as 11 pairs are also known.

This millipede was found in the Bunya Mountains of Queensland grazing on filaments of fungi from decaying wood. Millipedes from this area are yet to be described.

Silverfish and Earwigs

These little nocturnal insects often scuttle about in and around our homes—the primitive silverfish in dark corners and cupboards; earwigs under pots and rocks around our gardens. Several overseas species of both insects have established themselves in Australia but there are also at least 31 native silverfish and 85 native earwigs, with probably more still to be discovered.

Ever come across this curious creature zipping around in the bath or exposed in a drawer? This is an introduced silverfish and it will eat the glue and paper of your books. Native silverfish stick to the bush.

We most commonly encounter introduced species. With no traditional predators to keep their numbers in check, they are often the pest species, too. For example, the common household silverfish will nibble holes in your clothes and books and the European Earwig can cause serious damage to fruit, foliage and flowers.

Silverfish

These wingless, scaled creatures have a tapering body, long antennae and three long distinct tails. The main domestic species are silvery but others may be almost white, yellow or brown with dark stripes. Silverfish can run very fast but they cannot scale smooth surfaces. Native species are usually found under rocks, logs and leaf litter. Some shelter behind bark. A few species are known only from caves and still others, only a few millimetres long (less than $\frac{1}{10}$in), inhabit the galleries of ants and termites.

INSECT EVOLUTION

The evolution of primitive insects like silverfish to highly developed ones like butterflies, wasps and ants is reflected in how the young change as they moult. Young silverfish moult continuously, increasing in size but never altering their fundamental form. Insects like earwigs change gradually and subtly with each moult. The transformation from wingless larva to winged adult in advanced insects is so radical that it requires an intermediate stage, the pupa, in which the body can undergo a complete restructure.

Silverfish can live for up to five years. They moult throughout their lifetime. There is no larval stage; just increasingly larger versions as they grow. Although some species produce young from unfertilised eggs (a process known as parthenogenesis), most eggs are fertilised by sperm delivered in a packet by the male onto a surface over which he then encourages the female to crawl. When the packet contacts the reproductive opening on her underside, it snaps open and the sperm spills into her. She then eats the packet.

> **WILL SILVERFISH EAT CLOTHING?**
>
> Starch sometimes occurs in fabrics and silverfish love starchy food. They occasionally damage clothes in storage but this is not their preferred food.

Earwigs

Earwigs are small brown or black shiny-bodied insects. They have antennae and pincers at the tip of their abdomen, which are more curved in males. Some earwigs are wingless; others have a small front pair of wings and large membranous hind wings that compact neatly under small covers.

Earwigs can burrow but often they just shelter beneath bark, logs and rocks. They mostly eat plant matter but also take dead and some live invertebrates. They sometimes capture prey with their pincers but these are more often used to carry prey, defend themselves and in courtship rituals.

This native earwig from south-western Western Australia is one of the continent's most colourful species.

Female earwigs lay their eggs in a crevice or self-made burrow and guard them from predators. They regularly clean and turn them to keep them free from fungi. The nymphs that hatch look similar but not identical to small adults. After a couple of moults they move on or risk being eaten by their mother.

Australia's east coast wet forests contain one of the world's largest earwigs, the Giant Earwig, which is 5.5cm (2in) long. Another notable native is the Common Brown Earwig, a predator of caterpillars that is known to attack codling moth, a serious pest of fruit crops.

An earwig's pincers serve a number of functions. They can, as you see, be wielded with considerable flexibility. Males wave them about when courting females and fight off predators with them. They are also used for grasping, hauling and even killing small prey, but they are too small to inflict pain on a human.

Cockroaches

Many people view cockroaches with revulsion but the domestic scavengers we see skedaddling about in our kitchens are introduced species. There are probably a thousand native species of cockroaches in Australia, of which 530 have been named and described. They are all harmless and rarely venture into homes.

Some cockroaches are solitary insects but these arid-zone cockroaches congregate together beneath rocks, logs and clumps of spinifex. These individuals are probably all members of a single family.

DO COCKROACHES SPREAD DISEASE?

Home-invading cockroaches are not innately dirty. In fact, they groom themselves constantly to keep their bodies clean and in working order. However, they have the potential to carry diseases because they may scrabble about in places like sewers and then wander over our food. They can transmit organisms from one place to another on their feet and in their droppings but they are not vectors of specific diseases in the way that certain mosquitoes carry malaria.

Native species vary in length from a tiny 3mm (1/10 in) one to the world's largest cockroach, the 7cm (3in)-long Giant Burrowing Cockroach. The size of a small mouse, this uncharacteristically slow lumbering cockroach is from north Queensland and is sometimes kept as a pet.

Like the troublesome American or German Cockroaches, most Australian 'roaches' have flattened bodies so they are able to squeeze into narrow spaces such as under bark, stones or logs. They forage in the bush among leaf litter, vegetation, rotten wood, soil, foliage and flowers. Some, if not all, return nutrients to the soil by eating wood and dead leaves. While many are forest dwellers, there are desert cockroaches too, like the locally known Rain Beetles that burrow 60cm (24in) below ground. After rain they come to the surface in their thousands to look for new opportunities.

Not all cockroaches can fly. Some are forever wingless. Others have wings only for a while and in some species just the males are winged. Most female cockroaches carry their eggs in a capsule that projects from the tip of their abdomen. Abandoned in a sheltered spot, the capsule eventually dries and splits, leaving the hatched nymphs free to trundle off independently.

Cockroaches are vulnerable during moulting but most of the time their soft parts are protected beneath a hard exoskeleton. Some defend themselves from predators by rolling up while others use the secretion of pungent odours as an effective deterrent.

Some of Australia's bush cockroaches are colourful and many are beautifully marked. This Painted Cockroach is active during the day, unlike many other species, and can be found sunbaking in the morning across drier areas in southern Australia. It lives in all sorts of arid and semi-arid habitats, including caves, and searches for fungi in the cracks of decaying wood.

Stoneflies and Mayflies

As adults, these insects are winged but most of their lives are spent as nymphs submerged in cool, running fresh water. Stoneflies especially like cool alpine streams and 75 per cent of the 200 Australian species are endemic to Tasmania, although tropical species do exist. From temperate Australia, 100 mayfly species have been recognised to date.

At first glance adult stoneflies may look like elongated flies but note the long antennae, thread-like tails and how the two pairs of membranous wings fold flat against the abdomen. Stoneflies live mostly underwater feeding as nymphs and fly only during a relatively brief adulthood.

Nymphal mayflies and most stoneflies crawl and sometimes swim around stream beds. They usually draw oxygen from the water via gills in their thorax or abdomen but one family of stoneflies have gills that sprout like little tufts from the end of their abdomen. Nymphs feed on plants, organic debris, algae and sometimes tiny aquatic animals. They undergo many moults and while the mayfly's life cycle is often annual, stoneflies in cold mountain streams may remain there for two to three years before floating to the surface and clambering out to become winged adults.

Adult stoneflies can live for several weeks but adult mayflies survive for only a few hours or several days, during which time they do not eat—their digestive system is, instead, filled with air and used for balancing in flight.

NATURE'S ENVIRONMENTAL MONITORS

Stoneflies and Mayflies are sensitive to pollution and are often used to assess the health of fresh water.

FROM GILLS TO WINGS

Mayflies are ancient insects. The fossils of mayfly-like nymphs have been found with finely veined, highly mobile gills that may have been the progenitor of insect wings.

Mayflies are the only insects that moult with fully developed wings. The wings in the first (sub-adult or sub-imago) stage are opaque. This stage is known to fishermen as 'duns', and it may last only a few hours before, inflated with air, the insect moults again. This time its wings are translucent and filmy, like soft, veined glass. They are held vertically, the front pair being much larger than the back

A male sub-adult mayfly. The three thread-like tails and vertically held wings are typical of mayflies. Males have 'split eyes' which give them excellent, panoramic vision enabling them to pick out females when flying in a mating swarm. The claspers below the tails and their long front legs help them grasp their partner as they transfer sperm into her reproductive opening in mid-air.

pair. Extending from the tip of the abdomen are three stiff, thread-like tails.

While adult mayflies are proficient fliers and make the most of their time to participate in mating swarms above water, adult stoneflies have delicate wings and are reluctant to fly. They feed on algae, lichen and rotting wood and mate on vegetation or stones close to water. Some alpine species live in and around dense mosses.

Female mayflies and most female stoneflies drop their eggs into water, where they sink; some female stoneflies, however, struggle to the bottom of streams to lay their eggs.

FISHERMEN'S FRIENDS

Stoneflies and mayflies are a major source of food for many highly prized freshwater fish like trout. This is why so many artificial flies used by fly fishermen are carefully crafted to mimic various species and various life stages of these insects.

Damselflies and Dragonflies

On warm sunny days, especially in coastal and tropical areas, damselflies and dragonflies dash through the air. Of the world's 5000 species, 300 are known from Australia and up to 40 per cent of these species may have been flying around Australia when it was still part of Gondwana.

Damselflies and dragonflies are bound by a life cycle that depends on fresh water. Some species like fast-flowing rivers and creeks; others prefer swamps or lakes. Those inhabiting temporary pools have evolved a rapid life cycle.

During the few months of their winged adulthood, damselflies and dragonflies are impressive aerial acrobats and predators, snatching mosquitoes, butterflies and gnats in their spiny feet as they fly, consuming them in mid-air or while perched on aquatic vegetation. Most of their lives, however, are spent in obscurity as larvae submerged in freshwater streams and lakes.

Larval Life

Larvae vary in length from less than 1cm (⅓in) to more than 7cm (3in). Dragonfly larvae are chunkier and often larger than damselfly larvae. You can distinguish a damselfly larvae by the three paddle-shaped gills protruding from the end of its abdomen. These are absent in dragonflies, although there are sometimes one or two sharp prongs. The gills of dragonflies are located internally in their rectum, where muscular action continually sucks in and pushes out water.

Like the adults, larvae are ferocious predators. Armed with toothed jaws and large, scoop-like mouthparts, they stalk, ambush and lunge at small fishes, tadpoles, worms, crustaceans and the larvae of midges, mayflies and mosquitoes. In the murky habitat at the bottom of pools, they blend in with their surroundings, some even 'wearing' silt or algae on their back to disguise themselves.

They remain submerged for ten or more moults before crawling out of the water and pulling themselves up onto a stone or the vertical stem of an aquatic plant. Their skin splits down the back and as the insect drags itself free, a short, compressed body gradually extends to become long, slender and often brightly coloured. There are two enormous compound eyes and two pairs of thin, glassy wings that are fragile looking but stoutly veined and supported by powerful muscles on the thorax.

A Blue Skimmer Dragonfly rests beside its sloughed-off larval skin as its body elongates and its crinkled wings gradually expand. Once its body and wings have hardened in the air and transformation into a magnificent flying machine is complete, it will lift off in search of shelter among vegetation before taking to a life of aerial piracy and sexual gratification.

A DAMSELFLY WITH HISTORY

A small green damselfly species known as the Ancient Greenling is believed to be one of the earliest prototypes of this group ever to fly. It has been around for 270 million years and, although rare, it still flies through Australian airspace today.

Female dragonflies and damselflies are prodigious egg layers. Here Spot-winged Threadtails are participating in a communal egg-laying event. After mating, male damselflies retain their grasp on the female as she lays her fertilised eggs into water in order to ensure no other male intercedes and to lift her out of harm's way should a predator threaten them.

The three paddle-shaped gills at the end of the abdomen identify this larva as a damselfly. Larvae are usually brown or green to avoid detection by their prey. They can even sometimes change their colour after moulting to match their hunting habitat.

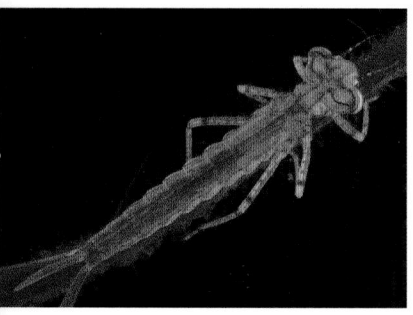

Knowing the Difference

As their name suggests, damselflies are distinctly thinner and daintier than dragonflies. When at rest, they usually fold their wings together along their body, the two pairs of nearly equal proportions. Dragonflies, on the other hand, hold their wings out perpendicular to their body like an aeroplane and the first pair is broader than the second. The enormous compound eyes of the dragonflies abut one another, while those of damselflies are well spaced.

Life on the Wing

These winged adults can fly long distances and at great speed: up to 50kph (31mph) in some cases. Their extensive travels in search of food and mates can take them long distances and often far from water. In the air their manoeuvrability is astounding; they can hover, fly upwards or downwards, to one side or another and even backwards.

Precision flying is invaluable during mating. Hovering above his female quarry, the male seizes his partner behind her head with claspers at the end of his abdomen. As they fly around together the female bends her abdomen down and forward to lift its end into his second abdominal segment. Their bodies now form a circle or 'wheel' and in this position they continue to fly as they mate.

MAKING A FRESH START

Females may mate with several males. A male tries to ensure that it is his genes that get passed on to the next generation by assiduously sweeping out his partner's reproductive tract to rid it of any residual sperm from past encounters before depositing his own.

Termites

The most striking feature of Australia's northern savannas are the termite mounds that dot the landscape. There are over 350 termite species in Australia, most inhabiting the northern tropics. Among them are the remarkable 'magnetic' termites that build their towering earthen mounds orientated north–south to regulate internal temperatures.

Workers and soldiers of Spinifex Termites mingle together, each on their separate missions. In this species the soldiers are smaller than the workers but easily distinguished by their hard, dark heads, from which protrude pointy snouts. Chemical defences can be squirted through these snouts to defend the colony. Both workers and soldiers are forever wingless.

Termites are colonial insects around 1cm (⅜in) long. Although commonly known as white ants, they are not ants at all. They eat wood and other plant material. The cellulose content of their food is hard to digest but they have special micro-organisms in their digestive systems to break down the fibres.

These highly social creatures live within colonies in nests. Individuals living in the colony are divided into castes and are physically differentiated to perform certain tasks. Nest building and food gathering is undertaken by the wingless, infertile worker castes. Fuelled by moulted skins and termite cadavers, these blind, soft-bodied creatures serve masticated dinner from both ends of their body to members of the

Built in northern Australia by Cathedral Termites, a rocket-shaped mound fluted by the passage of running water during the Wet season. These termites are remarkable architects, able to build high-rise structures up to 6m (20ft) tall.

MOUND MEDICINE

Traditional Aborigines sometimes take a pinchful of termite mound as a cure for diarrhoea, stomach aches and menstrual pain. It may be the high mineral content that settles the stomach. Kaolin, a well-known soother for tummy upsets, is also clay-based.

colony. They also patch and extend the mound and care for the eggs and larvae. Soldier castes defend the colony. They have large, heavily protected heads that carry modified mouthparts, part of which are fashioned into monstrous weapons.

There is also a fertile queen and several reproductive stand-bys, as well as a dutiful but unremarkable siring king. The grossly distended white abdomen of the queen, up to 3cm (1in) long, churns out as many as 3000 eggs a day. If nothing happens to her or the colony she may parent millions of termites over a lifetime of 20 or more years.

The life of a colony begins when virgin kings and queens, known as alates, fly out of an old nest at dusk on a warm summer night, often after rain. As they land they release pheromones to attract a mate and their wings drop off. Pairs then bury themselves in damp soil or tree trunks and nest. The earliest broods hatch into larvae that become the first workers and soldiers of the new colony. As the colony enlarges the queen becomes a full-time egg-laying machine and so the colony grows.

NOT ALL TERMITES EAT BUILDINGS

The scale of building destruction by termites is legendary and a survey by the Commonwealth Scientific and Research Organisation (CSIRO) reveals that about 30 per cent of homes have, or have had at some time, termites gnawing through their timbers. However, only six per cent of species infest wooden structures. Most termites are harmless so, before you call in the pest controllers, consult an expert who can identify the species you have.

Termite nests may be subterranean or extend into wooden structures, sometimes 'growing' out like carbuncles from tree trunks and branches. Still others rise from the ground like castles, reaching up to 6m (20ft) high. Honeycombed with galleries, cells and ducts, they are all remarkable feats of engineering, built to house millions of light-sensitive creatures at precisely regulated humidity and temperature levels. Nests are built from clay and plant fibre. The clay is often collected from subsoils rich in minerals and counters the leaching processes of heavy monsoonal rains.

Small as they are, termites play a major role in their environments. Their constant chewing up of wood, dead leaves and grasses provides an excellent recycling service for natural materials. Termites are also central to many food webs and a number of native animals depend upon them. For Short-beaked Echidnas, Numbats, blind snakes and some tiny frogs they are a staple food. Kookaburras, some goannas, Hooded Parrots and several kingfishers nest in termite mounds, while burrowing Pale Field-rats and Delicate Mice often dig into the 'basement'. The acoustic qualities of termite hollows amplify the calls of Northern Tree Frogs while certain geckos, pseudantechinuses, lizards, snakes, ants, beetles, silverfish and flies all avail themselves of the air-conditioned accommodation provided by termites.

DANCE OF THE TERMITES

After heavy rain on a warm balmy evening in summer, millions of fragile flying termites flutter silently through the air. Released from purpose-built escape hatches in the walls of their nests, their synchronised flight is a once-in-a-lifetime quest to establish new colonies. Few will make it. Most will be snapped up in mid-air by birds, netted in spider webs or die after crash landing and losing their wings.

The laterally compressed, wedge-shaped mounds of Magnetic Termites are orientated along a north–south axis. Known from nowhere else on Earth, they are built on northern Australia's floodplains. During the Wet season the resident termites, unable to live underground because the soil is inundated, occupy the above-ground portion of their structures. Remarkably, the magnetic alignment of the mounds provides a more or less constant temperature of 30 °C (86 °F), which is just comfortable for the thin-skinned, temperature-sensitive termites.

Stick and Leaf Insects

Coming across these thin, elongated insects is always a big surprise. Varying from 3–30cm (1–12in) long, they escape attention by masquerading as twigs or leaves, frequently on eucalypts or wattles. There are 104 described species from Australia, although more are likely to be described in the future. Only three of them are 'true' leaf insects and these are all restricted to the rainforests of northern Queensland.

These insects are collectively known as phasmids. They are vegetarians and, for the most part, nocturnal. The bodies of stick insects are long and thin, those of leaf insects are broad, almost flattened, to look remarkably like leaves. A phasmid's disguise goes beyond camouflage to mimic even the breeze as it sways about on long legs. While some phasmids fly (mainly males), many are wingless.

Eggs are sometimes fertilised by males attracted to females by their scent but

RAVENOUS STICKS

Populations of stick insects can grow to such large numbers that they become pests, defoliating entire stands of trees with their voracious appetites.

One of Australia's most spectacular insects is the Darwin Stick Insect that can grow up to 25.5cm (10in) long. While males can fly, this heavy-bodied female is incapable of flight. However, the scarlet stripe running along the underside margin of her rear wings, when revealed, is enough to startle and deter many potential predators.

often females completely dispense with male fertilisation (parthenogenesis) and lay unfertilised eggs to produce female clones.

While the female Macleay's Spectre swings her abdomen with gusto, flinging her eggs out like golf balls, dispersing them far and wide, other phasmids may just drop theirs one by one on to the ground. Eggs may resemble seeds with a tiny tasty knob to entice ants, which obligingly carry them off and bury them, thereby protecting them from predators, parasites and fire. When the nymphs hatch, they dig themselves out and hastily clamber up stalks or trunks to escape being eaten. Often a leg or two is lost in the rush but these regrow as the nymphs moult.

THE WORLD'S RAREST INSECT

Before Black Rats jumped ship onto Lord Howe Island (780km/500 miles north-east of Sydney) in 1918, there were giant stick insects, 12cm (5in)-long, festooning the canopy of forest trees at night. Locally known as Land Lobsters, they chomped away on leaves, hiding by day in tree crevices and hollows. Within a few decades the Black Rats had driven them to extinction, or so it seemed until three females were discovered on a spectacular sea stack called Ball's Pyramid 23km (14 miles) south-east of the main island. Now the focus of a recovery plan, these critically endangered insects may well make a comeback.

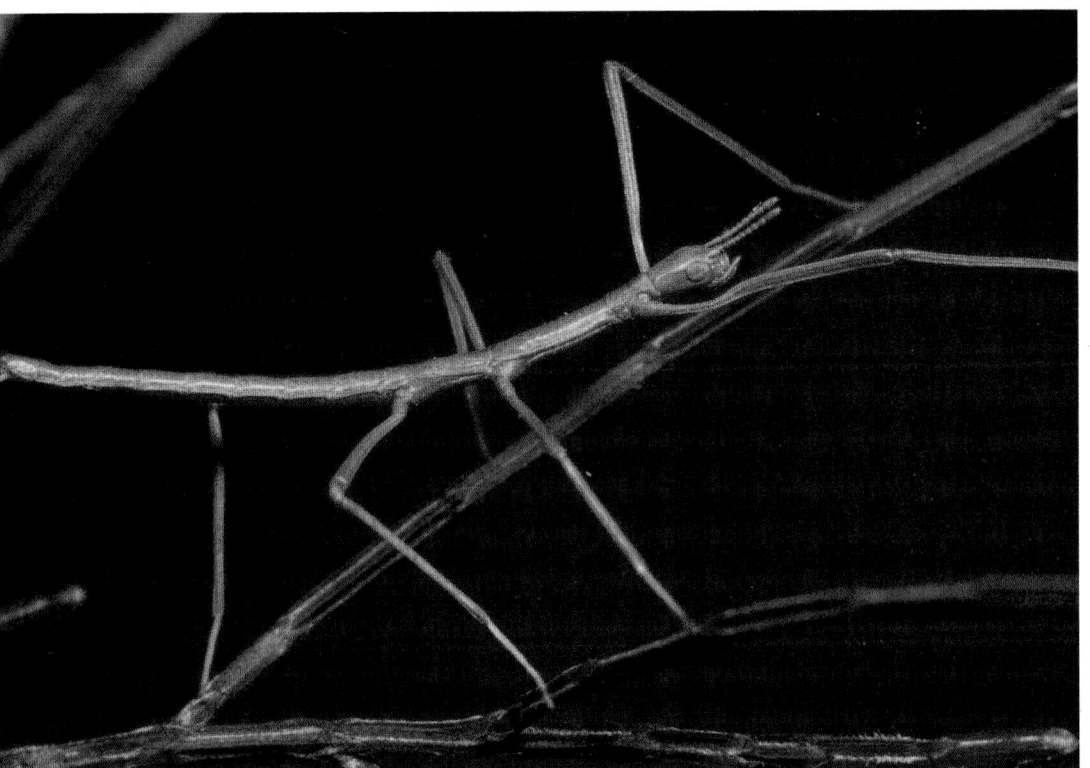

When a phasmid is threatened by a bird, its most feared predator, it usually freezes, stretching its front legs out to align with its body. If detected, it may flash open a pair of bright wings, hiss or kick with its back legs and spray the predator with a chemical deterrent.

These animals make popular pets, especially with children. They are harmless to humans but they are extremely fragile, so handle them with care.

It can be disconcerting to see a twig on the move. Here the young nymph of a stick insect matches the branches of a she-oak, even down to its leaf nodes. Only careful scrutiny of vegetation reveals the presence of a stick insect unless it is blown from its cover by wind.

Praying Mantids

Lurking beside ponds, outside lights and in among leaves and flowers are some of the world's fiercest insects. Stalkers and ambushers, the bodies of the praying mantids are built for surveillance and seizure. In Australia over 160 species of these miniature predators have been recorded.

This praying mantis lives in the mallee country of western New South Wales, north-western Victoria and the south-west. The thickened forelegs, lined with sharp spikes, are built for holding prey in a deathly embrace.

Adult mantids are usually 3–15cm (1–6in) long, although smaller and larger species are found. Mostly a cryptic green or brown, some have patches of bright colours, often on their underside. A few species are wingless but in most cases they have two pairs of wings: the front ones, hardened for protection, and large membranous hind wings for flying.

Keen eyesight and a panoramic view are provided by their two large bulging compound eyes, accompanied by three simple ones, mounted on a flexible swivelling head. A line or two of sharp spines fringe the mantid's muscular forelegs. As it stands alert, camouflaged among the leaves, these raptorial forelegs are poised, as if in prayer but in reality, ready to grasp passing insects. A mantid's attack is swift and usually fatal.

Savage Sex

Sex, too, can be a deadly affair. Females of some species often eat their partners after, or during, mating. The head is the first to go. The well-nourished female then produces a frothy liquid into which she lays up to several hundred eggs. She glues the whole structure to the underside of a leaf, a twig or bark and it quickly hardens into a protective egg case.

Parasitic wasps sometimes drill holes into these cases and lay their own eggs within. If the eggs survive, the nymphs that hatch look like miniature wingless adults. Only after their final moult into adulthood do mantids develop fully functional wings.

Superbly camouflaged, this female praying mantis is secreting an egg case (ootheca). This mass of white froth into which she will lay her eggs will soon harden. It will remain glued to the vegetation, withstanding all sorts of weather, long after the nymphs have hatched out.

Grasshoppers and Crickets

Of the world's 20,000 species, Australia has about 3000 grasshoppers, crickets, katydids and locusts. They are found throughout Australia, from alpine regions to rainforests, but the greatest diversity inhabit the arid inland. Just six species occasionally sweep across the country in migratory swarms known as locust plagues and from time to time several other species cause economic damage to crops.

Grasshoppers and crickets have powerful chewing mouthparts, two large compound eyes, three simple ones and antennae that are sensitive to smell, touch, humidity, vibration, wind velocity and direction. They range in size from 0.5cm (⅕in) to the native Giant Grasshopper whose body alone is 9cm (4in) long, but an average body length is between 3–6cm (1–2in).

These are mostly jumping insects powered by large muscular hindlegs. A few, like the mole crickets and sandgropers, have lost their ability to hop and taken to burrowing instead. Grasshoppers and crickets usually eat flowers, leaves and fruits but the tree and king crickets and some katydids are predatory.

Most adult grasshoppers and crickets can fly . . . to a point. Usually a large, membranous rear pair of wings are folded up like fans beneath the protection of a narrow, leathery front pair. Some, like the small ant

The mangled corpses of the Australian Plague Locust dashed against a car radiator. They are one of three native species that can form dense swarms and migrate long distances, wreaking havoc upon crops and pastures on their way. Strangely, these insects normally behave like solitary grasshoppers but after heavy rains mass emergence of nymphs from the ground and fresh green pick conspire to change their behaviour. Good feed increases fertility and consequently breeding more ravenous little eating machines are produced with devastating economic consequences.

The dashing Southern Pyrgomorph or Spotted Mountain Grasshopper. This grasshopper lives in the grasslands and heaths of alpine Tasmania, Victoria and New South Wales and can withstand temperatures of -2 °C (28 °F)

for long periods of time. It belongs to a family of bulky, slow grasshoppers with poor jumping ability. To protect itself from predators it makes itself distasteful by absorbing toxins from the plants it eats. Even little native carnivorous marsupials are wary of these grasshoppers whose colours advertise their noxious qualities.

crickets, however, have no need of wings since they live their entire lives inside the nests of ants.

Males serenade females by rubbing body parts together. Small tympanal membranes on the legs or abdomen act as ears. The female selects her partner based largely on his singing performance. Once paired, the male transfers a packet of sperm into her reproductive opening. Grasshoppers and crickets lay their eggs slightly differently but hatched nymphs of both look similar to their parents except for the absence of wings and their disproportionately large heads. Several features distinguish grasshoppers from crickets.

Grasshoppers

Grasshoppers have relatively short, robust antennae, usually less than half their body length. They are active by day, typically hopping along the ground and among grasses and low bushes. Males attract females with buzzes and rattles usually created by rubbing a row of peg-like structures on the thighs of their hindlegs against a hard ridge on their forewings.

To avoid being located by predators, the insects must blend into their surroundings. There are bright green, blade-shaped grass-eaters, sand-grained speckled grasshoppers, grey mottled bark dwellers and squat stone-like gibber-desert dwellers. All are vegetarians, although some specialise on the dead leaves of eucalypts, their vulnerable nymphs disguised as papery brown gum leaves.

At the tip of a female grasshopper's abdomen there are four small, hard, triangular plates, which she uses to drill deep down into soil to form an egg chamber. In this chamber she lays groups of eggs drenched in a frothy fluid that hardens to form a weatherproof egg case. She then plugs the chamber with soil. When the nymphs hatch, they burrow up to the surface. Before reaching adulthood they will moult five or six times.

A pair of mating toad hoppers. Most male grasshoppers are smaller than females and this species is no exception. Toad hoppers live in Central Australia. In stony country their squat shape and brick red colouring blend into the ground perfectly.

HOW LOCUSTS FIND RAIN

Locusts have an uncanny knack of finding rain and the new plant growth that inevitably follows. Migrating swarms sometimes even arrive before the rain. They migrate to find new food and to stay ahead of their predators. Lift-off is often at sunset. The winged adults appear to climb up several hundred metres to catch winds associated with low-pressure systems. Things don't always go to plan though, as kilometre-long drifts of locusts washed up on southern beaches and inland lakes bear witness.

A pair of raspy crickets mating.
The female hangs onto the
vegetation with two pairs of legs while
the male inserts his packet of sperm into
her reproductive organ, holding nothing
more than the feet of her hindlegs and
her sword-shaped ovipositor.

Crickets

Crickets have impossibly long, thread-like antennae, often twice the length of their bodies. Most are nocturnal and forage anywhere from the ground to the treetops. These species hide during the day, mostly in soil crevices, burrows, beneath leaf litter or logs. One group, the raspy crickets, is able to produce silk: some roll up and bind a leaf with silk in which to rest; others return each day to a burrow made of silk and sand.

More often heard than seen, male crickets court females with 'songs' they create by the resonating vibration by strumming a plectrum on one forewing with a file-like structure on the other. A narrow egg-laying tube called an ovipositor that sticks out from the abdomen easily identifies the female. With this she lays eggs one at a time into soil, crevices or along vegetation. Most crickets do not guard their eggs or young, although mole crickets are an exception. Cricket nymphs moult 10 times before reaching adulthood.

There is remarkable variety among Australia's crickets. Colours vary, even within species, and males frequently bare little resemblance to their female counterparts. Some species have adapted to living in many different types of habitat; others are specialists of spinifex, gum trees or rainforests, often bearing similarities to the vegetation they occupy.

Common on the east coast are Black Field Crickets and many species of mole crickets. Field crickets are dark brown, around 3cm (1in) long and often hop into houses. Mole crickets, on the other hand, spend much of their lives below ground. You may come across them when digging into soil or the compost heap or you may hear a piercing

---

THE COOLOOLA MONSTER

In 1980 an Australian entomologist came across a large (2.5–4cm/1–2in) primitive cricket-like creature in the coastal heathlands of Queensland's Cooloola National Park. Only after heavy rain does the mysterious subterranean Cooloola Monster come to the surface to look for a mate. Hunched, bright orange, with useless tiny wing buds but stout burrowing legs, its antennae are uncharacteristically short. Thought to be carnivorous, little is known of this unusual creature but several similar species have since been unearthed.

sound coming from the ground around dusk, especially after or just before rain. Mole crickets are dark brown, 3–4cm (1–2in) long, stout and with enormously strong forelegs adapted for digging. Females have no visible external ovipositor. They lay their eggs in a chamber at the end of a burrow and guard them from predators. They even stay with them through the early moulting stages of nymph-hood.

Although rarely seen, ferocious king crickets, relatives of the New Zealand giant wetas, roam the forests of the east coast and Tasmania on warm wet nights. Armed with enormous jaws they fight other males for access to females. Their diet is broad, from fungi to frogs, and they even cannibalise females of their own species. While some are only 3.5cm (1in) long, species up to 10cm (4in) long inhabit Queensland rainforests.

Katydids have very long antennae and adults are usually leaf green or brown. They are quite common in grasslands, heaths, woodlands and forests, including rainforests. Many are active during the day but they are rarely seen due to their cryptic appearance among the vegetation. The wings of those inhabiting gum trees often mimic the leaves, not just in colour and shape but even in the arrangement of their veins. The rasping mating calls of males are sometimes heard in Australia's suburban gardens but not all species are nocturnal.

A female Green Flightless Predatory Katydid is standing on tippy toes to lay her eggs. Her ovipositor, which would usually stick out vertically from her abdomen, is sunk into the ground as she delivers the eggs, one by one, through the hollow tubular structure and into the earth.

THE MIGHTY MOLE CRICKET

When held tightly in a fist, a mole cricket will use its front legs to wedge itself in between the fingers. The strength it exerts is totally unexpected.

A female Perth Balloon-winged Katydid devours a cicada.

Psyllids and Scale Insects

These minute insects are relatives of the notorious whiteflies, aphids and mealybugs that are regarded by gardeners and horticulturalists as serious pests of flowers, vegetables and fruit. Many psyllids and scale insects are native to Australia and they play an integral role in the life of the bush.

These tiny sculptured domes are the 'homes' of whitefly nymphs. The psyllids and scale insects are cousins of whiteflies and their nymphs, too, live in similar constructions. Secreted by the nymphs themselves and crowded onto bark or the underside of leaves, the miniature shelters protect them during their vulnerable wingless stage.

Stuck to the underside of eucalypt leaves you may find little round domes, often white, pink or brown. These are the shelters of immature psyllids and scales known as nymphs, which have hatched from eggs laid onto or into vegetation or, in the case of some scale insects, are born live. Wingless and defenceless, these nymphs secrete tiny domed shelters to protect themselves from the elements and predators. Psyllid shelters are known as lerps and those of scale insects as scales: lerps and scales may be waxy and soft or armoured.

Nymphs undergo five or so moults before attaining adulthood. Most adults are winged and look like minute cicadas which is hardly surprising since they, along with aphids and mealybugs, belong to the same insect group. All adult members of this group feed by sucking fluids, mostly from plants, with mouthparts designed to pierce tissue and draw up sap.

Tiny as psyllids and scale insects are, they reproduce fast and infest plants heavily. Most mature plants can withstand infestations but, robbed of moisture and nutrients, some plants weaken, become stunted in their growth or succumb to transmitted viruses, eventually loosing their leaves.

Many Australian psyllids and scale insects have co-evolved with native plants like

---

LERP LANGUAGE

Many psyllids are referred to as lerps. Strictly speaking, lerps are the shelters these insects build but rather confusingly the common names of many psyllids include the name 'lerp' in them, as in Red Gum Lerp.

These colourful and wingless Oleander Aphids are doing what psyllids, scale insects, whiteflies and mealybugs do best: sucking the sap out of a plant. Their secretions from these sweet plant fluids are known as honeydew, which is a favourite food of many ants. The presence of ants around these bugs deters many of the predators and parasitoids. Sooty mould, which grows well on honeydew, is often in evidence, too, as a black 'soot' on the surface of infested leaves.

eucalypts, wattles, she-oaks and figs. Inconspicuous as they are, they form important links in many food chains. Lacewings, ladybirds and spiders prey upon them and female parasitoid wasps lay eggs into living nymphs. Those little birds of the eucalypt canopy, pardalotes, feed almost exclusively upon lerps and swallows snatch winged adults in mid-air.

ANCIENT APHIDS

There are native aphids that date back to a time when Australia was part of Gondwana.

Cicadas

The sizzling sound of cicadas is the sound of summer in Australia. Although cicadas are essentially tropical insects and the rainforests of north-eastern Queensland certainly contain the greatest diversity, these magnificent large insects are found in rainforests, eucalypt forests and woodlands, grasslands, mangroves and arid shrublands all the way to the south coast. Of the 247 species described for Australia, only four are found anywhere else in the world.

More often heard than seen, an adult cicada takes its turn in the sun after years underground. Its journey has been hazardous, having emerged from the soil as a nymph, crawled its way into the cover of vegetation and moulted into this large fully-winged beauty. Weary from its adventure and with its body and wings still crinkled and soft, it could have been an early bird's breakfast. Now, with its body and wings stretched and hardened, it has a fair chance of surviving long enough to mate.

An early-morning chorus of cicadas signals a hot day ahead. Cicadas only 'sing' when it's hot and only the males sing. They sing to attract a mate. The sound is made by a pair of muscles, warmed by the sun, dimpling and popping back a ribbed membrane called a tymbal, which is located just behind the base of the wings. Often contracting at the rate of 100 pulses or more a second and amplified by the male's mostly hollow abdomen, the sound can be deafening.

If they are not snapped up by birds or abducted by Cicada Killer Wasps, cicadas have a few weeks of singing, flying, mating and sucking plant juice. The female then carves slits in bark with a saw-like protuberance from the end of her abdomen and slots eggs into them. When the tiny nymphs hatch out they tumble to the ground and must quickly burrow down into the earth. Once out of harm's way, they tunnel to some juicy young root and commence feeding.

Here cicada nymphs continue to grow and moult, often for several years, before tunnelling up to the surface and emerging into the air, usually under the cover of darkness. Their strong front legs pull them up into the nearest bush or tree for safety. The nymph then splits its skin. What crawls out is a beautiful creature in search of a mate.

NATTY NAMES

Australian cicada species have some very descriptive names. There are Cherrynoses, Double Drummers, Redeyes, Greengrocers, Yellow Mondays, Floury Bakers, Squeakers and Razor Grinders.

True Bugs

Although we think of any small creepy crawly as a bug, strictly speaking 'true' bugs are insects with sucking mouthparts belonging to the order Hemiptera. Because most suck plant sap, they are often considered pests. Australia has its share of cosmopolitan sap suckers but there are many native bugs too, some of which have been associated with native plants for tens of millions of years.

Bugs can vary in size from 0.4–7cm (⅛–3in) long, not counting their sometimes quite long antennae. Most adults, at least males, can fly. Their forewings are leathery at the base but membranous at the tip. This is a helpful distinction when trying to distinguish between some shiny black burrowing bugs and similar-looking beetles. A distasteful aspect of many bugs is their stink glands, which release a foul-smelling fluid when the insect is threatened.

Stink or Shield Bugs

One of the best-known native stink bugs is the Bronze Orange Bug (2.5cm/1in long). Anyone from the coastal regions of

These jewel bugs, photographed in Katherine Gorge in the Northern Territory, belong to a family of brightly coloured plant-suckers with a metallic sheen and a shield-like plate that hides their wings. Sometimes known as shield-backed bugs, they frequently cluster together on the underside of leaves to avoid predators. Like stink bugs, they can smell and taste bad, and their colouring is a reminder to potential predators. On the east coast native hibiscus plants, such as the Norfolk Island Hibiscus, are often infested with jewel bugs.

Life may look precarious for these shield bug nymphs (Eumecopus sp.) but this mid-air location for starting a family is out of the reach of many marauding predators. The nymphs have already undergone their first moult; their skeletons hang abandoned. The eggs from which they have emerged remain clustered and neatly sliced open.

eastern Australia who has a lemon tree in their backyard is likely to have encountered these bugs. Dark brown and bronze, with orange antennae, the hard and soft parts of its forewings are clearly visible.

Adults appear with young nymphs in early summer. They feed on the fresh juice of young leaves, which then wilt. They are slow-moving but tenaciously maintain their grip if you try to knock them off. In order to remove these bugs, wear garden gloves as they will spray you with a stream of horrible-smelling, skin-staining fluid when handled.

In common with other stink bugs, Bronze Orange Bugs mate end to end. The female lays her eggs in a cluster on the underside of a leaf. The first stage of life, called the first instar, is a minute wingless version of its parents but it is cryptically coloured green. As it moults and grows it changes colour, at first providing camouflage but later warning predators with its bright red pigment.

Assassin Bugs

The assassin bugs are predators that impale their prey on their long, sturdy feeding tubes which, instead of lying flat along their underside, as in most plant-feeding bugs, sit in an arc away from their body. Usually 1–3cm (⅓–1in) long, they ambush or stalk their quarry on vegetation, under bark or along the ground. Should an insect venture within striking distance the assassin bug stabs it through its cuticle, pumps saliva into the wound to paralyse it and liquefies its tissues. It then sucks up the 'soup' in its feeding tube. After its meal, only the skeleton of the victim remains.

Assassin bugs are a cunning lot. Some hang out in spiders' webs and steal enmeshed prey. Others stab termites through the walls of their mounds. There are bugs that mimic the scent of ants to lure them within striking distance. There is also a species from Cape York Peninsula that sucks blood from mammals and birds.

While some assassin bugs are conspicuously coloured, others are well camouflaged and some cover themselves in dirt and spider webs in order to disguise themselves. If they are harassed, they may bite a human, causing a stabbing pain like that of a bee or wasp sting.

> ### CROSS-BEARING BUGS
> Crusader bugs (2.5cm/1in long) look like elongated stink bugs but are distinguished by a yellow cross on their brown or grey backs. Like their relatives, the stink bugs, they emit a foul-smelling fluid. They are commonly found feeding on wattles and eucalypts, as well as citrus plants and roses.

Toppled and helpless, a ladybird is administered a deadly dose of fluid from the stout beak of an assassin bug. Not only will this paralyse the ladybird, it also acts like battery acid on its body, liquefying its tissues to a consistency suitable for drawing up through the bug's proboscis.

Aquatic Bugs

Many bugs have taken to fresh water and a predatory way of life, leading to some curious adaptations and non-conformist behaviour. These bugs usually have well-developed wings and are quick to colonise new wetlands, a useful trait in a land of unpredictable rainfall.

Water striders of more than one species often band together to hunt large prey. Here two species are sharing the spoils of a drowned praying mantid. Their forelegs grasp the prey as their proboscis stabs through the outer skeleton and into the flesh. Having liquefied the soft tissues, they will suck them up.

Water Striders or Pond Skaters

These spindly legged insects are often found in groups living in flowing water, where they scavenge on struggling and drowned insects floating downstream. Lightweight and covered in a fuzz of water-resistant hairs, they skate on water without breaking its surface tension. Their middle pair of legs paddle, while the back ones steer. The shorter front legs are reserved for grappling with prey. They can jump and move in quick bursts.

These insects sense potential prey from ripples picked up on their feet. They also communicate with one another by ripples, males sending out invitations to females and 'get lost' signals to other males. Coupling is piggy-back style. Males may stay and guard their partner or mate with other females. The fertilised eggs are laid on aquatic vegetation, floating flotsam or under water.

Backswimmers and Water Boatmen

These two aquatic families inhabit still or slow-flowing water. While rather similar-looking, they have some distinctive behaviours. Most notably the backswimmers swim upside down. They do a sort of backstroke with their elongated, hair-fringed hind legs. Their eyes are huge and their back is convex and usually a light colour to blend in with the sky so as to avoid detection from possible predators beneath them. They are fast swimmers and skilled predators, catching prey in their raptorial front legs. Eggs are laid in sliced plant tissue or attached to rocks. The flatter, oval-shaped water boatmen have two pairs of fringed hind legs with which they swim right-side up. Their smaller front legs are used to scoop up plant material from sediments or to catch small insects.

A backswimmer photographed underwater. Either the enormous eyes or the sensory hairs of its body locate prey. Once pinpointed, the powerful strokes of its long feathery back legs transport the backswimmer at high speed through the water as it gives chase.

Backswimmers and water boatmen are rarely more than 1.5cm (⅗in) long. They must regularly surface to collect air in a bubble. The back-swimmer's bubble is held in the hair-covered groove of its abdomen, while that of the water boatman is trapped under its wings. Males of both families emit sound, rubbing peg-like structures on their legs against prongs on their tube-like mouthparts to serenade females.

Water Scorpions

Water scorpions are quite big: up to 5.5cm (2in) long (not counting their tail). Their 'tail' is actually a telescopic breathing tube which pokes up into the air. Their front legs, held like a crab's at the very front of their body, are thickened to hold struggling prey before it is pierced by their tubular mouthparts.

Water scorpions live in debris at the bottom of shallow creeks where, brown and flattened, they look like fallen leaves. They usually only come to light when accidentally netted or after arriving unexpectedly in the swimming pool one night.

The top predator in many wetlands of eastern and northern Australia is the Giant Water Bug or Fish-killer Bug that grows to an enormous 8cm (3in) long. The tube at the back is a siphon through which is takes air from the surface above as it quietly hangs in among the aquatic vegetation, upside down and with its raptorial forelegs at the ready to grab passing prey. Slippery frogs and fish are gastronomic delights for this gigantic insect.

Lacewings

Adult lacewings are often exquisitely beautiful with brightly-coloured bodies, diaphanous wings and a metallic sheen to their bulbous complex eyes. However, as larvae, they are fierce little predators that ambush small invertebrates under leaf litter and bark and on stems and leaves.

An adult antlion lacewing, having recently left the cramped confines of its pupa underground and climbed up a plant. As it hangs from its legs, its soft, elongated body plumps up and its fragile wings, finely networked with tiny veins, unfurl.

Lacewings are common in most habitats of Australia. They undergo four stages of development: egg, larva, pupa and adult. As winged adults they are often seen in gardens resting among vegetation. While some are predatory, many others feed on vegetation and honeydew. As larvae, they are gardeners' friends, feeding on plant-sucking insects like aphids and scale insects. Some take honeydew and pollen, too. Others feed on mites and the eggs of butterflies.

The wingspan of adult lacewings ranges from 0.5–15cm (⅕–6in) and some of the largest have bodies up to 5cm (2in) long. Most are weak fliers that only fly at night. The moth lacewings of eastern Australia and the green lacewings are drawn to lights.

Adult lacewings have only a few weeks in which to mate and lay fertile eggs. They sometimes partake in mating swarms. While some females lay their eggs in soil, sand or mud, many lay them on the underside of living or dead vegetation, wood, windows and walls in distinctive arrangements. Commonly seen on thin long stalks are the little white eggs of the green lacewings and the U-shaped 'necklaces' of white eggs laid by the Blue-eyed Lacewing.

The Antlion Family

It is unusual for insects to be named after their larval stage but one family of lacewings is particularly well known for its larvae; these are the antlions. An antlion is a lacewing larva from the family Myrmeleontidae.

Having moulted three or four times over several months, an antlion spins out silk threads from glands located in its anus and cocoons itself in the silk to form a perfectly camouflaged pupa, which it buries underground. The pupal body within the cocoon gradually transforms into a winged adult, which eventually breaks free of its cocoon and drags itself to the surface and up the nearest plant. The adult lacewing is delicate

This rather unprepossessing creature will, one day, emerge as a dainty winged adult. What this antlion lacks in looks, however, it makes up for in subterfuge. Having constructed a conical pit of sand, it waits just below the bottom of the pit for a passing ant to lose its footing and tumble in. It senses the miniature landslide and lunges out to grab the ant with its stout pincers.

and soft-bodied, with two pairs of membranous wings of more or less equal size that fold tent-like along its body when at rest.

Although mostly unseen, antlions are a source of fascination to children. Their presence can be detected by small conical depressions in dry sand, which are pits designed to snare ants. When an ant stumbles into a pit and struggles to clamber out from its centre, a tiny pair of pincers belonging to a voracious little antlion emerge from just beneath the surface to drag the ant down.

The 'pincers' actually form part of the antlion's mouthparts; the other part is a feeding tube that sucks up the body juices of the ant. Antlions are usually around 1cm (½in) long and their pits about 5cm (2in) in diameter and 2.5cm (1in) deep. Pits are commonly found beneath overhangs where sand remains dry, such as on the floors of caves and under houses. Australia's dry sandy regions team with ants, making them a paradise for antlions.

Gauzy wings, a soft green body, shiny metallic eyes and long, thread-like antennae are all typical features of the green lacewing family. These lacewings commonly visit our homes on warm summer evenings; like moths, they are attracted by light. When disturbed, they may release a strong-smelling liquid.

Beetles

The order to which beetles belong, Coleoptera, contains more species than any other single order of animals. In Australia alone there are at least 29,000 species, but it is likely there are many more yet to be discovered.

A tropical Christmas beetle. Christmas beetles have developed close associations with native plants, especially the wattles and eucalypts. Infestations on trees and shrubs are quite common and a swarm can chomp their way through the foliage of a plant, stripping it bare within days. Usually plants recover from this seasonal assault but Christmas beetles have been implicated in a form of dieback, a common cause of death among eucalypt trees on farms.

Despite the multitude, beetles are not seen that frequently, partly because most of their lives are spent as larvae buried beneath bark, underground or within logs or tree trunks, but adults, too, are often inconspicuous. Many are nocturnal and many others with sombre colouring are hidden in soil, leaf litter and the homes of other animals. In Australia, however, there are some very bright and beautiful beetles that are quite easily seen, especially those inhabiting plants.

Beetles fly but only with their back pair of wings. The front pair, known as elytra, is hard and often shiny. They protect the membranous pair beneath and lift up to permit flight when necessary. In most beetles the elytra cover the entire abdomen, providing it with protection. Beetle larvae and adults have chewing mouthparts. Their antennae are highly variable and their shape and size often help with identification.

The eggs of beetles hatch out as larvae, sometimes known as grubs. As with all insects, the major preoccupation of larvae is feeding.

Once fattened up, they pupate before emerging, often after summer rain, as winged adults. Adults are primarily concerned with mating and ensuring the future of the next generation.

Because of their chewing habits, many beetles are considered pests of gardens, crops and plantations but some control other pests and nearly all of them, at one stage or another, are useful recyclers, keeping nutrients in leaves, wood, flesh, fungi, fur and waste in constant circulation.

The flowering eucalypts of Australia provide a bountiful source of nectar for many scarab beetles. Here a flower chafer feasts among the blossoms. Flower chafers are strong fliers and will travel long distances to find flowering trees. Many beetles target only one or a few native plants to feed upon.

Scarab Beetles

Members of the huge scarab family are solidly built beetles, 0.2–7cm (⅒–3in) long, with powerful front legs built for burrowing so they can lay their eggs in soil and decaying wood. You may have dug up their larvae when gardening: fat, white grubs, curled into a semi-circle, with a rusty brown head and six legs. Scarab larvae eat roots and decaying organic matter but many adults prefer leaves, nectar and pollen.

Soil-dwelling scarabs are usually black or brown but some of the flower chafers are brightly coloured. The fiddler beetles, marked with a distinctive violin motif, are exquisitely patterned. The elytra of Christmas beetles (1.5–4cm / ⅗–1½in) often have a metallic sheen. Each year their root-chewing larvae emerge from the soil as adults and take to the airwaves, often buzzing around lights, sometimes swarming into buildings. Despite the alarming clawed feet, they are harmless and will not bite.

PONGY PERFUMES

Many beetles defend themselves by producing fluids that smell and taste revolting. Those with glands able to produce these pongy perfumes are often brightly coloured to warn off potential predators.

The desert-dwelling geotrupid beetles are equipped with prominent horns similar to the unrelated rhinoceros beetles. These burrowers provide their larvae with balls of fungi, humus or dung in subterranean brood chambers. Both the larvae and adults can make hissing sounds by rubbing their hind legs on their abdomen.

Belonging to the scarab family, too, is a group of dark, round beetles that consume dung. Drawn by the pungent pong of fresh poo, adult beetles fly in to feed and toil among the droppings. Some species fashion small balls of dung, which they roll along with their forelegs before laying an egg into each ball and burying it in a brood chamber for their larvae-to-be to feast upon.

Ground Beetles

Most members of this large family of predatory beetles live on or in the ground but some live on tree trunks and leaves. Usually dark coloured and with long antennae, they run down insects and other invertebrates on their long, slender legs and attack them with their powerful jaws. The shiny metallic tiger beetles in this group can even catch flying prey. The larvae, too, are voracious predators, ambushing small invertebrates in the soil.

Most ground beetles are nocturnal and spend the day beneath logs or in leaf litter. Some are flightless and their elytra are often scored with subtle longitudinal furrows. They are widespread and highly adaptable insects, able to contend with the extreme conditions of snow country or deserts. Some discharge caustic secretions in self-defence. The Bombardier Beetle in particular excels in this department, squirting out a fluid from its anus that evaporates into a puff of 'smoke' on contact with air and makes an audible pop.

Jewel Beetles

The jewel beetles are among the most beautiful of all the beetles. Varying in size from 0.5–6.5cm (⅕–2.5in), they have an oval body and

You may have come across this flightless and nocturnal Burrowing Ground Beetle scurrying away having been revealed by the displacement of pots or logs in the garden. Like all ground beetles, it is well built for a life of chasing prey and grabbing it in its formidable jaws.

elytra that are lightly scored with longitudinal furrows. Bright contrasting colours and bold patterns make them highly visible in spring and summer when the adults fly about feeding on the nectar and pollen of flowers or the juices of leaves. A good place to look for jewel beetles is in the blossoms of native tea trees and eucalypts.

The larvae of most jewel beetles are wood borers and some are gall-makers, irritating the cells of plants they tunnel into to produce a protective covering in which they live until they eat their way out as adults. The heavily segmented bodies of the larvae are skinnier than those of longicorn larvae and taper from the head.

Jewel Beetles (above and below) are some of the prettiest beetles you will find. They are often found in the dish-like flowers of native plants, such as tea trees and eucalypts, where access to nectaries is easy.

FAKING DEATH

Beetles are on the menu of countless birds and those that are active during the day are especially vulnerable to being eaten. One ploy adopted by some of them is to play dead in the hope that a looming predator will pass them over in preference for something living. Flower-dwelling beetles often fall into the leaf litter as if dead, making a safer, speedier getaway than flying off.

A congregation of Southern Ladybirds. Ladybird beetles are a familiar, and usually welcome, sight in our gardens since most feed on aphids, mealybugs, scale insects and mites. Ants often attack ladybird beetles as they threaten their supply of honeydew produced by aphids. In addition to their warning colours and slippery bodies, ladybirds protect themselves by 'bleeding' a toxic, sticky yellow secretion from their leg joints.

A BUG OR A BEETLE?

It isn't always easy to tell the difference between a bug and a beetle. An important clue is how the front pair of wings close around each other. In bugs they usually overlap but in beetles the front wings, known as elytra, usually close against each other to form a single line down the middle of the back.

Ladybirds

Most people are familiar with the little ladybird beetles (0.2–1cm/⅒–⅓in long). Small, bright and shiny, their dome shape obscures their legs and their clubbed antennae are barely visible. Adult and larval ladybirds are predacious and serve gardeners and farmers well as most species feed on small but serious pests like aphids, mites and scale insects. A few, like the Twenty-eight Spotted Ladybird, however, are plant-feeders that damage tomatoes, potatoes and pumpkins.

Ladybirds lay their eggs close to a living source of food. As soon as they hatch the long-legged, spiny larvae start hoeing voraciously into their food. Several of the 300-odd Australian species have been exported to control pests overseas. Among them, the Cardinal Ladybird that successfully eradicated the Cottony Cushion Scale in California, where it was threatening the citrus industry, and the Black Ladybird that destroyed the Gum-tree Scale in New Zealand's Blue Gum plantations.

Fireflies

Despite their name, these are beetles, not flies. Australian fireflies are famous for the pale green winking lights the adult males produce while flying at night. The light is created by mixing oxygen from the air with a phosphate compound activated by an enzyme at the base of terminal segments of the beetle's abdomen. The light pulse lasts only as long as the oxygen; then another intake of oxygen fuels a new pulse.

The luminescence of males attracts flightless females resting on vegetation, who flash back in response. The sequence of flashes varies between species. Sometimes a group will produce a wonderful synchronised light show, perhaps to deter rivals or confuse predators. Larvae and even eggs of fireflies emit a glow, but why is a mystery.

Adult fireflies have small, elongate bodies, rarely 1cm (⅓in) long, with relatively soft elytra and big eyes. They live for only a few days and never feed but their heavily segmented larvae are predators of snails, injecting them with fluids that paralyse them and reduce their tissues to mush.

Australia's 26 or so species of fireflies are mostly inhabitants of rain-forests and mangroves, especially on the eastern seaboard. One species inhabits the Blue Mountains just outside Sydney.

Leaf Beetles

There are about 2200 species of leaf beetles in Australia. They come in all sorts of shapes but most are small with smooth elytra and many are brightly coloured with metallic hues. As their name suggests, they live among foliage and many inhabit native plants, especially wattles and eucalypts. Adult beetles feed on leaves, as do many of their larvae. Eggs are laid in clusters around shoots or on leaves, sometimes deposited around a stem in a circle so they resemble a miniature corn on the cob. Many leaf beetles do damage to such crops as citrus, stone fruit and members of the pumpkin family.

A Eucalyptus Leaf Beetle. Leaf beetles can severely defoliate eucalypts and, like the Christmas beetles, they are implicated in a type of dieback among eucalypts on farms. Certain species of leaf beetles will also defoliate wattles.

Clerid Beetles

Clerid beetles are a family of predators. Most inhabit bark and wood and are cryptically coloured but some brightly coloured ones live among flowers and foliage. Adults and larvae prey upon other insects. The long legs and good eyesight of the adults are useful for hunting. Some grow to 4cm (1½in) long and their bodies often sprout tufts of hairs.

Timber dwellers lay their eggs in crevices. The front part of the long larvae are reinforced with horny plates, protecting them as they chew

A clerid beetle forages for pollen among the stamens of a eucalypt blossom.

Despite appearances, these Plague Soldier Beetles do little damage to plants. Typically members of the soldier beetle family are black and yellow, or sometimes orange or red. They are small (0.5–1.5cm/⅕–⅔in), elongate beetles with soft, flattened bodies and elytra, distinct heads and thread-like antennae. In south-eastern and south-western Australia during warm weather, soldier beetles may congregate on flowers to mate and to prey upon soft-bodied insects visiting the flowers. Their larvae live under bark and often feed upon the eggs of locusts and flies.

their way into the tunnels of other wood-boring beetles, where they pick off the larvae. Longicorn larvae are especially prone to predation by clerid beetle larvae.

Quite a common sight is the widespread Yellow-horned Clerid Beetle that runs around tree trunks, its shiny black body glinting in the sunlight. Its yellow antennae wave around busily in a wasp-like fashion as it looks for prey. This mimicry may serve as a deterrent to potential predators.

Stag Beetles

Stag beetles (0.6–7cm/¼–3in) are ancient beetles, thought to have been around during the time of the dinosaurs. They are relatively rare in Australia with only about a hundred species known. They live in rotten wood on wet forest floors. Most inhabit eastern Australia, from Tasmania's cool temperate rainforests to north Queensland's tropical ones. Species are also known from the Northern Territory, the Kimberley and Victoria.

The males bear huge 'antlers' that are actually grossly distended parts of their jaw. These are used to fight other males. The contest involves trying to tip the opponent over by lifting him up from beneath with the jaws. Females have quite normal jaws.

A pair of male Golden Stag Beetles (right) wrestle for supremacy. They fight over territory and access to females. The idea is to get their horns underneath their opponent and topple it over.

Many stag beetles are plain brown but others have exquisite metallic bronze, blue, green and mauve elytra. The ends of their antennae are flattened and comb-like while their forelegs are stout, adapted for burrowing through wooden fibres. Females lay their eggs in decaying logs on the ground. The emergent white grubs feed on wood and pupate in oval timber chambers.

Stag beetles are highly sought after by collectors, making them vulnerable to extinction, as does logging in old-growth forests. The Broad-toothed Stag Beetle in Tasmania is currently under threat from such operations.

The sharp chewing mouthparts at the tip of a weevil's snout are wonderful precision instruments able to cut, drill and bore into fibrous plant material.

VIRGIN BIRTHS

Some weevils produce young without mating. Females lay unfertilised eggs and the larvae that hatch are all females with their mother's DNA. Producing clones like this can be useful when males are hard to find but fertilisation is important to the long-term wellbeing of any living species, as a mix of genes strengthens the stock.

Weevils

This is the largest beetle family in Australia, with over 8000 species. Weevils are recognised by their pronounced snouts, which may be short, long, straight, curled under, thin or broad. The often distinctly 'elbowed' antennae come off the snout and the mouthparts are at its tip. Varying in size from 0.1–6cm (³⁄₁₀₀–2½in) long, the well-armoured weevils are usually cryptically coloured and stippled.

Females lay their eggs into holes, which they drill in seeds, fruit, stems and even wood. The legless larvae are semi-circular and feed on roots or other plant tissue. Weevils are infamous for the damage they do to crops and stored grains but many inhabit native plants and Australian weevils have served well as biological controls of some weeds.

Some tiny wood-tunnelling weevils lack the distended snouts. Telltale furrows beneath bark are the work of bark beetles and small round holes in dead or dying timber of pinhole borers. Pinhole borers line the walls of their tunnels with fungi, which they cultivate for their larvae. If they relocate to a new log, they carry fungi with them to start a fresh 'garden' in their new home.

Longicorn Beetles

These attractive elongate beetles, varying in size from 0.5–8cm (⅕–3in) long, are easily recognised by their enormously long antennae that, in males, are sometimes longer than the length of their bodies. They have long legs, too, with distinct claws and large, powerful mouthparts. As adults, longicorns may nibble on bark and leaves but they do little damage compared to their wood-boring larvae, which chew extensive tunnels through wood just under the surface of bark.

A pair of White-spotted Longicorns mating. The female will deposit her eggs in a crevice or hole in a tree or bush and when the seemingly legless, wood-boring grubs hatch, they will tunnel into the water- and nutrient-conducting sapwood just under the bark. Tapping into the plant's life juices, they continue to chew and excavate, eventually emerging as winged adults from their oval-shaped tunnels.

Longicorn females usually lay their eggs only in weakened trees that already show signs of mechanical injury. Some species ringbark the branches of wattles, laying their eggs into indentations left by their chewing mouthparts. The top of the branch into which the grubs then tunnel is cut off from its food and water supply and dies.

There are over 1000 longicorn species in Australia and native species have evolved alongside the native flora, specialising in perhaps just Australian figs, banksias, wattles or eucalypts. Australia's largest beetle is Wallace's Longicorn from Cape York Peninsula that grows to 8cm (3in) long with antennae 12cm (5in) long.

The larva of a longicorn beetle, one of several species of larval moths and longicorn beetles known as witchetty grubs. Witchetty grubs are epicurean delights for traditional Aboriginal women and children who know where to dig and winkle out the grubs with hooks. Eaten raw or roasted in hot ash, they are reputed to have a delicate nutty flavour.

Rove Beetles

Rove beetles have elongate bodies, 0.1–2.5cm ($\frac{3}{100}$–1in) long, with tiny shortened elytra that leave their abdomen visible. Most are black or brown, blending into the soil and leaf litter, but there are brightly coloured species with metallic tinges, too. Their abdomen is hardened and movable, allowing them to raise their posterior segments as they run about. They are predators of small animals that scavenge and feed on rotting vegetation and carrion and they conveniently live beneath decaying plant, fungal and animal matter. Some rove beetles mimic ants and wasps and some live within the nests of termites and ants. If threatened they emit a pungent smell.

Where there's a corpse, there's bound to be maggots, and where there are maggots, expect rove beetles. These beetles also feed on fungi, plants, detritus, small invertebrates and their larvae and pupae. Sometimes mistaken for earwigs, rove beetles lack the posterior pincers.

A predacious diving beetle carries its bubble of air from the surface sandwiched between its elytra and abdomen. These beetles have no gills so periodically they rise to the surface backwards, poke their abdomen out of the water, raise their elytra and collect a bubble.

Water Beetles

Some beetles have pioneered the unlikely medium of water. In fact quite a number successfully live full-time in water. Two families in particular have adapted to a submersible life in fresh water: the diving beetles (0.5–2.5cm/⅕–1in), which are strong swimmers and active predators, and the scavenging water beetles (0.3–3.5cm/⅒–1½in), some of which prefer to crawl rather than swim.

Members of both families have streamlined smooth, oval bodies. They may be black, brown, green or golden, some with a metallic sheen. To propel themselves through water, the hind legs are flattened and fringed with swimming hairs. They operate like paddles, working in unison in the fast-swimming predatory diving beetles, and alternating in the less aquatically proficient scavenging water beetles. In order for these gill-less beetles to live under water, they must gather bubbles of air from the surface. Diving beetles are fierce predators of small fishes, tadpoles and aquatic invertebrates, while scavenging water beetles feed mostly on decaying plant and animal matter. The larvae of both families, however, are predators.

All water beetles have wings and they often fly to new aquatic territories. At night they are often drawn to lights and they occasional fall into swimming pools. They are quite harmless and play an important role in food chains, with many grubs and adults providing sustenance for waterbirds, turtles, frogs and fishes.

The predatory larvae of water beetles have formidable jaws. They usually inject their prey with flesh-melting enzymes and suck up the body fluids through hollow grooves in their mouthparts.

Whirligigs

Most people are familiar with whirligigs (1.4–2cm / ½–¾in), those frenetic beetles that zoom around the surface of water like crazed dodgem cars, and dive at the slightest hint of danger. Their short paddle-shaped middle and hind legs are modified for swimming, while their front pair point forward to grasp prey. Whirligigs mostly take creatures drowning on the surface. These they detect as ripples with their antennae and perhaps with their eyes, which are split, so they have vision both above and below water.

Whirligig larvae are equipped with feathery gills. They are predatory and stalk the bottom sediments for snails, mites and small insects. Holding prey in their well-developed mouthparts, they inject it with a liquidising enzyme that turns their bodies to an appetising slush. After their last moult, they crawl to the water's edge to pupate. When the pupa splits open, they return to the water. Whirligigs mate on the surface and the female lays her eggs on submerged vegetation. These beetles live for less than a year.

A female click beetle lays her eggs in the desert sands.

Click beetles

The elongate click beetles have larvae known as wireworms. Wireworms have a notorious reputation for ruining cereal crops and lawns by chewing the roots, although a few of them are carnivores that feed on wood borers. If they find themselves on their back, click beetles can jump out of trouble by flexing their body backwards until a peg on their undercarriage slips into a tailor-made cavity with a loud click and propels them high up into the air where they right themselves before landing.

Flies

There are 6500 described species of flies in Australia and, between them, they fill almost every terrestrial and freshwater habitat. While warm, damp environments where decomposition of organic matter is rapid are popular, some, like the ubiquitous Australian Bush Fly, have adapted to the arid conditions of the inland.

The pair of little straight rods ending with a knob behind the wings of this crane fly are balancing organs known as halteres. Halteres assist flight agility in all flies. Slender-bodied and with long legs and wingspans up to 7cm (3in), crane flies look a bit like giant mosquitoes. They are slow, rather awkward fliers that hang by their legs from vegetation near water. They live only a few days and never eat but their larvae feed in fresh water, damp soil or rotting plants. With over 700 species, this is Australia's largest family of flies.

Life in the Slush

Moist environments, such as those within forests or at the water edges, appeal to flies because their mouthparts are designed for sucking or mopping up decomposing plant or animal matter in liquid form. Some, like blood-sucking female mosquitoes, also have piercing mouthparts designed to puncture skin. Flies often soften their food with enzymes in their saliva to make it slushy. There are a few flies that lack mouthparts altogether and never feed, living only a few days as adults.

The larvae of flies, known as maggots or wrigglers, are another reason why flies favour moist habitats. All maggots are voracious feeders and their soft, segmented bodies, usually legless and with

Many of us have a very precise idea of what a fly looks like but this unusual and beautiful Banana Stalk Fly, with its long legs and horn-like antennae, defies the stereotype. In fact many flies are deceptive, some bearing a greater resemblance to wasps or ants in an effort to deter predators. Other flies in Australia are so small or obscure they completely escape our attention.

tiny heads, are designed for wriggling through rotting organic matter, waste, mud or water. They breathe through a couple of spiracles at the end of their abdomen. Some are predators and some parasitise the larvae and pupae of other insects. As they eat, maggots grow and slough off several skins before becoming a pupa. Some pupae are inactive and undergo metamorphosis within a barrel-shaped hardened larval skin, known as a puparium, before emerging as winged adults, but others have a bare pupal stage.

Adult Life and Development

Flies have large eyes and excellent vision. Almost all have a single pair of strong wings for sustained flight, the back pair having become a pair of club-shaped balancing structures called halteres. These assist manoeuvres in flight. A few flies have lost the power of flight, compensating with other skills such as wasp or ant mimicry.

Most flies are active by day. They are agile, strong fliers capable of long-distance travel. Many court and mate on the wing. Females need a protein meal to develop viable young. They lay either eggs or live maggots, often in hundreds, and life cycles can be rapid.

Some flies are instrumental in the transmission of human diseases but, despite their frequently unsavoury habits, many of them are important pollinators as adults, and nutrient recyclers as larvae. There are also entire families of flies that are beneficial to humans. The tachinid flies, for example, parasitise many agricultural and forest pests.

An adult tachinid fly feeds on nectar from a eucalypt blossom. Only as larvae do they parasitise other invertebrates, eating them from the inside out. Tachinid flies have been trialled as biological controls for a number of pest species.

Tachinid Flies

Tachinids are often seen on leaves, in flowers or walking up the trunks of eucalypt trees. Their larvae are parasitic on other invertebrates, especially beetles and caterpillars but also on some bees, wasps and bugs, at either the larval or adult stage. Females lay eggs or live larvae into or onto their hosts, or they may deposit them onto plants. The larvae burrow into their host and commence feeding on it, starting with the non-essential body bits but moving on until it eventually dies.

Mosquitoes

Not only humans are plagued by mosquitoes. Here a female mosquito extracts blood from a Saxicoline Tree Frog. Although female mosquitoes usually feed upon vertebrates, they are often choosy about which species. Males feed from plant juices but most females need a protein-rich blood meal to produce viable eggs.

Not everyone knows that mosquitoes are flies but they are, and nearly 300 species have been described from Australia alone. Diversity is greatest in tropical Australia but even in the Snowy Mountains and deserts there are mosquitoes.

They breed in still or slow-moving fresh or stagnant water, where females lay rafts of tiny eggs on the surface. Many are at large during dusk and dawn or at night but some 'mozzies' are active through the day. While males and some females feed on plant juices, most females require blood in order to breed successfully. They extract the blood through a long proboscis that pierces the flesh of their host, which is usually a warm-blooded animal such as a mammal or a bird. Certain species attack reptiles and frogs.

Quite a few mosquito species bite humans and a handful are carriers (vectors) of serious human viruses such as Barmah Forest virus or the most commonly transmitted mosquito-borne viral disease in Australia, Ross River fever. Although debilitating, neither are fatal; however, Murray Valley encephalitis can be. Most often reported from northern Australia, outbreaks of Murray Valley encephalitis occur occasionally in the south.

Another serious mosquito-borne virus that occasionally hits northern Australia is Dengue fever. Common in New Guinea and South-eastern Asia, outbreaks here are usually the result of an infected traveller arriving in the country. Australia is presently considered free of the infamous parasite carried by mosquitoes that causes malaria but there are fears that, with the effects of global warming, those mozzie species that act as vectors may migrate into northern parts of the country.

Mosquitoes also carry heartworm, a common and frequently fatal disease of dogs, and myxoma virus, which kills rabbits.

Metamorphosis is underway at the water's surface. On the left two mosquito larvae in their fourth moult take air through their snorkel-like breathing tubes. They commute up and down through the water, feeding underwater and breathing at the surface. The curled-up balls with tails are pupae, which do not feed but—unusually among insect pupae—they are active. They breathe at the surface through two horn-like tubes. Their skin splits after a few days and adults with only a few weeks to live emerge.

Robberflies

Robberflies are medium to large flies with a long abdomen and remarkable hunting abilities. They capture insects on the wing, grasping them in their strong legs and stabbing them with their stout proboscis. Some consume their prey on the wing but others return to a perch to inject flesh-melting saliva into their prey and lap up its body fluids.

Robberflies are quite common and are often seen on shrubs or tree trunks 1–2m (39–79in) off the ground, alert and on the look out for flying prey worth the chase. The hairs around their face are thought to guard them during struggles with potential victims.

Larvae live in the soil and are also predators. There are over 600 described robberfly species in Australia.

Robberflies are skilled and intrepid hunters. This handsome species, photographed near Lake Cronin in Western Australia, has pinned down a honeybee. From the size of the honeybee you can see that the fly is something of a giant, perhaps 8cm (3in) long.

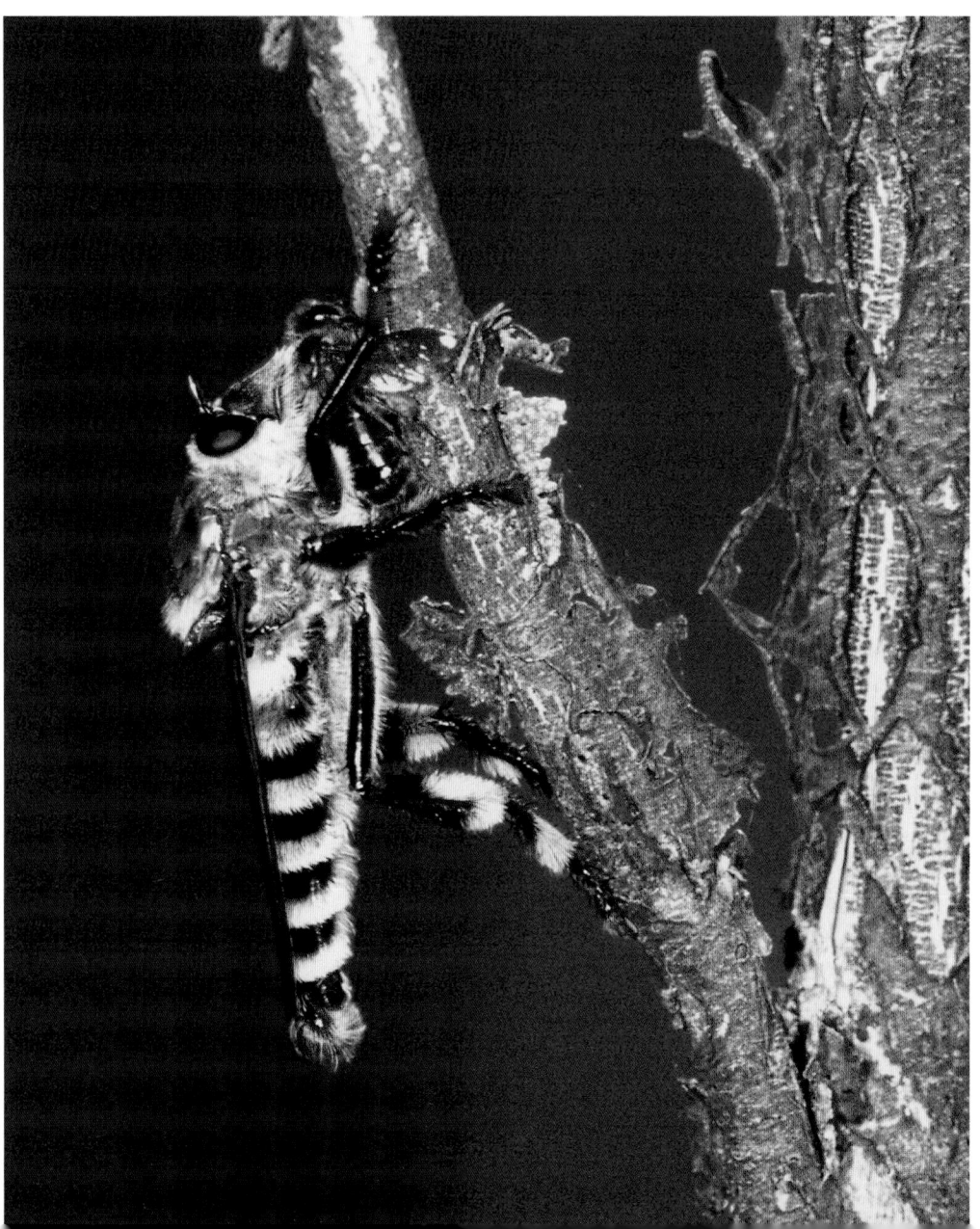

Fruit Flies

These tiny flies damage a wide range of commercial fruits and vegetables in Australia, as well as the fruits of native rainforest trees. Adult flies over-winter feeding on sweet juices such as honeydew. As temperatures rise, they lay their eggs just beneath the skin of fruit. Telltale pinpricks indicate where the female's ovipositor has punctured the surface. The larvae hatch and tunnel inwards, feeding as they go. The fruit rots, often as a result of larvae-borne infection, and may drop prematurely. The larvae then burrow into the ground, pupate and emerge as adults to repeat the cycle.

South Australia tries to protect its agricultural produce by operating quarantine inspections at road blocks and airports. Two species are troublesome: the introduced Mediterranean Fruit Fly in Western Australia and the native Queensland Fruit Fly found in the eastern states. Tomatoes, avocadoes, stone fruit, olives, quavas, citrus, figs and grapes may all be affected.

Bee Flies

Bee flies are hairy and stout and often look like bees or wasps but they have no sting. There are 400 species known in Australia, most of which are particularly well suited to arid and semi-arid habitats. While the adults feed on nectar and are undoubtedly important pollinators, the larvae parasitise the larvae of other insects, including those of bees and wasps, and may feed on grasshopper eggs. They are highly proficient fliers, often seen hovering above flowers or the ground in patches of sunlight.

> ### GASTRONOMIC TOES
> Flies trample over their meal in order to 'taste' it before tucking in.

A bee fly holds its wings out to the side in its customary manner. Australia is well endowed with bee flies, probably because of their ability to withstand arid and semi-arid environments.

A flesh fly consumes a recently departed hoverfly. These flies, so-called because of their diet, are early arrivals on the scene after death. They are usually black and grey with red eyes and recognised by three dark longitudinal stripes on the thorax. Females bear live larvae, some of which feed on carrion; others parasitise invertebrates or eat plant matter.

Vinegar Flies

These tiny yellow and brown flies are easily confused with fruit flies. Their larvae live within decaying fruit and adults are often seen flying above the fruit bowl or around trays at the green grocers. We are indebted to vinegar flies, especially to those from the genus *Drosophila*. Because they are widespread, small, easy and inexpensive to maintain and have rapid life cycles, they form the ideal laboratory animal and have proved invaluable in genetic experiments.

Horseflies and March Flies

There are over 200 species of these robust, large-eyed flies. The males feed on nectar but the females, like mosquitoes, nourish themselves on blood, which they draw through a stout proboscis that punctures skin. Humans are often targeted. The bite hurts but the flies are slow and easily swatted. Some are quite large. Larvae live in water or swampy places; the adults are most common during the summer in the south and during the tropical Wet season in the north.

Hoverflies

Hoverflies may be mistaken for bees or wasps due to their stripy black and orange, yellow or cream abdomens, which warn potential predators to keep their distance. They are often seen hovering among flowers in gardens. If disturbed, they dash away a couple of metres before hovering again. They feed on nectar and honeydew and pick up pollen on their hairy bodies.

The larvae of some of Australia's 169 species of hoverfly live in some curious places. For example, the larvae of native drone flies thrive in putrid deoxygenated puddles of decomposing flesh or vegetable matter. In order to breathe, they have long, extendable siphons that can reach to the surface; these are known as rat-tailed maggots. Other larvae that

A hoverfly feeding on nectar from a native lily. By unwittingly transporting pollen on its fuzzy body, it is an important pollinator of wild and cultivated plants.

> ### INVISIBLE BLOOD-SUCKERS
> Sand flies are known in the United States as no-see-ums for obvious reasons. Midges, both as adults and as larvae, are major sources of protein for fishes.

This is a mydid fly, a member of a family of handsome medium to large elongate flies with long club-shaped antennae. Many mydid flies disguise themselves as wasps. They are found throughout Australia, including Tasmania, often on sand where females lay their eggs.

hatch from little white eggs conveniently deposited beside aphids are wonderful aphid exterminators. There are also hoverfly larvae that live in the bulbs of plants, on fungi and in the nests of ants.

Sand Flies or Biting Midges

Sand flies are so tiny (less than 1mm/½sin long) you can barely see them with the naked eye but you sure know when you have been bitten. These biting midges cause animals, including humans, much persistent irritation when they are encountered around mangroves, estuaries and tidal flats, especially at dawn and dusk during still days. Both sexes feed on plant juices but the female seeks blood to provide protein for her eggs, which are deposited in the mud of tidal flats. The aquatic larvae live in brackish water where they feed on organic matter.

Non-biting Midges

Those clouds of tiny delicate flies that you see hovering erratically over water or above rocks by the sea on summer evenings are harmless, non-biting midges. These frenzied gatherings are of excitable males trying to attract the attentions of females who join the mosh pit for as long as it takes them to select a suitable mate. The pair then depart for nearby bushes in which to mate.

> ### NATTY NAMES
> Gnats and midges are terms used for tiny flies.

These jewel-like sticky beads dangle from silken threads spun by the larvae of little flies called fungus gnats. They are snares designed to entangle small flying insects drawn to pinpoints of bright blue light produced by the larva, which we call glow-worms. The light is the result of a chemical reaction activated by oxygen in the excretory organs of the glow-worms. Colonies put on spectacular light shows and in several humid caves, mineshafts and river embankments along the eastern seaboard, from northern Queensland to southern Victoria and Tasmania, they have become tourist attractions.

BATTLE OF THE DUNG PATCH

Bush Flies lay their eggs in dung. They reproduce much faster than their competitors, the trundling dung beetles that do likewise but not before they have laboriously rolled the dung in balls and buried it.

Their larvae are mostly worm-like aquatic creatures that swim by the energetic coiling and uncoiling of their bodies. Those of one of the most widespread and common species are bright red and known as bloodworms. While some larvae wriggle through soft sediment feeding on algae and bacteria, others are filter feeders that live in self-made tubes fitted with nets that are slung between struts protruding from the rim.

House Flies and Bush Flies

Before the introduction of the cosmopolitan House Fly, native Bush Flies dominated the Australian fly fauna, and in rural areas they still do. Both are robust, hairy members of the same family, of which there are another 180 species in Australia, including the blood-sucking Stable Flies and the Buffalo Flies.

House Flies frequently buzz around garbage. They lay a hundred or more eggs at a time, mostly in rotting vegetable matter. In warm weather, they can become sexually mature adult flies within eight days. This rapid life cycle, together with their sticky feet, hairy body and predilection for places where bacteria thrive, makes them transporters of many serious human diseases, including typhoid, salmonella and anthrax.

Bush Flies glean moisture and protein from the secretions of animals, including humans. They sponge up sweat, tears, mucus and blood from recent cuts and they lay their eggs in moist animal dung. Before the arrival of cattle in Australia, they relied on the

It's a good idea to keep your lips together on a warm day in the bush. These pesky Bush Flies are after saliva. Without water, they will die within a day. Despite their size differences, they belong to the same species; some just didn't quite get the nourishment of others.

dung of native animals, which is often quite dry and soon forms hard pellets. Since the arrival of the slushy cowpat, populations have soared, especially during hot weather.

As a rule House Flies infest houses, while Bush Flies stick to the bush, but Bush Flies are often carried into urban areas by winds. During the cold months the flies die off in southern Australia, as they cannot withstand low temperatures, but new waves arrive on warm winds from the inland and the north in summer.

Male bush flies can be differentiated from females by their large eyes. In males they almost touch at the top of their head while there is a space between those of females.

Most members of the blowfly family are brown, but metallic blue or green ones like this are commonly referred to as 'bluebottles'. Many of these robust hairy flies feed on plant fluids, including nectar, but their reputation in Australia is mostly based on the Australian Sheep Blowfly, whose larvae have developed resistance to all known sheep dip chemicals.

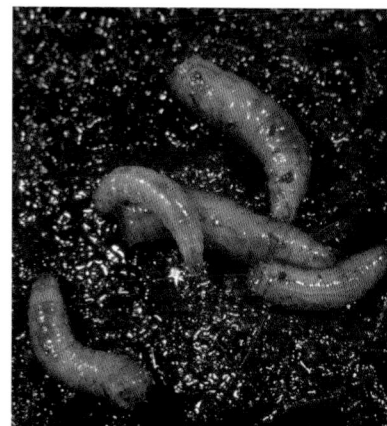

Like all fly larvae, or maggots, the introduced Australian Sheep Blowfly requires a moist habitat. These larvae are the most prevalent perpetrators of fly strike among sheep in Australia. The 5–8mm (⅕–⅓in)-long metallic green fly lays several hundred eggs into carcasses or onto the rotting fleece of live sheep affected by running sores. Larvae burrow through the fleece to reach the sores where they feed for three or four days before dropping off and burrowing into the soil to pupate.

MURDER CLUES

Blowflies infest carcasses, including those of humans. Different species are found at different stages of decomposition. By identifying the species, the time of a death can often be established, providing a useful clue to finding the culprit.

Butterflies and Moths

The majority of the 416 known species of butterflies in Australia live in tropical and subtropical regions. Nearly half of these are found nowhere else in the world and they include some exquisite and large species. There are, however, 50 times more moths in Australia—a phenomenal 20,000 species.

Three Chequered Swallowtails (wingspan 7.5cm/3in) settle to drink from the moist ground. Swallowtails occur mostly in rainforests. This species, however, has adapted to withstand the arid and semi-arid conditions of Central Australia. Fast flying and migratory, it is widespread and quite common but its movements are unpredictable.

Families of Australian moths are numerous but there are only six butterfly families. One consists of only a single species from the dense rainforests of Cape York Peninsula. The widespread 'blues', sometimes known as 'coppers' or 'azures', are the largest family of butterflies in Australia. They are tiny to medium butterflies, sometimes with tailed hindwings ('hairstreaks'). 'Skippers' are small to medium in size, mostly orange and brown butterflies that 'skip' or fly in short, erratic bursts, usually around low vegetation.

The large 'swallowtails' have conspicuous tailed hind wings and mostly inhabit tropical and subtropical areas of the east coast. Their wings are often black and white, green or turquoise, sometimes with red spots. The medium-sized, round-winged 'whites' or 'yellows' are indeed predominantly white or yellow. 'Nymphs' are medium to large, mostly orange or brown butterflies, prettily marked, often with false eyespots (little round circles).

The thousands of tiny overlapping scales that cover the wings of butterflies and moths set them apart from other insects. If a wing should lightly touch you, these scales will shed on your hands as a colourful powder. Many a butterfly and moth has made a lucky escape from a spider's web by loosing a few scales.

Another unique feature of these insects is their mouthparts. While some adult butterflies and moths never feed at all, most do drink water and sip nectar or fruit juices. They draw fluids into their mouth by means of a long, thin tube, known as a proboscis, that coils up like a spring when not in use but unfurls to reach into the throats of flowers. They then suck nectar up through the proboscis as if it were a drinking straw.

Within a single species of butterfly or moth there can be considerable variations in appearance. The vibrancy of colouring may alter in different seasons or regions. Patterns and colours between the sexes are often strikingly different; sizes, too, commonly vary, with females tending to be larger.

Butterfly or Moth: Telling the Difference

From an observer's point of view, there is no clear-cut distinction between a butterfly and a moth. Size can be deceptive. Butterflies in the 'blues' family have wingspans as tiny as 1.5cm (½in), while the wingspan of the Hercules Moth that lives in northern Queensland is a gigantic 25cm (10in). A better indicator is colour. Many butterflies have bright, and even iridescent, wings, while most moths come in subtle, sometimes sombre, colours.

Broadly we can say that if it flies by day with its two pairs of wings independent of each other and its antennae thickened at their ends or club-like, it is likely to be a butterfly. There are some day-flying moths, however, but their two pairs of wings are coupled by tiny hooks and operate as one. Moths are generally hairier and the antennae tend to taper at the ends or, in males, become feathery.

Typical of many skippers, the Western Grass-dart (wingspan 1.5–2cm / ½–¾in) makes short erratic flights close to the ground, resting frequently in patches of sunlight. Its colouring and its resting pose—with forewings up and hindwings spread, are also typical of skippers.

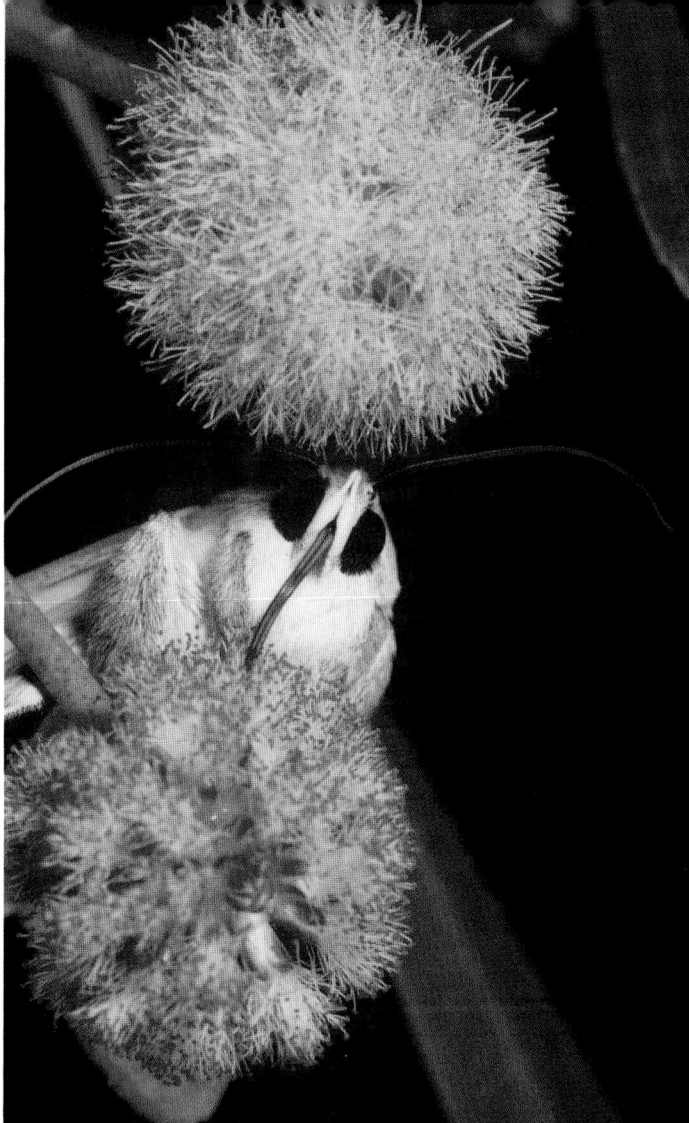

An owl moth extracting nectar from wattle flowers. Not too many nectar feeders can plumb the depths of a wattle's nectaries but that is where moths and butterflies, with their remarkably long proboscis, have the advantage. Several members of the owl moth family in their larval stage— when they are known as cutworms or army worms—chew through roots of cultivated grasses and crops, causing significant damage.

A Caper White absorbed in the business of laying her eggs. This pretty native butterfly, with a wingspan of 5.5cm (2in), has the typical colouring of its family. It is a common and widespread species, especially west of the Great Dividing Range. Although known to travel during the day, flying several metres above the ground, and to rest in bushes and trees by night, little is understood about its movements. Also in this family is the notorious Cabbage White.

Life Cycles

As with all of the more evolved insects, butterflies and moths undergo four stages of development: egg, larva, pupa and (usually winged) adult. The adult stage, although the most obvious to us, is frequently brief: sometimes only a week or two. There are butterflies, however, that live for a year or several, surviving hard times either sheltering beneath leaf litter or in caves in a state of dormancy, or migrating elsewhere to avoid harsh winter or summer conditions.

Most butterflies and moths lay their eggs onto plants, singly or en masse. The long, cylindrical larva that hatches is commonly referred to as a caterpillar. Some of Australia's caterpillars are as beautifully patterned, although not as elegant, as the butterflies or moths they will become.

The Lives of Caterpillars

Caterpillars live to eat. Almost all of them are vegetarians and usually leaf eaters. Species are often very particular about which plants they eat, so mothers take care to deposit their eggs on or beside desirable food plants (although some moths are known to scatter theirs while in flight). A female may lay less than 50 eggs or up to 10,000, depending on the species.

Not all caterpillars chomp at the edges of leaves; some burrow through them. Others, like many members of the swift or ghost moth family, gouge channels through bark, sapwood or the roots of plants. Root feeders living underground move up to just beneath the surface when they are ready to pupate, then break the surface as they emerge as adults. The branches of certain eucalypts in Queensland and New South Wales are mined by the larvae of the native Bent-wing Ghost Moth, a rather impressive pinkish brown moth with a wingspan of up to 23cm (9in).

GARDENING WITH BUTTERFLIES

If you are a keen gardener, you may think that butterfly caterpillars are something you'd rather be rid of but only caterpillars of the introduced Cabbage White Butterfly are seriously destructive in the garden. It is the caterpillars of moths that do the greatest damage.

Hawk moth caterpillars are stout and smooth, often striking in colour and markings, and most have one or two spine-like projections at their rear. Many, too, have large eyespots that are exposed at one end or the other of their body to frighten off predators. In this photo a hint of an eyespot peeps out just beyond the legs. The little black rings running like portholes down its sides encircle tiny holes known as spiracles, through which the caterpillar breathes.

Food Plants

Native larvae usually feed on native food plants and tastes are often very specific. For example, the larva of the Richmond Birdwing, a spectacular member of the swallowtail family, feeds only on two species of native vines that grow in the subtropical forests of south-eastern Queensland and north-eastern New South Wales. Many of these forests have been cleared for development, especially on the coastal lowlands, leaving the birdwings to starve in much of their former habitat. Fortunately, an imaginative awareness campaign has encouraged local gardeners to grow these native vines in their gardens to aid the recovery of this handsome butterfly.

Quite a few native butterflies and moths have adapted to introduced plants. Among them, the beautiful Orchard Swallowtail, whose larvae

All caterpillars have six stumpy legs at the front of their body but loopers also have four claspers at the back. Looper is a name given to the caterpillars of two families of moths that commonly infest garden or native plants. They often mimic the stalks on which they are feeding by standing upright and stock still on their claspers.

A female Orchard Butterfly (11cm/4in wingspan). In the cultivated gardens of all capital cities, from Cape York in Queensland to Adelaide in South Australia and as far west as Alice Springs, the loopy, languorous flight of this native swallowtail has become quite a familiar sight. Once solely dependent on native plants of the citrus family, it has taken happily to the cultivated exotic citruses. On inspection of your lemon tree, look for a caterpillar that looks suspiciously like bird poo.

A Chequered Blue or Saltbush Blue Butterfly displaying both the deep blue and rich coppery iridescent sheen so typical of many 'blues' or 'coppers'. This inhabitant of saltbush shrublands, mudflats and open woodlands, has a wingspan of only 1.8cm (¾in) and is one of many members of its family whose larvae associate with ants to the benefit of both parties.

masquerades as fresh bird poo on the leaves of citrus trees, and the dazzling Blue Triangle that has expanded its menu from native laurels to the introduced Camphor Laurel. Some introduced butterflies, like the Wanderer or Monarch of the Americas, only established in Australia with the arrival of their food plants, the milkweeds.

Many caterpillars eat toxic plants to make themselves distasteful to predators. For example, the native Common Australian Crow feeds upon the introduced and poisonous oleander to the extent that it has become commonly known as the Oleander Butterfly. There are also a few caterpillars that feed on small invertebrates, like scale insects and ant larvae, and cannibalism has been witnessed in a number of species.

Caterpillar/Ant Alliances

The relationship between many members of the blue butterfly family and ants is a remarkable and not uncommon phenomenon. These caterpillars have special glands able to produce a sweet exudate that ants love. In exchange for tasty exudates the ants provide protection to the caterpillars, sometimes welcoming them into their nests. Some ants even transport the caterpillars to their food plants where they feed and then ferry them back again to their shelters. Associations between caterpillars and ants are species specific on both sides and probably derive from alliances forged millions of years ago.

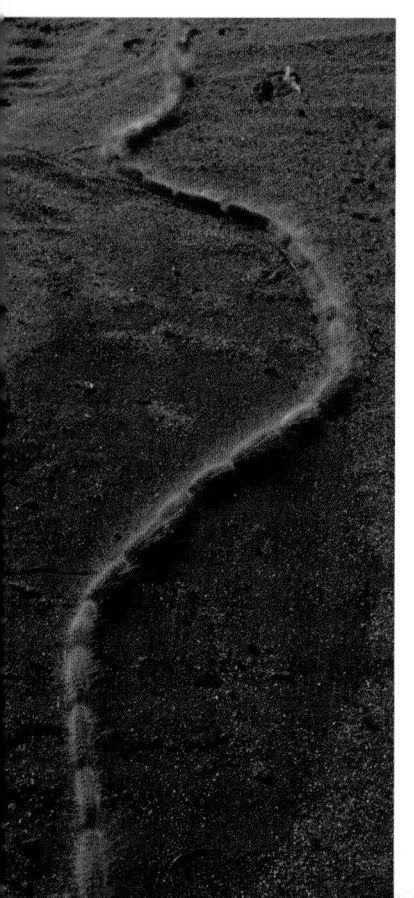

A line of Processionary Caterpillars keep to the straight and narrow by following a silken thread laid down by the leading caterpillar. These hairy caterpillars are quite common in the Australian bush. Having stripped the leaves from one wattle shrub, they are probably searching for another. Their hairs are long and barbed, protecting them from predators, including humans. It is inadvisable to touch them as they can cause intense irritation and allergic reactions.

Silk

Almost all caterpillars have silk glands. Silk extrudes from their mouths as wet strands and hardens on contact with air. Caterpillar silk is most commonly used to build cocoons in which to pupate but it is also used for safety lines should a caterpillar fall, as thread for securing the pupa and to weave shelters.

Some caterpillars carry their shelters with them. This is a feature of the case moth family, also known as bag moths or bagworms. While some shelters are silky smooth, those of other species have twigs or leaves woven into them for camouflage. The larvae pupate and transform into adults within. Some female case moths are wingless and never leave their shelter but males are winged and find females by scent. They have an especially long, expandable abdomen that reaches down into the female's 'case' in order to mate with her. She lays her fertilised eggs in the case and the larvae leave their mother's home to spin their own.

There are also caterpillars that build huge communal shelters of silk. Processionary Caterpillars spin multiple-occupancy nests that either rest at the foot of wattles in coastal regions or are suspended from the branches of wattles or eucalypts in inland areas. The suspended bag-like nests are conspicuous among the leaves and their builders, known as Bag-shelter Moths, may be a separate species from the coastal ground nesters. A curious feature of the Australian bush is the writhing hairy masses of Processionary Caterpillars at the base of trees or their single-file trains trundling across the landscape between feeding trees.

Case moths are cautious travellers. Here a larva trundles along carrying its shelter like a snail carries its shell; for both animals their portable bolthole is an indispensable means of protection, especially if it is as well camouflaged as the cases of these moths, spun from silk and thatched with floral debris.

Pupation

As caterpillars eat and grow, they moult and shed their skins over weeks and months. Some of the wood borers remain larvae for up to five years but eventually all larvae retire into a state of suspended or highly curtailed animation as pupae. The pupa of a moth or butterfly is often referred to as a chrysalis.

All the butterflies except the skippers pupate within a cocoon that hangs upside down from vegetation suspended by a girdle of silken

WITCHETTY GRUBS

The original witchetty grub was an 8cm (3in)-long moth caterpillar belonging to a single species of the giant wood or goat moth family. It was, and still is, dug up from around the roots of an inland wattle by Central Australian Aborigines who consider it excellent bush tucker. Nowadays the term witchetty grub refers to several large, juicy wood- or root-boring insect larvae, including some from the ghost moth family and even a species of longicorn beetle. Eaten raw or rolled in the hot ash of a fire, they are said to taste delicious.

The aerodynamic shape of the hawk moth's wings are built for speed and sustained flight. Narrow-winged species with strong thoracic muscles and a streamlined body like the hawk moth's can maintain a powerful and controlled flight and can even hover, while large, broad-winged butterflies tend to flap their wings in a languorous looping flight and make limited progress even in a gentle wind.

A pair of mating Black and White Tigers (wingspan 6cm/2⅜in). These butterflies live near swamps in northern and eastern Australia, as well as throughout South-east Asia. Their larvae feed on the trailing milkweeds that fringe rivers, creeks and mangroves.

thread. Wood-burrowing moth caterpillars pupate within the frass they have created while boring themselves out of branches and some root-devouring moth caterpillars pupate underground.

Taking to the Air

When temperatures rise or when the Wet season arrives in the north, the pupa splits or tears open and a crumpled long-legged creature crawls out of its casing. Hanging by its thin legs from a leaf or twig, its body gradually plumps up and two pairs of startlingly beautiful wings unfold and stretch. This remarkable process usually takes several hours, after which the adult butterfly or moth takes to the air.

The Mating Game

For a small insect in an enormous airspace, finding a mate can be problematic. Butterflies locate mates mostly by sight, which explains their propensity for exuberant colours. Although short sighted, they are sensitive to movement and colour, including ultraviolet. The mostly nocturnal moths have less need to show off as colours are not so visible in the dark; instead, they find one another by scents known as pheromones, which are released by females and received by the sensitive feathery antennae of males.

When looking for females, males narrow their search by focussing on likely spots. Many male butterflies flit around the food plants on which females emerge from their pupae. Sometimes they mate with females before they have even had time to dry their wings in the air. In species where pupae are not concentrated, males may search among nectar-rich flowers for feeding females.

Another strategy is to stake out a good vantage point from which to view passing females, perhaps near a clearing where visibility is good, or to patrol a promising stretch of vegetation. Such territories are hotly contested. A common phenomenon among moths and butterflies is hill-topping. This is when males of a single species congregate together at a prominent location, often at the top of a hill, in order to display themselves to females.

Some female butterflies only ever mate once; others mate just a few times. They have the capacity, however, to store sperm and fertilise their eggs over time.

Common Australian Crows (or Oleander Butterflies) over-wintering in a sheltered gorge. Up to 2000 may gather for protection in still, moist environments such as this. Here their metabolism slows right down so they can remain more or less dormant for weeks or months, rarely needing to feed or drink. Their dashing black and white colours are a warning to predators that they are poisonous.

Migration

Some long-lived butterflies and moths travel long distances to avoid seasonally stressful conditions. In Australia, no such migration is better recorded than that of the Bogong Moths, which is witnessed each year by the inhabitants of south-eastern Australia.

The caterpillars of Bogong Moths hatch from enormous clutches of eggs in the ground of the western plains and slopes of New South Wales, inland Victoria and the Darling Downs of Queensland. Known as cutworms because they cut the stems of their food plants at ground level, they feed on broad-leaved plants, including lucerne, and then pupate in the ground. In spring they emerge as sexually imma-ture, inconspicuous brown moths with a wingspan of 4cm (1½in).

As the heat builds up and the broad-leaved plants are replaced by unappetising grasses, they embark upon a nocturnal migration to the high country of New South Wales and Victoria. Under certain condi-tions, they may swarm into colossal clouds. Along their migration route, they are often misled into believing it is day by the light of fires, floodlighting and illuminated streets and houses. So they drop down to the ground to hide. The multitude of falling Bogongs occasionally accumulates into such enormous piles that their bulk clogs air ducts, lift pulleys and even railway lines. They are also sometimes blown off course by strong winds, coming to grief in the Bass Strait or winding up as far afield as Tasmania.

If they make it to the high country, they pile into crevices and caves at 1200m (4000ft) above sea level. Here they spend the summer hanging in dense clusters, bodies overlap-ping one another like roofing tiles, in a state of suspended animation. Come autumn they will return to their breeding grounds and, having mated and laid their eggs, they will die.

The highly sensitive feathery antennae of a male looper moth are fitted with tens of thousands of sensors. These pick up the wafting perfumes, or pheromones, of females from within a 1km (⅔mile) radius. They can also determine the direction from which the pheromones are coming by the intensity received at different sensors.

If you live in south-eastern Australia you may recognise these moths as summer visitors that fly into build-ings. Bogong Moths may not look very exciting but the scale of their nocturnal migrations is truly impressive.

A male whistling moth. Note the knob in the wing and the glassy corrugated crescent that surrounds it. Together these structures conspire to make a whistling sound when the moth flies. Males of some species are known to gather for collective whistling sessions.

Making Sounds

Butterflies and moths are usually silent but in Australia there is a family of day-flying moths whose males whistle. They bear a tiny knob on the outer edge of their front wing enclosed by a semi-circular, sculpted membrane. This membrane vibrates when the wing knobs clap together in flight, producing a whistling sound.

There is also the tiger moth family whose members not only repel predators with foul-smelling chemicals and striking colours but can stave off attacks from bats by producing ultrasonic sounds. Even larvae are known to make sounds, or at least vibrations, especially among those members of the 'blues' family that consort with ants. Some mimic the sounds of ant larvae in order to get the attention of adult ants.

Self-defence

The Meadow Argus is a common and widespread native butterfly with a wingspan of about 4cm (1½in). Its colouring and markings are typical of its family, the 'browns'. The false eyespots on the wings are designed to mislead a potential predator into believing they belong to a much larger animal and therefore one better left alone.

The bright colours of many butterflies and day-flying moths are not always just advertisements for mates. They are often warnings to birds, to which they are especially vulnerable, of their fowl taste or toxicity. Their unpalatability has been passed on to them by their larvae which, having eaten copious quantities of poisonous plants, become thoroughly distasteful or toxic themselves.

Butterflies disguise themselves from predators in several ways. The outline of many swallowtails and hairstreaks are broken up among the plants they frequent by wing patterns, frilly wing edges and 'tails' in the hindwings. False eyespots in wings confound those trying to focus on a potential meal. Even some caterpillars have false eyespots; most spectacular are those of the hawk moths.

Caterpillars are juicy enticements for many birds and, while some are smooth, others are hairy, among them hairy-mary caterpillars, Processionary Caterpillars and members of the tussock moth family. These 'urticating' hairs are pointed at one end and barbed along their length.

A larva of the Banksia Moth rears up and displays its retractable defence weapon: a glistening red appendage designed to intimidate predators. This species is widespread and the caterpillars are often found on the twigs or leaves of banksias, grevilleas, hakeas and dryandras. It pupates underground.

On piercing skin ,they cause intense itching, serving well as deterrents to many predators, including humans.

Cup moth caterpillars also sting when you brush against them but their effect is usually mild and short lasting. These chunky caterpillars are decked out in bright warning colours. On their upper surface they have eight nipples: four at the front and four at the back. In the face of adversity, each nipple everts in the form of a tiny bunch of poisonous spikes. These weapons are probably intended to deter parasitic wasps, another major threat to caterpillars, but they are prickly even to humans.

Some caterpillars, like those of the stripy black, red and white Common Australian Crow, have fleshy projectiles that look scary and break up the insect's profile against the light and shade of leaves and branches. Indeed soft projectiles can be truly menacing. For example, caterpillars of the swallowtail family, when alarmed, respond by everting a pair of bright fleshy prongs from behind their head. With these nasty smelling, miniature, glistening antlers, they rear up and lunge at their intruder. The native Banksia Moth caterpillar employs a similar strategy but its fleshy forked weapon shoots out of its mouth.

The warning colours of the tropical Cairn's Birdwing, a close relative of the endangered Richmond Birdwing. This is a male (12.5cm/5in wingspan). Females have a wingspan of 15cm (6in) but they lack the delicate peppermint green, which is replaced by white.

Sawflies

At one time or another most Australians come across a writhing knot of cater-pillar-like creatures huddled together, often beside or upon a eucalypt tree. These are commonly called spitfires and are the larvae of a family of sawflies. Sawflies are primitive stingless wasps that lack the typical narrow waspy waist.

An adult sawfly from the ancient family, Pergidae. Although wasp-like, it lacks the narrow waist of true wasps.

Most of the 176 species of sawflies in Australia are endemic. Best known are those species belonging to the Pergidae, a family that evolved on the supercontinent of Gondwana. The family of plants to which eucalypts belong, Myrtaceae, may also have evolved on Gondwana and it seems likely that, over millions of years, a close association between these trees and these sawflies has developed.

A Handy Egg-laying Tool

Sawflies acquired their name from the female's saw-edged ovipositor at the end of her abdomen. With this she delicately slits open the mid ribs of leaves or soft stems. Into the slit she deposits a series of eggs. Wedged between the plant tissues, the eggs are hidden from predators and shielded from the sun. After about four weeks the young larvae emerge and immediately band together for defence, arranging them-selves with their heads all pointing outwards.

The Inelegant Defence of Spitting

They feed by night, chewing at the edges of gum leaves, and communi-cate by tapping the ends of their abdomens against leaves. Before dawn one larva leads the way to a safe hiding spot; the others trundle after it. The last in line tweaks off the feeding leaf at its stalk, removing all evidence, including scent, of their presence on the tree.

At the slightest hint of danger, the larval mass writhes about in agitation; each animal's head and tail rearing up. Among the eucalypt

---

LENGTHY LARVAE

Sawfly larvae can grow quite big; up to 8cm (3in) long in the Steelblue Sawfly, a common woodland species of Victoria, coastal New South Wales and south-eastern Queensland. The winged adult, however, is only 2.5cm (1in) long.

These sawfly larvae have been disturbed. Their tails are raised in alarm and their shiny black heads face outwards ready to assault their attacker with eucalypt 'spit' if necessary.

sawflies, oily secretions are regurgitated as their foregut compresses with the bending of their body; sometimes liquid propels out of their mouth for a distance of up to 20cm (8in). This 'spitting' (which explains their common name) deters the small and timid, but large birds, such as currawongs, choughs and cuckoo-shrikes, relish juicy larvae, and some insects, such as tachinid flies, parasitise spitfires. There is a parasitic wasp that bypasses the seething mass but simply laying its eggs upon leaves in the hope that the larvae will swallow them. The wasp larva then hatches within the sawfly larvae and eats it way out.

Cloning the Next Generation

Having eaten their fill, the siblings bunch up and descend to the ground. They wriggle down into the earth to bury themselves. Underground they mash up soil, droppings and body secretions—frequently containing eucalyptus oil—and fashion individual papery pupal chambers they join together to form a honeycomb. Then each larva crawls into a chamber to undergo metamorphosis.

When the winged sawflies finally emerge the next season, or the one after, their gregarious lifestyle is over. As solitary 'wasps' they live only a short time, often without feeding. Many females emerge from their pupal chamber already carrying eggs. Although males certainly exist, it seems many eggs are never fertilised. They simply hatch as clones of their mother, a biological process known as parthenogenesis.

A NATURAL BALANCE

While native sawfly larvae chomp their way through prodigious amounts of foliage each season, they rarely seriously damage woodland trees. The trees may even benefit from the pruning. In eucalypt plantations and ornamental gardens, however, infestations may be too heavy and kill trees. Perhaps it is the absence of traditional predators in these situations that unbalances the natural relationship between insects and trees.

You are never alone if you are a sawfly larva. Siblings remain huddled together during daylight hours and never far from one another when eating. These hairy family members will support and defend each other during their most vulnerable moments: when they are moulting.

Wasps

In Australia there are 12,000 species of wasps, the vast majority of which are endemic to the continent. While adult wasps feed during the day on nectar and other sweet fluids, the majority of larvae are strictly carnivorous. Life cycles follow the conventional four stages of egg, larva, pupa and adult, but lifestyles vary considerably.

The social Common Paper Wasps busily build cells and stock them with living prey for the larvae to feed upon. Some empty cells await eggs to be laid by the queen, others already contain growing larvae. Still others have been plugged with silk spun by the larvae in preparation for their pupal development.

Winged Adults

While a few female wasps are wingless, most wasps have two pairs of wings but they appear as one because the smaller back pair is hooked to the front pair. Flies with just one pair of wings often disguise themselves as wasps, so telling the difference can be tricky. A wasp's abdomen is constricted into a narrow waist. Its mouthparts are adapted for biting and chewing, and sometimes sucking. The egg-laying tube at the end of a female's abdomen, which is known as an ovipositor, often doubles as a piercing or stinging weapon. Some wasps are so tiny you cannot even see them with the naked eye. Others, like the spider and cicada killer wasps, are very large.

Wasp Larvae

Wasp larvae are legless since they have no need to travel. Female wasps ensure their offspring have enough food to complete their entire larval and pupal stages. The widespread practice of delivering paralysed, but living, insect prey to larvae is typical of nest-building wasp families. The females immobilise their victims by anaesthetising them with their sting. They then transport them in their jaws, between their legs or even spiked on their stings, tucking them in beside their eggs as living, fresh food.

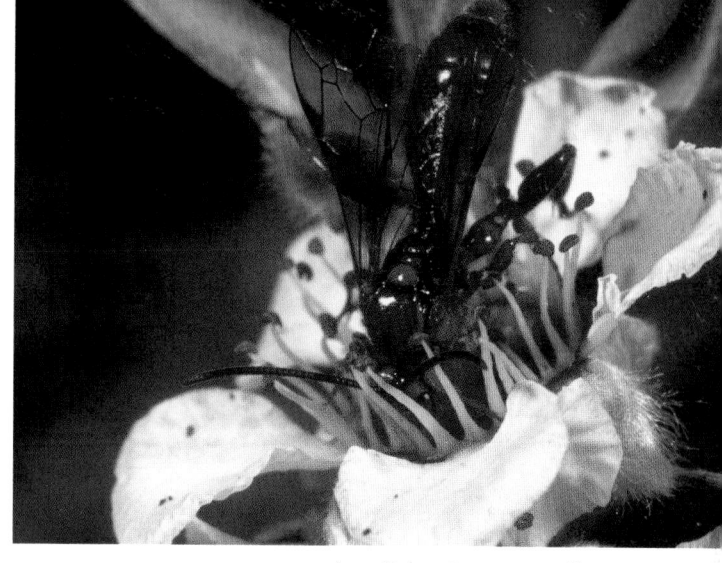

Australia's native wasps usually feed on the nectar of flowers and are important pollinators. They also provide indispensable services to humans by dispatching countless pest species. Most are not interested in stinging people but many have the capacity and they will certainly defend their nests if they are bothered.

Architecturally-minded Paper Wasps

Some wasps make elaborate nests for their larvae, among them the native paper wasps. These are social wasps (1–1.5cm/½in long) that live in colonies founded by a single female. In temperate Australia the males die off in winter but a few fertilised females see out the cold months holed up in protected cracks. As temperatures rise in spring these females grate old wood into a fine sawdust, chew it with saliva to a paste and fashion it into hexagonal cells, which dry to a papery texture.

The founding queen lays an egg into each cell. She feeds the hatched larvae, all of which are female, with mashed caterpillars. When they become wasps, her sterile daughters extend the colony with more cells into which only she, the queen, lays eggs. Her daughters now hunt and feed the young and build more cells. Towards the end of the season, males and fertile females are born. They mate and some females over-winter with their fertilised eggs ready for laying in the following year.

Mud-dauber Wasps

The solitary mud-daubers build a series of single nests. Females make countless trips to the edge of water to collect mouthfuls of mud that they form into single cells, audibly buzzing as they work. They pack each cell with paralysed, living spiders or caterpillars, then lay an egg in the cell, seal up the whole nest and fly away, never to return.

A common Australian mud-dauber is a black-and-yellow banded, 4cm (1½in)-long wasp with a thread-thin waist. It is a bold spider hunter. Holding the spider firmly but avoiding its jaws, it deftly swings its abdomen beneath its body to deliver a swift, precise injection of anesthetic to the spider's central nervous system.

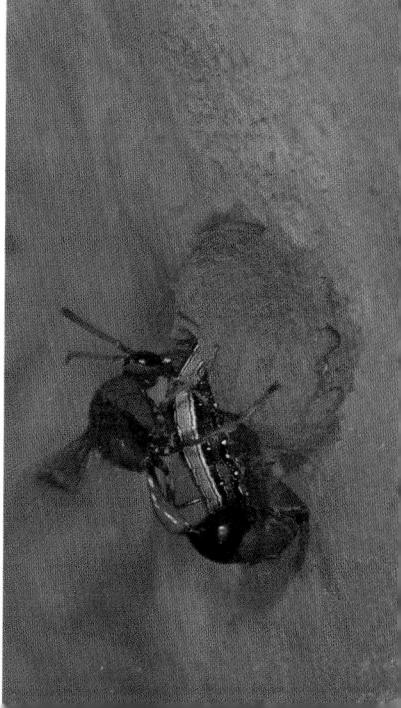

A female potter wasp stuffs a paralysed caterpillar into a cell. Like mud-daubers, potter wasps are solitary wasps that build single mud nests which they stock with paralysed prey for the larva to come.

Sand Wasps are commonly mistaken for bees. In sandy places, these lovely creatures sometimes occur in big numbers.

Sand Wasps

While paper wasps and mud-daubers construct their nests beneath rocky overhangs, suspended from vegetation or the eaves of buildings, or even within neglected furniture or implements, the sand wasps lay their eggs underground. They excavate their nests wherever there are sandy soils in heaths, woodlands or forests and feed their larvae in individual or shared nests, but cohabiting wasps never divide their tasks as do true social wasps like the paper wasps. Sand wasps are skilled pirates of the air, capturing flies on the wings as living food for their larvae.

Ichneumonid Wasps

Most wasps do not build nests for their larvae. One of Australia's largest families, the ichneumonid wasps, simply lay an egg directly onto or into the pupa or larva of another insect. When it hatches, it gradually eats its living host from the inside out, taking care not to kill it before it is ready to pupate. Caterpillars, beetle grubs and maggots (fly larvae) are all targeted, as are spiders and their eggs. These long-legged wasps have long, thin antennae and a slender, flexible abdomen that is able to curl beneath peeling bark to insert an egg into the living tissues of a wood-boring grub.

WASP COLOURS

Although black and yellow or black and orange are commonly the colours of wasps, there are many bees and flies with similar colouring and many wasps that are plain black, blue, green or grey and white.

BEWARE A NASTY STINGER

In Tasmania and south-eastern Australia the introduced European Wasp is abroad during warmer months. This yellow and black species is aggressive and will attack humans if its nest is approached. Nests are usually located in tree hollows, underground or in the cavities of walls and ceilings. If you find one in your home, leave the nest alone and contact professional pest controllers. Wasps are attracted to food and may crawl into drinks, so cover food and don't drink directly from cans or bottles.

Spider Wasps and Cicada Killers

The solitary spider wasps employ a similar technique to ichneumonids but on large spiders. Some leave larvae to hatch in the body tissues of spiders that are only temporarily immobilised. The spiders continue to toil, getting weaker each day as the larva grows stronger and larger. Eventually the spider dies. Other wasps drag enormous paralysed spiders down into specially prepared chambers. They then lay a single egg onto each spider before sealing the chamber and covering the burrow. Some spider wasps are said to be kleptoparasites because they lay their eggs exclusively on spiders that have been caught and immobilised by other spider wasps.

Spider wasps are quite common. They are restless insects that run to and fro on long legs, flicking their wings as they search for spiders beneath leaves and bark.

There are also large wasps that target cicadas. Paralysed by a hefty sting but still alive, cicadas are dragged down into underground dens and stuffed into cells. Beside each one, the Cicada Killer Wasp lays a single egg before sealing up the cell. When the wasp larvae hatch, they suck the life fluids from the living, but helpless, cicadas.

OUTWITTING WASPS

The males of at least 100 species of Australian wasps are regularly duped by orchids into believing they are mating with females when actually they are unwittingly pollinating the orchids. To trick male wasps, the orchids release female wasp pheromones and convincingly mimic their shapes and colours.

An intrepid Spider Hunter Wasp drags an enormous paralysed spider to its subterranean lair. Spider wasps commonly attack spiders much larger than themselves.

A tiny flightless female flower wasp performs a handstand on a paperbark nut. With her abdomen pointing skyward she emits pheromones that signal her readiness to mate. These scents waft on the air and are picked up by a passing male that responds by sweeping her up with his legs and carrying her around in the air. Some species mate on the wing; others land on flowers to feed and mate.

Wingless Females and Home Wreckers

In several wasp families, females are wingless but they are not without guile. The so-called velvet ants, which are really wasps, not ants, break into the nests of other wasps and bees. They deposit their eggs not only into the larvae and pupae within but also into the stored paralysed insects intended as food.

Blue Ants, a species of the flower wasp family, also only have wingless females. Unusually for wingless wasps, these females are metallic blue-purple. Their strategy is to burrow down to find mole crickets as hosts for their eggs.

Cuckoo wasps, like velvet ants, are home invaders, especially of the cells of mud-dauber and potter wasps. These small winged wasps are usually metallic green or blue. They hover slowly and feed on nectar. Females sneak into other wasps' nests and lay their own eggs there. These hatch before those of their host's and the cuckoo larvae quickly gobble up the host's eggs and stored food. A cuckoo wasp caught in the act by a returning mother protects itself from attack by rolling up and presenting an armour-like back to its challenger.

Ants

Australia has an astonishing diversity of ants. There are at least 4000 species, although not all are yet named. Many are endemic. They are widespread and abundant in terrestrial habitats, especially in the arid and semi-arid inland of Australia. Ants may play an invaluable role in seed dispersal and are an integral part of many Australians food chains.

Life Cycles

These social insects live in colonies or nests usually containing one egg-laying queen and hundreds or thousands of sterile female workers that care for the eggs, larvae and pupae. These workers are also responsible for building, maintaining and defending the colony. As the reproductive season approaches, activity in the colony increases and towards the end winged males and females are produced and leave the nest to mate. On landing, they lose their wings and the males die. The females that survive found new colonies or join established ones. Most ants nest underground but some nest in trees or disused termite mounds.

Green Tree Ants live in the vegetation of tropical Australia. Their nests are bundles of leaves pulled together and secured by silk. Only the larvae can produce silk so, while some workers draw the edges of leaves together, others hold larvae in their jaws and gently squeeze them to procure silk from their abdomens. Like tiny sewing machines they 'sew' the leaves together. Although Green Tree Ants do not sting, they do bite and the acidic secretions from their abdomen can cause irritation.

Some Unconventional Foraging Techniques

The diets of ants may be broad or specialised, and foraging times are often dictated by temperature. While adults can only ingest liquid food, the larvae happily take delivery of solid food.

Some ants are predators of termites or other ants. Others are scavengers, among them the abundant and widespread Meat Ants that dominate Australia. These dark red ants with black abdomens are about 1cm (⅓in) long. Their large conspicuous nests often join with others

A triumphant bull ant transports its booty back to the nest in its large pincer-like jaws. The prey, a winged ant of another species, has been stung to death with venom delivered from a sting at the end of its abdomen, which is only visible when in use. The primitive bull ants are a common feature of the Australian bush and found nowhere else. At 2–3cm (¾–1in) long and with such mighty defence equipment, they are best avoided. Their memorable sting delivers a sharp, strong pain that lasts up to half an hour and leaves a small red swelling.

and are scattered throughout open bushland in sandy and gravelly soils. They are aggressively defended. Meat Ants will bite, causing a short, sharp pain, so give them a wide berth.

Some workers obtain food by subterfuge, sneaking into the nests of invertebrates, including other ants, to steal their eggs, larvae or pupae. Another strategy employed by some ants is to 'farm' other animals. One nocturnal species, for example, takes bugs into its nest by day. Protected from daytime predators, the bugs relinquish their honeydew secretions to workers in return for a safe delivery back onto leaves to feed at night. Protection of more vulnerable creatures, such as aphids and caterpillars, in exchange for their sweet secretions is common.

Ants also strike 'deals' with plants. For example, the epiphytic ant-house plants in Australia's rainforests recruit ant protection in return for accommodation. To ensure the safe germination of their seeds, some plants have tiny tasty morsels at the end of their seeds that are relished by ants. Safely harvested within an ant's nest the seeds are unwittingly dropped into fertile dung heaps where their chances of germination are excellent. Many wattle seeds are dispersed in this way.

> **SWEET AND SOUR ANTS**
>
> The Aborigines of Central Australia value the sweetness of Honey-pot Ants and those of the tropical north enjoy the fizzing ascorbic acid (vitamin C) of Green Tree Ants.

Living Storage System

Ants sometimes store seeds in granaries and in arid Australia the Honey-pot Ants have turned themselves into living storage vessels. Certain workers in the colony that are fed honeydew from scale insects and psyllids retain the fluids in their vastly distended abdomens. Hanging from the ceilings of subterranean galleries, they regurgitate these fluids to quench the thirst of other workers.

The workers of sugar ants looking after pupae. Sugar ants may be tiny or up to 1.5cm (½in) long. They are stingless and have black heads and abdomens but orange or rusty-coloured middles. These ants love sweet food. They collect nectar and other plant juices and are commonly found in kitchens.

Introduced Ants

Some very troublesome ants have been introduced into Australia. The Yellow Crazy Ants that form super-colonies and eat everything that lies in their path are threatening the entire ecology of Christmas Island. In Brisbane's suburbs the fight is on to eradicate the small (mostly 3–6mm / ⅒–¼in long) but ferocious Red Imported Fire Ants of South America. In defence of their nests, workers launch coordinated and painful stinging attacks against intruders.

> **SCENT SIGNALS**
>
> Ants communicate with one another with scent signals. The paths to food are laid down as scent trails and formic acid, a strong scent, signals danger.

Bees

Over 1600 species of bees have been described for Australia so far and many more are likely to be discovered. The majority are endemic, having forged ancient associations with Australia's native flora over approximately 60 million years. Many, too, are small and solitary. As with the wasps, their two pairs of wings are hooked together to work as one pair.

The well-known introduced European Honeybee gathering nectar and pollen. Note the pollen 'baskets' on its hindlegs. These bees are renowned for their honey-making skills and remarkable levels of social organisation. They have adapted to Australia's native blossoms, competing with native bees and other insects dependent on native flora. They also successfully compete for suitable nesting sites, evicting nesting birds, native stingless bees and arboreal mammals from tree hollows and rock crevices.

Bees are vegetarians, adults feeding on nectar and larvae on pollen and honey. They are important pollinators and native species often specialise on native plants. Some have long tongues to reach into deep, narrow flower cups but many natives have short tongues and rely heavily upon the shallower, broader nectar cups of eucalypts, tea-trees and their relatives.

Introduced Social Bees

We usually associate bees with the throbbing activity of European Honeybee hives. Protected in tree hollows these colonies buzz with the comings and goings of workers as they fetch food on warm sunny days when flowers open and advertise their wares.

Within the centre of the hive lies the large, egg-laying queen and a few males, known as drones, which provide sperm when required. The sterile females, well named as workers, of which there are tens, if not hundreds, of thousands, tend the queen, the drones, the larvae and eggs. They produce wax from abdominal glands and work it into multiple hexagonal cells. They collect pollen, nectar and resin. Regurgitated and fanned by their wings, the nectar is reduced to honey and, when mixed with pollen, it feeds the hive's developing juveniles. Workers also extend and renovate hives, using the resin they gather to patch up cracks. Defence of the hive is the role of workers, too. They pierce invaders with a barbed sting at the end of their abdomen. Attached to the sting is a gland that pumps venom into the wound. The gland is ripped from the bee's abdomen in the process of stinging and so it dies.

This Dawson's Burrowing Bee is repairing her burrow entrance. These bees hatch underground. When females scramble to the surface, they are swept up by flying males ready to mate with them. They are then left to build their own nest, provision the egg chambers with a mixture of pollen and honey and lay their eggs.

Native Social Bees

Some native bees live in social hives with similar divisions of labour to the common European Honeybees. These black or brown bees are tiny, only about 4mm (⅙in) long, and around 50,000 individuals may form a colony. They live in the crevices of dead and living trees, and even in termite mounds. They make honey which is stored in spherical pots. They have no sting and defend the nest by wrestling with intruders and gluing them down with resin.

Aborigines in the north have always held the honey of these so-called Sugarbag Bees in high regard. Today they still collect nests. The honey, along with the wax, pollen, eggs and larvae, is scooped up and eaten raw and on the spot. They use the wax to smooth over the mouth pieces of didgeridoos.

Australian Aborigines have always known, too, of honey's therapeutic effects. Some communities drink honey or pollen mixed with water to cleanse the gut or they may smear it on sores and ulcers to heal the skin. Honey is especially good for healing eye sores from dust irritation.

Solitary Bees

Most of Australia's native bees build solitary nests. These bees can sting, although their sting is not barbed and they are not aggressive. Sometimes they join with others to form communities but each female lays her own eggs, builds her own nest and feeds her own larvae with honey and pollen.

Many solitary bees, such as the blue-banded bees, nest underground. Others, like the large, robust carpenter bees, bore into stalks or decaying branches to nest. The leaf-cutter bees cut neat circles out of leaves with their mouthparts to seal food-laden egg chambers which are packed into tunnels in plants, soil, fence posts and walls.

LOCKED OUT

Solitary males are excluded from nests. Some sleep curled up in flowers that close over them at night. Others, like the blue-banded bees, wrap their mouthparts around stalks and nod off in groups.

REMOVING A STING

The barbed sting of a European Honeybee comes with a gland that continues to pump venom after the skin is pierced. Rather than squeezing out the sting, which may increase the amount of venom in the wound, try to scrape the sting out with your fingernail placed under the gland.

A native Chequered Cuckoo Bee feeding on the nectar of a eucalypt flower. Cuckoo bees do not bother collecting pollen as they parasitise the nests of other bees. While a female solitary bee gathers food, the cuckoo bee nips into the nest, laying an egg into the pollen–honey mix stockpiled for the rightful owner's egg. The implanted egg hatches before the host's and the ensuing larva eats all the pollen–honey mix.

USEFUL INFORMATION

Websites

General

Australian Biological Resources Study (ABRS) Faunal Directory On-line: www.environment.gov.au/biodiversity/abrs/online-esources/fauna/index.html

Museum Victoria: museumvictoria.com.au/Discovery Centre

International Union for Conservation of Nature: www.iucnredlist.org

Queensland Museum: www.qm.qld.gov.au

South Australia Urban Forest Biodiversity Program: www.urbanforest.on.net

Dept of Environment and Conservation, Western Australia: www.calm.wa.gov.au

Dept of Primary Industries and Water, Tasmania: www.dpiw.tas.gov.au/inter.nsf/ThemeNodes/LBUN-5362MH?open

Wildlife of Sydney: www.faunanet.gov.au

Dept of Resources, Environment and the Arts, Northern Territory: www.nt.gov.au/nreta/wildlife/animals/index.html

Parks and Wildlife, Tasmania: www.parks.tas.gov.au/index.aspx?base=430

ABC Animal site: www.abc.net.au/schoolstv/animals

Mammals

Australian Platypus Conservancy: www.platypus.asn.au

Australasian Bat Society: ausbats.org.au

Birds

Australasian Raptors Association: ww.ausraptor.org.au

Australasian Wader Studies Group: www.awsg.org.au

Birds Australia: www.birdsaustralia.com.au

Australian Museum Bird Site: ww.amonline.net.au/birds

Parks & Wildlife Tasmania: www.parks.tas.gov.au/index.aspx?base=3049

Canberra Ornithological Group: ww.canberrabirds.org.au

Birdwatching in Sydney with the Cumberland Bird Observers' Group: www.cboc.org.au

NSW Field Ornithologists Club: www.birdingnsw.org.au

Bird Observers Club of Australia: www.birdobservers.org.au

Reptiles

Australian Reptile Park: www.reptilepark.com.au/animals.asp?catID=3

Society of Frogs and Reptiles: www.users.hunterlink.net.au/~sofar/id34.htm

Lizards of the Australian Wet Tropics: www.jcu.edu.au/school/tbiol/zoology/herp/wtlz/wtlz.html

Frogs

The Frogs and Tadpole Study Group (Sydney bae): www.fats.org.au/Welcome.html

Frogs in South Australia: www.frogatlas.com.au

Frogs Australia Network: www.frogsaustralia.net.au/frogs/links.cfm

Australian Dept of the Environment, Water, Heritage and the Arts: www.environment.gov.au/biodiversity/threatened/publications/frogs1.html

Frogs of the Australian National Botanic Gardens (Canberra): http://www.anbg.gov.au/anbg/frogs

Society of Frogs and Reptiles: www.users.hunterlink.net.au/~sofar/id34.htm

Fishes

Australian Museum Fish Site: www.amonline.net.au/fishes

Native Fish Australia: www.nativefish.asn.au

Invertebrates

CSIRO Entomology site: www.csiro.au/org/Entomology.html

University of Sydney Medical Entomology: medent.usyd.edu.au

Australian Museum, Invertebrates: www.amonline.net.au/invertebrates

Western Australian Museum, Crabs, Prawns, Barnacles and Other Crustaceans: www.museum.wa.gov.au/collections/natscience/aquaticzoology/crustaceans.asp

WA Museum, Insects: www.museum.wa.gov.au/collections/natscience/invertebrates/insects.asp

Brisbane Insects and Spiders: www.geocities.com/pchew_brisbane/index.html

Gordon's Entymological Glossary: www.earthlife.net/insects/glossary.html#3

New South Wales Dept of Health, Mosquito information: medent.usyd.edu.au/arbovirus

Plant Physiology Information Website, (honeybees): plantphys.info/plants_human/bees/bees.shtml

Butterfly website: www.staff.it.uts.edu.au/~don/larvae/nymp/villida.html

Books

Allen, G.R., Midgley, S.H. & Allen, M., 2002, *Field Guide to Freshwater Fishes of Australia*, Western Australia Museum, Perth

Anstis, Marion, 2002, *Tadpoles of South-eastern Australia*, Reed New Holland, Sydney

Barker, J., Grigg, G.C. and Tyler, M.J. 1995. *A Field Guide to Australian Frogs*. Surrey Beatty and Sons, Chipping Norton

Braby, Michael, E., 2004, *The Complete Field Guide to Butterflies of Australia*, CSIRO, Melbourne

Cogger, H.G. 2000. *Reptiles and Amphibians of Australia*. Reed New Holland, Sydney

Goodfellow, Denise Lawungkurr, 1993, *Fauna of Kakadu and the Top End*, Wakefield Press, South Australia

Goodfellow, Denise Lawungkurr, 2005, *Birds of Australia's Top End*, Wakefield Press, South Australia

Pizzey, Graham & Knight, Frank, 2008, *The Field Guide to the Birds of Australia*, 8th ed., HarperCollins, Sydney

Robinson, Martyn, 2000, *A Field Guide to Frogs of Australia: From Port Augusta to Fraser Island, including Tasmania*, Reed New Holland, Sydney

Simpson, Ken & Day, Nicolas, 2004, *Field Guide to the Birds of Australia*, 7th ed., Penguin Books, Ringwood, Victoria

Slater, P., Slater, P. and Slater, R., 2003, *Slater's Field Guide to Australian Birds*, Reed New Holland, Sydney

Swan, G. 2001, *Green Guide to Frogs of Australia*, Reed New Holland, Sydney

Swan, Gerry, Shea, Glenn and Sadlier, Ross, 2004, *A Field Guide to Reptiles of New South Wales*, 2nd ed., Reed New Holland, Sydney

van Dyck, Steve & Strahan, Ronald (eds), 2008, *The Mammals of Australia*, 3rd ed., Reed New Holland, Sydney

Wilson, Steve & Swan, Gerry, 2008, *A Complete Guide to Reptiles of Australia*, 2nd ed., Reed New Holland, Sydney

Zborworski, Paul, 2003, *A Field Guide to Insects in Australia*, 2nd ed., Reed New Holland, Sydney

Wildlife Parks and Zoos

New South Wales

Hunter Wetlands Centre, Newcastle (formerly Shortland Wetlands Centre) www.wetlands.org.au

Dorrigo Rainforest Centre, 02 6657 2309, www.dorrigo.com/attractions/rainforest

Taronga Western Plains Zoo, Dubbo, 02 6881 1400, www.zoo.nsw.gov.au/western-plains-zoo.aspx

Australian Wildlife Reptile Park, Gosford, 02 4340 1022, www.reptilepark.com.au

The Sydney Aquarium, Darling Harbour, 02 9262 2300, www.sydneyaquarium.com.au

Taronga Zoo, Mosman, 02 9969 2777, www.zoo.nsw.gov.au

Northern Territory

Alice Spring Desert Wildlife Park, 08 8951 8788, www.alicespringsdesertpark.com.au

Territory Wildlife Park, Berry Springs, 60km south of Darwin, 08 8988 7200, www.territorywildlifepark.com.au

Queensland

Lone Pine Koala Sanctuary, 07 3378 1366, www.koala.net/contact/index.htm

Mon Repos Conservation Park, (turtle watching), Bundaberg, 07 4131 1600, epa.qld.gov.au/parks_and_forests/find_a_park_or_forest/mon_repos_conservation_park/mon_repos_conservation_park__turtle_watching_guide/

Mareeba Tropical Savanna and Wetland Reserve, Mareeba, 07 4093 2514, www.mareebawetlands.com

Currumbin Wildlife Sanctuary, Gold Coast, 07 5534 1266, www.currumbin-sanctuary.org.au/content/home.asp?name=Home

South Australia

Cleland Wildlife Park, Adelaide Hills, 08 8339 2444, www.environment.sa.gov.au/parks/sanpr/clelandconservationwp

Seal Bay Conservation Park, Kangaroo Island, 08 8559 4207, www.southaustralia.com/9001050.aspx

Australian Capital Territory

Tidbinbilla Nature Reserve, 45km southwest of Canberra, 02 6205 1233, www.tams.act.gov.au/play/parks_forests_and_reserves/recreation_in_acts_parks_forests_and_bushlands/tidbinbilla_nature_reserve

Victoria

Melbourne Zoo, 03 9285 9300, www.zoo.org.au/MelbourneZoo

Healesville Sanctuary, 03 5957 2800, www.zoo.org.au/HealesvilleSanctuary

Serendip Sanctuary (bird sanctuary), 22km north of Geelong, 1800 620 888, www.parkweb.vic.gov.au/1park-display.cfm?park=182

Phillip Island Penguin Parade, 03 5951 2800, www.penguins.org.au

Tasmania

Trowunna Wildlife Park, 03 6363 6162,
www.trowunna.com.au
Bonorong Wildlife Conservation Centre, 03 6268 1184,
www.bonorong.com.au/joomla.index.php
East Coast Natureworld, Bicheno, 03 6375 1311,
www.natureworld.com.au
Tasmanian Devil Conservation Park, Taranna,
03 6250 3230, www.tasmaniadevilpark.com

Western Australia

Armadale Reptile Centre, Wungong, 08 9399 6927,
www.armadalereptilecentre.com.au
Monkey Mia, Monkey Mia Beach, via Denham,
www.sharkbay.asn.au/dolphins.html
Caversham Wildlife Park, Whiteman Park, Perth,
08 9248 1984, www.cavershamwildlife.com.au
Karakamia Sanctuary, 1 hour's drive east of Perth,
08 9572 3169, www.australianwildlife.org/
AWC-Sanctuaries/Karakamia-Sanctuary.aspx
The Perth Zoo, South Perth, 08 9474 3551,
www.perthzoo.wa.gov.au

GLOSSARY

Abdomen (in insects): the end section of the body, attached to the middle section, the thorax, which is attached to the head

Abundant: large number of individuals in a species

Aestivation: period of dormancy or inactivity during a hot or dry season

Amphibious: an animal that lives in water and on land

Arboreal: tree-dwelling

Arthropod: an invertebrate with segmented limbs e.g. crustaceans, centipedes, insects

Australasia: the region of Australia, New Zealand, New Guinea and neighbouring islands of the South Pacific

Baleen: the flexible whalebone plates in a whales' mouth that strain plankton

Billabong: branch of a river that has been cut off from the main channel

Blowhole: the one or two nostrils on the top of the head of dolphins and whales that allows them to breathe. On coming up for air, the animals spout water vapour

Blubber: the thick blanket of fat around a whale's body that stores energy and insulates it from the cold

Bow riding: riding the pressure waves created by forward-moving ships or large whales; a common occupation of dolphins

Brigalow: a distinctive type of woodland dominated by the wattle *Acacia harpophylla*, an extensive belt of which spans inland and eastern Queensland from Townsville to the New South Wales border

Broombush: *Melaleuca uncinata*

Bulkuru: *Eleocharis dulcis*, a tall, hollow-stemmed aquatic plant

Bush tucker: food derived from Australian native plants; often an important dietary component of traditional Aborigines

Canopy: the uppermost tree foliage

Carapace: a shielding plate covering the head, thorax and sides of a crustacean; also the top shell of turtles

Carbohydrates: important foods that provide the body with the fuel it needs for physical activity and for proper organ function. Examples are: honeydew, manna and nectar

Carpal joint: wrist joint; in birds, where the wings bend

Cay: a small low island or reef made of coral or sand

Chenopod shrubland: vegetation consisting of saltbushes, bluebushes and their relatives

Chitinous: made of chitin, a strong, lightweight natural plastic-type substance that protects softer body parts

Compound eye: an eye composed of a number of individual simple light receptors. Compound eyes can see shape, colour, movement, and tell the distance.

Copepod: a tiny aquatic crustacean

Corner Country: where the borders of Queensland, New South Wales, South Australia and the Northern Territory meet

Cosmopolitan: occurring in many parts of the world

Crepuscular: active at dawn and dusk

Dabblers: ducks that up-end their bodies in shallow water to feed on plants or animals below the surface

Diversity: in relation to animals, the variety of different species

Dorsal: Upper side

Dieback: the progressive decline in the health and vigour of trees, often leading to death; a common phenomenon on some Australian farms

Ear coverts: small feathers around the ears of birds

Elytra: (singular elytron) the hardened front pair of wings in beetles, designed to protect their membranous hindwings

Embryo: organism in early stage of development

Embryonic diapause: a period of suspended embryonic development

Endemic: unique to a particular geographical area e.g. an animal that is said to be endemic to Tasmania is found only in Tasmania

Entomologist: a scientists that studies insects

Ephemeral lakes: extensive shallow depressions in dry inland areas that fill with water intermittently. Prone to evaporation, they are more often dry.

Epiphyte: a plant that grows on another but feeds independent of it e.g. ephiphytic ferns on rainforest trees

Estuary: the place where a fresh-water river meets the sea

Exfoliating (rocks): the peeling away of the outer surfaces due to weathering etc.

Exoskeleton: the protective and supporting external skeleton of arthropods

Extinct: died out

Feral: living in the wild

Fledged (birds): totally or partially feathered and ready to leave the nest

Fledgling: young bird ready to fly

Flukes: the expanded tail 'fin' of a whale or dugong that propels it through water with an up and down movement

Forage: look for food

Gallery forest: a strip of forest that grows alongside a watercourse

Gibber desert or plains: large flat or flattish areas in Australia covered by small, rounded pebbles blasted smooth by wind and sand e.g. Sturt's Stony Desert

Gill net: a fishing net set vertically in the water so that fishes swimming into it are entangled in the mesh by their gills. Diving birds can also become entangled and die by drowning

Gondwana: a supercontinent that existed around 250 million years ago, consisting of many land-masses including Australia and New Guinea, Antarctica, South America and India. See Introduction.

Grizzled: streaked or mixed with grey

Habitat: the type of place where the animal usually lives

Hatchling: a recently hatched bird

Herbivore: an animal that eats only plants

Honeydew: a carbohydrate-rich secretion produced by sap-feeding insects

Hummock: grasses growing in raised mounds

Hypothesis: a proposition to be tested by further investigation

Insectivorous: feeds on insects

Invertebrate: an animal without a backbone e.g. an insect, worm, crab, starfish etc.

Kleptoparasites: animals that steal prey from other animals

Krill: tiny shrimps that swarm in their billions in cold polar waters and are food for baleen whales

Lamellae: in ducks, little plates that run along the edge of their bills. They may be fine for filtering food or coarse for cutting vegetation

Lateral: side

Lek (birds): a place where males maintain a territory to court and mate with females

Lerps: the scaly coverings of psyllid insects. Sometimes the insects themselves are referred to as lerps

Lignum: *Muehlenbeckia florulenta*, a tangled shrub that grows in ephemeral swamps, creeks and waterholes

Macropod: a member of the kangaroo and wallaby family

Mallee: a type of dry inland country found across southern Australia characterised by eucalypts whose main stems arise from, or close to, the ground as a single root stock.

Mandible: in birds, the upper or lower half of its bill

Mangrove: intertidal region where trees grow and are regularly inundated

Manna: an exudate of insects living on eucalypts

Maxilla: Upper jaw

Migration: in animals, a regular journey along a well-defined route, particularly one involving a return to breeding grounds

Mimicry: visual or audible imitation

Mistletoe: a parasitic plant of many other plants including eucalypts, she-oaks, paperbarks and wattles. Nearly 70 species of mistletoe are endemic to Australia

Mobbed: harassed

Molecular biology: the study of molecules in relation to living things, especial concerned with genetic material

Monsoonal: a climate of hot wet conditions alternating with cooler dry conditions

Morphological: based on physical form

Mulga: *Acacia aneura*, a species of wattle that dominates large expanses of central Australia, forming woodlands up to 14m high or shrublands as low as 1m

Native: naturally occurring; not introduced. It may occur naturally elsewhere, too. See **endemic**.

Nectar: a carbohydrate-rich produce of flowers

Nestling: a young bird still nest-bound

Niche: ecologically, a position occupied by a living species that avoids competition within an environment

Nocturnal: active at night

Nomadic: travelling irregularly in time, distance and direction

Nymph: an immature stage in some insects. Nymphs resemble adults but their wings are poorly developed.

Omnivorous: eats all kinds of food

Opportunistic: taking advantage of a temporary or locally abundant resource

Ovipositor: an egg-laying shaft that projects from the end of a female insect's abdomen

Palps: sensory appendages between the mouthparts and legs of spiders

Parasitoid: an organism that kills its host during or at the completion of its development

Parthenogenesis: the process by which viable young are produced from unfertilised eggs

Pectoral fins: fins that extend from the sides of the body

Pelagic: associated with the open water of the ocean

Pheromone: a chemical substance emitted by an animal to attract a mate or signal to other members of its species

Plankton: tiny plants and animals that drift around the world's oceans with little control over their direction

Plumage: feathers

Pod: a group of whales

Polygamous: the mating of one

male with several females or visa versa

Powder down: a powder derived from the disintegrated tips of old feathers used by some birds to clean and waterproof their feathers

Preen: in birds, to smooth, clean or distribute water-proofing oil to feathers with the beak

Prehensile: capable of grasping and gripping

Prey: animals caught and killed for food by other animals

Primate: a placental mammal that evolved as a tree-living animal with hands and feet adapted to gripping branches, e.g. humans, lemurs, monkeys and apes

Proboscis: in insects, a mouthpart that has become modified for the purposes of sucking up liquids e.g. plant sap or nectar

Protein: an essential component of food that helps grow, repair and maintain body cells

Pupate: to undertake the inactive stage that follows the larval stage and precedes the adult stage in some insects

Savanna: a flat expanse of dense grasses and scattered trees in tropical Australia. Savannas are prone to frequent fires. Those with mostly grasses are known as grassland savannas; those dotted with trees are called woodland savannas.

Seabirds: birds that rely on the ocean for food and come to land only to breed

She-oak: a native pine-like tree, sometimes known as casuarinas.

Shorebirds: birds that rely on shores and beaches for habitat, feeding and nesting

Speciation: the process whereby new species are generated

Species: similar individuals that can interbreed and produce fertile offspring

Spinifex: a name attributed to grasses belonging to the *Trodia* genus, commonly found growing inland and forming hummocks or tussocks

Spinnerets: organs at the rear of a spider's abdomen; they are composed of minute spigots through which silk is extruded

Storey: ecologically, a level of vegetation

Substrate: the earthy material at the bottom of a habitat e.g sand or gravel in a river

Swale: a dip between slopes where water may gather

Taxonomy: the systematic categorisation and naming of organisms

Temperate: climatic zone between the warm tropics and cold polar regions where summers are warm and winters cool

Terrestrial: ground dwelling

The Dry: the dry season in northern (monsoonal) Australia

The Wet: the wet season in northern (monsoonal) Australia

Thorax: in invertebrates, the body section between the head and abdomen to which appendages are attached

Top End: the top-most end of the Northern Territory from Daly Waters in the south and east and west to the Queensland and Western Australian borders

Torpor: a brief period of dormancy, often confused with hibernation. Hibernation is a much longer-term and more intense survival strategy

Tropical: hot humid regions near the equator, especially those lying between the Tropics of Cancer and Capricorn

Tussocks: in grasses, bunches of upward-pointing leaves derived from a compact root stock

Tympanum: a smooth piece of skin that acts an eardrum, commonly visible in reptiles

Upwelling: a process that occurs when strong winds blow surface water away and deeper water comes up to the surface to replace it. This deeper water may be rich in nutrients and so attract animals looking for food

Vagrant: in birds, a bird that has strayed beyond its normal range

Vent: in reptiles, the external opening of the reproductive and excretory duct

Ventral: underside

Vertebrates: animals with backbones

Vestigial traces: remains of body parts that have atrophied over the course of evolution

Waterfowl: a family of birds that includes swans, geese and ducks

Witchety grub (also Witjuti, Wichetty): see pages 393 and 411

Woodland: wooded land where trees are well spaced apart

SCIENTIFIC NAMES

Every species of animal that has been studied has a scientific, as well as a common, name. Scientific names are universal and are used among scientists of different regions and countries of the world. For readers searching for more information about animals mentioned in this book, it useful to be acquainted with the scientific names, so here is a list.

Scientific names of species are usually in italics and have two parts. The Koala, for example, is *Phascolarctos cinereus*. The second part, *cinereus*, is the species or specific name; it always begins with a lower case letter. The first part, *Phascolarctos*, is the genus or generic name; it always begins with an upper case letter. The genus is the name of the group to which this species most closely belongs.

Animals are grouped according to their relationships to one another and the rank above the genus (plural: genera) is the family. There may be many species and several genera in a family. Family names are not italicised, always begin with a capital letter and end with '-idae'. The Koala, for example, belongs to the family Phascolarctidae.

The rank above the family is the order, followed by the class and then the phylum (plural: phyla). Overarching all of these is the kingdom which, in animals, is known as Animalia. Animalia encompasses all animals and
separates them from other living groups such as plants which are in the kingdom of Plantae.

Occasionally there are some intermediary classifications, such as subfamily, superfamily and infraorder but they are prone to changes and need not be of great concern here.

Note: sp. = species (singular), spp. = species (plural), ssp. = subspecies

Mammals, class Mammalia

Monotremes, subclass Prototheria

Platypus, *Ornithorhynchus anatinus*, family Ornithorhynchidae
Short-beaked Echidna, *Tachyglossus aculeatus*, family Tachyglossidae

Marsupials, subclass Marsupialia

Koala, *Phascolarctos cinereus*, family Phascolarctidae
Northern Hairy-nosed Wombat, *Lasiorhinus krefftii*, family Vombatidae
Southern Hairy-nosed Wombat, *Lasiorhinus latifrons*, family Vombatidae
Common Wombat, *Vombatus ursinus*, family Vombatidae

Possums & Gliders

Common Brushtail Possum, *Trichosurus vulpecula*, family Phalangeridae
Mountain Brushtail Possum , *Trichosurus cunninghami*, family Phalangeridae
Short-eared Brushtail Possum, *Trichosurus caninus*, family Phalangeridae

Common Spotted Cuscus, *Spilocuscus maculatus*, family Phalangeridae
Southern Common Cuscus, *Phalanger mimicus*, family Phalangeridae
Scaly-tailed Possum, *Wyulda squamicaudata*, family Phalangeridae
Common Ringtail Possum, *Pseudocheirus peregrinus*, family Pseudocheiridae
Western Ringtail Possum, *Pseudocheirus occidentalis*, family Pseudocheiridae
Rock Ringtail Possum, *Petropseudes dahli*, family Pseudocheiridae
Striped Possum, *Dactylopsila trivirgata*, family Petauridae
Leadbeater's Possum, *Gymnobelideus leadbeateri*, family Petauridae
Daintree River Ringtail Possum, *Pseudochirulus cinereus*, family Pseudocheiridae
Herbert River Ringtail Possum, *Pseudochirulus herbertensis*, family Pseudocheiridae
Green Ringtail Possum, *Pseudochirops archeri*, family Pseudocheiridae
Lemuroid Ringtail Possum, *Hemibelideus lemuroides*, family Pseudocheiridae
Greater Glider *Petauroides volans*, family Pseudocheiridae
Yellow-bellied Glider, *Petaurus australis*, family Petauridae
Mahogany Glider, *Petaurus gracilis*, family Petauridae
Sugar Glider, *Petaurus breviceps*, family Petauridae

Squirrel Glider, *Petaurus norfolcensis*, family Petauridae
Feathertail Glider, *Acrobates pygmaeus*, family Acrobatidae
Honey Possum *Tarsipes rostratus*, family Tarsipedidae
Little Pygmy-possum, *Cercartetus lepidus*, family Burramyidae
Long-tailed Pygmy-possum, *Cercartetus caudatus*, family Burramyidae
Eastern Pygmy-possum, *Cercartetus nanus*, family Burramyidae
Western Pygmy-possum, *Cercartetus concinnus*, family Burramyidae
Mountain Pygmy-possum, *Burramys parvus*, family Burramyidae

Bettongs, Potoroos and the Musky Rat-kangaroo

Musky Rat-kangaroo, *Hypsiprymnodon moschatus*, family Hypsiprymnodontidae
Long-nosed Potoroo, *Potorous tridactylus*, family Potoroidae
Long-footed Potoroo, *Potorous longipes*, family Potoroidae
Gilbert's Potoroo, *Potorous gilbertii*, family Potoroidae
Northern Bettong, *Bettongia tropica*, family Potoroidae
Burrowing Bettong, *Bettongia lesueur*, family Potoroidae
Brush-tailed Bettong, *Bettongia penicillata penicillata*, family Potoroidae

Woylie, *Bettongia penicillata ogilbyi*, family Potoroidae

Rufous Bettong, *Aepyprymnus rufescens*, family Potoroidae

Tasmanian Bettong, *Bettongia gaimardi*, family Potoroidae

Kangaroos, Wallabies, Pademelons, Quokkas, Tree-kangaroos and Rock-wallabies, family Macropodidae

Red Kangaroo, *Macropus rufus*

Western Grey Kangaroo, *Macropus fuliginosus*

Eastern Grey Kangaroo, *Macropus giganteus*

Common Wallaroo, *Macropus robustus*

Eastern Wallaroo, *Macropus robustus robustus*

Euro, *Macropus robustus erubescens*

Northern Wallaroo, *Macropus robustus woodwardi*

Black Wallaroo, *Macropus bernardus*

Antilopine Wallaroo, *Macropus antilopinus*

Agile Wallaby, *Macropus agilis*

Red-necked/Bennett's Wallaby, *Macropus rufogriseus*

Swamp Wallaby, *Wallabia bicolor*

Parma Wallaby, *Macropus parma*

Tammar Wallaby, *Macropus eugenii*

Crescent Nailtail Wallaby, *Onychogalea lunata*

Bridled Nailtail Wallaby, *Onychogalea fraenata*

Northern Nailtail Wallaby, *Onychogalea unguifera*

Western Brush Wallaby, *Macropus irma*

Black-stripe Wallaby, *Macropus dorsalis*

Whiptail Wallaby, *Macropus parryi*

Quokka, *Setonix brachyurus*

Central Hare-wallaby, *Lagorchestes asomatus*

Eastern Hare-wallaby, *Lagorchestes leporides*

Spectacled Hare-wallaby, *Lagorchestes conspicillatus*

Rufous Hare-wallaby, *Lagorchestes hirsutus*

Banded Hare-wallaby, *Lagostrophus fasciatus*

Red-necked Pademelon, *Thylogale thetis*

Red-legged Pademelon, *Thylogale stigmatica*

Tasmanian Pademelon, *Thylogale billardierii*

Bennett's Tree-kangaroo, *Dendrolagus bennettianus*

Lumholtz's Tree-kangaroo, *Dendrolagus lumholtzi*

Yellow-footed Rock-wallaby, *Petrogale xanthopus*

Short-eared Rock-wallaby, *Petrogale brachyotis*

Cape York Rock-wallaby, *Petrogale coenensis*

Godman's Rock-wallaby, *Petrogale godmani*

Mareeba Rock-wallaby, *Petrogale mareeba*

Sharman's Rock-wallaby, *Petrogale sharmani*

Allied Rock-wallaby, *Petrogale assimilis*

Unadorned Rock-wallaby, *Petrogale inornata*

Herbert's Rock-wallaby, *Petrogale herberti*

Proserpine Rock-wallaby, *Petrogale persephone*

Brush-tailed Rock-wallaby, *Petrogale penicillata*

Nabarlek/Little Rock-wallaby, *Petrogale concinna*

Monjon, *Petrogale burbidgei*

Rothschild Rock-wallaby, *Petrogale rothschildi*

Black-footed Rock-wallaby, *Petrogale lateralis*

Purple-necked Rock-wallaby, *Petrogale purpureicollis*

Small Marsupial Predators, family Dasyuridae

Brush-tailed Phascogale/Tuan/Common Warbenger, *Phascogale tapoatafa*

Northern Brush-tailed Phascogale, *Phascogale pirata*

Red-tailed Phascogale, *Phascogale calura*

Atherton Antechinus, *Antechinus godmani*

Agile Antechinus, *Antechinus agilis*

Dusky Antechinus, *Antechinus swainsonii*

Fawn Antechinus, *Antechinus bellus*

Swamp Antechinus, *Antechinus minimus*

Fat-tailed Pseudantechinus, *Pseudantechinus macdonnellensis*

Fat-tailed Dunnart, *Sminthopsis crassicaudata*

Little Long-tailed Dunnart, *Sminthopsis dolichura*

Julia Creek Dunnart, *Sminthopsis douglasi*

Common Planigale, *Planigale maculata*

Long-tailed Planigale, *Planigale ingrami*

Kowari, *Dasyuroides byrnei*

Crested-tailed Mulgara, *Dasycercus cristicauda*

Brush-tailed Mulgara, *Dasycercus blythi*

Kaluta, *Dasykaluta rosamondae*

Kultarr/Wuhl-Wuhl, *Antechinomys laniger*

Dibbler, *Parantechinus apicalis*

Wongai Ningaui, *Ningaui ridei*

Pilbara Ningaui, *Ningaui timealeyi*

Southern Ningaui, *Ningaui yvonneae*

Quolls and Devils, family Dasyuridae

Eastern Quoll, *Dasyurus viverrinus*

Western Quoll, *Dasyurus geoffroii*

Northern Quoll, *Dasyurus hallucatus*

Spotted-tailed Quoll, *Dasyurus maculatus*

Tasmanian Devil, *Sarcophilus harrisii*

Bandicoots, family Peramelidae

Northern Brown Bandicoot, *Isoodon macrourus*

Long-nosed Bandicoot, *Perameles nasuta*

Western Barred Bandicoot, *Perameles bougainville*

Golden Bandicoot, *Isoodon auratus*

Bilby, *Macrotis lagotis*, family Thylacomyidae

Numbats, Thylacines and Marsupial Mole

Numbat, *Myrmecobius fasciatus*, family Myrmecobiidae

Thylacine, *Thylacinus cynocephalus*, family Thylacinidae

Kakarratul/Northern Marsupial Mole, *Notoryctes caurinus*, family Notoryctidae

Itjaritjari/Southern Marsupial Mole, *Notoryctes typhlops*, family Notoryctidae

Placental Mammals, subclass Eutheria

Megabats and Microbats

Spectacled Flying-fox, *Pteropus conspicillatus*, family Pteropodidae

Eastern Blossom Bat, *Syconycteris australis*, family Pteropodidae

Eastern Tube-nosed Bat, *Nyctimene robinsoni*, family Pteropodidae

Little Red Flying-fox, *Pteropus scapulatus*, family Pteropodidae

Gould's Wattled Bat, *Chalinolobus gouldii*, family Vespertilionidae

Ghost Bat, *Macroderma gigas*, family Megadermatidae

Dusky Leaf-nosed Bat, *Hipposideros ater*, family Hipposideridae

Western False Pipistrelle, *Falsistrellus mckenziei*, family Vespertilionidae

Rats and Mice, family Muridae

Delicate Mouse, *Pseudomys delicatulus*

House Mouse, *Mus musculus*

Black Rat, *Rattus rattus*

Brown Rat, *Rattus norvegicus*

Rock-rats, *Zyzomys* spp.

Common Rock-rat, *Zyzomys argurus*

Mitchell's Hopping-mouse, *Notomys mitchellii*

Dusky Hopping-mouse, *Notomys fuscus*

Fawn Hopping-mouse, *Notomys cervinus*

Spinifex Hopping-mouse, *Notomys alexis*

Northern Hopping-mouse, *Notomys aquilo*

Greater Stick-nest Rat, *Leporillus conditor*

Lesser Stick-nest Rat, *Leporillus apicalis*

Western Pebble-mound Mouse, *Pseudomys chapmani*

Giant White-tailed Rat, *Uromys caudimaculatus*

Golden-backed Tree-rat, *Mesembriomys macrurus*

Water Mouse, *Xeromys myoides*

Broad-toothed Rat, *Mastacomys fuscus*

Bush Rat, *Rattus fuscipes*

Swamp Rat, *Rattus lutreolus*

Dusky Rat, *Rattus colletti*

Pale Field-rat, *Rattus tunneyi*

Cape York Rat, *Rattus leucopus*

Canefield Rat, *Rattus sordidus*

Water Rat, *Hydromys chrysogaster*

Sea-lions and Fur Seals

Australian Sea-lion, *Neophoca cinerea*, family Otariidae

New Zealand Fur Seal, *Arctocephalus forsteri*, family Otariidae

Australian Fur Seal, *Arctocephalus pusillus*, family Otariidae

Subantarctic Fur Seal, *Arctocephalus tropicalis*, family Otariidae

Southern Elephant Seal, *Mirounga leonina*, family Phocidae

Leopard Seal, *Hydrurga leptonyx*, family Phocidae

Whales, Dolphins and the Dugong

Humpback Whale, *Megaptera novaeangliae*, family Balaenopteridae

Southern Right Whale, *Eubalaena australis*, family Balaenidae

Fin Whale, *Balaenoptera physalus*, family Balaenopteridae

Antarctic Minke Whale, *Balaenoptera bonaerensis*, family Balaenopteridae

Dwarf Minke Whale, *Balaenoptera acutorostrata*, family Balaenopteridae

Gray's Beaked Whale, *Mesoplodon grayi*, family Ziphiidae
Sperm Whale, *Physeter macrocephalus*, family Physeteridae
Killer Whale, *Orcinus orca*, family Delphinidae
Short-finned Pilot Whale, *Globicephala macrorhynchus*, family Delphinidae
Long-finned Pilot Whale, *Globicephala melas*, family Delphinidae
Indo-Pacific Bottlenose Dolphin, *Tursiops aduncus*, family Delphinidae
Offshore Bottlenose Dolphin, *Tursiops truncatus*, family Delphinidae
Short-beaked Common Dolphin, *Delphinus delphis*, family Delphinidae
Dugong, *Dugong dugon*, family Dugongidae

Introduced Herbivores and Carnivores

Rabbit, *Oryctolagus cuniculus*, family Leporidae
Goat, *Capra hircus*, family Bovidae
Horse, *Equus caballus*, family Equidae
Donkey, *Equus asinus*, family Equidae
Camel (One-humped), *Camelus dromedarius*, family Camelidae
Swamp/Water Buffalo, *Bubalus bubalis*, family Bovidae
Deer, family Cervidae
Pig, *Sus scrofa*, family Suidae
Dingo, *Canis lupus*, family Canidae
Fox, *Vulpes vulpes*, family Canidae
Cat, *Felis catus*, family Felidae

Birds, class Aves

Non-passerines

Emu and Cassowary, order Struthioniformes

Emu, *Dromaius novaehollandiae*, family Casuariidae
Southern Cassowary, *Casuarius casuarius*, family Casuariidae
Ostrich, *Struthio camelus*, family Struthionidae

Penguin, order Sphenisciformes, family Spheniscidae

Little Penguin, *Eudyptula minor*

Grebes, order Podicipediformes, family Podicipedidae

Great Crested Grebe, *Podiceps cristatus*
Australasian Grebe, *Tachybaptus novaehollandiae*
Hoary-headed Grebe, *Poliocephalus poliocephalus*

Albatrosses, Petrels and Shearwaters, order Procellariiformes

Southern Giant-Petrel, *Macronectes giganteus*, **family Procellariidae**
Wandering Albatross, *Diomedea exulans*, family Diomedeidae

Shy Albatross, *Thalassarche cauta*, family Diomedeidae
Wedge-tailed Shearwater, *Ardenna pacificus*, family Procellariidae
Fleshy-footed Shearwater, *Ardenna carneipes*, family Procellariidae
Short-tailed Shearwater, *Ardenna tenuirostris*, family Procellariidae

Pelicans, Gannets & Boobies, order Pelecaniformes

Australian Pelican, *Pelecanus conspicillatus*, family Pelecanidae
Australasian Gannet, *Morus serrator*, family Sulidae
Brown Booby, *Sula leucogaster*, family Sulidae
Masked Booby, *Sula dactylatra*, family Sulidae
Red-footed Booby, *Sula sula*, family Sulidae
Abbott's Booby, *Papasula abbotti*, family Sulidae

Frigatebirds and Tropicbirds, order Pelecaniformes

Greater Frigatebird, *Fregata minor*, family Fregatidae
Lesser Frigatebird, *Fregata ariel*, family Fregatidae
Red-tailed Tropicbird, *Phaethon rubricauda*, family Phaethontidae
White-tailed Tropicbird, *Phaethon lepturus*, family Phaethontidae

Cormorants and Darter, order Pelecaniformes

Black-faced Cormorant, *Phalacrocorax fuscescens*, family Phalacrocoracidae
Pied Cormorant, *Phalacrocorax varius*, family Phalacrocoracidae
Little Pied Cormorant, *Microcarbo melanoleucos*, family Phalacrocoracidae
Little Black Cormorant, *Phalacrocorax sulcirostris*, family Phalacrocoracidae
Great Cormorant, *Phalacrocorax carbo*, family Phalacrocoracidae
Australasian Darter, *Anhinga novaehollandiae*, family Anhingidae

Herons and Egrets, order Ciconiiformes, family Ardeidae

White-faced Heron, *Egretta novaehollandiae*
White-necked or Pacific Heron, *Ardea pacifica*
Pied Heron, *Ardea picata*
Great-billed Heron, *Ardea sumatrana*
Great Egret, *Ardea alba*
Intermediate Egret, *Ardea intermedia*
Little Egret, *Egretta garzetta*
Eastern Reef Egret, *Egretta sacra*
Cattle Egret, *Ardea ibis*
Bitterns, *Ixobrychus* and *Botaurus* spp.
Night or Nankeen Heron, *Nycticorax caledonicus*
Striated or Mangrove Heron, *Butorides striatus*

Ibises, Spoonbills and Jabiru, order Ciconiiformes

Australian White or Sacred Ibis, *Threskiornis molucca*, family Threskiornithidae
Straw-necked Ibis, *Threskiornis spinicollis*, family Threskiornithidae
Glossy Ibis, *Plegadis falcinellus*, family Threskiornithidae
Yellow-billed Spoonbill, *Platalea flavipes*, family Threskiornithidae
Royal Spoonbill, *Platalea regia*, family Threskiornithidae
Black-necked Stork or Jabiru, *Ephippiorhynchus australis*, family Ciconiidae

Swans, Geese and Ducks (Waterfowl), order Anseriformes, family Anatidae

Black Swan, *Cygnus atratus*
Cape Barren Goose, *Cereopsis novaehollandiae*
Australian Wood Duck, *Chenonetta jubata*
Plumed Whistling-Duck, *Dendrocygna eytoni*
Wandering Whistling-Duck, *Dendrocygna arcuata*
Australian Shelduck, *Tadorna tadornoides*
Pacific Black Duck, *Anas superciliosa*
Freckled Duck, *Stictonetta naevosa*
Grey Teal, *Anas gracilis*
Chestnut Teal, *Anas castanea*
Hardhead, *Aythya australis*
Musk Duck, *Biziura lobata*
Blue-billed Duck, *Oxyura australis*
Pink-eared Duck, *Malacorhynchus membranaceus*
Australasian Shoveler, *Anas rhynchotis*
Green Pygmy-goose *Nettapus pulchellus*
Cotton Pygmy-goose, *Nettapus coromandelianus*
Radjah Shelduck, *Tadorna radjah*
Magpie Goose, *Anseranas semipalmata*, family Anseranatidae

Eagles, Hawks and Falcons, order Falconiformes

Osprey, *Pandion haliaetus*, family Accipitridae
White-bellied Sea-Eagle, *Haliaeetus leucogaster*, family Accipitridae
Collared Sparrowhawk, *Accipiter cirrocephalus*, family Accipitridae
Whistling Kite, *Haliastur sphenurus*, family Accipitridae
Black Kite, *Milvus migrans*, family Accipitridae
Square-tailed Kite, *Lophoictinia isura*, family Accipitridae
Black-shouldered Kite, *Elanus axillaris*, family Accipitridae
Letter-winged Kite, *Elanus scriptus*, family Accipitridae
Brahminy Kite, *Haliastur indus*, family Accipitridae
Grey Goshawk, *Accipiter novaehollandiae*, family Accipitridae
Red Goshawk, *Erythrotriorchis radiatus*, family Accipitridae

Brown Goshawk, *Accipiter fasciatus*, family Accipitridae

Wedge-tailed Eagle, *Aquila audax*, family Accipitridae

Little Eagle, *Hieraaetus morphnoides*, family Accipitridae

Swamp Harrier, *Circus aproximans*, family Accipitridae

Spotted Harrier, *Circus assimilis*, family Accipitridae

Pacific Baza or Crested Hawk, *Aviceda subcristata*, family Accipitridae

Nankeen Kestrel, *Falco cenchroides*, family Falconidae

Brown Falcon, *Falco berigora*, family Falconidae

Australian Hobby/Little Falcon, *Falco longipennis*, family Falconidae

Black Falcon, *Falco subniger*, family Falconidae

Peregrine Falcon, *Falco peregrinus*, family Falconidae

Grey Falcon, *Falco hypoleucos*, family Falconidae

Black-breasted Buzzard, *Hamirostra melanosternon*, family Accipitridae

Moundbirds, order Galliformes, family Megapodiidae

Australian Brush-turkey, *Alectura lathami*

Malleefowl *Leipoa ocellata*

Orange-footed Scrubfowl, *Megapodius reinwardt*

'True' Quails (order Galliformes), Button-quails (order Turniciformes) and the Plains-wanderer (order Charadriiformes)

Stubble Quail *Coturnix pectoralis*, family Phasianidae

Brown Quail, *Coturnix ypsilophora*, family Phasianidae

King Quail *Coturnix chinensis*, family Phasianidae

California Quail, *Callipepla californica*, family Odontophoridae

Red-backed Button-quail, *Turnix maculosa*, family Turnicidae

Black-breasted Button-quail, *Turnix melanogaster*, family Turnicidae

Painted Button-quail, *Turnix varia*, family Turnicidae

Plains-wanderer, *Pedionomus torquatus*, family Pedionomidae

Rails and Crakes, order Gruiformes, family Rallidae

Lord Howe Woodhen, *Gallirallus sylvestris*

Tasmanian Native-hen, *Tribonyx mortierii*

Baillon's Crake, *Porzana pusilla*

Purple Swamphen, *Porphyrio porphyrio*

Chestnut Rail, *Eulabeornis castaneoventris*

Black-tailed Native-hen, *Gallinula ventralis*

White-browed Crake, *Porzana cinerea*

Red-necked Crake, *Rallina tricolor*

Buff-banded Rail, *Gallirallus philippensis*

Lewin's Rail, *Lewinia pectoralis*

Coot, *Fulica atra*

Dusky Moorhen, *Gallinula tenebrosa*

Brolga, Bustard (order Gruiformes) and Jacana (order Charadriiformes)

Comb-crested Jacana, *Irediparra gallinacea*, family Jacanidae

Australian Bustard, *Ardeotis australis*, family Otididae

Brolga, *Grus rubicundus*, family Gruidae

Sarus Crane, *Grus antigone*, family Gruidae

Waders, order Charadriiformes

Whimbrel, *Numenius phaeopus*, family Scolopacidae

Red-necked Stint, *Calidris ruficollis*, family Scolopacidae

Ruddy Turnstone, *Arenaria interpres*, family Scolopacidae

Bar-tailed Godwit, *Limosa lapponica*, family Scolopacidae

Eastern Curlew, *Numenius madagascariensis*, family Scolopacidae

Latham's Snipe, *Gallinago hardwickii*, family Scolopacidae

Double-banded Plover, *Charadrius bicinctus*, family Charadriidae

Red Knot, *Calidris canutus*, family Scolopacidae

Pied Oystercatcher, *Haematopus longirostris*, family Haematopodidae

Sooty Oystercatcher, *Haematopus fuliginosus*, family Haematopodidae

Banded Stilt, *Cladorhynchus leucocephalus*, family Recurvirostridae

Black-fronted Dotterel, *Elseyornis melanops*, family Charadriidae

Red-capped Dotterel, *Charadrius ruficapillus*, family Charadriidae

Red-kneed Dotterel, *Erythrogonys cinctus*, family Charadriidae

Hooded Plover, *Thinornis rubricollis*, family Charadriidae

Inland Dotterel, *Charadrius australis*, family Charadriidae

Banded Lapwing, *Vanellus tricolor*, family Charadriidae

Masked Lapwing/Spur-winged Plover, *Vanellus miles*, family Charadriidae

Oriental Pratincole, *Glareola maldivarum*, family Glareolidae

Beach Stone-curlew, *Esacus neglectus*, family Burhinidae

Bush Stone-curlew, *Burhinus grallarius*, family Burhinidae

Gulls, Terns and Skuas, order Charadriiformes, family Laridae

Silver Gull, *Chroicocephalus novaehollandiae*

Pacific Gull, *Larus pacificus*

Kelp Gull, *Larus dominicanus*

Crested Tern, *Thalasseus bergii*

Caspian Tern, *Hydroprogne caspia*

Fairy Tern, *Sternula nereis*

Little Tern, *Sternula albifrons*

Whiskered Tern, *Chlidonias hybridus*

Sooty Tern, *Onychoprion fuscata*

Bridled Tern, *Onychoprion anaethetus*

Noddies, *Anous* spp.

Brown Skua, *Catharacta antarcticus*

Arctic Jaeger, *Stercorarius parasiticus*

Pigeons and Doves, order Columbiformes, family Columbidae

Topknot Pigeon, *Lopholaimus antarcticus*

Wompoo Fruit-Dove, *Ptilinopus magnificus*

Diamond Dove, *Geopelia cuneata*

Superb Fruit-Dove, *Ptilinopus superbus*

Rose-crowned Fruit-Dove, *Ptilinopus regina*

Brown Cuckoo-Dove, *Macropygia amboinensis*

Peaceful Dove, *Geopelia striata*

Crested Pigeon, *Ocyphaps lophotes*

Rock Pigeon or Dove, *Columba livia*

Common Bronzewing, *Phaps chalcoptera*

Wonga Pigeon, *Leucosarcia melanoleuca*

Emerald Dove, *Chalcophaps indica*

White-headed Pigeon, *Columba leucomela*

Banded Fruit-Dove, *Ptilinopus cinctus*

Torresian Imperial-Pigeon, *Ducula bicolor*

Spinifex Pigeon, *Geophaps plumifera*

Cockatoos, order Psittaciformes, family Cacatuidae

Galah, *Eolophus roseicapillus*

Gang-gang Cockatoo, *Callocephalon fimbriatum*

Pink/Major Mitchell Cockatoo, *Lophocroa leadbeateri*

Cockatiel, *Nymphicus hollandicus*

Palm Cockatoo, *Probosciger aterrimus*

Yellow-tailed Black-Cockatoo, *Calyptorhynchus funereus*

Red-tailed Black-Cockatoo, *Calyptorhynchus banksii*

Glossy Black-Cockatoo, *Calyptorhynchus lathami*

Sulphur-crested Cockatoo, *Cacatua galerita*

Long-billed Corella, *Cacatua tenuirostris*

Little Corella, *Cacatua sanguinea*

Western Corella, *Cacatua pastinator*

Carnaby's/Short-billed Black-cockatoo, *Calyptorhynchus latirostris*

Baudin's/Long-billed Black-cockatoo, *Calyptorhynchus baudinii*

Lorikeets, Rosellas and Other Parrots, order Psittaciformes, family Cacatuidae

Rainbow Lorikeet, *Trichoglossus haematodus*

Scaly-breasted Lorikeet, *Trichoglossus chlorolepidotus*

Purple-crowned Lorikeet, *Glossopsitta porphyrocephala*

Varied Lorikeet *Psitteuteles versicolor*

Little Lorikeet, *Glossopsitta pusilla*

Musk Lorikeet, *Glossopsitta concinna*

Crimson Rosella, *Platycercus elegans*

Yellow Rosella, *Platycercus elegans flaveolus*

Adelaide Rosella, *Platycercus elegans adelaidae*

Western Rosella, *Platycercus icterotis*

Eastern Rosella, *Platycercus eximius*

Northern Rosella, *Platycercus venustus*

Pale-headed Rosella, *Platycercus adscitus*

Green Rosella, *Platycercus caledonicus*

Blue-winged Parrot, *Neophema chrysostoma*

Swift Parrot, *Lathamus discolor*

Orange-bellied Parrot, *Neophema chrysogaster*
Eclectus Parrot, *Eclectus roratus*
Red-cheeked Parrot, *Geoffroyus geoffroyi*
Double-eyed Fig-Parrot, *Cyclopsitta diophthalma*
Australian King-Parrot, *Alisterus scapularis*
Australian Ringnecks, *Barnardius* spp.
Hooded Parrot, *Psephotus dissimilis*
Golden-shouldered Parrot, *Psephotus chrysopterygius*
Paradise Parrot, *Psephotus pulcherrimus*
Budgerigar, *Melopsittacus undulatus*
Blue Bonnet, *Northiella haematogaster*
Regent Parrot, *Polytelis anthopeplus*
Mulga Parrot, *Psephotus varius*
Superb Parrot, *Polytelis swainsonii*
Rock Parrot, *Neophema petrophila*
Night Parrot, *Pezoporus occidentalis*
Ground Parrot, *Pezoporus wallicus*
Princess or Alexandra's Parrot, *Polytelis alexandrae*

Cuckoos, order Cuculiformes, family Cuculidae

Eastern Koel, *Eudynamys orientalis*
Channel-billed Cuckoo, *Scythrops novaehollandiae*
Oriental Cuckoo, *Cuculus optatus*
Pallid Cuckoo *Cacomantis pallidus*
Fan-tailed Cuckoo, *Cacomantis flabelliformis*
Shining Bronze-Cuckoo, *Chalcites lucidus*
Little Bronze-Cuckoo, *Chalcites minutillus*

Pheasant Coucal, *Centropus phasianinus*, family Centropodidae

Kingfishers and Kookaburras, order Coraciiformes

Laughing Kookaburra, *Dacelo novaeguineae*, family Halcyonidae
Blue-winged Kookaburra, *Dacelo leachii*, family Halcyonidae
Little Kingfisher, *Alcedo pusilla*, family Alcedinidae
Azure Kingfisher, *Alcedo azurea*, family Alcedinidae
Forest Kingfisher, *Todiramphus macleayii*, family Halcyonidae
Yellow-billed Kingfisher, *Syma torotoro*, family Halcyonidae
Collared Kingfisher, *Todiramphus chloris*, family Halcyonidae
Sacred Kingfisher, *Todiramphus sanctus*, family Halcyonidae
Red-backed Kingfisher, *Todiramphus pyrrhopygius*, family Halcyonidae
Buff-breasted Paradise-Kingfisher *Tanysiptera sylvia*, family Halcyonidae

Owls, order Strigiformes

Barn Owl, *Tyto alba*, family Tytonidae
Masked Owl, *Tyto novaehollandiae*, family Tytonidae
Grass Owl, *Tyto capensis*, family Tytonidae
Sooty Owl, *Tyto tenebricosa*, family Tytonidae
Lesser Sooty Owl, *Tyto tenebricosa*

multipunctata, family Tytonidae
Powerful Owl, *Ninox strenua*, family Strigidae
Rufous Owl, *Ninox rufa*, family Strigidae
Barking Owl, *Ninox connivens*, family Strigidae
Southern Boobook, *Ninox novaeseelandiae*, family Strigidae

Frogmouths, Nightjars and Owlet-Nightjars, order Caprimulgiformes

Tawny Frogmouth, *Podargus strigoides*, family Podargidae
Marbled Frogmouth, *Podargus ocellatus*, family Podargidae
Papuan Frogmouth, *Podargus papuensis*, family Podargidae
Large-tailed Nightjar, *Caprimulgus macrurus*, family Caprimulgidae
White-throated Nightjar, *Eurostopodus mystacalis*, family Caprimulgidae
Spotted Nightjar, *Eurostopodus argus*, family Caprimulgidae
Australian Owlet-Nightjar, *Aegotheles cristatus*, family Aegothelidae

Bee-eater and Dollarbird, order Coraciiformes

Rainbow Bee-eater, *Merops ornatus*, family Meropidae
Dollarbird, *Eurystomus orientalis*, family Coraciidae

Passerines, order Passeriformes

Pittas

Red-bellied Pitta, *Pitta erythrogaster*, family Pittidae
Blue-winged Pitta, *Pitta moluccensis*, family Pittidae
Rainbow Pitta, *Pitta iris*, family Pittidae
Noisy Pitta, *Pitta versicolor*, family Pittidae

Lyrebirds, Scrub-birds and Bristlebirds

Albert's Lyrebird, *Menura alberti*, family Menuridae
Superb Lyrebird, *Menura novaehollandiae*, family Menuridae
Rufous Scrub-bird, *Atrichornis rufescens*, family Atrichornithidae
Noisy Scrub-bird, *Atrichornis clamosus*, family Atrichornithidae
Western Bristlebird, *Dasyornis longirostris*, family Pardalotidae
Eastern Bristlebird, *Dasyornis brachypterus*, family Pardalotidae
Rufous Bristlebird, *Dasyornis broadbenti*, family Pardalotidae

Sittellas and Treecreepers

Varied Sittella, *Daphoenositta chrysoptera*, family Neosittidae
White-throated Treecreeper, *Cormobates leucophaeus*, family Climacteridae

Red-browed Treecreeper, *Climacteris erythrops*, family Climacteridae
Rufous Treecreeper, *Climacteris rufa*, family Climacteridae

Fairy-Wrens, Emu-wrens and Grasswrens, family Maluridae

Red-backed Fairy-wren, *Malurus melanocephalus*
Splendid Fairy-wren, *Malurus splendens*
White-winged Fairy-wren, *Malurus leucopterus*
Superb Fairy-wren, *Malurus cyaneus*
Purple-crowned Fairy-wren, *Malurus coronatus*
Variegated Fairy-wren, *Malurus lamberti*
Lovely Fairy-wren, *Malurus amabilis*
Blue-breasted Fairy-wren, *Malurus pulcherrimus*
Red-winged Fairy-wren, *Malurus elegans*
Southern Emu-wren, *Stipiturus malachurus*
Rufous-crowned Emu-wren, *Stipiturus ruficeps*
Mallee Emu-wren, *Stipiturus mallee*
Grey Grasswren, *Amytornis barbatus*
Black Grasswren, *Amytornis housei*
Striated Grasswren, *Amytornis striatus*

Australasian Warblers: Scrubwrens, Thornbills and Gerygones, family Pardalotidae

White-browed Scrubwren, *Sericornis frontalis*
Yellow-throated Scrubwren, *Sericornis citreogularis*
Shy Heathwren, *Calamanthus cautus*
Chestnut-rumped Heathwren, *Calamanthus pyrrhopygius*
Striated Fieldwren, *Calamanthus fuliginosus*
White-throated Gerygone, *Gerygone olivacea*
Western Gerygone, *Gerygone fusca*
Yellow-rumped Thornbill, *Acanthiza chrysorrhoa*
Chestnut-rumped Thornbill, *Acanthiza uropygialis*
Banded Whiteface, *Aphelocephala nigricincta*
Chestnut-breasted Whiteface, *Aphelocephala pectoralis*
Southern Whiteface, *Aphelocephala leucopsis*
Weebill, *Smicrornis brevirostris*
Pilotbird, *Pycnoptilus floccosus*
Rock Warbler, *Origma solitaria*

Pardalotes, family Pardalotidae

Striated Pardalote, *Pardalotus striatus*
Red-browed Pardalote, *Pardalotus rubricatus*
Forty-spotted Pardalote, *Pardalotus quadragintus*
Spotted Pardalote, *Pardalotus punctatus*

Honeyeaters, family Meliphagidae

Brown-headed Honeyeater, *Melithreptus brevirostris*
Blue-faced Honeyeater, *Entomyzon cyanotis*
New Holland Honeyeater, *Phylidonyris novaehollandiae*
White-cheeked Honeyeater, *Phylidonyris nigra*

Regent Honeyeater, *Anthochaera phrygia*
Little Friarbird, *Philemon citreogularis*
Singing Honeyeater, *Lichenostomus virescens*
Yellow Wattlebird, *Anthochaera paradoxa*
Red Wattlebird, *Anthochaera carunculata*
Little Wattlebird, *Anthochaera chrysoptera*
Noisy Miner, *Manorina melanocephala*
Bellbird or Bell Miner, *Manorina melanophrys*
Yellow-throated Miner, *Manorina flavigula*
Yellow-tufted Honeyeater, *Lichenostomus melanops*
Helmeted Honeyeater, *Lichenostomus melanops cassidix*
Eastern Spinebill, *Acanthorhynchus tenuirostris*
Western Spinebill, *Acanthorhynchus superciliosus*
Strong-billed Honeyeater, *Melithreptus validirostris*
Tawny-crowned Honeyeater, *Glyciphila melanops*
Singing Honeyeater, *Lichenostomus virescens*
Painted Honeyeater, *Grantiella picta*
Yellow-faced Honeyeater, *Lichenostomus chrysops*
Brown Honeyeater, *Lichmera indistincta*
Lewin's Honeyeater, *Meliphaga lewinii*
Gibberbird, *Ashbyia lovensis*
White-fronted Chat, *Epthianura albifrons*
Yellow Chat, *Epthianura crocea*
Crimson Chat, *Epthianura tricolor*
Orange Chat, *Epthianura aurifrons*

Robins, family Petroicidae

Jacky Winter, *Microeca fascinans*
Dusky Robin, *Melanodryas vittata*
Flame Robin, *Petroica phoenicea*
Scarlet Robin, *Petroica boodang*
Hooded Robin, *Melanodryas cucullata*
Red-capped Robin, *Petroica goodenovii*
Rose Robin, *Petroica rosea*
Eastern Yellow Robin, *Eopsaltria australis*
Western Yellow Robin, *Eopsaltria griseogularis*
Pink Robin, *Petroica rodinogaster*
Mangrove Robin, *Eopsaltria pulverulenta*
Lemon-bellied Flycatcher, *Microeca flavigaster*
Grey-headed Robin, *Heteromyias albispecularis*
Northern Scrub-robin, *Drymodes superciliaris*
Southern Scrub-robin, *Drymodes brunneopygia*

Chowchillas and Logrunners, family Orthonychidae

Logrunner, *Orthonyx temminckii*
Chowchilla, *Orthonyx spaldingii*

Babblers, family Pomatostomidae

Grey-crowned Babbler, *Pomatostomus temporalis*
White-browed Babbler, *Pomatostomus superciliosus*
Hall's Babbler, *Pomatostomus halli*
Chestnut-crowned Babbler, *Pomatostomus ruficeps*

Whipbirds, Wedgebills and Quail-thrushes, family Cinclosomatidae

Eastern Whipbird, *Psophodes olivaceus*
Western Whipbird, *Psophodes nigrogularis*
Chirruping Wedgebill, *Psophodes cristatus*
Chiming Wedgebill, *Psophodes occidentalis*
Spotted Quail-thrush, *Cinclosoma punctatum*
Cinnamon Quail-thrush, *Cinclosoma cinnamomeum*
Chestnut-breasted Quail-thrush, *Cinclosoma castaneothorax*
Chestnut-backed Quail-thrush, *Cinclosoma castanotum*

The Whistler Family, family Pachycephalidae

Crested Shrike-tit, *Falcunculus frontatus*
Crested Bellbird, *Oreoica gutturalis*
Golden Whistler, *Pachycephala pectoralis*
Mangrove Golden Whistler, *Pachycephala melanura*
Olive Whistler, *Pachycephala olivacea*
Grey Whistler, *Pachycephala simplex*
Gilbert's Whistler, *Pachycephala inornata*
Rufous Whistler, *Pachycephala rufiventris*
White-breasted Whistler, *Pachycephala lanioides*
Grey Shrike-thrush, *Colluricincla harmonica*
Little Shrike-thrush, *Colluricincla megarhyncha*
Bower's Shrike-thrush, *Colluricincla boweri*
Sandstone Shrike-thrush, *Colluricincla woodwardi*

Red-whiskered Bulbul, *Pycnonotus jocosus*, family Pycnonotidae

Flycatchers, family Dicruridae

Grey Fantail, *Rhipidura albiscarpa*
Willie Wagtail, *Rhipidura leucophrys*
Rufous Fantail, *Rhipidura rufifrons*
Mangrove Grey Fantail, *Rhipidura phasiana*
Northern Fantail, *Rhipidura rufiventris*
Spangled Drongo, *Dicrurus bracteatus*
Satin Flycatcher, *Myiagra cyanoleuca*
Leaden Flycatcher, *Myiagra rubecula*
Restless Flycatcher, *Myiagra inquieta*
Shining Flycatcher, *Myiagra alecto*
Broad-billed Flycatcher, *Myiagra ruficollis*
White-eared Monarch, *Carterornis leucotis*
Frill-necked Monarch, *Arses lorealis*
Pied Monarch, *Arses kaupi*
Black-faced Monarch, *Monarcha melanopsis*
Black-winged Monarch, *Monarcha frater*
Spectacled Monarch, *Symposiarchus trivirgatus*
Yellow-breasted Boatbill, *Machaerirhynchus flaviventer*
Magpie-lark, *Grallina cyanoleuca*

Cuckoo-shrikes and Trillers, family Campephagidae

Black-faced Cuckoo-shrike, *Coracina novaehollandiae*
White-bellied Cuckoo-shrike, *Coracina papuensis*
Ground Cuckoo-shrike, *Coracina maxima*
Barred Cuckoo-shrike, *Coracina lineata*

Cicadabird, *Coracina tenuirostris*
White-winged Triller, *Lalage sueurii*
Varied Triller, *Lalage leucomela*

Orioles and Figbird, family Oriolidae

Olive-backed Oriole, *Oriolus sagittatus*
Yellow Oriole, *Oriolus flavocinctus*
Australasian Figbird, *Sphecotheres viridis*

Woodswallows, family Artamidae

Black-faced Woodswallow, *Artamus cinereus*
Little Woodswallow, *Artamus minor*
Masked Woodswallow, *Artamus personatus*
White-browed Woodswallow, *Artamus superciliosus*
White-breasted Woodswallow, *Artamus leucorynchus*
Dusky Woodswallow, *Artamus cyanopterus*

Currawongs, family Artamidae

Pied Currawong, *Strepera graculina*
Black Currawong, *Strepera fuliginosa*
Grey Currawong, *Strepera versicolor*

Butcherbirds (family Artamidae) and Australian Magpie (family Artamidae)

Grey Butcherbird, *Cracticus torquatus*
Pied Butcherbird, *Cracticus nigrogularis*
Black Butcherbird, *Cracticus quoyi*
Black-backed Butcherbird, *Cracticus mentalis*
Australian Magpie, *Gymorhina tibicen*

Crows and Ravens, family Corvidae

Little Raven, *Corvus mellori*
Australian Raven, *Corvus coronoides*
Torresian Crow, *Corvus orru*
Forest Raven, *Corvus tasmanicus*
Little Crow, *Corvus bennetti*
House Crow, *Corvus splendens*

White-winged Chough and Apostlebird, family Corcoracidae

White-winged Chough, *Corcorax melanorhamphos*
Apostlebird *Struthidea cinerea*

Birds of Paradise, family Paradisaeidae

Magnificent Riflebird, *Ptiloris magnificus*
Paradise Riflebird, *Ptiloris paradiseus*
Victoria's Riflebird, *Ptilotis victoriae*
Trumpet Manucode, *Phonygammus keraudrenii*

Sunbird and Flowerpecker

Mistletoebird, *Dicaeum hirundinaceum*, family Dicaeidae
Yellow-bellied or Olive-backed Sunbird, *Nectarinia jugularis*, family Nectariniidae

Bowerbirds, family Ptilonorhynchidae

Regent Bowerbird, *Sericulus chrysocephalus*
Western Bowerbird, *Chlamydera guttata*

Spotted Bowerbird, *Chlamydera maculata*
Great Bowerbird, *Chlamydera nuchalis*
Tooth-billed Bowerbird, *Scenopoeetes dentirostris*
Spotted Catbird, *Ailuroedus melanotis*
Green Catbird, *Ailuroedus crassirostris*
Satin Bowerbird, *Chlamydera violaceus*
Golden Bowerbird, *Prionodura newtoniana*

Larks, Pipits, Wagtails and Warblers

Eurasian Skylark, *Alauda arvensis*, family Alaudidae
Horsfield's Bushlark, *Mirafra javanica*, family Alaudidae
Richard's or Australasian Pipit, *Anthus novaeseelandiae*, family Motacillidae
Wagtails, *Motacilla* spp., family Motacillidae
Brown Songlark, *Cincloramphus cruralis*, family Sylviidae
Rufous Songlark, *Cincloramphus mathewsi*, family Sylviidae
Tawny Grassbird, *Megalurus timoriensis*, family Sylviidae
Little Grassbird, *Megalurus gramineus*, family Sylviidae
Spinifexbird, *Eremiornis carteri*, family Sylviidae
Golden-headed Cisticola, *Cisticola exilis*, family Sylviidae
Zitting Cisticola, *Cisticola juncidis*, family Sylviidae
Clamorous or Australian Reed-warbler, *Acrocephalus stentoreus*, family Sylviidae
Oriental Reed-Warbler, *Acrocephalus orientalis*

Finches

Eurasian House Sparrow, *Passer domesticus*, family Passeridae
Eurasian Tree Sparrow, *Passer montanus*, family Passeridae
Common Greenfinch, *Carduelis chloris*, family Fringillidae
European Goldfinch, *Carduelis carduelis*, family Fringillidae
Painted Finch, *Emblema pictum*, family Passeridae
Zebra Finch, *Taeniopygia guttata*, family Passeridae
Blue-faced Parrot-finch, *Erythrura trichroa*, family Passeridae
Red-browed Finch, *Neochmia temporalis*, family Passeridae
Red-eared Firetail, *Stagonopleura oculata*, family Passeridae
Beautiful Firetail, *Stagonopleura bella*, family Passeridae
Diamond Firetail, *Stagonopleura guttata*, family Passeridae
Star Finch, *Neochmia ruficauda*, family Passeridae
Gouldian Finch, *Erythrura gouldiae*, family Passeridae
Zebra Finch, *Taeniopygia guttata*, family Passeridae
Yellow-rumped Mannikin, *Lonchura flaviprymna*, family Passeridae
Chestnut-breasted Mannikin, *Lonchura castaneothorax*, family Passeridae
Pictorella Mannikin, *Heteromunia pectoralis*, family Passeridae

White-eyes, family Zosteropidae

Silvereye, *Zosterops lateralis*
Yellow White-eye, *Zosterops luteus*
Slender-billed White-eye, *Zosterops tenuirostris*
White-chested White-eye, *Zosterops albogularis*
Christmas Island White-eye, *Zosterops natalis*
Pale White-eye, *Zosterops citronella*

Swallows Martins (order Passeriformes), and Swifts (order Apodiformes)

Welcome Swallow, *Hirundo neoxena*, family Hirundinidae
Tree Martin, *Hirundo nigricans*, family Hirundinidae
Barn Swallow, *Hirundo rustica*, family Hirundinidae
White-backed Swallow, *Cheramoeca leucosterna*, family Hirundinidae
Fairy Martin, *Hirundo ariel*, family Hirundinidae
Australian Swiftlet, *Aerodramus terrareginae*, family Apodidae
White-throated Needletail, *Hirundapus caudacutus*, family Apodidae
Fork-tailed Swift, *Apus pacificus*, family Apodidae
House Swift, *Apus affinis*, family Apodidae
Glossy Swiftlet, *Collocalia esculenta*, family Apodidae

Thrushes, family Muscicapidae

Common Blackbird, *Turdus merula*
Song Thrush, *Turdus philomelos*
Bassian Thrush, *Zoothera lunulata*
Russet-tailed Thrush, *Zoothera heinei*

Starlings and Mynas, family Sturnidae

Common Starling, *Sturnus vulgaris*
Common Myna, *Acridotheres tristis*
Metallic Starling, *Aplonis metallica*

Reptiles, class Reptilia

Crocodiles, family Crocodiylidae

Saltwater or Estuarine Crocodile, *Crocodylus porosus*
Australian Freshwater Crocodile, *Crocodylus johnstoni*

Freshwater Turtles

Western Swamp Turtle, *Pseudemydura umbrina*, family Cheluidae
Northern Long-necked Turtle, *Chelodina rugosa*, family Cheluidae
Eastern Long-necked or Snake-necked Turtle, *Chelodina longicollis*, family Cheluidae
North-west Red-faced Turtle, *Emydura australis*, family Cheluidae
Pig-nosed Turtle, *Carettochelys insculpta*, family Carettochelyididae

Sea Turtles

Flatback Turtle, *Natator depressus*, family Cheloniidae
Leatherback Turtle, *Dermochelys coriacea*, family Dermochelyidae
Pacific Ridley Turtle, *Lepidochelys olivacea*, family Cheloniidae
Loggerhead Turtle, *Caretta caretta*, family Cheloniidae

Green Turtle, *Chelonia mydas*, family Cheloniidae
Hawksbill Turtle, *Eretmochelys imbricata*, family Cheloniidae

Geckos, family Gekkonidae

Ring-tailed Gecko, *Crytodactylus louisiadensis*
Beautiful Gecko, *Diplodactylus pulcher*
Clawless Gecko, *Crenadactylus ocellatus*
Pilbara Dtella, *Gehyra pilbara*
Knob-tailed geckos, *Nephrurus* spp.
Pale Knob-tailed Gecko, *Nephrurus laevissimus*
Leaf-tailed geckos, *Saltuarius*, *Phyllurus* and *Orraya* spp.
Southern Leaf-tailed Gecko, *Saltuarius swaini*
Mourning Gecko, *Lepidodactylus lugubris*
Prickly or Bynoe's Gecko, *Heteronotia binoei*
Soft Spiny-tailed Gecko, *Strophurus spinigerus*
Barking Gecko, *Underwoodisaurus milii*

Legless or Flap-footed Lizards, family Pygopodidae

Worm lizards, *Aprasia* spp.
Scaly-foots, *Paradelma orientalis* and *Pygopus* spp.
Southern Scaly-foot, *Pygopus lepidopodus*
Excitable Delma, *Delma tincta*
Western Hooded Scaly-foot, *Pygopus nigriceps*
Burton's Legless Lizard, *Lialis burtonis*

Skinks, Family Scincidae

Great Desert Skink or Tjakura, *Egernia kintorei*
King's Skink, *Egernia kingii*
Garden Skink, *Lampropholis delicata*
Fence Skink, *Cryptoblepharus plagiocephalus*
Mountain Log or Southern Grass Skink, *Pseudemoia entrecasteauxii*
Pedra Branca Skink, *Niveoscincus palfreymani*
Gidgee or Stokes' Skink, *Egernia stokesii*
Cunningham's Skink *Egernia cunninghami*
Pygmy Blue-tongue, *Tiliqua adelaidensis*
Northern, Common or Eastern Blue-tongue, *Tiliqua scincoides*
Red-legged Skink, *Ctenotus labillardieri*

Unpatterned Robust Slider, *Lerista macropisthopus*
Western Blue-tongue, *Tiliqua occipitalis*
Bright Fire-tail Skink, *Morethia ruficauda*
Black Rock Skink, *Egernia saxatilis*

Dragons, family Agamidae

Jacky Lizard, *Amphibolurus muricatus*
Bearded Dragon, *Pogona barbata*
Mountain Heath Dragon, *Rankinia diemensis*
Pebble Dragon, Earless Dragon, *Tympanocryptis cephalus*
Frilled Lizard, *Chlamydosaurus kingii*
Eastern Water Dragon, *Physignathus lesueurii*
Central Bearded Dragon, *Pogona vitticeps*
Bicycle Lizard or Crested Dragon, *Ctenophorus cristatus*
Thorny Devil, *Moloch horridus*
Boyd's Forest Dragon, *Hypsilurus boydii*
Central Netted Dragon, *Ctenophorus nuchalis*
Dwarf Bearded Dragon, *Pogona minor*
Magnificent Dragon, *Diporiphora superba*

Goannas, family Varanidae

Lace Monitor, *Varanus varius*
Heath Monitor, *Varanus rosenbergi*
Short-tailed Pygmy Monitor, *Varanus brevicauda*
Perentie, *Varanus giganteus*
Mertens' Water Monitor, *Varanus mertensi*
Long-tailed Rock Monitor, *Varanus glebopalma*
Spotted Tree Monitor, *Varanus scalaris*
Pygmy Mulga Monitor, *Varanus gilleni*
Yellow-spotted Monitor, *Varanus panoptes*
Bungarra, *Varanus panoptes rubidus*
Sand (or Gould's) Goanna, *Varanus gouldii*
Glauerti's Rock Monitor, *Varanus glauerti*

Blind Snakes, family Typhlopidae

Southern Blind Snake, *Ramphotyphlops australis*
Beaked Blind Snake, *Ramphotyphlops grypus*

File Snakes, family Acrochordidae

Arafura File Snake, *Acrochordus arafurae*
Little File Snake, *Acrochordus granulatus*

Pythons, family Pythonidae

Carpet Python, *Morelia spilota*
Diamond Python, *Morelia spilota spilota*
Scrub or Amethyst Python, *Morelia amethistina*
Pygmy Python, *Antaresia perthensis*
Water Python, *Liasis mackloti fuscus*
Stimson's Python, *Antaresia stimsoni*
Green Python, *Morelia viridis*

Colubrids, family Colubridae

Slaty-grey Snake, *Stegonotus cucullatus*
Common Tree Snake, *Dendrelaphis punctulata*
Brown Tree Snake, *Boiga irregularis*
Macleay's Water Snake, *Enhydris polylepis*

White-bellied Mangrove Snake, *Myron richardsonii*
Bockdam, *Cerberus australis*
Keelback, *Tropidonophis mairii*

Elapids, family Elapidae

Bandy Bandy snakes, *Vermicella* spp.
Monk Snake, *Parasuta monachus*
Desert Banded Snake, *Simoselaps anomalus*
Whipsnakes, *Demansia* spp.
Yellow-faced Whipsnake, *Demansia psammophis*
Greater Black Whipsnake, *Demansia papuensis*
Olive Whipsnake, *Demansia olivacea*
Broad-headed snakes, *Hoplocephalus* spp.
Broad-headed Snake, *Hoplocephalus bungaroides*
White-lipped Snake, *Drysdalia coronoides*
Copperheads, *Austrelaps* spp.
Lowlands Copperhead, *Austrelaps superbus*
Highlands Copperhead, *Austrelaps ramsayi*
Pygmy Copperhead, *Austrelaps labialis*
Inland Taipan, *Oxyuranus microlepidotus*
Coastal Taipan, *Oxyuranus scutellatus*
Bardick, *Echiopsis curta*
'Black' snakes, *Pseudechis* spp.
King Brown or Mulga Snake, *Pseudechis australis*
Red-bellied Black-snake, *Pseudechis porphyriacus*
Tiger snakes, *Notechis* spp.
Death Adder, *Acanthophis antarcticus*
Brown snakes, *Pseudonaja* spp.
Eastern Brown Snake, *Pseudonaja textilis*

Frogs, class Amphibia, order Anura

Ground Frogs, family Myobatrachidae

Trilling Frog, *Neobatrachus centralis*
Turtle Frog, *Myobatrachus gouldii*
Sandhill Frog, *Arenophryne rotunda*
Crucifix Frog, *Notaden bennettii*
Nicholls' Toadlet, *Metacrinia nicholsi*
Western Banjo Frog or Pobblebonk Frog, *Limnodynastes dorsalis*
Quacking Frog, *Crinia georgiana*
Pouched or Hip Pocket Frog, *Assa darlingtoni*
Southern Gastric Brooding Frog, *Rheobatrachus silus*
Northern Gastric Brooding Frog, *Rheobatrachus vitellinus*
Red-crowned Toadlet, *Pseudophryne australis*
Lea's Frog, *Geocrinia leai*
Corroboree Frog, *Pseudophryne corroboree*
Giant Burrowing Frog, *Heleioporus australiacus*
Spotted Burrowing Frog, *Heleioporus albopunctatus*

Tree Frogs, family Hylidae

Motorbike Frog, *Litoria moorei*
White-lipped Tree Frog, **Litoria infrafrenata**
Javelin Frog, Litoria microbelos
Green and Golden Bell Frog, *Litoria aurea*

Dwarf Tree Frog, *Litoria fallax*
Water-holding Frog, *Cyclorana platycephala*
Spotted-thighed Frog, *Litoria cyclorhynchus*
Slender Tree Frog, *Litoria adelaidensis*
Dainty Tree Frog, *Litoria gracilenta*
Peron's Tree Frog, *Litoria peronii*
Magnificent Tree Frog, *Litoria splendida*
Main's Frog, *Cyclorana maini*

Ranids and Microhylids

Wood Frog, *Rana daemeli*, family Ranidae
Robust Frog, *Austrochaperina robusta*, family Microhylidae

Cane Toad

Cane Toad, *Chaunus marinus*, family Bufonidae

Fishes, class Osteichthyes, order Perciformes, (except for Lungfish)

Introduction

Giant Gudgeon, *Oxyeleotris selheimi*, family Eleotridae
Western Sooty Grunter, *Hephaestus jenkinsi*, family Terapontidae
Queensland Lungfish, *Neoceratodus forsteri*, family Ceratodontidae, sub-class Sarcopterygii, order Dipnoi

Murray–Darling Basin Fishes

Murray Cod / Ponde, *Maccullochella peelii*, family Percichthyidae
Trout Cod, *Maccullochella macquariensis*, family Percichthyidae
Freshwater Catfish, *Tandanus tandanus*, family Plotosidae
Silver Perch / Bidyan, *Bidyanus bidyanus*, family Terapontidae
Flathead Galaxia / Murray Jollytail, *Galaxias rostratus*, family Glaxiidae
Common Carp, *Cyrinus carpio*, family Cyprinidae •
Gudgeons, family Eleotridae
Southern Pygmy Perch, *Nannoperca australis*, family Nannopercidae
Australian Smelt, *Retropinna semoni*, family Retropinnidae
Golden Perch, Yellowbelly or Callop, *Macquaria ambigua*, family Percichthyidae
Goldfish, *Carassius auratus*, family Cyprinidae
Redfin, *Perca fluviatilis*, family Percidae

Fishes of the North

Rainbowfishes, family Melanotaeniidae
Fork-tailed catfishes, family Ariidae
Eel-tailed catfishes, family Plotosidae
Archerfishes, family Toxotidae

Barramundi/Giant Perch/Barra/Silver Barramundi/Palmer Perch/Sea Bass, *Lates calcarifer*, family Centropomidae

Saratoga or Spotted Barramundi, *Scleropages leichardti*, family Osteoglossidae

Gulf Saratoga, *Scleropages jardini*, family Osteoglossidae

Banded Rainbowfish, *Melanotaenia trifasciata*, family Melanotaeniidae

Other Coastal River Fishes

Queensland Lungfish, *Neoceratodus forsteri*, family Ceratodontidae

Mountain Galaxias *Galaxia olidus*, family Glaxiidae

Climbing Galaxias *Galaxias brevipinnis*, family Glaxiidae

Freshwater eels, family Anguillidae

Short-finned Eel, *Anguilla australis*, family Anguillidae

Lampreys, families Geotriidae and Mordaciidae

Inland Fishes

Desert Goby, *Chlamydogobius eremius*, family Gobiidae

Lake Eyre Hardyhead, *Craterocephalus eyresii*, family Atherinidae

Salamanderfish, *Lepidogalaxias salamandroides*, family Lepidogalaxiidae

Spangled Perch, *Leiopotherapon unicolor*, family Terapontidae

Bony Bream, *Nematalosa erebi*, family Clupeidae

Desert Mogurnda, *Mogurnda larapintae*, family Eleotridae

Estuarine Fishes

Freshwater Mullet, *Myxus petardi*, family Mugilidae

Australian Bass *Macquaria novemaculeata*, family Percichthyidae

Estuary Perch, *Macquaria colonorum*, family Percichthyidae

Gobies, family Gobiidae

Mudskippers, *Periophthalmus* spp., family Gobiidae,

Bridled Goby, *Amoya bifrenatus*, family Gobiidae

Introduced Fishes

Rainbow Trout/Steelhead, *Oncorhynchus mykiss*, family Salmonidae

Brown Trout/Sea Trout, *Salmo trutta*, family Salmonidae

Brook Trout/Brook Char/Fontinalis, *Salvelinus fontinalis*, family Salmonidae

Quinnat Salmon/King Salmon/Spring Salmon/Chinook, *Oncorhynchus tshawytscha*, family Salmonidae

Atlantic Salmon, *Salmo salar*, family Salmonidae

Redfin, *Perca fluviatilus*, family Percidae

Goldfish, *Carassius auratus*, family Cyprinidae

Common Carp, *Cyrinus carpio*, family Cyprinidae

Tench, *Tinca tinca*, family Cyprinidae

Roach, *Rutilus rutilus*, family Cyprinidae

Mosquito Fish/Gambusia/Plague Minnow/Top Minnow, *Gambusia holbrooki*, family Poeciliidae

Invertebrates, multiply phyla

Worms

Earthworms, class Oligochaeta, phylum Annelida

Giant Gippsland Worm, *Megascolides australis*, phylum Annelida

Flatworms, class Turbellaria, phylum Platyhelminthes

Leeches, class Hirudinidae, phylum Annelida

Velvet worms or Peripatus, phylum Onychophora

Land Snails and Slugs, phylum Mollusca, class Gastropoda

Giant Panda Snail, *Hedleyella falconeri*, family Caryodidae

Red Triangle Slug, *Triboniophorus graeffei*, family Athoracophoridae

Common Garden Snail, *Cantareus aspersus*, family Helicidae

Leopard Slug, *Limax maximus*, family Limacidae

White Italian Snail, *Theba pisana*, family Helicidae

Semi-slugs, family Helicarionidae

Otway Black Snail, *Victaphanta compacta*, family Rhytididae

Freshwater snails, families Lymnaeidae, Thiaridae, Viviparidae, Hydrobiidae, Planorbidae, Ancylidae (and Physidae, introduced)

Slaters, Shield Shrimps and Freshwater Shrimps, phylum Crustacea

Slaters, sow bugs, woodlice, *Porcellio* spp., *Haloniscus* spp., *Ligia* spp., order Isopoda

Pillbugs, *Armadillidium* spp., order Isopoda

Shield shrimps/tadpole shrimps, *Triops* spp./*Lepidurus* spp., order Notostraca

Common Freshwater Shrimp, *Paratya australiensis*, family Atyidae, order Decapoda

Fairy shrimps, *Branchinella* spp., order Anostraca

Brine shrimps, *Artemia* spp., *Parartemia* spp., order Anostraca

Cherabin, *Macrobrachium rosenbergii*, family Palaemonidae, order Decapoda

Anaspids, *Anaspides* spp., family Anaspididae, order Anaspidacea

Rock Pool Shrimp, *Palaemonites australis*, family Palaemonidae

Crayfish and Freshwater Crabs, order Decapoda, phylum Crustacea

Yabbie, *Cherax destructor*, family Parastacidae

Redclaw, *Cherax quadricarinatus*, family Parastacidae

Koonac, *Cherax preissii*, family Parastacidae

Gilgy or Gilgie, *Cherax quinquecarinatus*, family Parastacidae

Marron, *Cherax tenuimanus*, family Parastacidae

Giant Freshwater Crayfish, *Astacopsis gouldi*, family Parastacidae

Murray River Crayfish, *Euastacus armatus*, family Parastacidae

Large Gippsland Crayfish, *Euastacus kewshawi*, family Parastacidae

Inland Freshwater Crab, *Austrothelphusa* (formerly *Holthuisana*) *transversa*, family Sundathelphusidae

Lamington Spiny Crayfish/Lamington Plateau Crayfish, *Euastacus sulcatus*, family Parastacidae

Mites and Ticks, class Arachnida, order Acarina

Paralysis Tick, *Ixodes holocyclus*, family Ixodidae

Chiggers (larvae), family Trombiculidae

Scorpions, class Arachnida, order Scorpionida

Inland Robust Scorpion, *Urodacus yaschenkoi*, family Urodacidae

Rainforest Scorpion, *Liocheles waigiensis*, family Ischnuridae

Marbled Scorpion/Bark Scorpion, *Lychas marmoreus*, family Buthidae

Wood or Forest Scorpion, *Cercophonius squama*, family Bothriuridae

Primitive Spiders, class Archnida, order Araneae, suborder Mygalomorphae

Funnel-web spiders, family Hexathelidae

Sydney Funnel-web Spider, *Atrax robustus* Tree Funnel-web Spider, *Hadronyche* sp.

Trapdoor spiders, families Ctenizidae, Idiopidae

Mouse spiders, family Actinopodidae

Brush-footed spiders, families Barychelidae, Theraphosidae

Whistling or barking spiders, family Theraphosidae

Modern Spiders, class Archnida, order Araneae, suborder Araneomorphae

Huntsmen spiders, family Sparassidae

Wolf spiders, family Lycosidae

Garden Wolf Spider, *Lycosa godeffroyi*, family Lycosidae

White-tailed Spider, *Lampona cylindrata*, family Lamponidae

Jumping spiders, *Cosmophasis* spp., family Salticidae

Flower and crab spiders, family Thomisidae

Bolas and bird-dropping spiders, family Araneidae

Net-casting spiders, family Deinopidae

Black House Spider, *Badumna insignis*, family Desidae

Crinoline or Sombrero Spider, *Stiphidium facetum*, family Stiphidiidae

Daddy-long Legs, *Pholcus phalangioides*, family Pholcidae

Gum-footed spiders, family Theridiidae

Red-back Spider, *Latrodectes hasseltii*, family Theridiidae

Long-jawed spiders, family Teragnathidae

Golden Orb-weavers, *Nephila* spp., family Nephilidae

Leaf-curling spiders, *Phonognatha* spp., family Araneidae

Garden Orb Web Spider, *Eriophora transmarinas*, family Araneidae

St Andrew Cross Spider, *Argiope* spp., family Araneidae

Spiny spiders, *Austracantha minax* and *Gasteracantha* spp., family Araneidae

Centipedes, class Chilopoda

Earth Centipede, *Zelanion antipodus*, family Chilenophiliae, order Geophilomorpha

Giant Centipede, *Ethmostigmus rubripes*, family Scolopendridae, order Scolopendromorpha

'House' centipedes, *Allothereua* spp., family Scutigeridae, order Scutigeromorpha

Stone centipedes, order Lithobiomorpha

Millipedes, class Diplopoda

Black Portuguese Millipede, *Ommatoiulus moreletii*, family Julidae, order Julida

Pill millipedes, family Sphaerotheridae, order Sphaerotheriida

Spirobolid millipede, order Spirobolida

Silverfish, order Zygentoma

Earwigs, order Dermaptera

European Earwig, *Forficula auricularia*

Giant Earwig, *Titanolabis colossea*

Common Brown Earwig, *Labidura truncata*

Cockroaches, order Blattodea

Giant Burrowing Cockroach *Macropanesthia rhinoceros*

American Cockroach, *Periplaneta americana*

German Cockroach, *Blatella germanica*

Rain Beetle/Common Burrowing Cockroach, *Geoscapheus dilatatus*

Painted Cockroach, *Polyzosteria mitchelli*

Stoneflies, order Plecoptera

Mayflies, order Ephemeroptera

Damselflies and Dragonflies, order Odonata

Blue Skimmer, *Orthetrum caledonicum*

Spot-winged Threadtails, *Nososticta kalumburu*

Ancient Greenling, *Hemiphlebia mirabilis*

Termites, order Isoptera

Spinifex Termites, *Nasutitermes* spp., family Termitidae

Cathedral Termites, *Nasutitermes triodiae*, family Termitidae

Magnetic Termites, *Amitermes meridionalis*

and *A. laurensis*, family Termitidae

Giant Termites, *Mastotermes darwiniensis*, family Mastotermitidae

Stick and Leaf Insects/Phasmids, order Phasmatodea

Stick insects, family Phasmatidae

'True' leaf insects, family Phylliidae

Macleay's Spectre, *Extatosoma tiaratum*, family Phasmatidae

Land Lobster/Lord Howe Island Stick Insect, *Dryococelus australis*, family Phasmatidae

Darwin Stick Insect, *Eurycnema osiris*, family Phasmatidae

Mantids, order Mantodea

Grasshoppers and Crickets, order Orthoptera

Short-horned Grasshoppers and Locusts, family Acrididae

Australian Plague Locust, *Chortoicetes terminifera*

Spur-throated Locust, *Austracris guttulosa*

Migratory Locust, *Locusta migratoria*

Giant Grasshopper/Giant Valanga/Hedge Grasshopper, *Valanga irregularis*

Toad Hoppers, suborder Cantantopinea

Southern Pyrgomorph or Spotted Mountain Grasshopper, *Monistria concinna*, family Pyrgomorphidae

Katydids, family Tettigoniidae

Green Flightless Predatory Katydid, *Hemisaga* sp.

Perth Balloon-winged Katydid, *Tympanophora similis*

Raspy Crickets, family Gryllacrididae

Mole Crickets, *Gryllotalpa* spp., family Gryllotalpidae

Black Field Cricket, *Teleogryllus commodus*, family Gryllidae

King crickets, family Stenopelmatidae

Cooloola Monster, *Cooloola propator*, family Cooloolidae

Psyllids, Scale Insects, etc., order Hemiptera

Aphids, suborder Sternorrhyncha, family Aphididae

Mealybugs, suborder Sternorrhyncha, family Margarodidae

Psyllids, suborder Sternorrhyncha, family Psyllidae

Scale insects, suborder Sternorrhyncha, families Diaspididae and Coccidae

Red Gum Lerp, *Glycaspis brimblecombei*

Whiteflies, family Aleyrodidae

Cicadas, order Hemiptera, suborder Auchenorrhyncha, family Cicadidae

True Bugs, order Hemiptera

Stink or shield bugs, suborder Heteroptera, family Pentatomidae

Bronze Orange Bug, *Musgraveia sulciventris*, family Pentatomidae

Assassin bugs, suborder Heteroptera, family Reduviidae

Crusader bugs, suborder Heteroptera, family Coreidae

Jewel, harlequin or shield-backed bugs, family Scutelleridae

Aquatic True Bugs, order Hemiptera

Backswimmers, family Notonectidae

Water boatmen, family Corixidae

Water scorpions, family Nepidae

Water striders, family Gerridae

Pond skaters, family Gerridae or Veliidae

Giant Water Bug, *Lethocerus insulanus*, family Belostomatidae

Lacewings, order Neuroptera

Moth lacewings, family Ithonidae

Green lacewings, family Chrysopidae

Blue-eyed Lacewing, *Nymphes myrmeleonoides*, family Nymphidae

Antlions, family Myrmeleontidae

Green Lacewing, *Chrysopa* sp., family Chrysopidae

Beetles, order Coleoptera

Scarab beetles, family Scarabaeidae

Christmas beetles, *Anoplognathus* spp., family Scarabaeidae

Dung beetles, family Scarabaeidae and Aphodiinae

Ground beetles, family Carabidae

Burrowing Ground Beetle, *Scaraphites lenaeus*, family Carabidae

Geotrupid beetles, family Geotrupidae

Rhinoceros beetles, family Scarabaeidae, sub-family Dynastinae

Jewel beetles, family Buprestidae

Ladybirds, family Coccinellidae

Southern Ladybird, *Cleobora mellyi*, family Coccinellidae

Cardinal Ladybird, *Rodolia cardinalis*, family Coccinellidae

Black Ladybird, *Rhizobius ventralis*, family Coccinellidae

Twenty-eight Spotted Ladybird, *Henosepilachna vigintioctopunctata*, family Coccinellidae

Fireflies, family Lampyridae

Leaf beetles, family Chrysomelidae

Eucalyptus Leaf Beetle, *Chrysophtharta amoema*, family Chrysomelidae

Clerid beetles, family Cleridae

Yellow-horned Clerid Beetle, *Trogodendron fasciculatum*, family Cleridae

Soldier beetles, family Cantharidae

Plague Soldier Beetles *Chauliognathus lugubris*, family Cantharidae

Stag beetles, family Lucanidae

Broad-toothed Stag Beetle, *Lissotes latidens*, family Lucanidae

Golden Stag Beetle, *Lamprina aurata*, family Lucanidae

Weevils, family Curculionidae

Longicorn beetles, family Cerambycidae

Wallace's Longicorn, *Batocera wallacei*, family Cerambycidae
Longicorn Witchety Grub, *Eurynassa australis*, family Cerambycidae
White-spotted Longicorn, *Rhytiphora saundersi*, family Cerambycidae
Click beetles, family Elateridae
Rove beetles, family Staphylinidae
Water beetles, families Dytiscidae and Hydrophilidae
Whirligigs, family Gyrinidae
Bombardier Beetle, *Pheropsophus verticalis*
Twenty-eight Spotted Ladybird, *Henosepilachna vigintioctopunctata*

True flies, order Diptera

Tachinid flies, family Tachinidae
Crane flies, family Tipulidae
Banana Stalk Fly, *Telostylinus lineolatus*, family Neriidae
Mosquitoes, family Culicidae
Robberflies, family Asilidae
Fruit flies, family Tephritidae
Vinegar flies, family Drosophilidae
Horseflies and March flies, family Tabanidae
Hoverflies / Drone flies, family Syrphidae
Bee flies, family Bombyliidae
Sand flies or biting midges, family Ceratopogonidae
Flesh flies, family Sarcophagidae
Fungus gnats or Glow-worms, family Mycetophilidae
Non-biting midges, family Chironomidae
House flies, *Musca domestica*, family Muscidae
Bush flies, *Musca vetustissima*, family Muscidae
Stable flies, *Stomoxys calcitrans*, family Muscidae
Buffalo flies, *Haemotobia exigua*, family Muscidae
Blowflies and bluebottles, family Calliphoridae
Australian Sheep Blowfly, *Lucilia cuprina*, family Calliphoridae

Butterflies and Moths, order Lepidoptera

Metalmarks, family Riodinidae
Blues / Coppers / Azures / Hairstreaks, family Lycaenidae
Skippers, family Hesperiidae
Swallowtails, family Papilionidae
Whites and Yellows, family Pieridae
Nymphs, Browns, Crows, Fritillaries, Danaiids and Tigers, family Nymphalidae
Hercules Moth, *Coscinocera hercules*, family Saturniidae

Chequered Swallowtail, *Papilio demoleus*, family Papilionidae
Owl moths, family Noctuidae
Western Grass-dart, *Taractrocera papyria* ssp. *agraulia*, family Hesperiidae
Swift moth / Ghost moth, family Hepialidae
Bent-wing Ghost Moth, *Zelotypia stacyi*, family Notodontidae
Richmond Birdwing, *Ornithoptera richmondia*, family Papilionidae
Orchard Swallowtail, *Papilio aegeus*, family Papilionidae
Blue Triangle, *Graphium sarpedon* ssp. *choredon*, family Papilionidae
Wanderer or Monarch, *Danaus plexippus*, family Nymphalidae
Common Australian Crow or Oleander Butterfly, *Euploea core*, family Nymphalidae
Cabbage White Butterfly, *Pieris rapae*, family Pieridae
Caper White, *Belenois java teutonia*, family Pieridae
Cabbage White, *Pieris rapae*, family Pieridae
Loopers, families Geometridae and Noctuidae
Hawk moths, family Sphingidae
Case moths / Bag moths / Bagworms, family Psychidae
Processionary Caterpillars or Bag-shelter Moths, *Ochrogaster lunifer*, family Notodontidae
Witchetty Grub, *Endoxyla leucomochla*, family Cossidae
Giant Wood Moth or Goat Moth, family Cossidae
Chequered Blue or Saltbush Blue Butterfly, *Theclinestes serpentata*, family Lycaenidae
Bogong Moths, *Agrotis infusa*, family Noctuidae
Black and White Tiger, *Danaus affinis* ssp. *affinis*, family Nymphalidae
Whistling moths, *Hecatesia* spp., family Noctuidae
Tiger moths, family Arctiidae
Tussock moths, family Lymantriidae
Cup moths, family Limacodidae
Banksia Moth, *Denima banksiae*, family Notodontidae
Meadow Argus, *Junonia villida*, family Nymphalidae
Cairns Birdwing, *Ornithoptera priamus* ssp. *euphorion*, family Papilionidae

Sawflies, order Hymenoptera, suborder Symphyta

Spitfires (larvae), family Pergidae

Wasps, order Hymenoptera, suborder Apocrita

Paper wasps, family Vespidae
Common Paper Wasp, *Polistes humilis*, family Vespidae
Mud-daubers and sand wasps, family Sphecidae
Potter wasps, subfamily Eumeninae, family Vespidae
European Wasp, *Vespula germanica*, family Vespidae
Ichneumonids, family Ichneumonidae
Spider wasps, family Pompilidae
Spider Hunter Wasp, *Chirodamus* **sp.**, family Pompilidae
Cicada Killer Wasps, *Exeirus* spp., family Sphecidae
Velvet ants, family Mutillidae
Blue Ant, *Diamma bicolor*, family Tiphiidae
Cuckoo wasps, family Chrysididae
Sand wasps, family Sphecidae
Flower wasps, family Tiphiidae

Ants, order Hymenoptera, suborder Apocrita, family Formicidae

Meats Ant, *Iridomyrmex purpureus*
Sugar Ants, *Camponotus* spp.
Honey-pot Ant, *Camponotus inflatus*
Green Tree Ant, *Oecophylla smaragdina*
Bull ants or Bulldog Ants, *Myrmecia* spp.
Mulga Ant, *Polyrhachis macropus*
Red Imported Fire Ant, *Solenopsis invicta*

Bees, order Hymenoptera, suborder Apocrita, superfamily Apoidea

European Honeybee, *Apis mellifera*, family Apidae
Native social bees, *Trigona* spp. and *Austroplebeia* spp., family Apidae
Carpenter bees, family Anthophoridae
Burrowing bees, family Apidae
Dawson's Burrowing Bee, *Amegilla dawsoni*, family Apidae
Leafcutter bees, family Megachilidae
Short tongue bees, family Colletidae, and bees with short-pointed tongues, family Halictidae
Sugarbag bees, family Apidae
Blue-banded Bee, *Amegilla* sp., family Apidae
Cuckoo bees, family Apidae
Chequered Cuckoo Bee, *Thyreus caeruleopunctatus*, **family Apidae**

INDEX